Teachers' Schools and the Making of the Modern Chinese Nation-State, 1897-1937

Contemporary Chinese Studies

This series, a joint initiative of UBC Press and the UBC Institute of Asian Research, Centre for Chinese Research, seeks to make available the best scholarly work on contemporary China. Volumes cover a wide range of subjects related to China, Taiwan, and the overseas Chinese world.

Glen Peterson, *The Power of Words: Literacy and Revolution in South China, 1949-95*

Wing Chung Ng, *The Chinese in Vancouver: The Pursuit of Power and Identity, 1945-80*

Yijiang Ding, *Chinese Democracy after Tiananmen*

Diana Lary and Stephen MacKinnon, eds., *Scars of War: The Impact of Warfare on Modern China*

Eliza W.Y. Lee, ed., *Gender and Change in Hong Kong: Globalization, Postcolonialism, and Chinese Patriarchy*

James A. Flath, *The Cult of Happiness: Nianhua, Art, and History in Rural North China*

Christopher A. Reed, *Gutenberg in Shanghai: Chinese Print Capitalism, 1876-1937*

Erika E.S. Evasdottir, *Obedient Autonomy: Chinese Intellectuals and the Achievement of Orderly Life*

Hsiao-ting Lin, *Tibet and Nationalist China's Frontier: Intrigues and Ethnopolitics, 1928-49*

Xiaoping Cong, *Teachers' Schools and the Making of the Modern Chinese Nation-State, 1897-1937*

Diana Lary, ed., *The Chinese State at the Borders*

Xiaoping Cong

Teachers' Schools and the Making of the Modern Chinese Nation-State, 1897-1937

UBCPress · Vancouver · Toronto

15 14 13 12 11 10 09 08 07   5 4 3 2 1

Printed in Canada on ancient-forest-free paper (100 percent post-consumer recycled) that is processed chlorine- and acid-free, with vegetable-based inks.

Library and Archives Canada Cataloguing in Publication

Cong, Xiaoping, 1954-
Teachers' schools and the making of the modern Chinese nation-state, 1897-1937 / Xiaoping Cong.

(Contemporary Chinese studies, ISSN 1206-9523)
Includes bibliographical references and index.
ISBN 978-0-7748-1347-1 (bound); 978-0-7748-1348-8 (pbk.)

1. Teachers colleges – China – History – 20th century. 2. Teachers – Training of – China – History – 20th century. 3. Educational change – China–History – 20th century. 4. Social change – China – History – 20th century. 5. Education and state – China – History – 20th century. I. Title. II. Series.

LB1727.C5C65 2007   370.71'051   C2007-900028-2

This book has been published with the help of a grant from the Chiang Ching-kuo Foundation and with a Small Grant from the University of Houston.

UBC Press
The University of British Columbia
2029 West Mall
Vancouver, BC V6T 1Z2
604-822-5959 / Fax: 604-822-6083
www.ubcpress.ca

In memory of my father
Cong Yiping (1917-1998)

And to my mother

Contents

Tables

Acknowledgments

This book is the result of a long journey of intellectual inquiry. My interest in China's teachers' schools began in the early 1970s, arising from connections between these schools and my family. However, it was not until I attended the University of California in Los Angeles that my general interest in teachers' schools became one of scholarly inquiry and academic research. I will always be indebted to the stimulating academic community at UCLA.

I owe my greatest intellectual debt to my PhD advisor at UCLA, Benjamin Elman, whose scholarship and academic vision had a strong influence on the perspective of this book. It was his different approach to Chinese education and intellectual history that ignited my desire to work on a topic that had been sleeping in my mind for decades. Without his inspiration and unfailing help, I would not have been able to accomplish this work.

My sincere gratitude goes to John Hawkins, my co-advisor, for his generous support and academic encouragement. I would also like to thank Kathryn Bernhardt, Theodore Huters, and Perry Anderson. Their preeminent scholarship, in addition to the classes I have taken from them, has broadened my understanding of historical studies. I am particularly grateful to Richard J. Smith at Rice University, whose encouragement helped me to get out of the postdissertation quandary and to continue pursuing my work.

In the process of writing this book, I have received many invaluable comments from colleagues. Particular gratitude goes to Joan Judge for reading my work and for her many suggestions. I greatly appreciate Charlette Furth, Ruth Hayhoe, Susan Mann, Liu Chang, Dorothy Ko, Meng Yue, Qian Nanxiu, Elizabeth Littell-Lamb, Xia Xiaohong, Chen Pingyuan, Mary Kay Vaughan, Robert Culp, Christopher Reed, Keith Schoppa, and Sun Yi for reading parts of my work and providing many useful insights and suggestions.

I am grateful to my friend Sam Gilbert, who read the manuscript and offered comments. He also helped polish the prose. Cyndy Brown worked on the majority of the manuscript to correct grammatical problems and catch editorial errors, and Angie Kirby-Calder helped edit one chapter of this book. Their efforts are most appreciated.

Special thanks go to my colleagues in the Department of History at the University of Houston. Joseph Pratt, who served as chair, helped me get financial support for summer research and freed me from some of my teaching load so that I could work on the manuscript. Sue Kelloge, present chair of the department, skillfully guided me through the final stages of completing this work. Kairn Klieman, Sarah Fishman, Catherine Patterson, Martin Melosi, Roberta Bivins, John Hart, Lupe San Miguel, and Kathleen Brosnan read parts of my work and offered their comments and suggestions on proposals, grant applications, and the publication process. Steve Mintz deserves special mention since he read an early draft of the manuscript and provided valuable comments. Landon Storrs, Andrew Chesnut, Eric Walter, James Martin, and Stone Bailey also offered me their support in various ways.

I would also like to express my gratitude to the staff members of the History Department – Lorena Lopez, Gloria Ned, Donna Bulter, Christine Womack, and Richard Frazier – who helped me with travel arrangements, grant and conference paperwork, mail deliveries, photocopying, and class paperwork. Special appreciation also goes to John Antel, the Dean of the College of Liberal Arts and Social Sciences, for his warm support and assistance that made the publication of this book occur sooner than planned.

I greatly appreciate the comments and criticism from all of the above colleagues and friends who have offered their opinions and ideas. Nonetheless, none of them is responsible for any errors or ommisions in the book.

Many thanks are due to the staff of the following libaries and archives for their kind assistance in finding many precious documents that have enriched my research: Research Library and East Asian Library at UCLA; University of Houston Library, especially its Interlibrary Loan Department; the National Library in Beijing; the Second Historical Archives in Nanjing; the Shanghai Municipal Library and Archives; the Hebei Provincial Archives; Shandong Provincial Archives; and Shaanxi Provincial Archives and Library.

It was my great pleasure to work with UBC Press editors who provided gracious and professional assistance during the publication process. Senior editor Emily Andrew selected this manuscript and believed in its value. She also helped me apply to the Chiang Ching-kuo Foundation for a publication grant. Managing editor Holly Keller worked patiently on the manuscript. I also would like to thank the anonymous readers selected by UBC Press. Their critical comments and constructive suggestions have made this a better book.

It was an honour to receive a fellowship from the Spencer Foundation, which generously provided me with a grant for a full year to focus on my writing and the completion of the manuscript. Acknowledgment also goes to the Center for Chinese Studies, which supported my archival research in China, and to the Department of History at UCLA, which supported part of my writing. I am grateful to have received financial support from the University of Houston, which not only financed my additional archival work but also partially funded the book's publication. I would also like to express my gratitude to the Chiang Ching-kuo Foundation for its financial support for the publication of this book.

Finally, my deepest gratitude is directed to my own family – my mother and my sisters, Wanping and Lixin, for their boundless support and unconditional love. With their encouragement, I have been able to release myself from many family duties and to concentrate on my writing and career. The spirit of my father, his experience and his expectations for me, have always been the inspiration for my life. This work is the best memorial that I could give him.

Teachers' Schools and the Making of the Modern Chinese Nation-State, 1897-1937

China in the 1930s

Introduction

In 1997, a series of magazine and newspaper articles and radio and television broadcasts heralded the centennial of the establishment of China's first teachers' school. One year before the Hundred Days of Reform, Shanghai's Nanyang Public School (*Nanyang gongxue*) first opened the doors of a new section – *shifan yuan* (an institutional label that would soon be applied to new schools all over China – which had been created to train primary and secondary schoolteachers. Between 1897 and today, China has experienced reforms and revolutions; at every turn, the place of the teacher in society has shifted and, with it, efforts to create suitable teachers' schools. The modernization of education has followed a tortuous path, never straying far from the political and social transformations of the past century.

This book addresses one part of that story – the development of teachers' schools from 1897 to 1937, when the outbreak of the Anti-Japanese War obliged many schools to close. I have written an account of the transformation of both institutions and society in the politically tumultuous decades of the early twentieth century, focusing on the unique nature of Chinese teachers' schools, which were a hybrid model that bridged Chinese and Western educational systems and ideals. Although based on a modification of Western models, these schools, through utilizing a local cultural and institutional inheritance that honoured the role of teachers as socio-political leaders, constantly adjusted themselves to the needs of Chinese society. One might say that teachers' schools propelled the age-old tradition of linking politics and education into the twentieth century.

The industrial age was marked by the emergence of education as central to modernity. By establishing modern schools, the state penetrated local society. Education, traditionally left to religious, kinship, and occupational organizations, became a public affair. As Ernest Gellner has noted, modern schools imparted a standardized national "high culture" to the masses, making modern economic, political, and social interaction possible.[1] Eugen Weber showed in his famous study of the "modernization of rural France" that mass education led peasants to identify with the nation, integrate into the modern world, and become conversant with urban official culture.[2] And in Southeast Asia, modern education created an imagined community crucial to the spread of nationalism.[3] Although certain features have proven general in the development of modern education, each country has travelled its own particular road, producing distinct results.

The modern teacher has been both the creation of this momentous transformation and its instrument. In France, teachers were "harbingers of enlightenment and of the Republican message that reconciled the benighted masses with a new world, superior in wellbeing and democracy."[4] During the Third Republic, pioneering female teachers challenged a predominantly male profession and advanced the cause of sexual equality.[5] Teachers also played the part of rabble-rousers: they educated and mobilized peasants in the early twentieth-century Russian and Mexican Revolutions.[6] In spite of being a product of industrial society, the formation of teachers as a professional corps, their methods of training, and the role they played in the social and political arena varied in each society due to different cultural heritages and sociopolitical settings.

Unlike most Western states, at the turn of the nineteenth century, China already possessed a countrywide network of schools, supplemented by state and private academies and by the community and family schools that had for over a millennium prepared young men to sit for the civil and military examinations. Until the abolition of the civil service examination system in 1905, teachers were generally the by-product of these examinations. As early as the Tang Dynasty (618-907) the Confucian master Han Yu (768-824) had defined the responsibilities of the teacher as "passing down the essence of Confucian doctrine" (*chuan Dao*), "transmitting knowledge" (*shou ye*), and "elucidating the subtle meaning" (*jie huo*).[7] The Chinese term for teachers' schools, *shifan*, can be traced back over a thousand years. In late imperial times, it came to be applied to Confucian teaching officials (*ruxue jiaoguan*), who had a heavy moral responsibility to "serve as role models for people" (*wei ren shibiao*).[8] The term was revived at the turn of the twentieth century and applied to modern professional teachers.[9] Due to the high expectations associated with them, teachers' schools were given a special position in the modern Chinese educational system.

In the late nineteenth century, Japan and many Western countries established special teachers' schools to staff their expanding educational systems. Over time, the schools were replaced by teacher training courses in the regular education system, and programs were developed to certify teachers. Since their beginnings in the early twentieth century up to the present, Chinese teachers' schools have maintained a vast independent system.[10]

The Chinese teachers' school system was parallel to, but separate from, the regular system of secondary and higher education. It included secondary teachers' schools, colleges, and universities as well as less formal training programs. This system extended from the capital to provincial cities and county towns. For most of the twentieth century, students preparing to work as teachers paid no tuition, received government stipends, and were obliged to accept the posts assigned them after graduation. In contrast to regular secondary schools and colleges, the curricula of teachers' schools were designed to meet the pedagogical needs of primary and middle schools. A stricter than normal moral training was part of young teachers' training, in the expectation that they would reform the common people and disseminate state ideology. The students and recent graduates of teachers' schools took on the political and social projects of each succeeding regime as Chinese political life zigzagged across the early twentieth century.

Previous Studies

Modern Chinese education has been a favourite topic of scholarly research in the West, in Japan, and in China. Western studies began by describing how a dynamic Western system displaced a static Chinese system, thus assigning the birth of modern Chinese education to the period during which Western-style schools were introduced. In his study of a small number of schools established by the officials of the Self-Strengthening Movement (Yangwu Yundong) in the 1860s to train engineers, military technicians, and translators, Knight Biggerstaff flatly stated that this was the beginning of modern education in China.[11] John Cleverley, on the other hand, claimed that the missionary schools marked the beginning of modern education.[12] This perspective implies that "modern" means "Western," and it tends to assume an inevitable opposition between "modern" and "traditional." Histories based on these assumptions have tended to overlook the internal dynamics of Chinese society, which produced the continuous development of the education system long before the advent of Western-style schools, and which continued to drive the transformation of Chinese education in the nineteenth and twentieth centuries. Moreover, in these accounts, the destruction of Western-style schools in local riots, the refusal of some families to send their children to these schools, and the existence of experimental schools in which traditional links to the local community were revived are often simply viewed as a reactionary defence of tradition. Chinese experiences and programs that do not fit the modern Western model are often overlooked altogether.

Decades ago, Benjamin Schwartz perceived the problem of the "tradition versus modernity" model and pointed out its limits with regard to explaining the transformation of Chinese intellectuals, especially the May Fourth generation.[13] Scholars have subsequently tried to avoid this dichotomous model by examining the interaction between Chinese and Western influences on education and, increasingly, by looking for the indigenous paths to innovation. For example, Sally Borthwick's excellent study of traditional *sishu* schools juxtaposes them with China's modern Western schools, reminding us that the two types had existed side by side since the beginning of the twentieth century. Borthwick suggests that the dichotomous division between "modern" and "traditional" schools in China was artificial as modern and traditional educational practices interacted with each other and continued until the early Communist period.[14] Wen-hsin Yeh's study of Western-style universities in Shanghai from the early twentieth century to the 1930s points out that the rise of new universities in Shanghai was the result of the traditional network of the imperial Jiangnan gentry-elite. These newly established academies displayed a cultural continuity that, though largely adopted from Western curricula, gave Confucian training an important position and sought to harmonize tradition and modernity.[15] Ruth Hayhoe, examining the Republican period, perceived the influence of tradition. Concerns about geographic distribution and the equal distribution of educational resources were deeply rooted in the imperial system.[16] Her study of China's universities presents a process of conflict, interaction, and adaptation, in which the Western concept of the university never made more than a partial appearance. The Western ideals of academic freedom and autonomy were transformed into a quintessentially Chinese tradition that emphasized the political responsibility of intellectuals.[17] Joan Judge's examination of the textbooks used by the Qing government for women's education proves that "modern" and "traditional" are inadequate analytical categories. Among the role models presented in these books were not only famous Western women but also Chinese paragons of womanly virtue.[18] Suzanne Pepper considered education from the angle of social equality, seeing modern education as a long-term conflict between formal, elite education and those who provided a radical critique of this approach.[19]

Most recent studies of local history attest to the interactions between traditional and modern schools. For instance, Stig Thøgersen's outstanding study of Zouping County tells the story of a fully engaged local society that embraced a range of educational practices offered by both traditional and modern schools. He hoped to go beyond the division between traditional and modern by viewing the changes and continuities in local schools through the eyes of the local people.[20] In his study of the educational reformer James Yen (Yan Yangchu) and his experiments of the 1920s and 1930s in northern Chinese villages, Charles Hayford convincingly shows that modern educators "were not passive victims of foreign influence, but active adapters and creative developers."[21] Helen Chauncey's study of county level educational practices in Jiangsu demonstrates how modern schools "became instruments in elite strategies to assert control over social and material wealth" in the early Republican period.[22] Traditional collectivities, such as lineages, were also involved in the establishment of modern schools. In his comparative study of two counties in Zhejiang Robert Culp shows that members of both the gentry and the new elite responded to the state's call with regard to school-building enterprises.[23]

Unfortunately, very few English language accounts have examined teachers' schools and their role in the development of Chinese education and the transformation of Chinese society.[24] While some have acknowledged the cultural and political importance of teachers as representatives of new concepts and the modern state in local communities,[25] teachers' schools have generally been viewed as quite insignificant, simply an attachment to the general educational system.

General educational institutions – elementary schools, middle schools, and colleges and universities – are still at the centre of all studies of Chinese educational history, undoubtedly because this segment of the educational system provides a good basis for comparison with the systems in Europe and America. In other words, scholars have treated Western institutions as a window through which to view China. From this window, teachers' schools, which lack a counterpart in today's Western system, have been invisible. An assumption that China's teachers' schools, like their nineteenth-century predecessors in the West, were designed to accomplish the pedagogical training of teachers, to function as an undifferentiated part of a modern educational system, has erased from the general narrative of modern education the special features and the unusual role of these schools in Chinese society.

The small number of English language works that focus on teachers' schools has been written by Chinese scholars. Chuang Chai-hsuan, who completed a doctorate at Columbia University's teachers' college in 1922, dedicated a chapter of his dissertation on Chinese education to the teacher training system. Chuang outlined teachers' status, the certification system, and the various teachers' schools that opened during the late Qing dynasty and the early twentieth century.[26] An article by J.P. Chu, "Normal School Education in China," appears in the 1923 *Bulletin on Chinese Education,* compiled by the Chinese National Association for the Advancement of Education.[27] In this summary, written for non-Chinese readers and based on official Qing documents, Chu briefly reviews the education of teachers before the establishment of the Republican government and provides detailed information about the administrative system, the curricula, and the distribution of normal schools and students during the first decade of the Republican era. Finally, a thin volume published in 1960 documents the development of teachers' schools during the first decade of Communist rule.[28] These works barely scratch the surface of the subject.

Japanese scholarship on Chinese teachers' schools has also been limited. A study by Igarishi Shoichi of the establishment of teachers' schools in the late Qing, published in 1969, reviews such early schools as Nanyang Public School and evaluates the place of teacher training in the new educational system established between 1902 and 1904. Limiting himself to the pedagogical function of the new educational system, Igarishi overlooked the social significance of establishing teachers' schools during a transitional era.[29] Kobayashi Yoshifuni's recent study of Chinese teachers provides a detailed picture of the lives and social activities of primary schoolteachers in urban areas during the 1920s. Although he offers a brief description of teacher training, teachers' organizations and teachers' struggles against qualifying examinations and for financial security occupy centre stage.[30]

Chinese scholarship has treated the topic of teachers' schools more extensively than has other scholarship and has recognized their distinctive qualities. Several book-length studies provide basic histories of teachers' schools, with sections on curricula and state policy.[31] Rather reductively, these repetitive histories view teachers' schools as loci for the inculcation of official ideology. By focusing on government plans but rarely considering how they were implemented, such studies assume too much about the relationship between rules and schools. Like their Western and Japanese colleagues, Chinese scholars rarely cross the threshold of the schoolhouse to examine its social, cultural, and political role and the part it played in the transformation of Chinese education and society.

The Narrative: Interaction, Penetration, and Hybridization

After studying the Indian caste system, Lloyd Rudolph and Susanne Rudolph concluded that when modernization encountered tradition it did not so much supersede it as penetrate it and then yield, in turn, to being infiltrated.[32] Long before the coming of the Western powers in the nineteenth century, China had an immense and elaborate school system. In the transformation of that vast imperial system, what part became modernized and what part remained traditional? Could "the modern" combine with "the traditional"? How were local cultural resources adapted to a foreign institution? How did traditional ideas about education and the role of teachers influence modern schools and modern teachers?

I view both modernity and tradition as complex and changing concepts.[33] In the early twentieth century, many Chinese intellectuals, educators, and officials viewed Western countries as the embodiment of modernity and believed that, to the extent that China could emulate those countries, it, too, could become strong and wealthy. But they were facing a changing and diverse West.[34] Many Chinese educators, especially those trained in European and American universities, believed that modernizing Chinese schools had to involve using Western theories, models, curricula, pedagogies, and even textbooks. Within this mindset, various educational systems – including French, German, British, American, and Japanese ones – were studied and introduced to China. When an imported model did not work out, educators would search for a new one. Although the British model played an important role early on during this period of the Self-Strengthening Movement,[35] it was the Japanese model that, in 1904, left the deepest mark on the first modern Chinese educational system. An American model was adopted in 1922, a French model in 1928, and a Soviet model after 1949. Clearly, modernity was an overlapping, multicultural work in progress.

Tradition, seen as a reactionary force by most modernizers, is, in fact, multifaceted. By the time the first modern educational system was established, the reformers were facing an already altered "tradition," which included newly established Western-style schools dedicated to the self-strengthening programs, missionary schools, and reformed academies; contemporary topics had even been introduced into the civil service examination. At the same time, tradition was entering the first modern school system in the form of awarding graduates degrees with imperial titles. Nor was the traditional emphasis on moral cultivation abandoned: teachers generally clung to age-old pedagogy in classes devoted to the Confucian classics. The "tradition" that the 1922 reformers perceived in the previous educational system involved centralization and uniformity. The critics of the 1922 educational system also attacked what they saw as exclusive, urban schools in which students were being nursed by traditional, bookish study, with the idea of one day turning them into rich officials. Tradition had various faces and was perceived differently by different people.

As "modernizers" and "traditionalists" searched for solutions, they surveyed the social conditions of the day. Both struggled for dominance, and neither group won a decisive victory. Whether one joined the New Culture Movement, which repudiated tradition, or clung to Confucian values, it was clear that everyone was fighting on the same ground and facing the same issues.[36] To the modernizers, the previous Western models did not overcome the problems of traditionalism and would need to be replaced with a newer model. The traditionalists, on the other hand, blamed the problems they faced on the tinkerings of the modernizers. By the 1920s, when popular educational and rural construction movements were emerging, the first generation of graduates from China's modern educational system was already being viewed as part of traditional rural communities and was becoming an obstacle for the newer wave of social change. Radicals like Tao Xingzhi and conservatives like Liang Shuming both thought that modern schools retained too many (bad) traditional elements. Tao and Liang also agreed that the answer lay in the countryside, where local resources and traditional practices could be turned to account. It was in this environment of mutual blame, interaction, infiltration, experimentation, and innovation that some modern models and ideas were modified and tradition was revived and reformed. The result was a hybrid.

The development of modern schools, and teachers' schools in particular, played a part in the two processes that most influenced China's twentieth-century transformation: "localizing the global" and "nationalizing the local." The former involved a dynamic process in which institutions and educational traditions were transformed through a series of negotiations, interactions, infiltrations, and compromises with new ideas and methods, and from this process there emerged a hybrid model of Chinese education. Producing a modern Chinese educational system involved more than simply replacing Chinese models, textbooks, curricula, and pedagogy with their Western equivalents. Local educators experimented, creating a new approach to pedagogy that included aspects of both foreign and domestic cultures. The process of "nationalizing the local" involved efforts to culturally and politically unify and "nationalize" local communities through education – efforts that saw teachers' schools assigned a key role. The state used education and modern schools to create political unity, to train citizens, to promote national identity, and to extend state power to local communities.

In the late nineteenth century, acute domestic and international problems led members of the ruling class to call for reform. Even as Japan and the Western powers proved themselves utterly inimical to China's well-being, 1902 and 1904 saw the adoption of educational reforms drawn from Western and Japanese models. Key aspects of the reforms were designed to deal with the institutional and human legacies of the examination system and the schools established to feed it. The national teachers' school system that was introduced in 1904, which borrowed much from the Japanese system, was created on the institutional foundations of the imperial schools. One of its key mandates was the transformation of examination-trained literati into professional teachers and educational administrators.

Declaring a school "modern" or "Western-style" did not magically exorcise all traces of the examination system, dogmatic pedagogy, and the obsession with a small number of ethical and political texts written many centuries earlier. In fact, Western-style modern schools largely incorporated such educational traditions: when the modern educational system was established, many traditional academies and dynastic schools were converted into Western-style schools. This conversion ensured a strong continuity between the new and the old. On the other hand, while traditional schools were integrated into their locales, both institutionally and morally, Western-style schools were intentionally set apart. Moreover, the creation of Western-style schools in coastal cities exacerbated the already problematic gap between the literate elite and the masses. The new schools did not provide a means to educate the vast population of China; rather, they transformed a small part of the traditional elite into a modern elite. In other words, modern education took over and enhanced the role that traditional education had played in reproducing elite status and domination.

The radical experiments initiated in the late 1920s, such as Xiaozhuang Village Teachers' School, attempted to address the problems that examination culture was extended into Western-style schools and new schools were misfit in Chinese communities. These experiments challenged the urban-oriented system of new schools by bringing to the rural masses a modern education that sought to incorporate rural traditions and resources and to accommodate rural needs. Radical reformers promoted the Western emphasis on practical knowledge and tried to uproot the dogmatic and examination-oriented traditions that persisted in many new schools. The practical knowledge that was promoted included rural, local, and traditional knowledge – subjects ignored and often scorned by Westernized urban educators. Radical intellectuals also attempted to integrate schools into rural communities in order to make them centres of rural leadership and reform. Teachers would do more than teach new subjects: like the Confucian gentry, they would try to be village leaders and to exemplify moral values. The influence of such experiments would be profound, going far beyond the educational domain, strictly construed, to merge with the movement to transform rural society. Their echoes can be found in some of the more radical policies implemented by both Nationalist and Communist regimes.

From the eighteenth century, a time of rapid educational expansion, state and local governments expanded their control into primary education by encouraging the establishment of community schools and local academies. The establishment of teachers' schools at the beginning of the twentieth century served the same purpose. These schools, sponsored and controlled by the state, provided teachers and administrators who were trained to impart a unified curriculum that had been designed by state officials. Standardized examinations controlled entrance into and graduation from teachers' schools, ensuring a certain level of professionalism. Since the schools would carry out certain administrative duties in local education and governance, the state saw them as a way of reaching local communities.

In the early Republican period, education was regarded as a means of unifying the country, and the value of teachers' schools was generally acknowledged. It was in these schools that many teachers learned the vernacular language, Mandarin, whose universal use was considered to be a crucial element in building a stronger nation. Even when contending warlords atomized the polity, many of those who had been trained in teachers' schools clung to the pedagogical ideals they had absorbed. These educated elites influenced the state by staffing the bureaucracy, operating professional organizations, and continuing to build national unity at the local level, with or without the supervision of a centralized state.

The state and ambitious administrators saw teachers' schools as a means of modernizing local communities in a way that was in keeping with their distinctive visions of modernity. Radical intellectual reformers attempted to use village teachers' schools to carry out rural social reform. Xiaozhuang Village Teachers' School, which I discuss at some length in Chapter 4, was not only a pedagogical experiment but also an effort to create a new social structure that would enable economic development and local democracy. The Nationalist government was quick to appreciate the political value of this enterprise, and it prescribed the Xiaozhuang model for all village teachers' schools. As state agents that penetrated rural communities, these teachers' schools displayed the "soft" side of the state-building process. They were expected to be naturally resistant to the pitfalls of an entrenched bureaucracy and to bring changes directly to villages.

But extending modern education to the village proved a fateful step. When hundreds of thousands of rural youths entered modern educational institutions, they brought with them their concerns and their discontent with the state – concerns and discontents that would eventually remap the politics of the day and reorient the direction of society. In the 1930s, once political radicalism had won the battle for the hearts and minds of those enrolled in local teachers' schools, these schools became centres for Communist recruitment. The re-emergence of the Chinese Communist Party in the mid-1930s, and its success in the 1940s, can be traced to the rural educational experiments of the 1920s.

The story of teachers' schools also follows the narrative line of women's changing social position in twentieth-century China. Traditionally, mothers had been children's first teachers – a role that drove gentry families, who hoped that their daughters would marry well, to see that girls learned to read and write. Efforts to expand the state's role in primary education and kindergarten for boys helped open the doors of public education to women and provided them with a legitimate role as professional teachers. This largely unintended development forever altered the position of women in Chinese society. As women crept higher and higher up the teaching hierarchy, the state was driven to hire more women to staff higher levels of women's teachers' schools, thus opening secondary and tertiary education to women. For decades, female teachers' schools provided a socially acceptable bridge that enabled educated women to extend their talents, influence, and activities to other parts of society.

Documents and Methodology

In searching through a number of Chinese archives, I discovered a large quantity of valuable sources for this book, including local historical documents, school records, personal correspondence, and data collected by education officials. Although I sometimes use government regulations and decrees to sketch the kind of policy making that was not always reflected in the classroom, for the most part, I depend on other official records to fill this gap. For instance, I often turn to the immense number of bulletins issued by the central government and the provincial bureaus of education.[37] Previous scholars, who emphasize official regulations and educational policies, have overlooked these invaluable publications, which chronicle official communications (including instructive notes, memoranda, school requests, and official responses), inspectors' reports, annual school reports, school budgets, personnel files, school records, student lists, and much more. I focus on those documents that provide detailed information concerning what was actually happening in the schools. I also supplement and check these materials with archival documents, contemporaneous magazine articles, the memoirs and diaries of students and educators, local histories, and a number of important biographical collections.

Since the 1980s, many documents relating to education have been opened to the public, and Chinese scholars have made a great effort to compile a number of documentary collections containing a large quantity of original materials. Some of my material comes from these collections, most of which are of high quality (although intellectual predispositions have, as ever, impinged on the selection and organization of materials). I have also studied the tremendous output of Chinese intellectuals of the Republican era, who, with great excitement, recorded their visions of what education might become in China.

Teachers' Schools and the Making of the Modern Chinese Nation-State covers educational change throughout most of China and provides a broad view of the trajectory of teachers' schools. Although a case study focusing on a particular region or school would have permitted the use of greater detail, the extreme institutional instability of the four decades under consideration would mitigate its value. As Stig Thøgersen points out, the concerns of local society with regard to the goal of education differed from those of state and national reformers. Therefore, educational practices at the local level, which often had to meet personal goals, sometimes drifted away from the intention of official policies and the general tendency of educational development at the national level.[38] This difference sometimes reveals the limitations of the case study method. Since teachers' schools were secondary and tertiary establishments, their fate, by and large, was in the hands of central and provincial governments. Their pedagogy and curricula were as tightly controlled by the state as were those of any other kind of school. In order to evaluate the overall development of teachers' schools and their relation to social transformation, this book examines the history of these schools, from the establishment of the first teachers' schools in coastal areas to the merger of most such schools with regular schools in the 1920s, to the rise of experimental village teachers' schools in the latter part of that decade, to the Nationalist government's development of a system of more stable village teachers' schools in rural and inland areas in the 1930s, to the expansion of women's normal schools from big cities to inland towns, to, finally, Communist efforts to train teachers in their revolutionary base areas.

In order to understand the history of teachers' schools during this period, the reader should supplement this book with case studies, thus ensuring that breadth is leavened by depth. Case studies – focused on specific schools, specific regions, specific moments – help us to understand the connection between policy and practice. Readers should consult Richard Orb and David Buck's early studies of education in Zhili and Shandong, respectively; Marianne Bastid's study of Zhang Jian's educational activities in Tongzhou, Jiangsu; Helen Chauncey's study of educational elites in Jiangsu; Stig Thøgersen's studies of Zouping, Shandong; Robert Culp's study of Zhejiang; Ruth Hayhoe's interprovincial comparative study; and Elizabeth VanderVen's recent dissertation on Haicheng, Liaoning.[39] These show that, from the beginning of the twentieth century up to the 1930s, local elites actively promoted educational projects proposed either by the central government or by national educational organizations. Most government regulations were carried out at the local level; the interests of local elites and the capacities of local governments invariably necessitated adjustments and refinements. Overall, these case studies suggest a fairly high degree of uniformity in educational development throughout China. Drawing on these works as well as on my own archival discoveries, I attempt to combine the broad view with the close-up view. In each chapter, I describe a single teachers' school, thus giving a national story solid grounding in a specific reality.

Because this book analyzes the role of teachers' schools in the social transformation of twentieth-century China, I look less at pedagogy than I do at the wider relationship between schools and society. In adopting a functionalist perspective, I am able to assess professionalization while avoiding the pitfalls of essentializing. I avoid most pedagogical issues involving curricula, schooling, textbooks, examinations, institutions, teaching, and so on as I believe that discussing these issues would distract from my focus on the social and political role of teachers' schools. This is a study of institutions and their relations with a broader society; it is not a study of teachers as a professional corps. An evaluation of teachers as a social group and of their activities in both school and society would require a different set of documents, a different approach, and a different book.

Summary of the Book

Chapter 1, which reviews the imperial school system, delineates the factors leading to the expansion of education during the Ming and Qing dynasties. It describes the efforts of the Qing imperial court to reform education and the civil service examination system, arguing that the social and political crises of the second half of the nineteenth century provided the incentive for the educational reforms we see at the turn of the twentieth century. Reformers hoped that Western schemas might supplant an inefficient bureaucracy and an impractical educational system. This chapter also assesses women's education and women's traditional role as family educators in late imperial China, and it argues that the development of a new style of women's schools in the last decade of the nineteenth century was not primarily the accomplishment of Western missionaries (as is conventionally contended) but, rather, was deeply rooted in the survival strategy of an elite class and was developed in late imperial times.

Chapter 2 examines the political and educational reforms launched by the Qing court in the early years of the twentieth century, after military defeats at the hands of Japan and some Western states. The establishment of a new school system became one of the most important projects of the New Policy Reform. Though Japanese models inspired the leading reformers, these models were deliberately modified to reduce the chaos attendant upon political reform and the 1905 abolition of the civil service examinations. An analysis of data from the Liang Guang Advanced Teachers' College (1902-11) shows that teachers' schools provided expectant officials and surplus literati with a channel through which to achieve new identities as educational administrators and modern professional teachers. During this period, Chinese women's education also experienced an important transformation. In order to prevent educated women from turning into a subversive force, the Qing court built female teachers' schools, thus channelling women's education into training "the teachers of citizens," thereby supporting the state-building project. Thus, the task of educating women was transferred from the domestic sphere to the public realm, and traditional ideology, which espoused educating mothers to ensure the family's prosperity, was extended to training female teachers to ensure the nation's prosperity. These schools provided, for the first time, a legitimate role for women as educators in the public domain.

Chapter 3 explores the role that teachers' schools played in counteracting the instability that followed the 1911 Revolution and the steady growth of female teachers' schools. As regional warlords fought among themselves, professional educators tried to maintain the integrity of the existing educational system and hold the country together by separating education from politics. Educational bureaucrats, most of whom had been trained in teachers' schools, collaborated with local elites to continue implementing a unified educational policy. These educators formed a national network that was centred in teachers' schools and in the national and regional educational associations that functioned as an alternative system for educational administration (thus helping to hold the country together). Through the examination of 1,700 resumes of local educational officials, I attempt to show that "state and society" in the early republican period were not clearly divided realms, rather they were overlapping and mutually penetrated. During the 1910s, these newly professionalized educators pushed through a series of reforms that advanced women's education and that provided more chances for girls and women. The transformation of the Beijing Female Teachers' School into the Beijing Female Teachers' College is an example of the expansion of women's education. This not only made public higher education accessible to women but also gave them the opportunity to teach at a higher level in the public schools.

Chapter 4 analyzes the efforts made by Chinese educational reformers in 1922 to modernize China's educational system by adopting American models. The struggle, which centred on teachers' schools during this period, represented Chinese intellectuals' different perceptions of modernity. Contrary to the intention of its framers, who hoped to lay the foundation for a democratic polity, the 1922 reform actually widened the educational gap between urban and rural areas. To fend off such growing disparities, radical reformers created hybrid village teachers' schools to challenge the Westernized system that was being implemented by the state, largely in big cities. A case study of the Xiaozhuang Village Teachers' School, and a reinterpretation of Tao Xinzhi's educational practice, shows that, by introducing traditional resources into modern schools, the radical reformers were attempting to develop a model of social organization that could reform and reorganize a disintegrating rural society. This chapter also looks at how female teachers' schools fared under the influence of the 1922 education reform. Although the reformers made provisions for upgrading female teachers' colleges to teachers' universities, in the area of women's education, the emphasis was on building regular female secondary schools in urban areas. This was a shift away from the policy followed through previous decades (which made preponderant investments in female teachers' schools), and it gradually undermined the importance of female teacher training at the secondary level and reduced women's opportunities in society. On the other hand, the newly invented village teachers' school developed a program for training female teachers for village schools, and this was seen as the first step towards the liberation of women in rural areas.

Chapter 5 examines how, during the 1930s, the new Nationalist government (also known by its Chinese name – Guomindang), established in 1927, built up a network of various types of local teachers' schools across the nation. Planning to reshape and control the countryside, the Nationalists, by expanding local teachers' schools, extended secondary education into rural areas. The schools were directed to engage in social reform programs and to assist the state in reconstructing rural communities. Three village teachers' schools – Xianghu in Zhejiang, Huangdu in Jiangsu, and Baiquan in Henan – illustrate the various techniques the government used to penetrate rural communities. They show that the teachers' schools of the 1930s were an important vehicle through which the state built a power base in various villages. Chapter 5 also looks at the development of local female teachers' schools in rural and inland areas. Encouraged by the rural reconstruction movement, educators criticized the shortcomings of the 1922 reform and turned their attention to rural and working-class women. An examination of the Shandong Provincial Women's Normal School Number One shows that provincial female teachers' schools were one of the very few legitimate avenues through which rural and inland women could win a degree of social and economic independence. Moreover, teachers' schools introduced women to other professions, such as writing, editing, journalism, the arts, and the law, thus carving out more public space for them.

Chapter 6 examines the sociopolitical consequences of the expansion of rural education under conditions of economic decline and the surge of nationalism before the Japanese invasion of 1937. In this crucial period, rural teachers' schools became not only channels of social mobility for youth from less well-to-do rural families but also centres for Communist organizing. Using data taken primarily from teachers' schools in Shandong and Hebei provinces (two provinces that were the Chinese Communist Party's most important revolutionary bases in the 1930s and 1940s), I analyze the factors that made local teachers' schools the training centres for Communist revolutionaries as well as the venue for bringing to the countryside a revolution that had begun in the cities. After converting to the revolutionary creed in the local teachers' schools, young teachers returned to their home villages to ignite revolution and to become local guerrilla leaders. This helps to explain how the Communists were able to re-emerge after their major defeat in the mid-1930s to develop a powerful underground organization in rural areas.

The story of China's teachers' schools does not end in 1937. Substantial chapters could be devoted to the period from the Anti-Japanese War to the radical changes that followed the 1949 Revolution. The political role of the schools was endorsed by the Nationalist government during wartime but, under the Communist government after 1949, was superseded by other types of revolutionary organizations. On the other hand, their free tuition policy continued to help rural youth move up in society. The teachers' school system was revived in the late 1970s, after having been closed down during the Cultural Revolution, and it continued to prepare professional teachers during the reform era. But a series of threats has recently surfaced. The tuition-free policy has been abolished, a new plan for transforming teachers' schools into regular colleges has appeared, and college students of rural origin are having difficulty paying tuition. It seems that teachers' schools are once again facing an uncertain future.

1

The Imperial School System and Education Reform in the Second Half of the Nineteenth Century: A Historical Review

At the turn of the twentieth century, a confluence of forces indigenous and exotic drove China's leaders to heed the call of educational reformers. A series of shocking blows to the imperial body politic inspired statesmen to study European schools; however, as Chang Hao has pointed out, it would be wrong to underestimate long-term developments that originated within Chinese society.[1] During the Ming dynasty (1368-1644) an array of new types of schools had opened, starting a trend that continued under the Qing dynasty (1644-1911). The introduction of Western-style schools in the second half of the nineteenth century and the beginning of the twentieth was part of a long period of experimentation, innovation, and reform. Throughout this period, many officials believed that China's social and political travails would only end if its educational institutions were reformed so that they could produce more able men to help the state deal with practical problems. As education expanded in late imperial society, it served an ever larger segment of male society, and female literacy increased among gentry-elite families in China's richer, more sophisticated regions. The story of the transformation of women's education at the turn of the twentieth century cannot be told without spotlighting late imperial female learning.

Schools and Teachers in Late Imperial China

During the late sixth century and the early seventh century, China formalized its civil service examination system, selecting imperial officials based on objective tests of knowledge that emphasized the Confucian classics. From that time on, education gradually came to be equated with preparation for the state examinations, which produced a class of literati-officials.[2] Teachers in imperial society formed a marginal group that was either directly or indirectly attached to the state bureaucracy. From the seventeenth century to the nineteenth century, the educational system expanded until a countrywide network of schools extended from the Imperial University in

Beijing down to the village level. This expansion gradually changed the position of teachers and affected the nature of the educational system.

The School System in Late Imperial China: Ming and Qing

The school system in late imperial China was composed of dynastic schools (*guanxue*) and various types of unofficial and semi-official schools, including academies (*shuyuan*), clan and family schools (*zushu* and *jiashu*), charitable schools (*yishu* or *yixue*), and community schools (*shexue*). During the Ming dynasty, the *guanxue* school system formed an empire-wide network that was divided into two sections: central schools and local schools. The central schools included two imperial universities (*guozijian*), the highest imperial educational institutions in the Ming capital cities of Beijing and Nanjing,[3] and other schools for imperial clan descendants. Local schools were composed of prefectural schools (*fuxue*), district schools (*zhouxue*),[4] and county schools (*xianxue*), which were built in every jurisdictional region.[5] Previously, dynastic schools existed only at the prefectural level (*fu*); after the founding of the Ming dynasty, dynastic schools were set up in every county (*xian*) – a huge undertaking. The number of schools varied over the course of the Ming because, from time to time, administrative districts underwent rezoning. Based on the number of jurisdictions, contemporary scholars estimate that there were from 1,000 to 1,200 local dynastic schools in the fourteenth century and 1,471 after 1573.[6]

These government schools – which recruited local students known as licentiates (*shengyuan*), who had already passed the lowest level examination, in keeping with the county quota system (*xue'e*)[7] – were the most important element of the Ming (and the Qing) educational system. The main task of these schools was to prepare students for the civil service examinations and to support them with government subsidies.[8] During the first half of the Ming dynasty, teaching officials (*jiaoguan*) periodically gave lectures on the Confucian classics, checked attendance, assigned and assessed writing assignments, and evaluated student talent and behaviour. But from the middle of the Ming, due to the decline in the qualifications of teaching officials and in their pedagogical activities, the quality of education in these local dynastic schools degenerated quickly.[9]

The Manchu rulers of the Qing adopted the Ming school system with only slight modifications.[10] Although lectures and both monthly and quarterly examinations were maintained at a minimal level until the Yongzheng reign (1723-35), dynastic schools gradually became the places where, from a bloated pool, the central government charitably placed those expectant elderly officials who had never received any job assignments. This policy further impaired the pedagogical function and activities of dynastic schools and turned them into places where students signed up for subsidies.[11]

In addition to the government school system, another stream of education in late imperial society was formed by the academies (*shuyuan*), which had originated as early as the Tang (618-907) and developed during the Song (960-1127) and the Yuan (1271-1368) dynasties. The spread of private academies during the late Ming gradually drew students away from the dynastic schools. Like the dynastic schools, most academies aimed at preparing students for the civil service examinations, though some derived their prestige not from association with the state but, rather, with a famous scholar and/or with innovative academic activities. Many *shuyuan* were destroyed or banned by the Ming court due to their dissident scholarship during the mid-Ming and their deep involvement in political protest during the late Ming factional struggles.[12] The recovery of *shuyuan* during the Qing started with the Yongzheng regime, when the emperor ordered local officials to rebuild and develop them. The academies of the Qing period differed in some respects from those of the Ming. First, the Qing governments had a much stronger influence over them than had the Ming governments. Under the Qing, the academies lost their autonomy and became de facto organs of the state: most received financial support from local government, and most headmasters were appointed or hired by government officials.[13] Second, the academies, formerly located in remote areas, far from political centres, were now relocated to cities and towns near administrative centres, allowing tighter government surveillance.[14] Eventually they formed a provincial-prefectural-county hierarchical system that was parallel to the dynastic school system.[15] Third, as their numbers increased, academies expanded to new areas, including rural communities.[16] Although frequent openings and closures make it difficult to estimate the total number of academies nationwide during the Qing, that number definitely rose over the eighteenth and nineteenth centuries.[17] Compared to the dynastic schools, the academies had more accommodating curricula, no quota limits, looser restrictions on students' geographic origins, and more flexible admissions standards. Still, dynastic schools maintained a basic institutional connection to the civil service examinations, from which they received annual quotas. These distinct features determined how private academies and dynastic schools would fare under the educational reforms of the twentieth century.

As is mentioned above, young men often began their formal education at clan and family schools, charitable schools, private schools (*sishu*), and community schools (*shexue,* in some places called *weixue*).[18] Some scholars have suggested that village academies (*xiangcun shuyuan*) performed a similar function.[19] Other scholars assert that, during the early Qing, charitable schools functioned as academies for advanced study, becoming elementary schools only later.[20] Some charitable schools in local communities taught only basic reading skills.[21] Although debates have recently occurred regarding the names, characteristics, and functions of elementary schools in late imperial society, no one disputes that elementary education during the Ming and Qing expanded greatly, penetrating even into rural communities. During this period, several kinds of schools carried out the task of teaching basic literacy and advanced study.[22]

While it did not intervene in the affairs of village-sponsored schools or family schools, the state did encourage the work of community schools and certain types of charitable schools.[23] Imperial edicts promulgated by both the Ming and Qing courts, following a tradition inherited from the Yuan, ordered local governments to establish either a charitable school or a community school in every village and, in frontier regions, to promote literacy and moral education. As Sarah Schneewind has pointed out, such educational interventions sometimes conflicted with local religious forces and the fluctuating private interests of local officials.[24] It is true that the effectiveness and longevity of these schools varied, depending on the enthusiasm of local officials and the local economy;[25] in some cases, civil servants did more harm than good to the spread of literacy.[26] In any case, the appearance of community and charitable schools in late imperial society represented an effort by the state to oversee both elementary education and local society. Through these schools, the state tried to fill the cultural vacuum that private schools ignored.[27] This effort failed for a number of reasons, including social instability, the limited interest and authority of local officials, and a shortage of qualified teachers. Among these, lack of funds and teachers was probably key. Teachers were often poorly paid, and no formal standards were ever established for their professional qualifications, treatment, and occupational stability. As we will see, the modern school system, which was constructed after 1904, systematically tried to solve these problems by providing elementary schools with state-trained and state-supported teachers.

Teachers in Late Imperial Society

While the shortage of competent teachers for China's dynastic schools was immediately evident, no professional training was ever provided by the state. Teachers, at all levels, were either low-level bureaucrats or by-products of the examination system. In imperial society, educational personnel were divided into three types: officials and teachers in the dynastic school system; teachers in private academies; and teachers in family schools, private schools, charitable schools, and community schools. Very little scholarly work has been done on the training, selection, origin, educational and social background, and number of teachers in this period.[28]

In addition to the faculty at the two universities in Beijing and Nanjing and the provincial education commissioners, the Ming court also named numerous other education officials, including district (*zhou*) education directors (*jiaoshou*), prefectural education directors (*xuezheng*), and county education directors (*jiaoyu*) as the head of schools in each jurisdictional region. The teaching officials at each level were aided by two to four teaching assistants (*xundao*).[29] With the exception of the post of provincial education commissioner (*duxuedao*), which the Qing court renamed director of studies (*xuezheng*) in 1684, the successors to the throne retained all of the terms assigned in the Ming.[30] The duty of the provincial education commissioner was to promote and supervise educational affairs within the province; he did not have any actual teaching duties. Theoretically, educational officials were in charge of the educational affairs of their respective administrative areas and also served as teachers and headmasters at the dynastic schools.[31] As previously mentioned, the schools declined in the latter half of the Ming, educational officials did virtually no teaching throughout the Qing, and the position of "educational official" became a nominal title, a sinecure that the court benevolently assigned to elderly literati or expectant officials.[32] Not true teachers, these officials were still responsible for local educational administration and had the power to rank students in seasonal and yearly examinations. These special duties later helped these people to transfer into the modern educational bureaucracy.

The number of imperial teaching officials is also worth examining. According to Wu Zhihe, over 4,000 teaching officials swelled the ranks of officialdom during the Ming dynasty.[33] While the exact number of Qing educational officials has not been the subject of scholarly research, an approximation can be estimated from the organization of the school system at each jurisdictional level. After 1884, the Qing divided its territory into twenty-three provinces. During the reign of the Guangxu emperor (r. 1875-1908), there were 185 prefectures, 218 districts (73 of these were under the direct jurisdiction of provincial governments, giving them the same status as prefectures, while 145 were under prefectural governments), and 1,314 counties.[34] Adding up these various posts, one arrives at 1,735 educational officials. Each would have had two to four teaching assistants, possibly totalling 5,151. Taking into account that some frontier regions and small counties were too remote or too small to be assigned an educational official, and that many probably got by with few regular teaching assistants, we may safely say that there were about 6,000 educational officials during the Qing period.

The decline of teaching in dynastic schools may be related to the low status of teaching officials and to the method used to select them. Ming regulations decreed that no official with a rank higher than "the second class of the ninth rank" (*cong jiupin*) – the lowest level on the bureaucratic ladder – could serve as a prefectural education director. Later, the rank of the prefectural education officials was demoted to "unranked" (*wu pinji*) and then to "miscellaneous positions" (*zaliu*).[35] Thus, teaching officials were actually excluded from the official bureaucratic system. If promising students were to enjoy the most favourable intellectual climate, their teachers should have been drawn from the most brilliant pool. According to Wu, the ruler of the early Ming did indeed make a plan to select teaching officials from a pool of "advanced scholars" (*jinshi*) by adding a special title, *fubang jinshi* (the supplementary list of *jinshi* degree; *jinshi* was the highest degree) to the civil service examinations. This plan, however, soon failed because everyone with an advanced degree tried to avoid teaching assignments since they led to miserable professional status and the paltry income of the dynastic schools. The Ming government was reduced to recruiting "university students" (*jiansheng*), "contributed students" (*gongsheng*), and provincial degree holders (*juren*, the secondary degree) to serve as teachers.[36] Little changed in the Qing: although the rank of teaching officials was raised to the "regular seventh rank" (*zheng qipin*), the highest rank for teaching officials at the prefectural level was still barely equal to that of a county magistrate.[37] The situation deteriorated over the course of the dynasty: since, by the mid-Qing, many teaching posts were sold for a fixed price (*juanna*), many of those who held these positions did not possess even the most rudimentary qualifications.[38] As we can see, the low qualification of teachers in dynastic schools was only to be expected.

Those who taught in private academies (referred to by a variety of titles, such as *shanzhang*, *yuanzhang*, *zhujiao*, and so forth) had achieved far greater academic distinction than had their official counterparts. Thanks to Liu Boji's research on private academies in Guangdong Province during the Qing period, we know a great deal about the teachers in these institutions. While the majority had passed the palace or provincial examinations (these were the highest and intermediate level examinations), a few had only passed the qualifying examination. Many had retired from officialdom, had been excused from government service to observe the traditional period of mourning a dead parent, or had previously taught in government schools.[39] Research has also shown that, inevitably, there were some poorly qualified academy teachers who got their positions due to favouritism.[40] But, overall, the academies had to maintain their reputations by hiring noted teachers and, thus, attracting students.

Throughout the Ming dynasty, teachers at elementary schools were divided into two types (though sometimes they could be both). Teachers at the primary level (*mengshi*) were distinguished from those at the advanced level (*jingshi*).[41] This division corresponded to two levels of elementary education, defined by contemporaneous ideas about children's intellectual development. Primary schools (*mengxue*) educated younger male pupils and, in some family schools, young females were taught basic reading and writing skills (I treat female education in another section). Advanced elementary education (*jingshi*, named for the principal subjects taught) trained students who already possessed basic skills and who displayed the intellectual talents required to pass the examinations. Liao T'ai-ch'u's study of traditional schools in the 1930s suggests that primary schooling could sometimes last for ten years, during which time students memorized a set curriculum of Confucian texts, the meaning of which was explained to them by their teachers only when memorization was complete.[42] During advanced study, teachers continued to present rote interpretations of important books.

What little is known about those who taught in Ming-era clan schools, charitable schools, and community schools comes from contemporaneous works of seventeenth-century fiction.[43] In stories and novels, one routinely encounters schoolteachers who lived in abject poverty. If they held a degree at all it was the licentiate's degree; many had failed the examinations time after time. Recent research indicates that most schoolteachers were drawn from the local literati and that their employment conditions varied considerably depending on professional achievements, the type of school in which they worked, and the generosity of the school's management.[44] It is true that some of the local teachers who are mentioned in historical records enjoyed better working conditions, but these exceptional individuals entered the record only because they later won high office through civil service examinations. Almost by definition, those who did not pass the examinations and who remained trapped in village teaching jobs disappeared without a trace. However, the conditions in which they lived may be glimpsed through looking at documents concerning Qing-era village teachers.

The situation of schoolteachers in rural communities did not change much during the Qing. Evelyn Rawski's research shows that most schoolteachers were selected by school administrators or clan or village leaders from among the local literati who held the lowest degrees or who were preparing to sit for the lowest examinations. A teacher, the role model for the young men of the community, was expected to be both well educated and highly ethical.[45] Data on the educational backgrounds of the teachers in Zhili Province reveal that as many as 69 percent of elementary schoolteachers in one fortunate county were degree-holders, while in another county it might be only 23 percent. The data also show that the more teachers there were in a given county, the lower the percentage of degree-holders.[46] These numbers tell us very little regarding the question of the relative competence of primary and advanced elementary teachers, and they shed no light on how they divided the teaching of basic literacy and the teaching of advanced texts.

A range of factors, including social origins, educational background, and closeness to well placed officials, influenced the lot of teachers in late imperial society. Those who taught in academies (some of which were state-sponsored) enjoyed higher salaries thanks to their distinguished performance in the examinations and the status that accompanied their elite jobs.

The director of an academy could draw from several hundred to 1,000 silver taels annually, supplemented by student gifts. But an assistant teacher in the same school might only make forty taels.[47] Paltry official salaries obliged some state teachers to rely on donations from students.[48] Teachers in village schools received very low pay; and, when they were paid, it was often in kind – perhaps with a bag of rice, a piece of meat, or a bundle of vegetables. For instance, teachers in Guizhou village schools received only ten taels per year, and most teachers in clan and family schools and community schools were paid between ten and forty taels per year, probably determined by the level of the students they taught.[49] The vast discrepancies among teachers' income in premodern China, and the hardships suffered by those who taught in rural communities, foreshadowed the problems that would be faced by modern teachers (see Chapter 4).

Since the mid-Ming, a deep gap has opened between those members of the imperial bureaucracy who held real political power and those who attended to educational matters. The educational group was gradually marginalized through the demoting of ranks, the lowering of salaries, and the extension of terms of service. Ming educational officials occupied such low official status that they had no say in local administrative affairs or in county political activities. Whereas administrative officials normally served three-year terms before being considered for promotion or relocation, educational officials served for nine years, which effectively deprived them of any hope for political power.[50] Although the Qing court tempted educational officials with the prospect of being promoted to county magistrate, the large number of officials waiting for a position reflects a bleaker reality.[51] Since some faculty of the academies were drawn from off-duty officials and those who held no official rank, they, too, lacked any direct connection to political power.[52] When we examine the birth of the modern educational system and the first cohort of professional teachers, we should remember that, for centuries, teachers had been the most marginalized group in Chinese officialdom.[53] This helps us to understand just how important the establishment of independent teachers' schools was to the modern schooling structure. The marginalization of teaching officials in imperial times paved the way for the modern separation of the educational group trained in teachers' schools and the government officials who held real political power.

Liang Qichao and Educational Reform in the Late Nineteenth Century

The nineteenth century's educational crisis stemmed not only from weaknesses endemic to the schools and the examination system but also from wider social problems, such as demographic growth, social unrest, and military disasters. In the second half of the nineteenth century, the appearance of missionary schools, with their distinct style, curricula, and tendency to promote female education, suggested a new option for would-be educational reformers. When "Self-Strengthening" officials began opening new-style schools in the 1860s, they included Western learning in the curriculum. Still, the influence of Western learning and the appearance of modern schools were confined to coastal areas and treaty ports. Most proposed reforms focused on recycling suggestions that stressed education itself rather than political change and systemic reform. These proposals failed to address the challenges posed by social change and political crisis in late imperial society as well as the newly arrived foreign threats. As problems continued to pile up, prominent officials began to believe that China needed to pursue a more radical approach. Drawing on decades of ambitious proposals, Liang Qichao (1873-1929) drew up a comprehensive plan for starting afresh: his would be an educational transformation aimed at bringing real social change.

Problems with the Late Qing Educational System

The first problem of late Qing education was the tension between expanded education and the limited quotas of the dynastic schools. The conflict between increasing literacy and the number of candidates for the examinations, along with the limited quotas of dynastic schools, left the path for social mobility via the examination system very narrow indeed. Benjamin Elman has recently pointed out that, although the court responded affirmatively to local requests to increase the examination quotas and the number of students enrolled in dynastic schools, such cosmetic changes were far outstripped by population growth.[54] In 1741, China had a population of about 143 million, but, by 1850, it had reached about 430 million.[55] With the expansion of education, the number of literate people (with and without degrees) was growing. The quota for dynastic schools, however, did not increase until after the mid-nineteenth century, when the Qing court suppressed the Taiping Rebellion.[56] According to Chang Chung-li, prior to the rebellion, 1,741 state schools throughout the empire had enrolled 25,089 students in examinations that were held twice every three years. After the rebellion had been put down, the number of schools increased to 1,810 (due to the remapping of administrative districts), and the quota for total enrolment was increased to 30,113.[57] The total number of candidates competing for the licentiate's degree in any given year was approximately two million.[58] The rate of passing the lowest level examination stood at only 1.25 percent before the Taiping Rebellion and at 1.5 percent afterward.[59] In this situation, dynastic schools were forced to expand by producing many informal titles. Besides the "regular student" (*linsheng*), formal students who received financial support from the government (as the quota system promised), there were informal students. These included the "supplementary student" (*fusheng*) who received no financial aid and whose numbers were not limited by quotas, as well as the "added student" (*zengsheng*), the "specially appointed student" (*yisheng*),[60] and the "selected student" (*basheng*).[61] The number of these informal students sometimes exceeded the maximum number of formal students (as indicated by the original quota figure). For example, in 1836 Zouping County was assigned a quota of thirty students, but the number of supplementary students was over 400.[62] The overpopulated dynastic schools disabled the quota system.

The odds of succeeding in the next test, the provincial examination, were just as daunting as were the odds of succeeding in the first test. Elman's research shows that, before the 1850s, the success rate at the provincial level was about 1.5 percent.[63] Many endured several consecutive failures (the provincial examinations were held every three years during the Qing) yet remained enrolled in dynastic schools in order to collect their subsidies. From 1865 to 1872, the Qing court gave some prefectures and counties more quotas as a reward for their financial support for the war against the Taiping rebels.[64] However, this only marginally increased their chances of success in the empire-wide competition for primary degrees, and it had the unpleasant effect of increasing the competition at the provincial level.[65]

An educational system developed to feed the extraordinarily competitive examinations inevitably yielded huge numbers of surplus literati who never held official positions. Each time an examination was held, 98.5 percent of those taking it failed. How could these people make a living? Many turned to teaching.[66] The surplus literati who became teachers assisted the expansion of elementary education and of literacy, which, in turn, made examinations even more competitive. At the same time, rising examination quotas and the increasingly common practice of selling degrees and official titles created an overflow of fully qualified men who held no office. This group of marginalized official-literati became a force that advanced to fill the new schools and the school administration during the late Qing educational reform.

As dynastic schools became little but registration offices for local examinations and dispensaries for educational welfare payments, as well as a charitable place to house elderly literati and expectant officials, the court began to feel that it was losing control over local society, which it had formerly been able to monitor through educational institutions. The winnowing away of any meaningful function for dynastic schools was of particular concern because of the traditional role of the teacher as the ethical torchbearer for the community. The imperial state depended on the school system to inculcate and spread its ideology, and the dynastic schools were used to pacify local communities. Dynastic schools were typically situated in local Confucian temples, within which local gurus and worthies were worshipped. Wu Zhihe's remarkable research shows that, during the Ming, these schools functioned as centres for spiritual, cultural, and moral correctness. Local records, artistic works, and books were stored in schools, and important ritual events took place in them – seasonal sacrifices, social ceremonies, community assemblies, and the paying of homage to wise elders, filial sons, and faithful wives. Ideally, every teacher and student was expected to serve as a moral examplar for the local people, while teaching officials were expected to supervise the moral and social order of local communities.[67] When the schools became saturated with disqualified teachers and frustrated students, the image of the school leader as ethical examplar collapsed.

The late Qing also saw the conflict between examination-oriented education and popular education, whose goal had deviated from what the state had intended for it. The spread of elementary educational institutions, such as clan schools, private schools, community schools, charitable schools, and village *shuyuan*, resulted in an increasing number of youth with basic literary skills.[68] As Woodside points out, popular literacy was a double-edged sword: it helped to reinforce community security and it also helped to develop some rebellious consciousness. Meanwhile, failed efforts to move up the social ladder also created intense social instability.[69] In the late Qing, unhappy literati and migrating peasants created a national crisis that lasted over a decade. Therefore, during the Tongzhi Restoration after the Taiping Rebellion, the reinstallation of dynastic schools and the examination system was an important way of rebuilding local order.[70] Social stability became a pressing concern, and this inspired educational reform during the second half of the nineteenth century.

On the other hand, some literati and government officials tried to find an outlet for a basically literate populace. They considered community and charitable schools not as a means of supplying talented people to the bureaucracy but, rather, as a means of keeping good people content with their lot in life.[71] In 1826, Zhou Kai, the governor of Xiangyang Prefecture, issued a regulation for prefectural charitable schools:

> [We] do not expect every child of the poor to reach [great literary] achievement [because they] have to learn farming when they are fourteen or fifteen. If they can read these three books,[72] [they] will know in their hearts that "filial piety, brotherliness, loyalty, faith, rites, righteousness, honesty and a sense of shame" are the principles for managing a family. [These principles] will be of benefit all their lifetime. Although [they] could not go to [higher-level] schools to become refined literati [*xiushi*], they will be obedient people content with their life [*anfen zhi liangmin*].[73]

At the same time, scholars who were promoting charitable schools for children from poor families also suggested a change in the goal of education: "Charitable schools are specifically established for children of poor families. If [the schools] teach them to read all the Classics, this will not only be beyond their capacity, but also will not meet their urgent needs ... This [East Guangdong Primary] Charitable School is established for the purpose of teaching children from poor families to know basic principles of morality. Therefore, the curriculum [of this school] does not include contents related to the examinations."[74]

The purpose of basic education no longer simply involved "selecting talented people for the state" but also involved providing students with "skills to support their families" (*yi wei yangshi fuyu zhi zi*)[75] and moral training to ensure that the empire was populated by "obedient people." We will see that this two-level system in elementary education, which established different types of education for different social sectors, was inherited by the modern educational system. The establishment of the modern school system, along with vocational training institutions, tried to address this long-standing problem.

The problems that the state faced in expanding education led to the decentralization and privatization of education, which undermined state power in local communities. Woodside believes that the state's gradual withdrawal from public education since the mid-Qing period and the increasing privatization of primary education fostered a strong discontent among the intelligentsia.[76] Since the state's efforts to extend its influence into local communities by encouraging community schools and charitable schools gradually withered due to lack of funding and teachers, great lineages concentrated their resources on training their brightest young men to win honour for their clans. The evidence from local gazetteers shows that, facing the extraordinary competition of the examinations, large families and clans adopted a strategy that invested resources in the most promising young men. The clan would arrange for students who did not have the talent to pass the examinations to learn practical skills, such as money management, farming, and a knowledge of the family business.[77] This strategy resulted in concentrating wealth and power in the hands of large families, and it left those from lower social strata struggling, thus increasing dissatisfaction with the privatization of education. Woodside points out that the desire to revive the legendary system of state controlled education that had existed before 1840 inspired political opposition and, in the early twentieth century, provided reformers with a strong motive for establishing a countrywide public school system.[78]

Tentative Reforms of the Late Qing Educational System

Prior to the New Policy (1902-11) reform, the court modified the content of the civil service examinations, mandated pedagogical changes in old academies, and built new ones. As early as the 1880s, articles and memorials by reform-minded literati such as Feng Guifen (1809-74), Xue Fucheng (1838-94), and Zheng Guanying (1842-1922) broached the subject of radical change; however, it was not until 1895, when China was defeated in the Sino-Japanese War, that significant numbers of literati and officials started to take the issue of reforming the examinations seriously. The court approved wide-ranging reforms only after 1901.[79]

One area that did undergo substantial change in the second half of the nineteenth century was the academy. During the reign of the Tongzhi emperor (1862-74), 366 new academies were built; over the next thirty-four years, 671 more were erected.[80] Only a few of these, such as the Polytechnic Academy (*Gezhi Shuyuan*), placed Western learning at the centre of their curriculum, thus marginalizing Chinese learning.[81] Some academies tried to shift the focus of learning away from the single purpose of passing the civil service examinations, giving greater scope to rediscovering how the traditional classics could provide answers to contemporary problems. Examples include Longmen Academy in Shanghai, Weijing Academy in Shaanxi, Zunjing Academy in Sichuan, and Nanjing Academy in Jiangsu. A small number of academies, such as Zhengmeng Academy in Shanghai and Chongshi Academy in Zhejiang, added Western learning to their curricula and were thus gradually transformed from old-fashioned academies into new-style schools (*xuetang*). Before 1895, the impact of Western learning on the daily lives of most Chinese literati was negligible, and what stimulus for reform they felt was engendered from within their own traditional frames of reference. The new and reformed academies produced a group of literati whose solid classical training had occurred in an environment committed to innovation; they would support the more dramatic reforms to come.[82] After 1895, with the rise of the new nationalism, modern academies opened in the wealthy and progressive Jiangnan area at a dizzying pace, and many added Western learning to their curricula. In other parts of China, major changes did not take place until after 1900.

During this same period, many officials associated with the Self-Strengthening Movement established modern professional schools. Though few in number, these new schools produced engineers, linguists, and military officials who were needed for the government's self-strengthening projects. Examples are the Capital Foreign Language School (*Jingshi Tongwen Guan*, 1862) in Beijing, the Shanghai Foreign Language School (*Guang Fangyan Guan*, 1863) in Shanghai, the Guangzhou Language School (1864), the Fujian Shipbuilding School (1866), and a number of military academies.[83] Progressive provincial governors in Fujian, Zhejiang, Guangdong, and Hubei took leading roles in founding, funding, and staffing such schools during the 1890s.[84] While it could be argued that these schools failed to adequately strengthen China, they did provide a generation of mathematics, physics, chemistry, geology, and foreign language teachers for the schools that constituted the next stage in the transformation of Chinese education.

Despite an environment rich in practical innovation, dynastic schools did not respond to any proposals for change. Before there could be complete educational reform there would have to be political reform.

Liang Qichao and the 1898 Reform

In October 1896, after China's defeat in the Sino-Japanese War, Liang Qichao, a prominent scholar and one of the leaders in the famous Hundred Days of Reform in 1898, published a long article on political and educational reform in a famous reformist newspaper, *Current Affairs* (*shiwubao*). In this noteworthy reform manifesto, "A general proposal for reform" (*Bianfa tongyi*), he proposed three alternatives for China's political and educational future. In the first, the court would eventually replace the current examination system with an empire-wide school system. Only this, he wrote, would ensure the success of reform. In the second, the court would enlarge the examination curriculum by adding more questions about practical skills and Western knowledge. He noted that this amounted to a compromise measure and could only achieve limited success. In the third, the court would reform the content of the examinations by adding a question about contemporary issues and practical topics. As Liang pointed out, this could only produce minor rewards.[85]

Liang pioneered the idea of teachers' schools, possibly inspired by Japanese educational reform, from which he seized on the teachers' school, or normal school, as the "foundation of mass education." Anticipating the shortfall of qualified teachers for modern schools, he advocated establishing a teachers' school in every county and one at each jurisdictional level above the county. He hoped that the students who graduated from these schools would go on to teach in elementary schools. Other teachers' schools would prepare teachers to teach secondary students and college students.[86] Liang's proposal did not address either the ongoing shortcomings of the examination system or the dynastic schools; it simply showed how the huge number of surplus literati could be employed. No single plan could solve the problems that had hobbled China's political system for centuries.

Other reformers of the 1898 generation, including Kang Youwei (1858-1927), Li Duanfen (1833-1907), and Sheng Xuanhuai (1844-1916), also dodged the problems besetting the dynastic school system. In a memorial submitted during the reform, Kang suggested replacing academies and "improper shrines" (*yinci*) with Western-style schools; he mentioned nothing about dynastic schools.[87] The Guangxu emperor accepted Kang's suggestion and issued an edict urging all provincial governors to act.[88] The Hundred Days of Reform turned a blind eye to the dynastic school system and tried to revolutionize the examination system by transforming the academies into a national school system. Perhaps the reformers were wary of inciting conflict with conservative groups who had interests in the state school system. Many conservatives viewed academies, whose history was spotted here and there with anti-establishment activities, with distrust and insisted that the state's political stability was enshrined in the dynastic schools. Any change in that system would have affected the selection of officials as a whole and might have mitigated the inculcation of state ideology. Though they had long since ceased to have any practical educational function, the dynastic schools remained a formidable obstacle to educational reform.

Women's Education in Late Imperial Society

Although the expansion of education in the eighteenth and nineteenth centuries largely benefited male students, women were also affected, especially in economically and culturally advanced areas. Because of the important role mothers played in early education, the late Qing's intensification of the examination system encouraged gentry families to invest in their daughters' education. By the end of the nineteenth century, Chinese gentry began actively promoting women's education along lines borrowed from missionary schools. However, the ideological rationale for the changes in female education was deeply rooted in the traditional idea that women were the primary family educators. The driving force for this transformation was reform-minded gentry who were responding to a rising nationalism.

Women's Learning in the Inner Chambers

Recent scholarship suggests that the old adage "a woman is virtuous only if she is untalented" indicates the discontent that arose as women began to gain access to education in late imperial China. Beginning in the seventeenth century, women from gentry families in Jiangnan were involved in literary activities, and a group of female writers became fairly well known in elite circles. In the cultured urban milieu, courtesans were expected to cultivate elegant literary tastes.[89] Rawski estimates that nineteenth-century female literacy was between 2 percent and 10 percent but that it could have been as high as 25 percent in wealthy and progressive regions.[90] Slight by comparison with the population as a whole, literate women nonetheless managed to carve out a distinctive cultural realm.

Female education was also offering women a change in context, even exposing them to market forces as they began to profit from their literary skills. Susan Mann suggests that late Qing female education involved both literate and non-literate learning. Both forms of learning were strictly limited to the domestic sphere, and there was no government involvement.[91] While women's education took place only in the home, literate women significantly expanded the bounds of learning. Their curriculum, which included classical texts, was not limited to moral instruction. Girls from elite families generally studied the same texts as did their brothers.[92] Ko's research shows that, in the eighteenth century, some women were not only erudite but also taught in family schools and sold their artistic works to bring in much-needed income.[93] The appearance of women teachers and published writers reflected the changing position of women in late imperial society.

Women of all classes received non-literate education, which, according to Mann, included moral inculcation and domestic skills training.[94] Different rituals, such as foot binding, the celebration of Double Seven Festival, the sacrifices to Leizu, and dowry preparation taught girls that being good wives and mothers meant staying at home, taking care of children, and putting to use the domestic skills they had learned.[95] It is worth noting that the three traditional elements of women's education – moral inculcation, literary study, and training in domestic skills – were maintained as three principal parts of the curriculum in early twentieth-century modern women's schools.

In the late Qing, changing conditions obliged both men and women to revise their vision of women's education, and a trend of nurturing talented women (*cainü*) in literary creation gradually emerged among the Jiangnan gentry-literati families.[96] Since the late Ming, some male literati had promoted the education and literary activities of their wives, concubines, daughters, and even daughters-in-law.[97] An education could do many things for a woman, including improving her ability to express herself and communicate with the outside world, improving her appeal as a prospective wife, and improving her ability to impart knowledge to her children, support her husband by managing the family wealth, and maintain family order by following Confucian teaching. In light of the fierce competition of the civil service examination, the education of gentry women was seen as strictly utilitarian: it would help maintain family prosperity by helping one's sons pass the examinations. Mothers played an important role in children's early education and were often expected to teach their sons their first characters. The woman who could do this and more could give her son an edge in the examination culture that would soon engulf him. On the other hand, mothers were also expected to be the primary educators of their daughters, teaching them to read, to behave ethically, and to perform their domestic labors.[98] Chen Hongmou, who wrote a treatise on the importance of women's education, believed that "a wise daughter will make a wise wife and mother. And wise mothers rear wise sons and grandsons."[99] It was indeed the consideration of "indigenous statecraft tradition," according to Paul Bailey, that assigned women "as guarantors of household virtue and prosperity".[100] However, Nanxiu Qian points out that women's education in the modern era also had another tradition, the tradition of "*xianyuan*" (worthy ladies), which emphasized a literate culture of elite women in imperial history.[101] Given this, the idea that the mother should play the role of teacher within the family received a great deal of support among many male literati during the late Qing period, and it became key to the transformation of women's education at the turn of the twentieth century.

New Factors in Female Education: Missionary Schools and Overseas Students

In the mid-nineteenth century, Western missionaries introduced the first girls' schools in China. Before 1900, however, this development took place primarily in coastal areas. The first opened in 1844 in Ningbo, Zhejiang Province;[102] by 1877, 524 pupils were enrolled in thirty-eight Protestant missionary schools for girls.[103] By 1896, the total number of female pupils in missionary schools reached 6,798; there were 308 schools at the time.[104] Historical records show that, before 1895, missionaries also sent a handful of girls overseas for study.[105]

In the second half of the nineteenth century, the students at missionary girls' schools, and female overseas students who were sponsored by missionaries, were quite distinct from the image I presented earlier of genteel Jiangnan girls. From 1842 to the early 1880s, missionary schools encountered great difficulties in enrolling girls from well-to-do backgrounds. To attract students, early missionary schools provided free tuition and board, even paying girls' families to permit them to attend. Such arrangements had special appeal for poor families.[106] The situation shifted a bit during the 1880s since, by then, a small number of female students attended not because of financial need but because of religious conviction.[107] Starting in 1890, the missionaries were able to adjust their recruitment strategy and turn their attention to female students from the upper classes.[108]

One sign of the changing class background of the girls who enrolled at missionary schools was the introduction of a tuition system. The earliest girls' school in Ningbo, for example, began charging for board and tuition at the end of the 1880s.[109] St. Mary's Hall in Shanghai, a girls' school established in 1881, was not very successful even though classes were free and students were supplied with a stipend. By 1890, the school had only thirty-two students; it started charging tuition after 1900.[110] The most famous women's school, the McTyeire School for Girls (*Zhongxi Nüshu*), which was established by missionaries in 1892 in Shanghai, was specifically for Chinese upper-class women. "It was the first school which charged parents regular fees for the board and tuition of their daughters while in school."[111] The American Methodist Church established a girls' school in Fuzhou in 1859; during the early years of its existence, it had only one student, but, by 1888, it had thirty students. No student was charged tuition until 1894. In 1894, about one-third of the students in this school were child-brides (*tongyangxi*), but, by 1909, this group of students had become insignificant, constituting only one-eightieth of the student body.[112] This change implies two possible tendencies between the 1890s to 1900s: (1) more students and (2) fewer students from the lower social strata. American Methodist missionaries reported in 1907 that their school for girls would soon begin charging tuition, regardless of students' marital status or financial condition.[113]

The gradual exclusion of poor girls from missionary schools through the imposition of tuition fees indicates that the strategy of turning to the upper classes had begun to pay off.

Still, it would take time for this strategy to show results. Enrolment records indicate that missionaries did not attract many upper-class female students until after 1900. The McTyeire School for Girls in Shanghai enrolled only seven students in its first year,[114] and, in 1900, it had only three graduates.[115] St. Mary's Hall had the same experience: in 1900, the school had only one graduate.[116] And, with regard to the American Methodist school for girls in Fuzhou, "Not till 1896 did it cease to be necessary to seek students and become possible to select students."[117] It seems that missionary schools only really began to develop after 1900, when they turned to recruiting students from among upper-class women. This was also the time when girls' schools run by Chinese gentry took off.

As these schools trained girls to assist in missionary enterprises, the curriculum emphasized religious courses, languages, world history, and a basic knowledge of the natural sciences.[118] English language classes and Bible reading were given priority over study of the Chinese language.[119] In the missionary schools, the domestic skills Chinese society considered crucial to serving as an exemplary wife and mother were only extracurricular activities.[120] Women sent overseas studied medicine, which was most appropriate with regard to the agenda of the religious mission but was utterly unheard of in Chinese society. In her study of an early group of women who studied abroad, Ye Weili said, "Rather than seeing their medical practice as a self-fulfilling career in the modern sense, they looked at it essentially as a Christian service."[121] Upon their return to China, these remarkable doctors both worked in and established Christian hospitals.[122] Most of them never married and never became wives and mothers.[123] Not only did the missionary schools prepare women for lives that were aberrational by conventional Chinese standards, but the overseas education they provided Chinese women differed from the teacher training sought by the young women who, some years later, would be sent abroad by the Chinese government.

Despite their atypical nature, the girls' schools established by Western missionaries and missionary-sponsored overseas training were of significance for women's education in China in two ways. First, missionary schools brought the issue of female education, formerly confined to the domestic domain, into the public domain and raised the possibility of female education as a public undertaking. Second, missionary schools provided an example of girls' schools, some aspects of which the Chinese gentry adopted in setting up their own women's schools.[124] As change swept across China at the turn of the twentieth century, two distinct pedagogical streams converged, and the missionary experience blended with Chinese elite education to produce something new.

The Transformation of Women's Education: 1895-1900

While Zheng Guanying has been identified as the first spokesman for the general education of Chinese women, his ideas did not go much beyond training "virtuous women, virtuous wives and virtuous mothers (*liangfu, liangqi, liangmu*)."[125] The publication of Liang Qichao's famous manifesto of 1896, "A General Proposal for Reform," played a more significant role in the transformation of women's education. In a section entitled "On Women's Schooling" (*Lun nüxue*), Liang linked women's education to the very survival of the nation. While it is difficult to unravel the patriarchal from the radical in this piece, Liang ambiguously asserts that "the weakness in this country [*tianxia*] is rooted in the fact that women are not educated."[126] As Nanxiu Qian points out, blaming women for China's weakness was representative of the 1898 male reformers' view of women's education, as they saw women only as economic resources. Therefore, educating women, in the eyes of male reformers, like Liang himself, was a way "to restore Chinese pride, despite the recent humiliations."[127] From this approach, Liang accepted traditional ideas about mothers as the primary teachers of young children but, inspired by nationalism, he claimed, less ambiguously, women's key role in children's education and mothers' importance with regard to raising decent male citizens.[128] It was Liang who transformed these ideas in a way that would help break the bonds of domesticity.

In 1897, Liang wrote a statement for the Jingzheng Girls' School (*Jingzheng nüxue* – literally, the girls' school of classical principles), which was opened that year in Shanghai by a group of local gentry. He declared that educated women benefited society in four ways: by assisting their husbands, by teaching their children, by helping their families, and by improving the [Chinese] race (*xiangfu, jiaozi, yijia,* and *shanzhong*).[129] Liang belonged to the tradition of late imperial literati, which promoted female education for the sake of training wise mothers. But one finds something new in Liang's articles. First, in referring to "two hundred million" women,[130] Liang shifted the focus from the elite class to all women. Second, he related the significance of women's education to the fate of the country and assigned men and women equal responsibility. Third, he promoted the idea that women's education should take place outside the family and should be based on the traditional (i.e., male) curriculum. Physical training was also necessary, he wrote, to improve women's health so that they would have strong bodies to carry strong babies.[131] By binding the nation's fate to women's education, Liang created a rationale for bringing women's education into the public domain as well as providing an ideological basis for elite groups to begin building women's schools. This link, however, was established on the basis that Liang excluded the *"cainü"* tradition from late imperial female learning, as Harriet Zurndorfer has pointed out.[132] Female reformers, on the contrary, embraced Western knowledge while maintaining their own tradition of *"cainü"* and *"xianyuan"* that emphasized women's self-expression and intellectual independence.[133] Unfortunately, as shown below, women reformers' voices were inundated under the high tide of nationalism and the urgent state-building program in the 1902 New Policy Reform, which adopted the male approach of 1898 in promoting a women's public educational system.[134]

Indeed, the prominent men who collaborated to found Jingzheng Girls' School had been inspired by such ideas. The school admitted girls from gentry families, ages eight to fifteen, who already possessed basic reading skills. The school regulations stated: "Although the school advocates equal education for all classes and opposes discrimination on the basis of social status, opening this school is regarded as a pioneering action: this school is training teachers for the future. Therefore, it is necessary to select women from good families (*liangjia guixiu*)."[135] The founders and financial supporters of the school were all from literati-official families, and the first cohort of students was drawn exclusively from their ranks.[136] The school regulation that forbade students from "bringing their own maids to live with them" gives us an indication of just who was enrolled there.[137] Education for the upper classes followed the late imperial tradition of schooling women of the gentry. As we will see in Chapter 2, the imperial tradition as it applied to female education (which included literary study, moral training, and domestic skills training) was not soon shaken off.[138] By this time, as we saw above, missionary schools for girls had also become schools for the elite. From 1898 on, enrolment in both missionary schools and private schools run by Chinese gentry expanded. Something had changed: perhaps it was a new strategy on the part of missionaries, perhaps it was a revolution in elite attitudes, perhaps it was both. Missionary schools had an impact, but, ultimately, it was the Chinese elite that was the driving force in the transformation of Chinese women's education.

2
Education and Society in Transition: The Rise of Teachers' Schools, 1897-1911

The failure of the 1898 reform was followed by a series of imperial edicts abrogating educational reform. However, this political relapse did not last long. After the disastrous Boxer Rebellion and the foreign invasion in 1900, the Qing court once again grew convinced of the urgent need for reform. The major projects in the 1898 reform were revived in the New Policy of 1902. In 1902, the Qing court promulgated the Imperial Regulations for a Modern School System (*Qinding xuetang zhangcheng*)[1] as the most important part of the New Policy Reform. One year later, in 1904, the regulations were reissued in a considerably revised form as the Imperially Approved Memorial on Modern School Regulations (*Zouding xuetang zhangcheng*) to announce the nationwide establishment of a new-style school system. Then, in a fateful move, in 1905, the Qing court announced the abolition of the thousand-year-old civil service examination system, which was to be replaced by a modern school system on the Western model.

Amidst these social changes, Liu Dapeng (1857-1942), a member of the Shanxi gentry who taught privately in his village, was anxiously watching this series of drastic conversions and recorded their impact on his small community. Very much a product of late Qing examination culture, Liu had been teaching at local private and family schools (*si shu*) off and on for almost twenty years. He had managed to pass the provincial examination in 1894 but had failed the metropolitan examination three times. His sons followed his example, studying for the examinations while teaching. A work entitled *Diary from a Retreat* (*Tuixiang zhai riji*) features Liu's record and vividly conveys the difficulty teachers and students had in adjusting to a new age.[2]

When the final curtain on the examinations was rung down, the way of being of numerous scholars vanished. The establishment of new schools threatened the livelihood of every older teacher. In the late Qing, the imperial civil service examination system had produced 20,000 to 30,000 licentiates nationwide each year as well as thousands of provincial and national degree-holders (*juren* and *jinshi*) in triennial examinations. In addition, numerous candidates studied for the examinations while the state supported over 6,000 education officials in offices. At the same time, the number of expectant officials – people who had titles but no actual offices – was several times greater than what the imperial offices could hold. The rise of a new educational system precipitated a break, both educationally and socially. The literati, like Liu and his sons, were facing a serious challenge.

This chapter examines the rapid expansion of teachers' schools in the first decade of twentieth-century China and analyzes the social and educational transformation brought about by their establishment. These institutions were used as a means to transform the old dynastic schools and to provide some older literati with a new social identity. They also became a political arena for superfluous imperial officials by allowing marginal candidates for bureaucratic positions to become educational officials and to regain prestige and power by controlling government-run teachers' schools. This new system of teachers' schools further institutionalized the long-standing split between educational circles and the government bureaucracy, and it legitimated the position of teachers as a professional group. In the newly built modern educational system, which emphasized training for modern citizenship, the Qing state attempted to extend its influence into the previously private education of young boys. An unexpected result of this state-building project was the establishment of public schools for women and girls, including teachers' schools and elementary schools. This meant redefining the meaning of women's education: from being an investment in the family it became an investment in the nation, and it legitimated women's position in the public domain.

Teacher Training and Social Transformation

China's first teachers' institution in Shanghai was established in 1897 by Sheng Xuanhuai, under the strong influence of the thinkers who later led the 1898 reform.[3] The teachers' school (*shifan yuan*) of Nanyang Public School (*Nanyang gongxue*), a pilot program largely copied from Japanese teacher training programs, was not a public institute but an organization-funded school. With its limited influence, it survived the tumult of the aborted reform movement, the disorder of the Boxer movement, and the occupation of Beijing by European powers, only to close in 1903.[4] In 1902, the teachers' college (*shifan guan*) at Capital University (*Jingshi da xuetang*), a public school, was established in Beijing and soon superseded the function of the Nanyang Teachers' College with regard to training teachers for the nation. Between 1897 and 1903, only a few teachers' schools sprang up nationwide, and each was quite isolated from the others.[5] But the Qing court's 1904 proclamation of the Imperially Approved Memorial on Modern School Regulations triggered a massive change. According to incomplete statistics collected by the Board of Education (*xue bu*), the number of modern schools increased from 222 in 1902 to 16,895 in 1907.[6] Teachers' schools were a rapidly growing component of the new educational system: they constituted almost half of all schools above the elementary level.[7] In 1907 there were 541 teachers' schools,[8] compared with 74 specialty colleges (*zhuanmen xuetang*), 137 vocational schools (*shiye xuetang*), and 398 regular middle schools (*putong zhong xuetang*).[9]

Teachers' Schools in the 1904 School System

The 1904 school system showed some correspondence to the imperial school system, although the former had a new appearance. The designers of the 1904 system kept the old system in mind; for them, establishing a new system did not mean completely destroying the old system. The resilient semi-official *shuyuan* system became the foundation of the regular educational system (i.e., elementary, middle schools, colleges/universities) under the 1904 reform.[10] The 1904 system suggested that regular middle schools be set up in each administrative city and town, at the provincial, prefectural, and county levels. In practice, due to the lack of financing, most local governments took a shortcut, converting the academically advanced *shuyuan* in provincial capitals into colleges and middle schools, the *shuyuan* in prefectural cities into middle schools, and the *shuyuan* in county towns into higher primary schools.[11] All of these conversions maintained an approximate correspondence between the academic levels of postreform and prereform institutions. These regular schools, like the *shuyuan* in the prereform period, received only a portion of their funds from local governments and had to depend on students' paying for tuition, fees, boarding, textbooks, and clothes.[12] Meanwhile, existing community, charitable, village, and private schools, which taught basic reading and writing skills, were now brought into the lower primary school network. During this transition, many new schools were established by officials and local gentry, but many old schools remained and retained their traditional curricula. The 1904 system set up regulations for training and selecting teachers for lower and higher primary schools.[13] Under the 1904 system, the state, for the first time, made a consistent effort to maintain control over local elementary education by providing state-trained and government-financed teachers.

The 1904 regulations established an independent system of teachers' schools. These schools operated at both secondary and tertiary levels of education, but it was the former that made up the majority of the teacher training system. These schools differed from regular middle schools not only in training and curricula but also in many other respects. Unlike with regular middle schools and colleges, with teachers' schools, governments had full control, reinforcing school regulations, selecting teachers, admitting students, and appointing principals and presidents. Unlike regular middle schools, teachers' schools were entirely financed by the governments; their students not only enjoyed a tuition-free policy and free boarding but also received subsidies and sometimes even textbooks and uniforms. Middle schools had no restrictions on students' geographic origins, but teachers' schools only accepted students from their own regions. While regular middle schools prepared students for a range of options, whether continuing on to higher education, entering government service, or engaging in business, the teachers' schools prepared students for teaching in primary schools. In other words, the curricula of these two types of schools were designed to achieve distinct goals: middle schools focused on meeting college requirements while teachers' schools focused on the needs of elementary schools. Middle schools graduates were facing a free job market, while teachers' school graduates were required to accept government-assigned teaching positions. At the tertiary level, teachers' colleges were parallel to specialty colleges, with the exception of being financed by the government, accepting only regional students, and obliging their graduates to teach. The curricula of teachers' colleges attempted to meet the needs of secondary education, and graduates were assigned to teach in middle schools.[14]

It was clear that the modern Chinese educational system used the Japanese system as a model, but the designers and the Qing court took into account conditions particular to China. Most scholars have focused on the similarities between the Chinese and Japanese school systems. Some have gone so far as to say that Chinese reformers "copied Japanese education in all aspects, including the system, its purpose, contents, and methodology."[15] Chinese scholars Qian and Jin, however, detect a considerable difference between the 1904 Chinese school system and that of Japan, and contend that the former refashioned extant models, including Japan's, to suit the conditions and needs of Chinese society. In the adapted Chinese school system, particularly as it applied to teachers' schools, students had to attend school for several more years than did those in the Japanese system, the Confucian classics were ubiquitous, and there was a range of refinements made to teachers' training.[16] Most important, the modifications were based on what the model of the old dynastic schools, particularly in terms of financial support; admissions policies; restrictions on student status, age, and geographic origin; student subsidies; postgraduate employment; and quotas.

In the early days of constructing the modern school system, the framers of the 1902 regulations devoted little attention to teachers' schools, which were designed as small accessories attached to secondary education, as Borthwick shrewdly notices.[17] The 1904 system, however, specified a separate teacher training system, including both secondary and tertiary levels, independent from the regular secondary and higher education system. This change may well have emerged from the widely shared sentiment that, having failed to provide the most basic mechanism for expanding education – namely, the training of a large corps of teachers – the 1902 plans had been doomed to failure.[18] But an equally significant concern was how the old system could be modified to accommodate new functions.

Between 1901 and 1904, the fate of the dynastic schools remained uncertain. The 1902 regulations carefully avoided the issue of state schools and the examination system by emphasizing, instead, the transformation of academies into modern schools. Since the government did not provide financial support to the students of the modern middle schools and the examination system was abolished, the tie between the state and the graduates of middle schools loosened. The graduates of the regular middle schools and colleges were free to choose their own careers, and the government could no longer assign jobs to them. If future bureaucrats still came from the graduates of modern schools, then the government would no longer be able to exert direct control over the source of future officials by assigning their curricula and moulding their ideological propensity. Moreover, the abolition of dynastic schools meant discharging over 6,000 educational officials and tens of thousands of officially registered imperial students, not to mention affecting the far larger numbers of literati who spent their lives studying for the examinations. This left room for considerable unrest.

The architects of the 1904 system fretted about the rupture that would result from abolishing an examination system that had lasted over a millennium. The original plan for replacing the old school system with the new one was much more moderate, however. In 1904, Zhang Zhidong (1837-1909), modern China's most famous educational reformer who, at the time, was serving as a minister of education (*guanxue dachen*), submitted a memorial to the emperor on this issue.[19] He proposed a temperate course, gradually whittling away the examinations while promoting the new schools. Zhang estimated that this transition could take place over the course of three of the triennial metropolitan examinations. By the time the examination system had been phased out, graduates from the newly established modern schools would step into the positions formerly held by examination degree holders. Zhang provided detailed steps for reducing quotas at each level of the examinations and described the ideal form of final examinations at each level of the modern schools. He also proposed transferring provincial educational commissioners to analogous posts overseeing the new school system.

Zhang Zhidong also outlined a mechanism for reassigning those who had passed all but the final level of the traditional examinations: they would transfer into the new schools at the level dictated by their previous achievements. Those above the age of thirty would complete their education in teachers' schools, following an abbreviated curriculum. Anyone over fifty would be assigned to an assistant post in local government after passing a special examination. Those who had studied for the examinations all of their lives and had reached the age of sixty without earning a degree were to be assigned to lower-level teaching positions. Degree holders from this older cohort were to be teachers or examiners.[20] Zhang had clearly devoted a fair amount of thought to providing for the generations who had invested so much in a system soon to vanish. In reality, his slow-paced reform plan was ruled out by an appeal for more rapid change, but its concerns definitely affected the way in which teachers' schools were regulated. The 1904 system replaced the examination system and teachers' schools were specifically built to parallel the regular school system.

After the promulgation of the 1904 reforms, the Board of Education urged each province to implement them. The establishment of teachers' schools had a direct and urgent motivation: teachers were desperately needed.[21] Other motives also drove the reforms as teacher training was considered to be the foundation of the entire modern educational system. Controlling teachers' schools would enable the state to mould the modern school system according to its terms. Towards the end of 1903 or the beginning of 1904, in "A Program for Educational Affairs" (*xuewu gangyao*), Zhang Baixi, Zhang Zhidong, and Rong-qing, prominent Qing education officials, expressed their concern over the lack of state control of education: "Although there are some middle schools and colleges in a number of provincial cities," they wrote, "[we should] not let them create their own pedagogical methods, as they might mislead students in the future."[22] The state had to intercede. Through the 1904 measures, the state guaranteed that the entire teacher training system remained in the hands of the state, just as it had within the dynastic school system.

The 1904 regulations offered the flexibility to carry out a smooth social and educational transformation. Local governments were granted the authority to modify the regulations to suit local conditions, especially in the early stages. The 1904 regulations required that each prefecture, district, and county set up one lower teachers' school (*chuji shifan xuetang*), but they also stated that, initially, one in the provincial capital would suffice. Once the advanced teachers' colleges (*youji shifan xuetang*) were producing enough teachers, lower teachers' schools were to be established at the county level.[23] The regulations for advanced teachers' colleges allowed lower teachers' schools to merge with them to form combined teachers' schools.[24] From 1904 to 1910, the country built nineteen teachers' colleges nationwide in twenty-three provinces.[25] Efforts were also made to provide teacher training in those provinces and regions that did not yet have proper teachers' schools. Estimating the number of lower teachers' schools is very difficult since records were categorized on the basis of programs rather than on the number of schools. Incomplete statistics suggest that, by 1909, there were about ninety-two complete programs (*wanquan ke*) and 112 simplified programs (*jianyi ke*).[26] The total number was still less than the sum of all of China's counties. However, if we count the number of short-term teachers' schools (*chuanxi suo*, or *jiangxi suo*), which numbered 303 in 1908, the campaign to open teachers' schools across the country may, to a certain extent, be counted a success.[27]

Local governments were ordered to allocate funds for teachers' schools from their fiscal budgets. Nothing would be recouped from students, as tuition was to be free.[28] Rather than erect new buildings, local officials very often assigned a new function to examination halls (*gongyuan*, or *shiyuan*) and government-financed academies. Sichuan Provincial Teachers' College (*Sichuan tongsheng youji shifan xuetang*) and Liang Guang Advanced Teachers' College (*Guangdong and Guangxi youji shifan xuetang*) were both housed in former examination halls, while Jiangsu Teachers' School (*Jiangsu shifan xuetang*) and Liang Hu Teachers' College (*Hunan and Hubei youji shifan xuetang*) were built on the ruins of academies that had previously been sponsored by the government.[29]

Teachers' schools had special requirements on students' status and their geographic origins. Students who had attended dynastic schools and literati who had studied for the imperial examinations were to be admitted to teachers' schools before other applicants. Administrators at teachers' schools in the provincial capitals, districts, and counties were ordered to "select students from among contributed students (*gongsheng*), regular students (*linsheng*), added students (*zengsheng*), supplementary students (*fusheng*), and imperial university students (*jiansheng*) within the province" – in other words, men who already held degrees in the prior examination system.[30] Furthermore, the modern schools would draw their students from the same area as had the dynastic schools.[31] Baoding Lower Teachers' School (*Baoding chuji shifan xuetang*) specified that no student would be admitted without holding a degree from the now defunct examination system.[32] Other schools, not quite as strict, required degrees from most students (e.g., teachers' schools in Sichuan and Zhejiang).[33] Data from Liang Guang Advanced Teachers' College show that, in 1904, 100 percent of the students in the "administrator training program" were degree holders, and over 70 percent of the students who were in accelerated and simplified programs before 1907 held imperial degrees and titles.

Teachers' schools applied quotas based on administrative level and local population. The regulations stated that quotas had to be in keeping with the number of local children eligible for elementary education. Since no reliable census figures existed, each province was provisionally allowed to set its quota at 300 students and each district and county at 150; advanced teachers' colleges at the provincial level were to admit 240.[34] These quotas were sometimes adjusted. For example, due to Zhili's special position in the traditional administrative and educational systems, Zhili Teachers' College

(*Zhili shifan xuetang*, a provincial college) set its quota at 800, with each of its counties being allowed a certain number of slots. Each large and each medium county was to enrol eight students, and each small county was to enrol four.[35] Due to its leading position in northern China in the late Qing, Beiyang Advanced Teachers' College (*Beiyang youji shifan xuetang*), established in 1906, admitted 160 students each year. Of these, sixty were assigned to other provinces in northern China, where teachers' schools had not yet been established.[36]

Students who wished to attend advanced teachers' schools had to be recommended (*jianju*) by local government officials before taking an entrance examination.[37] Some advanced teachers' schools had local governments set a special quota for some students who would be guaranteed admission (*baosong*) after passing the entrance examination.[38] Although the 1904 system required an entrance examination for all students and did not require recommendations, out of habit all schools continued the recommendation system along with entrance examinations.[39]

The 1904 regulations also set up an honour system that granted imperial degrees and titles to those graduating from new schools.[40] The students who graduated from universities would receive "advanced scholar" (*jinshi*) degrees and official titles that were equivalent to those held by previous *jinshi* degree winners. These people could work for various departments in the central government. Those who graduated from specialty colleges and teachers' colleges would be given a "recommended literatus" (*juren*) degree along with the official titles that had previously been given to *juren* degree-holders at the prefectural and district office levels. The graduates of secondary vocational schools, middle schools, and primary teachers' schools were awarded "special contributed student" (*bagong*), "excellent contributed student" (*yougong*), and "yearly contributed student" (*suigong*) degrees. Of these new degree-holders, those from vocational and middle schools were not promised any official title or position but were simply "allow[ed] ... to find jobs for themselves" (*ting qi zi ying sheng ye*).[41] In contrast, the graduates from primary teachers' schools were assigned the official titles of *jiaoshou*, *jiaoyu*, and *xundao*, the titles of teaching officials in the dynastic school system at prefectural, district, and county levels.[42] Although the court barely had a chance to put it into practice, this system of awarding titles indicated the state's view on the correspondence between teachers' schools (and various types of modern schools) and the imperial school system.

The regulations published in the 1904 system required graduates of teachers' schools to become teachers. Graduates from lower teachers' schools who had benefited from government financial support had to teach for three to six years (depending on the program in which students were enrolled), while those who had partially paid their way had to teach for two to three years.[43] Provincial officials could send graduates of provincial lower teachers' schools to teach in distant areas if this became necessary, but the expectation was that they would work in local schools.[44] Those who graduated from advanced teachers' colleges were expected to teach for six years. During their first two years of teaching, new teachers worked wherever provincial officials sent them. Those who did not fulfill their teaching obligations were required to repay their educational fees and tuition.[45] Records from Liang Guang Advanced Teachers' College show that a majority of graduates did indeed become teachers or administrators after graduation.

In 1904, teachers' schools replaced dynastic schools, transferring students and teaching officials. By regulating the source of the nation's teachers, the government maintained control over education. It is not difficult to understand why the early Republican government also assigned teachers' schools the responsibility for educational development in their regions (see Chapter 3).

Different Types of Teachers' Schools

Unlike regular secondary and tertiary schools, where a rather strict system regulated the promotion of students from one level of study to the next, late Qing teachers' schools were more flexible about academic progress and other matters. Unable to muster the staff and money needed to meet the demands of the new regulations, many areas opened combined teachers' schools that consisted of a teachers' college program and a lower teachers' school course (*liangji shifan xuetang*). This was a way of harbouring financial resources and providing a reliable pool of students for the higher level. In 1905, Baoding Advanced Teachers' College (*Baoding youji shifan xuetang*) chose the ninety-six best students from the 1,280 graduates of its primary teachers' school to continue on to college. The rest of the graduates were sent to teach in middle and elementary schools.[46] Data from other schools suggest that new teachers' colleges widely practised the custom of skimming the cream off the top of local middle schools.

At the tertiary level, by 1911, thirteen independent teachers' colleges had opened in the provinces, some of which were combined teachers' schools.[47] First opened in 1904, the School of Teachers' Training at Capital University (*Jingshi da xuetang youji shifan ke*) recruited students from the entire country (see Table 2.1).[48]

In these colleges, future teachers were assigned to a number of different programs, from a thorough course of study (*wanquan ke*) that lasted six years, to the selective major program (*xuan ke*) that took two years, to the single specialized program (*zhuanmen ke,* or *zhuanxiu ke*) that lasted one year, to a one-year preparatory program (*yu ke*). According to the 1904 regulations, a proper teacher training program, besides one year of preparatory courses, would include one year of general courses (*gonggong ke*), three years of courses in a major (*fenlei ke*), and one year of advanced training (*jiaxi ke*)

Table 2.1

Teachers' colleges established before 1911

	Name of college	Date started	Location	Description	History
1	Department of Teacher Training at Capital University	1904	Beijing	College level only; the highest national college to recruit students, nationwide	Transferred from the School of Teachers' Training (1902) at Capital University; changed into the Capital Advanced Teachers' School (1908)
2	Zhili Teachers' College	1902*	Baoding	When established in 1902, this school was designed as a combined teachers' school. In 1905, the school became college level only.	The name of the school changed to Baoding Teachers' School in 1905
3	Jiangsu Teachers' School	1904	Suzhou	A combined teachers' college.	
4	Beiyang Teachers' College	1906	Tianjin	A college-level-only school that recruited students from all of northern China	Merged with Baoding Teachers' College in 1911
5	Shandong Advanced Teachers' College	1910	Ji'nan	College level	Upgraded from a provincial teachers school, built in 1903, to a college-level school
6	Shanxi Combined Teachers' College	1906	Taiyuan		Upgraded from a teachers' school built in 1905

►

◂ *Table 2.1*

	Name of college	Date started	Location	Description	History
7	He'nan Advanced Teachers' College	1907	Kaifeng	College level	Upgraded from He'nan Teachers' School, built in 1905
8	Sichuan Provincial Teachers' College	1905	Chengdu	A combined school	Changed into college-level-only in 1910
9	Liang Hu Teachers' College	1906	Wuhan	A combined school	
10	Zhejiang Compound Teachers' College	1907	Hangzhou		Degraded to a secondary teachers' school in 1910
11	Liang Jiang Teachers' College	1905	Nanjing	A combined school that recruited students from Jiangsu, Jiangxi and Anhui	Transferred from Sanjiang Teachers' School, built in 1903
12	Hu'nan Advanced Teachers' College	1908	Changsha	College level	
13	Fujian Advanced Teachers' College	1907	Fuzhou	College level	
14	Liang Guang Advanced Teachers' College	1906	Guangzhou	College level only	

* *Zhong wai shifan jiaoyu cidian* indicates that this school was established in 1903. That might be true because some schools began their building process earlier but started to enrol students one year later.

Source: Li Youzhi (compil.), *Zhong wai shifan jiaoyu cidian* [Compendium of teachers' education in China and the world] (Beijing: Chinese Broadcasting and Television Press, 1994), 314-84; Ju Xingui, Tong Fuyong, and Zhang Shouzhi (compil.), *Shiye jiaoyu, shifan jiaoyu* [Vocational education and teacher training] (Shanghai: Shanghai jiaoyu chubanshe [Shanghai Education Press], 1994), 628-733.

– a total of six years.[49] As one might expect, during the first few years under the 1904 system, most schools were unable to build a complete six-year program and, therefore, the length of programs offered varied from school to school. Most colleges had only a selective program, a special major program, and a preparatory program to meet the urgent need for teachers. Jiangsu Teachers' College, established in 1904, had only a two-year selective program and a one-year preparatory program.[50] Baoding Teachers' School, designed for the secondary level, also added three types of college programs, ranging from one-half year to three years.[51] Although Beiyang set up a complete program, the emphasis of the school, as called for explicitly in Yuan Shikai's memorial, was on the elective program, which provided teachers for a number of different provinces.[52] Zhejiang Teachers' College had a similar emphasis, but it offered only a three-year selective program.[53]

In 1907, there were 527 students in four-year complete programs, 2,603 students in two- or three-year selective programs, and 894 students in one-year special major programs.[54] With this flexibility, these colleges produced a large number of teachers in a short time. Nonetheless, given the population of China, the number of teachers being produced would not be able to meet the needs of the new schools, especially the rapidly growing Western-style schools.

From 1904 to 1909, these colleges, which were intended to train teachers for secondary education, were actually producing elementary schoolteachers. For example, Jiangsu Teachers' School had both an accelerated program (*sucheng ke*) and a short-term program – each lasting one year.[55] Beiyang Teachers' College had a simplified program (*jianyi ke*) that trained older students for one year before sending them off to teach in elementary schools.[56] Sichuan Provincial Teachers' College had two departments for training elementary schoolteachers: the department for primary teacher training (*chuji bu*) was for younger students, and the simplified training department (*jianyi bu*) was for older students. By 1908, there were only sixty students in the advanced (college level) department, but there were 109 in the primary and 173 in the simplified training departments.[57]

In general, lower teachers' schools offered both a four-year complete program and a simplified program.[58] The 1904 regulations did encourage local governments to build simplified programs but did not provide rules for operating them. Most schools set up simplified programs that lasted from one to two years. In 1907, there were 64 lower teachers' schools attended by 6,390 students, and there were 179 simplified programs with 15,833 students.[59]

The 1904 regulations encouraged those areas that did not qualify for formal teachers' schools to set up short-term teacher training schools (*chuanxi suo*, or *jiangxi suo*). Teachers' colleges designed their programs with different students in mind. Some colleges had a special department to provide practical training to those who were already teachers (*jiaoshou lianxi suo*, or *jiaoyuan jiangxi suo*). Jiangsu Combined Teachers' College set up a special training program (*jiangxi suo*) that provided short-term training for elementary schoolteachers.[60] Liang Guang Advanced Teachers' College also had a practical training program (*danji jiaoshou lianxi suo*).[61] Teachers who had been employed in old-style local schools were often enrolled in these new schools for a short period of training in order to learn new pedagogical methods and educational theories. The type of program available at these short-term training schools offered students between six months and one year of intensive training, enabling them to receive credentials for specific subjects, such as physical education, drawing, or music. In 1907, the total number of these institutions reached 276 and they enrolled 9,844 students: there were more of these schools than there was of any other sort of teacher training facility.[62] And, more than other schools (with their multi-stage programs and modern curricula), these small local schools maintained continuity with the old system. They dominated the national teachers' training program for the first five years after 1904. After being immersed for six to twelve months, teachers from lower-level academies, community schools, charitable schools, and so forth not only received new credentials that enabled them to teach in modern schools but also gained a new identity: they were modern teachers.

Elastic Curricula

The curricula of the teachers' schools established under the 1904 system had some resemblances to those of regular middle schools and colleges, but they involved a greater degree of flexibility. Future teachers studied a range of subjects before launching into their properly pedagogic studies, and certain courses required at regular schools were minimized or left out entirely.

Before starting courses in their major, future teachers were required to take general courses for one year. These included moral studies, Confucian classics, literature, foreign languages, logic, mathematics, and physical education. There was no similar requirement for regular college students. In addition to the courses required by their own majors, students at teachers' colleges were required to take specifically pedagogical courses such as theory of education, teaching methods, and psychology. Such courses were, of course, absent from regular college curricula.[63]

The curricula of lower-level teachers' schools were based on the needs of the elementary schools to which the young teachers would be sent. The basic courses were similar to those offered in regular secondary-level schools: the 1904 regulations called for study of moral cultivation, Confucian classics, literature, history, geography, mathematics, natural science, physics, chemistry, and physical education at both middle schools and teachers' schools. Nevertheless, teachers' schools often emphasized moral cultivation and Confucian classics while reducing the hours of study devoted to other courses. In addition, teachers' schools offered a special course that covered the history of education in China and abroad, educational and psychological theory, a survey of recent edicts on education, and educational administration. Nearly as many class hours were dedicated to education courses as to classics, the course with the most class hours.[64] Unlike Japanese teachers' schools, most Chinese teachers' schools did not require the study of foreign languages (as these were rarely taught to young students).[65] Compared to regular middle schools, all teachers' schools were weak in foreign language training; instead, they provided special courses in calligraphy, painting, handicrafts, and introductions to agriculture, industry, and commerce – all courses that were in the elementary curriculum. Another special course, "practising the official spoken language" (*xi guanhua*), offered guidance in how to teach the official national language to children who had grown up speaking one of China's hundreds of local dialects.[66] The education courses and other courses related to teaching primary school cut into the time for in-depth study of courses that were generally required for regular secondary students. This became an important topic of educational debate in the late 1910s and early 1920s as some critiques of the teacher training system directly addressed the low quality of the graduates of teachers' schools (see Chapter 4).

All types of teachers' schools were permitted to add or omit courses based on the conditions of the school and/or the needs of the students. Since most students at teachers' colleges had previously attended dynastic schools, the former were expected to emphasize courses that had not been taught under the examination system (such as mathematics and natural sciences).[67] To meet the urgent need for certain types of elementary and middle school teachers, teachers' schools offered special short-term programs in such areas as physical education and music training.[68] In 1907, twelve college-level elective programs were offered, compared with only two complete programs. At teachers' schools, there were 179 simplified programs and only sixty-four complete programs. This ratio continued into 1908, when, at the tertiary level, the number of selective programs and special programs increased to twenty-eight, while the number of complete programs levelled off at five. At the same time, although the number of complete programs at lower teachers' schools increased to eighty-one and the number of simplified programs fell to 110, the number of short-term schools for teacher training increased to 303.[69] This kind of flexibility facilitated the rapid transformation of students drawn from the old literati into modern teachers.

Women's Education and State Building, 1907-11

Women's education was severely repressed when, during the halcyon days of 1898, Empress Dowager Cixi dismantled all of the reform measures adopted by her nephew, the Guangxu emperor. Four years later, the Qing court's New Policy reforms brought about another revolution in the educational system but continued to exclude women from public schooling. From 1902 to 1906, private schools for girls and women advanced so quickly that they constituted a challenge to the Qing court's control over education and social order. Pressed by reform-minded gentry and officials, in 1907, the Qing court issued regulations that, for the first time, assigned Chinese girls and women a place in public schools.

Women's Education at the Crossroads, 1900-6

To the ambitious young women of the day, the regulations of 1904 can hardly have sounded promising: "The aim of education [*jiao*] is to teach women the principles of being wives and mothers ... Young girls absolutely must not walk along the street to get to school. It is also improper for them to read Western books, thereby picking up foreign customs. They might wish to choose their own marriage partners and defy the orders of their parents and husband." Still, the government did acknowledge that women had to be educated. "If none of the women in the country learn, the educational level of mothers will not improve, children will not grow strong, and their character and behavior will not be good." But the education the reformers had in mind for these future mothers would not take place in public schools: "Girls can only be taught at home, either by their mother or by a tutor, so that they may become literate." [70] The government hoped to control female education by publishing special textbooks for home study.

Despite all of the concern about the impropriety of girls, attending school, the 1904 regulations acknowledged that new public kindergartens needed female teachers and caretakers who had been trained in new-style schools. Now that young boys, who, at least in elite families, had always been taught at home by their mothers, would be attending public kindergartens, there was both an opportunity for the state to begin early indoctrination and a need for women to step up as salaried civil servants. The attempt to start male formal education at a younger age had unintended consequences. Although in reality only a few kindergartens were established in the 1900s and only a handful of boys may have attended them, their existence resulted in a legitimate reason for reform-minded elites to endorse female schooling.

In the early twentieth century, women's education displayed a great diversity in theory and practice. Western ideas concerning women's rights to education and Japanese ideas concerning training "good mothers and virtuous wives" (*xianmu liangfu*) attracted both male and female reformers.[71] The government, on the conservative side as always, encouraged the publication of textbooks that were peopled with both traditional and updated female moral exemplars and that advised women to study at home.[72] A range of different views circulated regarding the role of women and their duty to the nation.[73] An article published in *Dongfang zazhi* (Eastern miscellany) highlighted the original Japanese idea of "good mothers and virtuous wives," contending that morality had to be central to women's education lest they overlook their duties to the family. After all, a woman's duty to her country was principally a duty to her family.[74] In 1902, an article published in *Nü bao* (Women's newspaper) entitled "On Promoting Women's Schools" echoed Liang Qichao: the country's fate depended on women's education and the time had come for the government to establish a national school system for girls.[75] The moderate group believed that the purpose of women's education was to educate mothers for a new body of citizens and inculcate a new spirit of citizenship.[76] During the same period, a small group of radicals advocated educating women as a way of encouraging revolution. It fiercely denounced the policy of educating women to become "good mothers and virtuous wives": this sort of schooling only turned women into "high-class slaves to men." These revolutionaries looked forward to the day when women would free themselves from men's control and dedicate themselves to destroying the Qing government.[77]

It is worth discussing the voices of female writers during this period and their views on the purpose of women's education. Although the rhetoric of women as "mothers of the citizen" was prevalent in the discussion, as Xia Xiaohong points out, most female writers developed a strong sense of education as a means of taking responsibility and being independent.[78] A brilliant female student, Zhang Jianren, wrote at age sixteen that the purpose of women's education was for equality, "to take personal responsibility same as men, to share responsibility to support family like men and to enjoy all natural rights that men have."[79] In answer to the question of what women's education should do to empower women, Zhang stressed the importance of improving individual liberation and the physical strength of women. Zhang drew attention to the urgent task of eliminating foot-binding and implementing physical training for a strong body so that women would have more freedom and be able to carve more social space.[80] This idea was entirely different from the concerns of many male elites and educators who prioritized moral training in women's education.[81]

Between 1902 and 1907, many women's schools were established in the Jiangnan area and the Zhili region as well as in inland provinces such as Hunan, Sichuan, Guangxi, Jiangxi, Shandong, and even Guizhou and Yunnan.[82] To examine how ideas about women's education were put into practice in the late Qing, I have selected several of the most famous women's schools for closer attention.

Nurturing Roots Women's Academy (*Wuben nüshu*), established in Shanghai in 1902, was a pioneering effort on the part of open-minded elites who clung to the idea of the 1898 reformers that women's education could lay a foundation for a strong nation.[83] The school enrolled women in their teens to early twenties who had basic literacy but later expanded into elementary education and enrolled girls at lower ages. Most students were expected to enter the school's teacher training program after completing their elementary studies.[84] The school was dedicated to teaching women the basics of literature and Western knowledge, how to improve household skills, and how to teach children. Among the subjects studied were morality, science, and domestic work skills. The curriculum at the lower elementary level emphasized basic literacy, arithmetic, and moral cultivation as well as singing, physical education, drawing, sewing, and handicrafts. Courses such as history, geography, science, physiology, physics, and chemistry were taught in the last years of elementary school.[85]

Inculcating Doctrine Women's School (*Yujiao nüxuetang*) represented a rather conservative approach to education. The school was established in Beijing by a group of Manchu and Han gentry-officials in 1904 and declared that its sole purpose was to train "good mothers and virtuous wives" – a purpose that differed from that of Wuben Academy. The regulations of the school indicated no intention to train students to work in the public or to become teachers. This was also evident in the curriculum: besides basic reading skills and a few courses on the basics of Western knowledge, the emphasis was on sewing, handicrafts, and other household skills.[86] It added a teacher training program only after the Qing promulgated the new regulations on building female normal schools in 1907.[87]

Revolutionary and anarchist leaders, on the other hand, turned to women's education as a way of training spies and assassins. Patriotic Women's School (*Aiguo nüxue*), founded in Shanghai in 1902, was to serve as a base for revolution. When students were not studying reading, natural science, physical education, and family management, they discussed revolutionary and anarchist theories and practised making bombs.[88]

Besides these famous women's schools, there were also other types of schools for women. A small number of more practical educators believed in teaching women survival skills and helping them to be self-reliant. They opened sericulture schools in Shanghai, Fuzhou, and Hangzhou; handicraft schools in Shanghai, Yangzhou, and Hangzhou; and nursing schools in Shanghai, Beijing, and Hangzhou.[89] Other educators created alternative professions for women. For example, three medical schools were opened for female students in Shanghai (1905), Beijing (1904), and Tianjin (1906), and a midwife school for women was opened in Hangzhou (1906).[90] In 1906, a female language school was built in Beijing, named Yiyi Nü xuetang (Girls' School of Language Translation), specifically training students to be translators.[91] The multifaceted aspects of girls' schools built during this period offered girls and young women diverse choices.

During this period, the majority of women's schools shared several common features. First, during this early age of women's education, most schools were elementary schools and emphasized basic literacy and functional training, including arithmetic and household skills.[92] Students who qualified for secondary education were rare: Beiyang Women's Normal School in Tianjin had to import students from Shanghai.[93] Second, most students came from the elite classes. At Patriotic Women's School, the students were drawn entirely from the founders' families.[94] A gentry family school, Nurturing Roots Women's Academy, required that students exhibit the "good manners of grand families" (*dajia fengfan*).[95] The entire student body of Inculcating Doctrine Women's School in Beijing was made up of the wives, concubines, daughters, nieces, and sisters of Manchu and Han Chinese officials.[96] In 1904, a county magistrate in Shandong Province opened a school for girls from literati-official families: it was reported that only 1 percent of the people in the neighbourhood had even heard of the school as information circulated almost exclusively among local gentry families.[97] As can be seen, female education began as an entirely elite affair.

Moreover, the curricula of most women's schools exhibited the strong influence of tradition. Moral cultivation and the study of classical literary works were universally emphasized.[98] Unlike boys' education, which at its lowest official level presumed basic literacy, girls' schools, even at the middle school level, had to allocate many hours to teaching basic reading skills. Western knowledge was conveyed rather sketchily, and scientific knowledge was conveyed through examples from domestic life: family hygiene was a standard "science course." Household skills were also widely taught: girls studied cooking, sewing, handiwork, and family management (*jia shi*).[99] New subjects included physical education, games (*youxi*), and singing to enhance women's capacity to nurture children. Schools strictly prohibited the practice of foot-binding. If a student bound her feet prior to entering the school, she would be forced to unbind them after she enrolled. Nurturing Roots Women's Academy gave students detailed instructions on how to unbind their feet and provided samples of special shoes they could wear during their recovery.[100] The schools became a model of what women could do after they unbound their feet and entered the public sphere.

During this period, the ambiguity of the central government's attitude towards women's education provided local governments with some flexibility. Many local governments oscillated between supporting and banning women's schools. Some state institutions became involved in women's education but tended to limit it to teacher training. In 1904, Hubei provincial governor Duan-fang established a women's school in Wuhan to train childcare workers.[101] In 1905, Hunan's provincial government sent twenty female students to Japan to attend teacher training programs; Fengtian and several other provincial governments followed suit.[102]

Each time a new girls' school opened, more female teachers were needed. Local governments began opening women's normal schools. In 1906, Beiyang

Women's Normal School (*Beiyang nüzi shifan xuetang*) opened in Tianjin.[103] The Education Bureau of Fengtian (present-day Liaoning) established a women's normal school in 1906, recruiting students between the ages of twenty and thirty.[104] Local government involvement in women's schools had a decisive effect: government officials envisioned women's secondary education exclusively in terms of training teachers for the public education system. During this period, women's education was transformed from a private family practice to a public undertaking.

Local governments also placed restrictions on women's schools, sometimes even closing them in response to pressure from conservatives. Some women's schools in Guangdong were forced to close; others had to change their names and regulations.[105] The Number One Hunan Women's School had to close in 1904 after an attack by Wang Xianqian, a leading member of the conservative gentry, who had been rebuffed in his efforts to force one of the school's students to be his concubine.[106] The Hubei girls' school established by Governor Duan-fang was closed by the order of Governor-General Zhang Zhidong after a great deal of pressure from a group of conservatives.[107] The Jiangsu Education Bureau refused to register Cuihua Women's School (*Cuihua nüxue*) as school authorities had defied convention and propriety by hiring male teachers.[108] Local governments exercised absolute power over these schools, which, for obvious reasons, had to be far more carefully monitored than did boys' schools. A variety of reasons could be given for delaying the approval of an application. For example, the Liang Guang Education Bureau criticized a school's curriculum for offering few courses on women's domestic duties. Permission to open was withheld until the curriculum had been expanded.[109]

Although government authorities had initially planned to limit women's education to the inner chambers, the rapid development of private women's schools began to escape their control. Authorities then changed their approach, monitoring the development of women's education to ensure that it met the needs of the state.

Women's Normal Schools and State Building, 1907-11

By 1906, women's schools were widely encouraged by reform-minded elites. In 1907, the Qing court decided to promulgate regulations on women's education as a supplement to the 1904 Imperially Approved Memorial on Modern School Regulations: women's education would become part of the public school system. When the first imperial statistics on education were published in 1907, they recorded over 400 women's schools.[110] Although the number of female schools opened before 1907 was miniscule compared to the number of male schools, their existence put the issue of creating public women's schools on the agenda and prompted debate among imperial officials. The Qing court was profoundly concerned about the moral impact of women's schools, their educational aims, their curricula, their textbooks, and the changes that education would bring to women's lives and thinking.

In 1906, an official of the Ministry of Works (*gongbu zhushi*), Liu Xun, sent a memorial urging the court to promote regulations regarding women's schools. He pointed out that, if there were no women's schools, kindergartens would lack teachers and family education would suffer. He believed that, if women's schools were allowed to multiply without government supervision, the women of China would suffer. "Chinese women's education is in an embryonic stage," he said, "but we have already seen unfortunate results. It is not unusual to see newspaper reports about women's misconduct." He proposed that the government issue special textbooks for girls and women, select teachers on the basis of morality, and set up strict rules to keep males and females separate at school.[111]

Similar concerns were expressed in a memorial from the minister of the Board of Education regarding the regulation of women's schools. The minister admitted that many people were applying to open women's schools and that many such schools had recently been opened by officials, merchants, and gentry. If there were no regulations, the honest people who wanted to build schools would have no guidelines, and those who built schools only to win fame would lead women's education into disrepute. Clearly, it was imperative that the central government set up rules for women's education.[112]

The central government was growing increasingly concerned about the need for professional women teachers in kindergartens and private homes. Since women from ordinary families were not well enough educated to teach their daughters to be "good citizens," local governments were expected to provide tutors for this purpose.[113] After the promulgation of the 1904 regulations, Tianjin County sent its draft regulation on women's schools to the Board of Education, urging the central government to open the door for women's public schooling.[114] Acting on his own authority, a Zhejiang financial official used provincial revenues to subsidize the efforts of local gentry to establish a female school for childcare workers.[115]

Pressure continued to mount in 1906, as more local officials urged the central government to take a stand on women's normal schools. As the first group of female students finished its elementary education, there were demands to provide more. By the time the 1907 regulations on women's education were promulgated, a small number of private teachers' schools had opened for women. Some women's schools, including Nurturing Roots Women's Academy, Zhounan and Jingzhu Girls' Schools in Hunan, and Lize Women's Normal School in Jiangsu, also provided teacher training programs.[116] In 1906, Duan-fang called on the central government to establish regulations for women's public education. In his opinion, establishing women's normal schools ought to be the government's "top priority" (*di yi yaowu*).[117]

In 1907, the government promulgated the Imperially Approved Regulations on Women's Normal Schools and Girls' Elementary Schools (*Zouding nüzi shifan xuetang ji nüzi xiaoxuetang zhangcheng*), officially recognizing women's place in the public school system. The public schools for women and girls had two components: primary schools for training girls and secondary schools for training female teachers (*nüjiaoxi*). Officially, the women's normal school became the highest institution for women's education and the only kind of secondary public school women could attend. Graduates would teach in girls' elementary schools and would serve as kindergarten caretakers. Each township and county was to have its own women's normal school. Like men's normal schools, women's normal schools would be founded by local governments and tuition would be free. The regulations also made provisions for private normal schools, though these could be opened only with the special permission, and under the supervision, of local government. Having received a free education, the graduates of women's normal schools were obliged to teach at public girls' schools and kindergartens; those who elected not to do so were liable for the entire cost of their education.[118]

With the 1907 regulations on women's education, local governments began to establish elementary schools for girls and, a more pressing issue, women's normal schools at the secondary level. At times, local officials took a shortcut, directly converting previously private or government-sponsored schools for women into government-run schools. Jiangsu Cuimin Women's School opened in 1905 as a private school, but when Duan-fang became governor-general of Jiangsu, Jiangxi, and Anhui in 1908, he imposed government controls and made it a public teachers' school.[119] From 1907 to 1911, local governments set up Jingshi Women's Normal School (1908) in Beijing, Wuchang Women's Normal School (1909) in Hubei, Jiangsu Women's Normal School (1911), Hunan Women's Normal School (1911), and Henan Women's Normal School (1911).[120]

The 1907 regulations stressed four aspects of women's education. First, the students of women's normal schools were expected to adopt the traditional morality of virtuous daughters, wives, and mothers. The regulations stressed that "all ideas of freedom (such as eliminating the demarcation between men and women, women selecting their own spouses, women giving speeches in public political assemblies, and so on) must be prohibited in order to maintain social morality ... Women should always obey their parents and husbands."[121] Second, the students were to be trained to be good mothers, whose contribution to their families would increase the prosperity of the country. Third, students were expected to learn practical skills for daily life, including housework. Fourth, as women engaged in physical exercise and learned about personal hygiene, it was expected that their health would improve. The regulations announced, once again, that the practice of foot-binding was prohibited.[122]

The government carried out a policy of sex segregation intended to limit women's participation in social activities and to prevent improper behaviour. Girls' and boys' schools were to be separated, and all teachers and administrators in the former were to be women. Men over the age of fifty could serve on the managerial staff, but their offices could not be situated in the school building proper.[123] Life in women's normal schools would be strictly controlled. Students were allowed to go home on weekends only when accompanied by a male family member. Visits to the school by relatives of faculty and students had to be approved in advance. The Board of Education issued a regulation on students' clothing: faculty and students were prohibited from wearing silk, colourful or Western-style clothing, jewellery, and makeup.[124] Women's conduct was far more rigidly defined by school regulations than was men's conduct.

Women's course of study in teachers' schools did not last as long as did men's and was not as advanced. While men might go on to teach in higher primary school and middle schools, women were being trained to provide only lower primary school and preschool education. Female curricula and course requirements were also simplified. Table 2.2 compares the curricula of male and female secondary-level teachers' schools, where students were trained to teach primary school.

The differences in the curricula indicate that women would only be assigned to teach the lower grades. The fact that female students were not designated to take the "reading classics" course implies that the government considered female teachers unsuitable to teach those classics designed for primary school curricula. A little bit of history, geography, and science might be appropriate for women's role in the lower grades but not physics, chemistry, botany, or zoology, which were included in upper primary school curricula. Women were trained to teach "feminine" subjects such as music and household skills. This gender segregation with regard to curricula, which was set up by the Qing court, continued into the Republican period.

The framers of the 1904 reforms had declared that "[male] preschool education ... is the primary foundation of citizens' education" (*Mengyang ... wei guomin jiao yu zhi di yi jizhi*).[125] Three years later, however, the designer of the 1907 regulations on women's education would declare that "women's education is the foundation of citizens' education" (*Nüzi jiaoyu wei guomin jiaoyu zhi genji*).[126] This shift reveals the extent of state power, which now formally encompassed the traditional domain within which women provided their sons and daughters with a basic education.

Through the 1907 regulations, the Qing court hoped to achieve a compromise between the reformists and the conservatives. By giving local governments power over women's education, the court checked the ire of conservatives who had attacked the new women's schools as a source of moral corruption. Local "evil gentry" (*e shen*) were singled out in the regulations as an element against which girls' schools had to be defended.[127] The schools provided women with an escape from the bonds of domesticity and assigned them a legitimate role in the public realm.[128] But, as women's normal schools reinforced the traditional role of the female as family educator, their role was not entirely new. The regulations deterred women from engaging in more radical social activities and suggested no avenues by which women might participate more fully in public life.

With the state involvement, however, the multifaceted tradition of women's education was transformed exclusively into training female teachers. During this transformation, the specific tradition of the mother as the primary educator for her children was emphasized, whereas women's study of prose and poetic writings was suppressed. Using the slogan "Women's education is the foundation of citizens' education," the dynasty placed women's education on the state agenda. By establishing women's normal schools, the state brought women's education into the state-building process: fledgling, decentralized, private schools were recast within a unified state project. Taking over the traditional idea of providing mothers with knowledge for the sake of family prosperity, the government now advanced a project that turned mothers into a public resource. The establishment of women's normal schools permitted women to receive an education beyond the elementary level and legitimated their work as teachers. This was an unprecedented change in Chinese society and profoundly influenced later generations.

Transforming Literati-Officials into Modern Teachers: The Case of Liang Guang Advanced Teachers' School, 1904-10

The 1904 reforms strengthened the system of teachers' schools at the secondary level, where elementary schoolteachers were trained. Establishing a new public school system at the local level created a unified education system staffed by modern professional teachers with specialized training. Teachers ceased to be a by-product of the civil service examination system, and the establishment of teachers' schools finally institutionalized state efforts to separate the training of teaching officials from the training of bureaucrats – a process begun in the Ming dynasty.

Liang Guang Advanced Teachers' College (*Liang Guang youji shifan xuetang*) was established the same year that the 1904 regulations on education were promulgated. Under its initial name, Liang Guang Accelerated Teachers' Academy (*Liang Guang sucheng shifan guan*), the school recruited its first cohort of students into a six-month accelerated program. The selection of the provincial examination hall as the location of the school signalled the connection between the academy and the imperial examination system. Liang Guang Accelerated Teachers' Academy also provided a short-term program for training school administrators (*guanliyuan lianxi suo*). Soon, other programs were set up for the old literati, who needed new identities in an age of transition. In its second year, after the abolition of the imperial examinations in 1905, the school adopted what would become its permanent name – Liang Guang Advanced Teachers' College.[129] A close study of this school may help provide an understanding of how, at the beginning of the twentieth century, teachers' schools became special institutions for transforming old literati-officials into modern teachers.

Opening Another Arena for Power: Educational Administration

The rising surplus of expectant officials worried late Qing rulers. In addition to those who had never held actual office (*shi que*), there were many officials who languished between assignments. Like educational officials, this group longed for power and saw the new school system as an opportunity to seize it. In the late Qing, the educational arena offered several opportunities for ambitious expectant officials. These people, who had strong government connections, could be appointed as the heads of newly established schools. A group of former bureaucrats who had left their government jobs moved to the educational field, where their new responsibilities provided a sense of connection to officialdom (teachers' schools were run by the local government). Those who had fewer connections could begin by taking a special teachers' school program and progressing to being appointed as school administrators or as officials in the local educational administration.

Liang Guang Advanced Teachers' College was established by the Bureau of Education for Guangdong and Guangxi (*Liang Guang xuewu chu*). The chancellor of the school, Wang Zhouyao, was appointed by Guangdong and Guangxi's governor-general, Cen Chunxuan, who later suggested that the school be upgraded to an advanced teachers' college.[130] Most of the school's administrators held official titles, but these were preceded by the terms "candidate" (*houbu*, or *buyong*), "with the title of" (*zhixian*), and "equal to the title of" (*tong ... xian*). These were, in fact, expectant officials. In the school's early years, it employed a faculty and staff of forty-seven (Japanese teachers not included), twenty-eight of whom were expectant officials, four of whom held proper offices, and thirteen of whom held imperial degrees. Of the remaining two faculty members, one graduated from a Japanese school and one from Capital Teachers' College.[131] Possession of an official title bound them to the government, but the emptiness of the title relegated them to the political margins. Some must have believed that running a government school would give them a chance to exercise actual power.

Table 2.2

Comparison of curricula at female and male secondary-level teachers' schools

	Class hours per week								
	Year 1		Year 2		Year 3		Year 4		Year 5
Name of course	F	M	F	M	F	M	F	M	M
Moral cultivation	2	1	2	1	2	1	2	1	1
Education	3	4	3	6	3	8	15	14	15
Reading classics		9		9		9		9	9
Chinese language and literature	4	3	4	2	4	2		1	2
History	2	3	2	3	2	3		1	1
Geography	2	2	2	2	2	2		2	1
Mathematics	4	3	4	3	3	3	2	3	3
Physics and chemistry		2		2		2		1	
"*Bowu*" (botany and zoology)		2		2		2			
"*Gezhi*" (science)	2		2		2		2		
Calligraphy		3		2		1		1	1
Painting and drawing	2	2	2	2	2	1	1	1	1
Household management	2		2		2		2		
Sewing	4		4		4		3		
Handicrafts	4		4		4		3		
Music	1		1		2		2		
Physical education	2	2	2	2	2	2	2	2	2
Total	34	36	34	36	34	36	34	36	36

Source: Xue bu, "Zouding chuji shifan xuetang zhangcheng," "Zouding nüzi shifan xuetang hangcheng," The Board of Education: *Xue bu guanbao* [Official Bulletin of the Board of Education, 1904-11], 398-411, 575-81.

During the same period, expectant officials in other provinces underwent the same process. The administrators at Hunan and Hubei Teachers' College (*Liang Hu shifan xuetang*) had been in a similarly marginal position. Eight of the twelve administrators, including the chancellor, the dean, the chief accountant, and the medical doctor, possessed official titles; the remaining four were degree holders. The eight official title holders were either "candidate officials" or "officials on trial" (*shiyong*). Among the forty-five faculty members, sixteen held various imperial degrees and twenty-four possessed both imperial degrees and official titles. Of these, twenty-one had only empty titles.[132] Many of the forty degree holders (sixteen degree holders and twenty-four officials with degrees) had also studied either at a new-style academy or at a Japanese school.[133] The first administrators of the Zhejiang Combined Teachers' College (*Zhejiang liangji shifan xuetang*) had similar backgrounds. In 1905, the governor of Zhejiang, Zhang Zengyang, advocated building a teachers' college on the location of the previous examination hall and appointed a prefect candidate (*houbu zhifu*), Lu Guixing, to supervise the project, and the school opened in 1908.[134] At Liang Jiang Teachers' College, all seven administrators held official titles but no office.[135] In all of these provinces, officials who had been marginalized under the imperial bureaucratic system took roles in the rapidly expanding field of education.

The programs organized by teachers' schools provided a fast track through which degree holders could become school administrators. Table 2.3, derived from the brochure of Liang Guang Advanced Teachers' College (*Liang Guang youji shifan xuetang yi lan*), shows that all of those who enrolled in the short-term programs specially designed for training school administrators possessed degrees or official titles; most had been regular students (*linsheng*) or supplementary students (*fusheng*) in previous dynastic schools. Data on this group of graduates show that many of them became administrators or teachers at various educational levels. Of the sixty-four graduates about whom information on subsequent employment was available, thirty-seven served as school administrators or teachers.[136] Under the imperial system, this group of students would have had to pass the next level of the examinations in order to qualify for a government assignment; under the new system, these people studied in teachers' schools for six months or a year and then became educational administrators. Clearly, their satisfaction was an important issue for the early twentieth-century Qing court.

Schooling Older Literati

The educational transformation of the late Qing inevitably altered the careers of older literati. While traditional private academies and dynastic schools had always been open to the young and the old, modern regular schools set up strict age limits with regard to promotion from one grade to the next. Beginning in 1905, all those above the age of twenty-five were barred from attending regular new schools at the primary and secondary levels. As a result, a large number of literati had little choice but to turn to the new teachers' training programs.

Data from Liang Guang Advanced Teachers' College (see Tables 2.4 and 2.5) reveal that the school enrolled many older students in its administrator training program. Most of the students in that program were between twenty-six and forty years old. In the accelerated program, ages ranged from twenty-one to thirty. In the teachers' licensing program, the age range was broader, from twenty to seventy-three, with most students falling between twenty-one and thirty-five.[137] The 1904 school regulations required that students at both advanced teachers' colleges and lower teachers' schools be no older than twenty-five and no younger than eighteen. Students between the ages of twenty-five and thirty were allowed to enrol in the simplified program. At Liang Guang Advanced Teachers' College the average student

Table 2.3

Imperial titles possessed by graduates of Liang Guang Advanced Teachers' College

	Programs							
Imperial titles	Administrator Training Program (1904)	Accelerated Program (1904)	Simplified Program (1906)	Simplified Program (1907)	Physical Training Program (1907)	Advanced Elective Program (1909)	Advanced Specialty Program (1910)	Totals
Juren (Recommended scholar)	8					1		9
Jiansheng (University student)	13	11	6	11	10	16		67
Gongsheng (Contributed student)	2	2	9	4	1	5		23
Bagong (Special exam student)	3		2	2				7
Fugong (2nd class *Juren* list)	6	1						7
Fugong (Supplementary *Juren* list)	3	2	3	2		1		11
Lingong (Special contributed student)			3	1				4
Linsheng (Regular student)	40	3	32	23		2		100
Zengsheng (Added student)	16	2	9	7		1	1	36
Fusheng (Supplementary student)	49	22	103	127	6	26	9	342
Yisheng (Specially appointed student)			1	2	2	2	1	8
Basheng (Selected student)				1				1

Xundao (Assistant teaching official)	2			2				4
Wubin zhixian (Fifth rank title)	1							1
Xunjian (County security officer)	2							2
Xiancheng (Assistant county magistrate)	1							1
Zhoutong (Assistant district magistrate)		1			1			2
Jingli (Financial official)				1				1
Congjiu (2nd class of the ninth rank)				1				1
Wuju (Recommended military officer)					1			1
Shixi Qidouwei (Inherited military title)					1			1
Wupin jungong (Fifth rank for military credit)					1			1
No title/degree	0	16	55	260	87	148	116	682
Total number of graduates	146	60	223	445	110	203*	126	1,313
Total number with title /degree	146	44	168	184	23	54	11	659
Percentage with title/degree	100%	73.3%	75.3%	41.4%	20.9%	26.6%	8.7%	50.1%

* Although the total number should be 203, the original document has only 202 students' names on the list.

Source: Liang Guang youji shifan xuetang yi lan [Brochure for Liang Guang Advanced Teachers' College (1910)], Shanghai Metropolitan Archives, file Q0-12/1086.

age dropped over time. Presumably, most older literati attended less expensive short-term schools closer to home. And, as students finished their elementary training, the school admitted much more qualified younger students. In some areas, this process was slow; until 1918, former private school teachers continued to be admitted to teachers' schools in Shandong's Zouping and Changshan Counties, and some went on to teach students who were over seventy years old.[138]

Teachers' schools applied a liberal age policy. A teacher involved with Zhejiang Combined Teachers' School wrote in his memoir that the school attached little importance to age, permitting students from eighteen to forty to enrol in the lower teachers' schools.[139] The 1904 regulations also gave teachers' schools some leeway in terms of their programs. For example, schools were encouraged to allow older students and impoverished rural scholars (*xiangjian laosheng hanru*) to audit classes. Short-term schools were to give precedence to admitting former schoolteachers who were between the ages of thirty and fifty and who had taught in the old-style elementary schools.[140] The growth in the number of short-term teachers' schools may indicate the efficacy of this policy. In 1907, these schools numbered 276 and enrolled 9,844 students; by the following year, they numbered 303 and enrolled 10,558 students.[141] In 1909, however, there were only 187 such schools, and they enrolled only 7,670 students. The following year showed continued declines, and the average student age also decreased.[142] One possible explanation for this is that these special programs had fulfilled their historic task of transforming old literati into modern professional teachers. The teachers' school system could now be developed into a more formal system. This would be a task for the next decade, the 1910s.

Creating Modern Professional Teachers

The rise of teachers' schools in the first decade of the twentieth century not only reformed the old educational system but also transformed a portion of the old literati class. Women's education shifted from the family to the public domain, and women's role as the primary educators of their children was incorporated into the state agenda. The educational system quickly accomplished two goals: the establishment of new schools and the creation of modern teachers as a professional group. Helen Chauncey's study of the educational elites of Jiangsu notes that the changing of social status was closely related to modern education and that the graduates of new schools gradually replaced the old gentry.[143] During the late 1900s and the early 1910s, imperial degrees and modern school credentials were often juxtaposed in various documents so that educators could claim their educational qualifications. In the next chapter, however, I show that, by the end of the 1910s, this phenomenon had changed. Educational administrators at provincial and county levels omitted their imperial degree-holding experience

Table 2.4

Age distribution of graduates from Liang Guang Advanced Teachers' College

	Program							
Age of students	Administrator Training Program (1904)	Accelerated Program (1904)	Simplified Program (1906)	Simplified Program (1907)	Physical Training Program (1907)	Advanced Elective Program (1909)	Advanced Specialty Program (1910)	Totals
Under 20	2	7	23	26	33	1	13	105
21-25	20	29	101	227	58	86	70	591
26-30	52	20	92	153	19	108	43	487
31-35	32	2	3	36		7		80
36-40	25	2	1	3				31
41-45	11		1					12
46-50	4							4
51-55			1					1
Total	146	60	223*	445	110	203**	126	1,313

* The original record was missing one student's age.

** Although the total number was 203, the original document has only 202 students' names on the list.

Source: Liang Guang youji shifan xuetang yi lan [Brochure for Liang Guang Advanced Teachers' College (1910)]. Shanghai Metropolitan Archives, file Q0-12/1086.

Table 2.5

Age distribution of enrolled students in 1910

	Departments						
Age	Chinese and foreign languages	History and geography	Mathematics and chemistry	Natural science	General courses	Special teacher training program	Totals
Under 20	1		2		10	10	23
21-25	15	18	36	30	36	49	184
26-30	4	37	17	24	13	62	157
31-35						24	24
36-40						19	19
41-45						4	4
46-50						1	1
51-55						1	1
Over 70						1	1
Totals	20	55	55	54	59	171	414

Source: Liang Guang youji shifan xuetang yi lan [Brochure for Liang Guang Advanced Teachers' College (1910)]. Shanghai Metropolitan Archives, file Q0-12/1086.

and only mentioned their modern school qualifications. Sometimes, people only admitted to imperial degrees if they did not have any modern school experience.[144]

We do not have statistics for the total number of teachers who graduated from teachers' colleges and teachers' schools during this period. However, it is possible to estimate the number of graduates based on the number of registered students who attended teachers' schools (see Table 2.6).

From 1907 to 1909, short-term teachers' schools sent at least 28,852 graduates to teach at elementary schools. Based on my estimate, by 1909, at least 29,707 graduates from primary teachers' schools were working in elementary schools. There may have been about 60,000 graduates from various types of teachers' schools working in elementary schools. In the same year, about 6,758 graduates of advanced teachers' colleges would have become

Table 2.6

Overall number of enrolled students, 1907-9

	Advanced Teachers' School			Primary Teachers' School		Short-term Teachers' Schools	
Year	3-year program	2-year program	2-year program	3-year program	1-2 year program	6 month-1 year program	Totals
1907	527	2,686	894	6,640	15,833	10,028	36,608
1908	1,103	3,243	1,678	7,347	9,332	10,838	33,541
1909	1,504	3,233	691	8,441	7,195	7,986	29,050
Totals	3,134	9,162	3,263	22,428	32,360	28,852	99,199
Estimated graduates*	718	4,307	1,733	6,875	22,832	28,852	65,317

* Since the data only provide the numbers of students in schools or the number of graduates, each year's total may count students who had been counted the previous year. One student might be counted two or three times if he or she entered school in 1907 or 1908. There is no number for total students graduating from teachers' schools as a whole. My method of estimating the number of graduates is as follows: since the complete program required three years to graduate, about two-thirds of the students who were counted in 1907 should have graduated by 1909. One-third of students who were counted in 1908 should have graduated by 1909. In a two-year selective program or specialty program, the students who were counted in the 1907 data should have graduated in 1909, and one-half of the students who were counted in 1908 should have graduated in 1909.

Sources: Xuebu zongwusi, *Guangxu san shi san nian di yi ci jiaoyu tongji tubiao* [The first compilation of statistics on education, 1907], *Guangxu san shi si nian di er ci jiaoyu tongji tubiao* [The second compilation of statistics on education, 1908], and *Xuantong yuan nian fen di san ci jiaoyu tongji tubiao* [The third compilation of statistics on education, 1909], in Ju Xingui, Tong Fuyong, and Zhang Shouzhi (compil.), *Shiye jiaoyu, shifan jiaoyu* [Vocational education and teacher training] (Shanghai: Shanghai jiaoyu chubanshe [Shanghai Education Press], 1994), 615-27.

middle school teachers. In 1907, there were 1,955 higher primary schools, 29,199 lower primary schools, and 2,451 primary schools for both levels in the provinces, and, on average, each elementary school would have had about two teachers who had been trained in teachers' schools.[145] By 1907, according to the first survey on teachers carried out after the reforms, the percentage of teachers who had graduated from teachers' schools had already reached 34.2 percent in advanced elementary schools and 39.8 percent in primary elementary schools.[146]

The situation of teachers' schools improved in 1909. Of the teaching staff in normal schools, 43 percent had graduated from teachers' schools, while only 24 percent had no modern educational training. The remaining 32 percent of teachers in teachers' school were graduates of overseas schools or other types of educational institutions or they were foreign teachers.[147] From 1904 to 1911, this group of modern teachers gradually replaced the old literati in educational institutions, especially in those above the advanced elementary level. Therefore, 1904-10 can be considered the critical transitional period for both Chinese education and the Chinese literati.

This is not to say, however, that teachers' schools were the only avenue open to old literati who wished to gain new identities in the late Qing. The path for transforming literati-officials varied, depending on the individual's age, family finances, personal status and fame, and connection with power. Literati accounted for only a small portion of the graduating class of any given school. However, the teachers' schools played a crucial role in the vocational training of those literati whose age barred them from attending newly established regular schools, military schools, and vocational schools or who were too poor to study abroad or in big cities and too marginal to be involved in political institutions.[148] Many in this group had already been teaching for a living and lacked professional alternatives. Some older literati did not make the transition to the modern educational system during the late Qing at all; during the Republican period, other institutional reforms were made in an effort to co-opt this minority. This process lasted for several decades.

To see how one family adapted to the rapidly changing educational environment, consider Liu Dapeng. He arranged for one son to teach at the private school he ran, which maintained the traditional Confucian curriculum, and sent another son to the provincial teachers' school to study Western subjects. After the 1911 Revolution, as a provincial celebrity who was engaged in the prior constitutional movement, Liu himself switched pedagogical allegiances and became the principal of one of the new-style primary schools.[149] Liu and his family adapted to a momentous change that not only fundamentally altered education but revolutionized elite society as a whole.

3
Pursuing Modernization in Trying Times: Teachers' Schools, 1912-22

The 1911 Revolution overthrew the Manchu regime and ended the imperial system. Intent on building a strong nation and a progressive modern polity in China, the revolutionaries were, from the outset, hindered by many obstacles in their attempt to establish a true republic. Conflict between President Yuan Shikai, the head of the postrevolutionary regime, and liberal elites (consisting mainly of local gentry leaders, returned overseas students, and revolutionaries) dominated the politics of the early Republican era.[1] The liberals designed a new educational system that was promulgated in 1912, followed by a series of regulations and national curricula that were published in 1913. These made up the formal framework for public education in China until 1922. Liberal educators saw reconstructing the nationwide network of teachers' schools as crucial to the construction of a unified nation. These schools would facilitate the spread of a single spoken and written language throughout China. They would also contribute to training "good mothers and virtuous wives," which was still the dominant ideology behind women's education, even as programs that encouraged women to enter the working world and to exercise their civil rights filtered into the curriculum. Liberal arguments pressured women to stick to their traditional role as teachers: their big step into professional careers would permit them to serve the country by educating citizens-in-training in the public schools. Then President Yuan Shikai decided to restore the imperial system, thus precipitating a political crisis. After Yuan's dictatorship collapsed, military officers vied for control of the central government, and Beijing lost control over local governments. The Republicans' hopes for a strong and modern nation suddenly seemed premature.

Many studies of Chinese education have rightly stressed the fact that modern schools grew out of the determination to enhance state power and to promote nationalism.[2] These connections are particularly visible during periods when education is directed by central state authorities, as it was before the collapse of the Qing court in 1911 and after the Nationalist Party (Guomindang [GMD]) established control over all of China in 1927. During the intervening period, central authority disintegrated and regional warlords seized power. Provincial self-governance groups sprang up; the New Culture Movement gnawed away at the ideological basis of the old political order; Western ideas such as anarchism and socialism also undermined existing authority. When central state authorities had little power to impose their will on local education officials, did schools continue to play a role in promoting the state-building project? And, if they did, did a specific institution play a key role?

When political strife and warlordism paralyzed the central government between 1916 and 1927,[3] provincial and county educators formed a decentralized but national network to replace the dysfunctional national education bureaucracy. These educators understood that their goal was to promote the education of the citizenry from the bottom up, which included building schools for girls and advancing female teachers' schools, with or without state guidance.

Unifying the Country through Education

In 1912 and 1913, the new Ministry of Education began to design a school system that would manifest the Republican spirit. Its first edict was terminological: the modern schools established in the late Qing period would now be called "schools" (*xuexiao*) rather than "study halls" (*xuetang*).[4] The ministry tried to erase all traces of imperial education by banning official Qing textbooks, the terms that referred to the imperial system and the Qing court, the study of Confucian classics in primary school, and the practice of awarding imperial titles to graduates.[5] The unified educational system was meant to create enlightened citizens (*guomin*) for the new republic.

Reconstructing Teachers' Schools to Unify the Nation

In 1913, when the political situation had stabilized, the Ministry of Education launched an ambitious educational inspection program that covered twenty-two of a total of twenty-three provinces. The inspectors chalked up the poor results of Qing efforts at educational modernization to fragmentation and inconsistency. Government leaders believed that, if they could unify the nation's education system, they would unify the country. The minister of education declared:[6]

> I believe that running a state has two components: dealing with internal and external affairs. Without excellent education, we cannot compete with other countries; without unified education, we cannot eliminate domestic disturbances. Recently our country has experienced a series of incidents, and internal affairs have become more pressing than external affairs. In

> establishing the goals of education, we should make unifying education our first priority. When education is unified the citizens' thinking will be unified; when the citizens' thinking is unified domestic disturbances will not take place ... [I]f education is not unified there will be no unified thought; if citizens' thinking is not unified it will be impossible to build a unified country.[7]

Measures to unify and centralize teachers' schools included nationalizing higher teachers' colleges[8] and placing secondary teachers' schools under the control of provincial governments. In addition, teachers' schools took charge of developing and supervising local education.

When the Qing court established teachers' schools in the first decade of the twentieth century, provinces, especially economically and educationally advanced ones, were encouraged to set up their own advanced teachers' colleges. By 1911, there were fourteen college-level teachers' schools, including combined colleges (see Table 2.1). This system reflected the political conditions of the late Qing: more responsibilities devolved to the provinces as the central government gradually collapsed.

The Republican system put power over higher education in the hands of the central government, and teachers' schools – at both tertiary and secondary levels – drove the enterprise. Setting up a unified teachers' school system would, it was hoped, unify the Chinese educational system. The first step was to nationalize teachers' colleges. In 1913, the minister of education stated:

> Teachers who will serve in secondary teachers' schools are to be trained in higher teachers' colleges [*gaodeng shifan xuexiao*], so [these colleges] are the foundation of the foundation [*genben zhi genben*] ... Only if we nationalize higher teachers' colleges and administer them through the central government ... making the state's spirit their spirit and the state's principle their principle, will we be able to achieve unity ... So, to unify education we should set up national higher teachers' colleges immediately: this is indeed the best plan for setting the country on a firm footing [*shi wei guojia genben zhiji*].[9]

The central government was intent on regaining control over the provinces. At the end of the Qing, there were only three public universities: Capital University in Beijing, Beiyang University in Tianjin, and Shanxi University in Taiyuan. At the same time, each province also had various higher colleges (*gaodeng xuexiao*) and preparatory schools (*yuke*), which functioned as bridges between middle schools and universities (or specialized colleges). The higher colleges were abolished in 1912, and the three public universities were added around 1920.[10]

In 1913, the Ministry of Education planned to reduce the previous fourteen teachers' colleges to six national ones – located in Beijing, Wuchang, Nanjing, Shenyang, Guangzhou, and Chengdu – that would supplant the provincial higher teachers' colleges. In 1914, only two higher teachers' colleges, those in Beijing and Wuchang, were in the hands of the central government.[11] Between 1915 and 1917, the other four were established in Nanjing, Chengdu, Guangzhou, and Shenyang. (Shenyang Higher Teachers' College was originally a local secondary teachers' school with several college programs. Thanks to the efforts of the Ministry of Education, initiated in 1916, it became a higher teachers' college in 1918.)[12] During that period, a number of provincial teachers' colleges were either demoted to provincial secondary teachers' schools or closed.[13] The Ministry of Education long planned to establish a higher teachers' college in Xi'an to provide teaching personnel for northwestern China, an educationally backward region. But financial difficulties and political instability kept Shaanxi Teachers' College from opening until the 1930s.[14] Although all of the efforts to achieve political unity were frustrated during the 1910s, progress on the educational front can be measured by the discussions held in 1918 by the presidents of the national teachers' colleges. Their united mission to see normal colleges spread across the map of China and their willingness to distribute student quotas across the country symbolized China's desire to be a unified nation.[15]

Even as the Ministry of Education nationalized teachers' colleges, it ordered that the administration of secondary teachers' schools set up in the last decade of the Qing be transferred to provincial governments.[16] The new order for teachers' schools also stipulated that, once they had been granted permission from the heads of the provincial and national departments of education, county governments could establish secondary teachers' schools. The order also permitted private teachers' schools, and it was during this period that missionary schools for teachers were set up.[17] Private teachers' schools were few, however, compared to government schools (which were free of charge).

In most provinces, the secondary teachers' schools previously run by prefectural governments officially became provincial teachers' schools and were given numbers.[18] From 1912 to 1917 the number of teachers' schools actually decreased (see Table 3.1).

A combination of factors precipitated the decline evident in Table 3.1. Schools had merged and budgets had shrunk. Some of the elementary and short-term teachers' schools opened by counties in the late Qing were integrated into provincial teachers' schools as secondary departments, while those considered to be substandard were closed.[19]

And all the time provincial governments planned more schools. In 1917, Fujian and Zhejiang adopted plans for their own teachers' schools.[20] The

Table 3.1

Numbers of teachers' schools and students, 1912-17

	Number of schools	Number of students
1912	253	28,605
1913	314	34,826
1914	231	26,679
1915	211	27,975
1916	195	24,959
1917	148	23,382

Sources: The Ministry of Education: *Di er ci Zhongguo jiaoyu nianjian* [The second yearbook on the education of China, 1948] (Beijing: Shangwu Yinshuguan [Commercial Press], 1948), 3: 311. The data for 1917 are drawn from Jiaoyu bu, "Minguo liu nian quanguo shifan xuexiao yi lan biao" [Chinese Historical Archives Number Two in Nanjing], file no. 1057, vol. 68. However, Chuang Chai-hsuan, based on the List of Normal Schools issued by the Ministry of Education in 1918, indicates that there were 194 teachers' schools nationwide in 1917. See Chai-hsuan Chuang, *Tendencies toward a Democratic System of Education in China* (Shanghai: Commercial Press, 1922), 104-6. The difference may have been caused by the administrative chaos of the time.

frontier province in the northwest, Xinjiang, established a teachers' school in 1916, which had fifty-seven students and became the highest level modern educational institution in the entire province.[21] In 1920, one of China's most remote provinces, Qinghai, established its first teachers' school with an enrolment of over 100 students. It became the most advanced modern educational institution in the province.[22]

The plan the Ministry of Education drew up for teachers' schools was intended to establish national control over all teachers' colleges and provincial control over all secondary teachers' schools. County governments had little influence over schools: all power at the secondary level and above was concentrated in the hands of the provincial and central governments. The minister of education had the right to appoint the presidents of national teachers' colleges, while provincial governors had the right to appoint principals of provincial secondary teachers' schools and county teachers' schools.[23]

To improve central control, in 1914 the Ministry of Education attempted to establish a new system of districts for teachers' schools (*shifan qu*). Most of the country was to be divided into six districts organized around the six extant national teachers' colleges.[24] Each college would draw students from its district and train the teachers who would serve there. The colleges were also in charge of the development of education within the district. Each president or dean was required to inspect the local middle and primary schools and to guide improvements.[25] For the president of Beijing Teachers' School, this meant visiting innumerable schools in Jingzhao (the capital zone), Zhili, Shandong, Henan, Rehe, Chahar, and Suiyuan – a very large area that includes parts of present-day Hebei, Liaoning, Inner Mongolia, and Shanxi. The Wuchang district covered most of Hunan, Hubei, and Jiangxi; Nanjing covered Jiangsu, Zhejiang, and Anhui; Guangzhou covered Guangdong, Guangxi, and Fujian.[26]

Similar administrative responsibilities were given to provincial teachers' schools. The Ministry of Education required that each province create a number of "teachers' school [sub]districts," ensuring that one teachers' school was located within each subdistrict. The school's administrators were to oversee educational affairs in the subdistricts, direct the implementation of education policy, and work to coordinate schools, thus promoting much-valued national unity.[27]

The program relating to teachers' school districts was never implemented at the national level. After Yuan's fall in 1916, the Ministry of Education never mustered the authority to impose such grand schemes; none of the subsequent warlord regimes had the power to implement the program, and local provinces did not cooperate with the Ministry of Education in order to put it into practice.

While the teachers' college districts never functioned satisfactorily, the provincial program survived the collapse of the Yuan regime and thrived well into the 1930s. Between 1914 and 1918, most provinces created teachers' school subdistricts and established or planned to establish a corresponding teachers' school for each district.[28] Some provinces, such as Fengtian, Shanxi, Anhui, Shaanxi, Jiangxi, Jilin, Henan, Zhejiang, Zhili, Jiangsu, and Guangxi, sent documents to the Ministry of Education to report having accomplished this project.[29] In those provinces that could not set up their teachers' school subdistricts, such as Heilongjiang, the Ministry of Education instructed the principals of the teachers' schools to make efforts to direct local education by periodically visiting primary schools in their neighborhoods.[30] In 1917, when contending forces in Jiangxi province were fighting over the site for a new teachers' school, the Ministry of Education intervened and helped decide the location in accordance with provisions relating to teachers' school subdistricts.[31] In 1921, when Henan's Bureau of Education decided to increase the number of its teachers' schools, the plan was to determine the site of new schools in accordance with teachers' school subdistricts.[32] In the midst of this drive to enrich rural education, the Association for Research on Primary Education of the Jiangsu Teachers' School District Eight (*Jiangsu diba shifan qu xiaoxue jiaoyu yanjiu hui*) held its third annual conference in 1925. In addition to requesting that Provincial Teachers' School Number Eight set up a branch specifically to train teachers for rural primary schools, the association requested a summer teacher-training program, a clear explanation of the educational regulations of 1922, textbooks for teaching Mandarin Chinese, and examples of the sort of material the new regulations would require teachers to convey to their students.[33]

As Hayhoe points out, throughout the Republican period, great efforts were made to reallocate educational resources to ensure a more geographically equitable distribution.[34] The mechanism that would permit this democratization of educational opportunity was the teachers' school district system: teachers' schools would function as midwives and nurture modern education in their districts. While I have found evidence that the district system functioned in the provinces despite its collapse at the national level, the situation may not have been as rosy in other parts of China. The district system was still being pursued in the 1930s under the Nationalist government. *Regulations for Teachers' Schools* (*Shifan xuexiao guicheng*), published in 1931 by the Ministry of Education, reinforced the system (see Chapter 5). The surviving records from this period are sparse and do not allow a full evaluation of the practical impact of the teachers' school subdistrict system in the provinces. In the absence of a viable central government, the provincial authorities had limitless power over education – particularly, as will be seen, after 1916.

Teachers' Schools and Language Unification

Those who envisaged a new China unified through education dreamed of a time when every inhabitant of the huge country would speak a single language, one of the key elements of the modern nation-building project. The teachers' schools were designed to be the central vehicle for attaining this goal. In this section, I examine how the teachers' schools were used to promote language unification.

Written Chinese has been used throughout the Chinese cultural zone since the centralizing projects of the first Chinese dynasty, the Qin (221-207 BCE). But, over time, the gap between literary Chinese and spoken Chinese grew into a huge trench, and regional variations in the latter are so great as to render regional dialects mutually incomprehensible.[35] In the late Qing, as elite reformers searched for ways to educate the masses and the state began to reinforce its control over localities, the idea that a single vernacular language might become a national standard, and that the literary language might correspond to it, became a sort of holy grail.

Many viewed the diversity of local dialects as an obstacle to modern education. As long as local dialects were used in classroom instruction, teachers and students could not easily move from place to place. In 1913, when an inspector from the Ministry of Education visited Fujian Province, he discovered that, because most of the teachers' schools were located in the provincial capital, Fuzhou, the local dialect had become the lingua franca of the classroom. Since the Fuzhou dialect was only spoken in the immediate neighbourhood of the city and was incomprehensible in other parts of the province, few students from outside Fuzhou were likely to thrive at its schools.

Furthermore, the graduates of Fuzhou's teachers' schools faced a serious language barrier when sent off to teach.[36] When the presidents of the national teachers' colleges met in 1918, they saw that the same problem was afflicting National Guangzhou Higher Teachers' College: despite the adjective, it could not attract students from outside Guangdong Province because all the teaching was done in Cantonese.[37]

During the twilight of the Qing dynasty, at the same time that reformers were establishing the new school system, some turned their attention to the creation of a national language. One of the courses required at the new teachers' schools was "practising Mandarin" (*xi guanhua*). The revolutionaries of 1911 endorsed the project as well. When the Republican Ministry of Education held a national conference on educational reform in 1912, the adoption of a national language was much discussed.[38] The participants decided that the first step was to unify pronunciation. So the ministry established the Committee on Unifying Pronunciation (*Duyin tongyi hui*). Ongoing political friction made it impossible for the committee to attain great success: its only achievement was putting together a document containing a set of symbols for conveying pronunciation (*zhuyin zimu*).[39] Within months, the committee published a proposal that suggested that the Ministry of Education issue this document as the official pronunciation key for the unification of national pronunciation (*guoyin*).[40] The committee also proposed that the Ministry of Education set up a school offering brief courses in the *zhuyin* system.[41] Such a school was finally established in 1915.[42]

Prodded by the New Culture Movement, the national language campaign took off after 1916. That was the year a group of intellectuals organized the National Language Study Society (*Guoyu yanjiu hui*), hoping to use state power to establish a single national language and to unify the written and spoken languages (*wen yan tongyi*).[43] The initiation of the movement for a national language (*guoyu yundong*) has been attributed to two factors. First, the leaders of the New Culture Movement advocated the widespread adoption of the written vernacular.[44] Second, at the request of the National Federation of Educational Associations (NFEA), in 1917 the Ministry of Education ordered teachers' schools to take the lead in promoting the national language.[45]

Encouraged by the New Culture Movement, in 1917 the Ministry of Education set up the Preparatory Committee for National-Language Unification (*Guoyu tongyi choubei hui*), which was dominated by members of the National Language Study Society.[46] By 1919, the committee had drawn up a basic proposal and had insisted upon installing a course on the national language in all teachers' schools.[47] In the same year, the National Federation of Educational Associations met for the fifth time and urged the Ministry of Education to adopt six measures to promote a national language. The first was the addition of a course in the national language to the curriculum of all teachers' schools; others included training educational administrators and schoolteachers, replacing literature courses with language courses, and establishing branches of the Preparatory Committee for National Language Unification in each province.[48]

Beginning in 1918, the Ministry of Education called on the six higher teachers' colleges to establish a national language program (*guoyu ke*) that would prepare teachers to carry out language instruction in regular middle schools and secondary teachers' schools.[49] Beijing and Nanjing's colleges set up their programs that same year.[50] The National Federation of Educational Associations and the Preparatory Committee for National-Language Unification had a more ambitious plan: expanding the teaching of the national language into the secondary teachers' schools. But development was uneven, and a lack of qualified teachers inevitably provoked delays. For instance, when Chengdu Teachers' College reported that it could not find anyone to teach the national language course, the Ministry of Education allowed the school to postpone setting up the program until students in the short-term program at Beijing Higher Teachers' College had mastered the *zhuyin* system.[51]

Through the efforts of teachers' schools, the *zhuyin* system started filtering down to the county level. In 1919, the Nanjing Teachers' College announced its plan to train primary school language teachers for the sixty counties of Jiangsu Province.[52] The Ministry of Education opened a school to provide intensive instruction in the *zhuyin* system and requested that all provinces send their literature teachers to Beijing to attend the course. In addition, the Ministry of Education instructed teachers' schools in each province to develop courses modelled on the training school; primary schoolteachers would be sent to summer language schools.[53]

In 1920, the national language movement won a major victory. The Ministry of Education announced that, starting with that year's fall term, the classical Chinese class (*guowen*) taught in the first and second grades of all primary schools would be replaced with a vernacular Chinese class (*yuti wen*).[54] This marked the transformation from teaching the *zhuyin* system to teaching a standard written language in vernacular style. To implement this change, the Ministry of Education required that all teachers' schools, including secondary and tertiary schools, begin teaching the national language in courses such as vernacular writing, the *zhuyin* system, standard pronunciation, history and grammar of the national language, and pedagogic methods. To set the courses on a solid footing, the ministry also suggested that all teachers' schools reduce the number of class hours devoted to classical Chinese and increase the number devoted to national language classes.[55]

Many teachers' schools implemented the program as instructed. Even before the Ministry of Education issued its detailed requirements for language teaching at teachers' schools, some had already added the national language to their curricula. For instance, by 1918, the curriculum of Fujian Teachers' School Number Two offered courses on written national language, spoken national language, pronunciation practice, and conversation.[56] At Hubei Teachers' School Number Two, the national language course was divided into three parts: classical literature (*wen yan wen*), vernacular literature (*yuti wen*), and spoken national language (*guoyu*).[57]

Local educational associations also actively promoted the teaching of the national language. In 1918, Jiangsu's Education Association established short-term national language training classes with the help of Nanjing Higher Teachers' College.[58] Furthermore, the province summoned eighty county education inspectors for four weeks' intensive language training.[59] Zhejiang's Bureau of Education required schoolteachers from sixty counties to attend a language training course at Nanjing Higher Teachers' College.[60] In 1922, Anhui and Jilin Provinces established branches of the Preparatory Committee for National-Language Unification under the direction of provincial education bureaus. They planned to promote the national language by training teachers and increasing the number of hours devoted to it in teachers' schools. Moreover, Jilin's provincial education officials also suggested that a national language test be included in the licensing examination for primary schoolteachers and that county education inspectors add the teaching of the national language to the criteria they use when evaluating schools.[61] In 1924, the Ministry of Education required that all those applying to teach in primary schools take a national language test.[62]

Nation Building through Independence of Education

As provincial elites witnessed the withering away of the central state, which began in the late Qing and accelerated after the 1911 Revolution, they snatched power for themselves.[63] After 1916, many in the provinces called for complete autonomy in all educational matters, including budgets. Provincial elites acted with increasing disregard for the warlords in the capital and the provinces, organizing regional and national associations to develop policies for local education. Local educational associations worked with increasingly professionalized local administrations to create uniform curricula and standards.

Divorcing Education from Political Instability: The National Federation of Educational Associations and the Provincial Educational Associations

The Ministry of Education suffered from crippling administrative discontinuities during the warlord period. From 1916 to 1922, no fewer than eighteen ministers and acting ministers of education came and went; seven flashed past in 1922 alone.[64] The very idea of a consistent national education policy during this period seemed to be absurd.

Most warlords were utterly indifferent to educational development, and, as Ka-che Yip has shown, they regarded intellectuals as a threat to their interests. A crucial contributing factor was the lack of financial resources: in 1919-20, education accounted for a mere 1 percent of the national budget.[65] But Yip's conclusion that education in China stagnated during this period fails to appreciate that power over education was in the hands of provincial governments and local elites. His thesis must be modified in view of surviving educational records.

Statistics show that, during the first decade after the 1911 Revolution, the number of middle schools grew from 359 in 1912 to 435 in 1915. They suffered a dramatic setback in 1916, dropping to 342 when Yuan's regime collapsed. By 1925, there were only 404 middle schools.[66] On the other hand, primary schools grew from 86,318 with 2,793,633 students in 1912 to 128,525 with 4,140,066 students in 1915. After a slight setback in 1916 (schools dropped to 120,103 and students to 3,843,455), primary schools increased to 177,751 with 6,601,802 students in 1922.[67] The data sets demonstrate that secondary education stagnated while primary education grew at fast pace.

Higher education developed rapidly during the warlord period. In 1916, there were only ten universities nationwide (this includes both public and private); by 1925, there were twenty-one national universities, nine provincial universities, and ten registered private universities.[68] Several famous universities were established between 1917 and 1925, including Beijing Teachers' University (1923), Beijing Women's Higher Teachers' College (1919), Southeast University (now Nanjing University) (1921), and Tongji Specialized College (1917).

While political disorder did have a negative impact on educational development, other factors mitigated this. In his study of education in Republican Shandong, David Buck depicts a series of cooperative ventures between the Ministry of Education and the local educational associations, whose expertise facilitated policy making. Recommendations and policies emanating from the centre were put into practice in Ji'nan (Tsinan) only when they met with the approval of local officials and associations.[69] Buck's work has subsequently been confirmed by other studies and extended to other areas. For example, Bailey has shown that the development of local education did not depend entirely on financing from central and provincial governments: district governments spent more money on education than did provincial governments.[70] This may explain the stagnation in secondary education noted above since that sector depended heavily on provincial financing, whereas primary education tended to rely on district and county government support. As Thøgersen's research shows, at the local level, governments worked with the gentry, both modern and traditional, to successfully promote elementary education in a time of national crisis.[71]

While Buck shows the central government working fruitfully with local partners, studies of local elite activities published in the following decades show something else. Most scholars have noticed that the growth of local education under the warlords was the result of vigorous local educational associations, while weak state power provided opportunity for local elite activism in education.[72] These studies on the activities of local educational associations most likely reflect the reality of educational development at the time. Many of these local associations were established in the late Qing period and actively participated in the constitutional and self-governance movements. In the early years of the republic, they suffered a severe setback, but, by 1915, the newly created National Federation of Educational Associations held its first national conference in Tianjin, drawing representatives from educational associations in twenty-four provinces, special regions, and Beijing.[73] By the late 1910s, educational associations nationwide had formed a hierarchical network that tied national, provincial, and county organizations together and functioned as an alternative to the central, provincial, and county government education bureaus.

A review of the relevant documents from this period shows that it was these professional educators who dominated education. Starting in 1915, the National Federation of Educational Associations held a national conference every year to discuss national education policies and reforms. By and large, the Ministry of Education simply served as a rubber stamp for the recommendations that emerged from these conferences. For instance, when the federation's 1918 meeting ended with a call for improving women's education, the Ministry of Education simply issued an order advocating women's education, attaching the federation's proposal in lieu of instructions to provincial administrations.[74] The role of the National Federation of Educational Associations was clearly central in creating a national language. Resolving the continuing dispute over which dialect would become the standard was utterly beyond the capacity of the Ministry of Education. So when, in 1920, provincial representatives of the National Federation of Educational Associations agreed that Beijing would serve as the standard, the Ministry of Education simply ratified the decision, eventually publishing a dictionary that provided the Beijing pronunciation of most commonly used Chinese characters.[75] A review of ministry records from this period shows that, after approving them at their annual meetings, the National Federation of Educational Associations regularly sent proposals to the Ministry of Education to be distributed through its administrative network.

The federation's domination of educational policy reached its apex with the 1922 reforms. In 1921, a new educational system, copied from American models, was drafted at the federation's seventh conference. The following year, officials of the Ministry of Education presented an alternative proposal, but members of the federation protested furiously until finally the cowed officials were obliged to give in and accept the federation's version.[76] It is telling that National Federation of Educational Associations representatives did not go to the Ministry of Education to sell their proposal; rather, state officials came to them to try to influence the direction of reform. After the 1922 educational guidelines were issued, the Ministry of Education did not even make a pretence of drafting regulations; instead, the federation organized a committee to flesh out the guidelines.[77] Evidently, a non-state body had effectively replaced the Ministry of Education.

As their power over policy grew, professional educators moved to wrest control of financial resources from the political authorities. The movement drew wide publicity in 1921, when the faculty and staff of Beijing's higher educational institutions went on strike, demanding the return of educational funds that had been embezzled for military expenses.[78] In 1917, the National Federation of Educational Associations had already called on the national and provincial governments to increase funding for education.[79] At the sixth annual meeting, representatives proposed that the Ministry of Education set education funding independently.[80] Provincial educational associations organized many protests to demand fiscal independence for education; however, as Pepper points out, these efforts met with very limited success.[81] Since the shortage of education funds and the separation of educational funds from other government funds were national issues, not specific to teachers' schools, I provide only a brief summary.

Educational Uniformity and Regularity through Professionalization

The establishment of teachers' schools at the beginning of the twentieth century institutionalized the separation of political bureaucrats and educational administrators (see Chapter 2). Educational independence began with the restructuring of educational administration. In the late 1910s, initiated and supported by the National Federation of Educational Associations, the Ministry of Education started restructuring provincial and county bureaucracies. In this plan, provincial educational bureaus, *jiaoyu ting* (bureaus of education), were no longer subordinate to provincial governors (as was the case under the early Republican system) but, rather, reported directly to the Ministry of Education. The commissioners of these bureaus only communicated with provincial governors when educational affairs were involved with provincial administration.[82] Most provincial education commissioners, who were appointed directly by the Ministry of Education, were local elites and many of them had been leaders of provincial educational associations.[83] As expected, this reform was not welcomed by some provincial warlords; however, the Ministry of Education insisted on it as it was supported by educational associations at all levels.[84] At the county level the Ministry of

Education's plan to restructure the educational bureaucracy did not go well. In 1918, the ministry decided to temporarily preserve the Education Exhortation Offices (*quanxue suo*), which had been established in the late Qing as county education administrations. But, after 1923, reconstruction was eventually accomplished when, nationwide, county education offices became education departments (*jiaoyu ju*).[85]

The establishment of educational independence during the 1910s and 1920s was based on the professionalization of educators. These educators gradually came to dominate all decision making and policy implementation with regard to education in China.[86] As educational associations seized centre stage, professional educators gradually replaced members of the gentry in positions related to local educational administration. Despite excellent studies of these educational associations, the extent of professionalization in the educational bureaucracy, and its influence on education, remains unclear. We need to know more about the people in this group of educational officials: their educational background, their experience in education, and their positions. Such details would facilitate our understanding of how their professional training kept local schools running, especially after the collapse of central power.

By around 1920, the effect of teachers' school training on teachers and administrators was evident in the field of education. The data from the résumés of over 1,700 education officials – sent to the Ministry of Education between 1917 and 1923 by the educational bureaus of nineteen provinces, numerous counties, and the capital region – indicate this trend. These résumés include the officials' names, their places of origin, and their titles; their educational background and work history in the field of education; and the various positions they had held.[87] County-level officials who appear in the cluster of résumés are the directors (*suozhang*) and staff (*shixue*, or *shixue yuan*) of the educational exhortation offices (*quanxue suo*). Provincial officials include the branch director and the staff of the bureaus of education (*jiaoyu ting kezhang* and *keyuan*), the provincial education inspector (*sheng shixue*), and directors and members of the examination committee for elementary teachers (*jianding xiaoxue jiaoyuan weiyuan hui zhuren/weiyuan*). Of these 1,700 educational officials, more than 50 percent had graduated from various teachers' schools either at home or abroad. About 20 percent had graduated from other types of modern schools, ranging from universities to primary schools. Not surprisingly, during this period of transition, about 10 percent of education officials still held only an imperial title, while the rest chose not to reveal their credentials. Understandably, the percentage of teachers' school graduates among these officials was gradually increasing while the number of traditional degree-holders was decreasing.[88] This shows that, in the field of education, the new professional elite (who were educated in modern schools), were gradually replacing the old gentry. Clearly, modern school credentials had become the key to acquiring a position in educational administration.

An Overlapped State and Society in the Educational Circle

The studies of local elites provide us with a clear picture of the educational activities of these people and their achievements. Most research, however, focuses on the activities of village elites, whose interest was in building elementary schools and who left secondary education to provincial and county elites. In their villages, these elites enjoyed a socio-cultural network that was reinforced and expanded through their participation in educational activities, whether they resisted or accepted state penetration.[89] Nonetheless, at the county level, the relationship between the educational elite and the government is not clear. These elites and their associations were very often seen as forces that existed apart from the state, and their relations with state power have been described as being in opposition to it but nonetheless interacting with it.[90] On the other hand, the so-called "state," which was represented by provincial and county bureaucratic organs such as provincial "education bureaus" and county "educational exhortation offices," often had an extremely vague face. Although Chauncey notes that some local elites in Republican Jiangsu counties had served the former regime as members of the imperial educational bureaucracy, she gives no indication that this connection to the state continued into the Republican era.[91] And once this connection was erased, the model of state versus society became applicable. However, as Thøgersen points out (based on his study of Zouping), the relations between state power and local elites in the field of education were "far too complicated to be reduced to any simple state versus society model."[92] The information contained in the data on provincial and county educational officials reveals the same complexity.

The personnel connection between the state bureaucracy and local educational associations continued even after the Revolution and persisted through the time of the warlords. These two institutions actually overlapped, and educational bureaucrats and local educational elites were very often comprised of the same group of people. In 1912, the Ministry of Education promulgated regulations on educational associations, stipulating that people who held educational positions, who had experience in education, and who had specialized knowledge could be members of provincial educational associations.[93] In 1919, the Ministry of Education revised the regulations, stipulating that those people who were active teachers or educational administrators, or who had a certain number of years of experience with education or educational administration, could be members of educational associations.[94] Based on this regulation, as well as all school teachers, both provincial and county administrators could be included in the associations. Although there are no membership lists of country educational associations to examine, the information from the reports has indeed shown that many educational bureaucrats were former heads (*huizhang*) or vice-heads (*fu huizhang*) of local educational associations.

The data from the résumés of education officials sent to the Ministry of Education seem to indicate this overlapping. Many local administrators were also former teachers and members of local educational associations. For example, one of the Henan provincial education inspectors, Li Yujie, graduated from Beijing Advanced Teachers' College in the late Qing. After teaching at an upper primary school, a middle school, and a vocational school, he became a staff member of the Education Exhortation Office of Zhengyang County and then, in 1918, an inspector at the provincial education bureau.[95] Most of his colleagues had similar experiences, as did educational officials in other provinces and counties.[96] Another example, Fan Zizhan, a staff member (*shixue*) of the Education Exhortation Office of Dangshan County, Jiangsu Province, in 1920, had graduated from a teachers' school. His professional experience included teaching at a middle school, being the principle of an elementary school, and being in charge of teacher training for a vocational program. Fan was also once the head of the county educational association (*xian jiaoyu hui huizhang*).[97] This kind of experience was not unusual for these educational officials. Among the 1,700 educational administrators listed in the reports to the Ministry of Education, over 90 percent had either taught in or administered primary schools or secondary schools (as principals or deans), and about 7 percent of them had been the head or vice-head of a local educational association. The data show that, after graduating from teachers' schools or other types of modern schools, most of these people taught in local schools and then gradually moved up to become principals or deans and members of local educational associations. Some of them were heads or vice-heads of local educational associations and then worked in county educational offices, and some moved up to the provincial level. These people could shift between being teachers, education activists, and administrators. Thus, there was significant overlap among members of local educational associations, educational administrators, and teachers; teaching practice, administrative operation, and the study and discussion of policy were closely linked through the educational associations. This explains why education continued to develop during times of political disorder.

The limitations of the documentary record, however, make it difficult to analyze the extent and depth of the overlap between local schools and local educational administrators. Considering the rapid development of primary education nationwide during this period, the role of professional education administrators who had been trained in teachers' schools should not be underestimated.

Teaching as a Profession for Women: Female Teachers' Schools in the 1910s

The regime that emerged out of the 1911 Revolution declared its commitment to gender equality, including in the sphere of education.[98] Still, society had changed far less than the official rhetoric would indicate. Bailey shows that the debates over women's education during the late Qing and the early Republic were "fraught with ambiguity and contradiction."[99] And Borthwick's study of changing ideas regarding the role of women in the 1910s and 1920s paints a dim picture of progress in female education.[100] Though the Republican advocates of female education lacked the pioneering spirit of the late Qing innovators, and though women's education was overshadowed by boisterous political struggles, newly professionalized educators pushed through a series of reforms to women's education. These differed from those of the late Qing, through which the purpose of training female teachers was clearly stated in the Qing court's regulation that female teachers assist family education and young citizens' education. Also, an unintended result was that women worked as teachers in the public domain in the late Qing (see Chapter 2). However, in the early Republican society, the question of the "proper" profession for females became a topic of public debate. This was an indication that the society had begun to normalize women's position in the public realm. Teaching was no longer just an unintended consequence of promoting male education, but a profession for women.

Discourse on Women's Education in Early Republican Society

In 1914, the Ministry of Education set out to define the official goals of women's education. It announced that, rather than pursuing lofty goals, women's education should emphasize the "principle of training virtuous wives and good mothers" (*liang qi xian mu zhuyi*).[101] In the cultural landscape of the 1910s, official ideology reaffirmed the importance of conservatism while the New Culture Movement did the opposite. Yet the old idea of "virtuous wives and good mothers" continued to serve the state. Elizabeth VanderVen's research on Haicheng County, Fengtian (now Liaoning Province), shows that, in the 1910s, the national debate on "virtuous wives and good mothers" had already spread to the villages of northeastern China. Members of the village elite used this discourse when pleading with county authorities for the funds they needed to open girls' schools.[102]

Moreover, since this discourse was both widespread and strongly nationalist, it drew many women to educational activism. This was unlike what had occurred in the last decade of the Qing, when male literati were the main advocates of female education and when some of the bold women who took up the cause suffered such pressure and abuse that they killed themselves.[103] When the first issue of *Women's Magazine* (*Funü zazhi*) was published in 1915, many women were invited to contribute; in the first few years of the magazine's existence, there appeared a number of articles by women studying in teachers' colleges. These women consistently voiced the opinion that women's education would make China a strong nation.

In one article, Liu Sheng, the female director of Heilongjiang's Provincial Reformatory Institute for Women (*Shengli nüzi jiaoyang yuan*), stated that the power of Western countries (which took the form of gunboat diplomacy) was a purely external form of power, while the education of wise mothers, virtuous wives, and gentle daughters (*xianmu, liangqi, shunü*) was an internal form of power.[104] In 1915, a female educator succinctly states the rationale for women's education: "Whether or not the country is strong depends on its citizens. Whether or not the citizens are good depends on mothers' education. In order to set mother's education on the right track, women's education must be promoted."[105] Ding Fengzhu, a student of Jiangsu Female Normal School Number Two, wrote to *Women's Magazine* and pointed out that whenever women's education flourished the country was strong, and that when women failed to get the education they wanted the country was weakened. She believed that the goals of women's education were to "foster the teaching of motherhood [*long mu jiao*], to expand teacher's training [*hong shizi*], to fortify the national teaching [*zhen guojiao*], and to improve household management skills [*zheng jiazheng*]."[106] Of course, such remarks were hardly innovative: what they showed was that the idea of "virtuous wives and good mothers" had been embraced by a broad constituency.

In the 1910s, the discussion of women's education that was taking place in popular magazines heated up, and educators raised difficult questions about the utility of the current curriculum.[107] The Ministry of Education had yet to design a separate course of study for women's schools, and much of the debate on women's education centred on the different educational needs of women and men. An article published in 1915 in *Women's Magazine* criticized the women's schools for teaching their students "dragon butchering skills" (*tu long shu*) – that is, skills of a high order but of little practical use. According to Zhan Lu:

> [Female students] will not be translators but they are learning foreign languages; they will not engage in surveying but they are studying trigonometry; their handicrafts class stresses crafts, but they cannot make a pair of shoes ... [They] are not going to participate in the civil service examinations [*wenguan kaoyan*], but they are taught to discuss the lessons of history; there is no chance for them to take the palace examination [i.e., the

> highest level of the abolished civil service examinations], but they are required to practise fine calligraphy; they are very familiar with stories about Napoleon, but they cannot remember their grandfather's names; they are acquainted with foreign geography, but do not know the names of nearby rivers and mountains.[108]

Zhan Lu captures a key dilemma facing women's education. According to Republican principles, female students should study subjects similar to those studied by their male counterparts, including mathematics, literature, foreign languages, physics, chemistry, foreign geography and history, politics, and so forth. But there was no place where women might exercise such knowledge.

This contradiction prompted calls to limit women's education to subjects of immediate – that is, domestic – applicability. In the 1910s, most women's schools found that female students and their families expected a curriculum emphasizing "feminine courses." The Ministry of Education made a compromise, offering special courses on "family management," sewing, and gardening and scaling back or cancelling courses that were not so "important," such as trigonometry and English.[109] Many women's secondary schools devoted less attention to mathematics, foreign languages, and Chinese literature than they had done previously. An educator who visited the Jiangsu Provincial Women's Normal School Number Two in Suzhou in 1919 reported that it had cancelled all its English classes in order to devote more hours to literature and family management. Proud of the policy of emphasizing family affairs, the school displayed the results of students' needlework on its classroom walls. The visitor praised this policy, commenting that, for women, no skill was more important than sewing.[110] The Nanjing Women's Normal School, for its part, opened a demonstration kitchen decorated with various charts describing the chemical ingredients of foods. Thus, if its students learned anything about chemistry, it was as an adjunct to their study of nutrition and cooking.[111]

Producing model citizens was a sound national goal, but educators had to face reality and address what women would be allowed to do once they received a modern education. The distinction between appropriate and inappropriate activities for women was spelled out quite explicitly in a 1912 letter written by a female student who had just returned from studying in the United States. This letter was addressed to the then minister of education, Cai Yuanpei. Gao Guiqiao championed the establishment of more teachers' schools, which she saw as providing a proper channel for women's "pent-up energies." To illustrate the danger of failing to provide this channel, she referred to a recent incident in which a group of women led by Tang Qunying stormed the newly organized Republican Congress, demanding women's suffrage.[112] She explained her position in English:

> Now while China is considering her undeveloped resources she must not overlook womanhood which has within it great potentialities. Today we have women by the tens of thousands who are so nearly a dead weight upon our nation, if these women become usefully employed China will be far on the way toward the ideal China. Many of our women are eager and longing for an outlet for their pent-up energies but they lack vision. Some of them take up the wrong path of thinking as you have already seen. They are anxious to do something for the country and have equal rights, and so they go out as suffragettes, leave their homes and families, go window smashing as in the case of Nanking, and clamouring for the presidency and other offices which are adapted to men.
>
> Our women should have a school to teach them that women can have equal rights without following their brothers to the ballot box or doing any thing that is manly enough for a man yet not womanly enough for a woman. They should have the opportunity to learn to direct their pent-up energies toward the three great fields of work particularly adapted to women – home, philanthropy, and school.
>
> The Normal School which is greatly needed in China and which I am pleading for your help is one which will prepare the women for their inheritances of usefulness and will embrace the three departments of home, philanthropy, and school.[113]

While Gao did not think that participating in politics was proper for women, she did believe that women could be excellent teachers.

Echoing this letter, Bai Yun divided women's professions into two categories: noble (*gaoshang*) and generic (*yiban*). She believed that teaching was, for women, a noble profession (as were medicine, law, journalism, and writing, though several of these were not yet open to women), particularly primary school teaching, because women were gentle by nature and good with children.[114] In a similar vein, in 1917 Hou Hongjian, once the principal of a female normal school, published an article in the popular magazine *Chinese Educational Circle* (*Zhonghua jiaoyu jie*). While he believed that women ought to acquire skills that would make them self-reliant, he argued that their curricula ought to reflect the reality of their lives. Hou endorsed the study of household management, childcare, teacher training, medicine, nursing, sewing, and sericulture. He pointed out that it was widely recognized in educational circles that teaching younger primary-school students was a fitting vocation for women. He suggested that more women's teachers' schools be opened: since women surpassed their male counterparts in teaching young children, increasing the number of women teachers would improve Chinese education overall.[115]

The Advancement of Women's Education: From Beijing Female Normal School to Beijing Women's Higher Teachers' College

During the 1910s, more schools for girls and women opened, following the trend established in previous decades. Women's education, referred to as the "foundation of citizens' education" during the late Qing, was now referred to as the "embryo of citizens' education" (*guomin jiaoyu zhi peitai*), suggesting its relationship to the birth of new citizens.[116] One of the new schools for women was Beijing Women's Higher Teachers' College (*Beijing nüzi gaodeng shifan xuexiao*), the first teachers' college in China that admitted only women. This was a landmark in women's education and moved it up to tertiary level within the public educational system.

The opening of primary schools for girls in the 1900s served to prepare for the increase in secondary women's normal schools in the 1910s. The path taken by the private Qiming Girls' School (*Qiming nüzi xuexiao*) in Pingjiang County, Hunan, was typical of the gradual development of women's normal schools. Qiming was established as a lower primary school for girls in the last years of the Qing. Four years later, it was expanded so that students could take upper primary classes when they completed the lower school. Graduates were invited to continue in a teacher training program. After this program grew to include four classes of students and a fully developed curriculum, the school became a simplified teachers' school. In 1916, an application was made to the Ministry of Education to make Qiming a full-fledged teachers' school.[117] A selective review of the history of female normal schools in Henan suggests that the gradual expansion seen with Qiming was typical. For example, the female normal school in Runan County was originally built as a primary school for girls in 1911, then upgraded to a one-year simplified female normal school in 1918. In 1929, the school became a three-year normal school.[118] (Note that the disorder of the 1910s and 1920s worked against the expansion of secondary education, which relied heavily on the provincial government for financial support.)

In general, women's secondary-level teachers' schools grew faster than did regular middle schools for women. In the waning years of the Qing, there were about twenty female teachers' schools.[119] By 1917, there were forty-five public and private women's teachers' schools at provincial and county levels, with 4,712 students.[120] The general agreement on the value of women teachers had done its work. Remarkably, among the 400 public and private middle schools nationwide in 1919, only ten were women's middle schools.[121] By 1923, thanks to the encouragement of the 1922 reform, the number of women's middle schools had increased to twenty-five, while the number of women's teachers' schools had reached sixty-seven.[122] Women's normal schools remained the major path by which women received anything other than a primary education. During this period, many girl students saw female teachers' schools as their chance for future development.[123]

The future of female normal schools was spelled out by the evolution of Beijing Women's Higher Teachers' College. The college began as a secondary-level teachers' school in 1908, originally named Capital Women's Normal School (*Jingshi nüzi shifan xuetang*) and directed by Fu Zengxiang, the former principal of Beiyang Female Normal School. In its first year, 145 students enrolled, coming from Beijing, Hubei, Jiangsu, and Tianjin. Attached to Capital Women's Normal School was an elementary school for girls used for teaching practice. By the time of the 1911 Revolution, the normal school had graduated 106 students. Only briefly interrupted by the revolution, the school changed its name to Beijing Women's Normal School (*Beijing nüzi shifan xuexiao*). In 1915, it enlarged its campus and added a kindergarten. Up until 1917, the school had been recruiting from 40 to 70 students each year; in 1916, it reached its largest enrolment, with over 270 students. The following year, that number had shrunk to 190, possibly due to budget cuts.[124]

The school's curriculum expanded significantly over the years. From a single two-year simplified course of study (*jianyi ke*) offered in 1908, the school's offerings expanded the following year to include a complete program (*wanquan ke*), in which forty-three students enrolled, and an advanced program (*gaodeng ke*), in which 130 students enrolled. In 1911, the complete program was changed to "full program" (*ben ke*) – a four-year training program for primary schoolteachers and kindergarten caretakers – and forty-seven students graduated. Two years after the Revolution, a two-year advanced program at college level was devoted to household management and skills (*jiashi jiyi zhuanxiu ke*), and in the following year, a course to prepare female secondary education teachers was inaugurated. Over the next two years, two more programs were added: a preparatory course for the complete program (*yuke*) and a two-year childcare program (*baomu jiangxi ke*). In 1917, the school moved to a new location, and new buildings were constructed for the constantly expanding institution. At the same time, a new three-year college-level program devoted to education and literature was added to train teachers and administrators for female middle schools and teachers' schools. Many of the courses now offered at the Capital Women's Normal School went far beyond what was usually offered at such schools and were, in fact, college-level courses. In 1917, a regular female middle school was added to the other affiliate schools, where student-teachers could practise teaching at secondary school level.[125] More development occurred in 1918, when two special programs were added in preparation for transforming the school into a proper teachers' college: drawing and handicrafts was one, natural science the other.[126]

In the leap from a secondary school to a college, the National Federation of Educational Associations played a significant role. In 1916 and 1917, the federation constantly returned to the idea of opening a female teachers' college and urged the Ministry of Education to take on the project.[127] Although there were several higher educational institutions for women before 1919, all were missionary schools.[128] By the late 1910s, the time for establishing a Chinese higher educational institution for women was arriving. It was at the high point of the New Culture Movement and the May Fourth Movement that China's first public college for women opened. In June 1919, the ministry issued a special order that the Beijing Women's Normal School be promoted to the Beijing Women's Higher Teachers' College, and the school began to recruit students for the fall term.[129] The programs under the secondary school structure now developed into disciplines and included departments devoted to literature; history and geography; foreign languages; mathematics, physics, and chemistry; mineralogy and biology; and household management. Special programs included drawing and handicrafts and caring for children as well as music and physical training.[130]

The establishment of Beijing Women's Higher Teachers' College had a ripple effect. In the summer of 1920, the fact that China's top university, Beijing University, allowed nine women to audit courses was the main topic in the national media.[131] In the same year, Nanjing Higher Teachers' College followed suit, and in the following decades most colleges began accepting female students.[132] Compared to the sensational events occurring at Beijing University, the establishment of Beijing Women's Teachers' College was a quiet, but pioneering, move in the promotion of female higher education.

A Curriculum for Domesticity or for a Career?

One important change in female education witnessed in the early Republican period was the inclusion in women's curricula of such "feminine courses" as household management, gardening, sewing, and the like. Some scholars have seen this as moving towards "a more comprehensive view of education," while others have seen it as nothing but a conservative backlash.[133] Did expanding the curriculum provide women with the chance to play a more active role in society?[134] As it turns out, studying domestic skills may have led many to public careers and helped them to enlarge their role in public life.

At Beijing Women's Normal School, the students in every program had to take courses such as handicrafts (*shougong*), household management and gardening (*jiashi yuanyi*), and sewing. But the number of class hours devoted to such subjects was insignificant. In the preparatory program, four hours per week were devoted to sewing, while literature involved ten, math five, and English three. In the complete program, handicrafts and sewing involved two and four hours, respectively, per week during the first two years, while household management and gardening (three hours weekly) were not even studied until the third and fourth years. Compared with literature, education, mathematics, science, physics, chemistry, and English – any one of which required between three and six hours weekly – the time devoted to "feminine courses" was trivial.

It is important to point out that these courses were designed to fit the curricula of elementary schools. The students in female normal schools studied these courses for the purpose of becoming professional teachers, not housewives. The childcare program was not aimed at improving motherhood but, rather, at training teachers for lower primary schools and training caretakers for kindergartens. According to the Ministry of Education, the reason for the establishment of a college program (*zhuanxiu ke*) was to meet the urgent demands from female middle schools and teachers' schools: they needed female teachers to teach household management, sewing, and other feminine courses.[135] The importance of training was specified in the description of the "household management and skills" program. When female normal schools first opened in 1907, graduates were expected to work as primary schoolteachers. By studying household management, education, and literature, female teachers were able to teach at secondary schools: the passage to equality had widened a bit more. It is interesting that one of the principal skills women had to acquire in order to enter a realm previously occupied by men was household management – a peculiarly female traditional specialization. It would appear that Jiang Weiqiao was right: studying household management courses provided women with new careers.[136]

But were there jobs for the graduates of female normal schools? According to the incomplete data from Beijing Women's Normal School, thirty-three students graduated in 1911, of whom eight went on to work either as teachers or as principals of elementary schools. Of the 1914 graduates of the simplified program, twenty-three out of thirty-two went on to teach in elementary school or female teachers' schools. In 1917, twenty-one out of thirty-two full-program graduates became schoolteachers. Data from two Jiangsu provincial female normal schools show their graduates finding employment. From 1914 to 1921, a majority of the graduates of Female Normal School Number One went on to teach. During the same period, the provincial Female Normal School Number Two sent 4 percent to 10 percent of its graduates to higher education and 73 percent to work as teachers (20 percent opted to return home without jobs).[137] Of course, opportunities for women in the 1910s were still very limited as most women were facing pressures from society and families. The path to skilled professions was narrow and the range of occupations restricted. Some graduates elected not to take jobs – some would marry and never teach any children but their own – but others contributed to a new aspect of the twentieth-century Chinese woman, who was becoming a professional and working within a very public realm.

4
Modernity and the Village: The Emergence of Village Teachers' Schools, 1922-30

Beginning in 1920 the fledgling system of Western-style modern schools in China became the target of severe criticism on the part of progressive intellectuals, education experts, local elites, and radical activists.[1] These critics argued that the centralization, elitism, and fusty pedantry of the schools distanced them from local communities and, hence, the real needs of the people. An even broader consensus rejected the state's centralized control over the schools, which was too easily exploited by Yuan Shikai's monarchist pretensions. The concentration of Western-style schools in cities meant that a new urban privileged class enjoyed educational opportunities that were largely denied to the vast rural population.

In the early 1920s, a group of intellectuals trained in European and American universities spearheaded a movement to reform the system of state schools. This movement led to the adoption of the 1922 Educational Reform, a bid for an advanced and flexible system that would meet the needs of society by redistributing policy-making power to local society. As it turned out, this resulted in an even more urbanized and elitist educational system, and it increased the educational gap between cities and villages. Although the reformers of 1922 made provisions for upgrading female teachers' colleges to teachers' universities, in the area of women's education, the emphasis was on building regular female secondary schools – a shift away from the previous decades' preponderant investments in female teachers' schools. The 1922 reform produced an unexpected consequence: a shortage of teaching personnel, especially in the rural areas, due to reduced funding for teacher training.

Many of those who had been dissatisfied with the existing educational system immediately complained about the shortcomings of the 1922 Educational Reform. With the influence of the New Culture and May Fourth Movements, they hoped to expand education to the majority of the population through rural education programs that would contribute to the democratization of China. The success of such programs depended on responding to the problems of widespread illiteracy, poverty, and the lack of educated leaders in rural communities.

Xiaozhuang Village Teachers' School (*Xiaozhuang xiangcun shifan xuexiao*), founded by Tao Xingzhi in 1927, was the embodiment of an experimental program sponsored by educated elites. People continued to hope that teachers' schools could play an important role in reforming education and society. In this social and educational experiment, local cultural and institutional resources played a key role in supporting Xiaozhuang's use of Western ideas and models of education and knowledge. This experiment was not confined to the educational realm: it also addressed problems caused by political disorder, rural poverty, and village disintegration. The Xiaozhuang model placed village teachers' schools at the centre of a rural reconstruction movement, with teachers serving as community leaders.

The 1922 Educational Reform: Teachers' Schools in the 1920s

Frustrated by the failure of Yuan Shikai and his warlord successors to establish a truly republican polity, a group of progressive intellectuals, most of whom had graduated from American and European universities, opted to take matters into their own hands.[2] The power struggle among warlords weakened central political control and lessened financial support to local education. Amid the New Culture Movement, Euro-American ideas of democracy and liberalism gained adherents among progressive Chinese intellectuals. In this atmosphere, the architects of the 1922 reform drew on the American model of schooling as opposed to the centralized Chinese model, which was seen as abetting the conservative politics of Yuang and his successors.[3] Instead, the new school system granted local communities greater autonomy in making decisions about schools.

The Changing Position of Teacher Training in the 1922 Educational Reform

The ideas of the American Progressive Movement strongly influenced the framers of the 1922 Educational Reform. From May 1919 to July 1921, the philosopher John Dewey visited China, working as a visiting professor at Beijing University and Beijing Higher Teachers' College and giving a series of lectures. A collection of his lectures was quickly translated and published, and his ideas were discussed in China's intellectual circles; among the pithy mottoes and phrases associated with Dewey's thinking were "education is life," "school is society," "learning from doing," and "child-centred education."[4]

In 1921, Paul Monroe, professor of education at Columbia University's teachers' college, also visited China. He attended the seventh conference of the National Federation of Educational Associations in 1922 and discussed the outline of that year's reform proposal with its drafters.[5] This document, largely based on American models, not only became the model for school organization but also influenced textbook selection, curriculum creation, and teaching methods.[6] Most striking was the introduction of the "6-3-3" system: six years of elementary school, three years of junior high school (*chuzhong*, lit., lower middle school), and three years of senior high school (*gaozhong* upper middle school). The university model was also based on the American system.[7]

The 1922 Educational Reform outlined changes to the teacher training system. The length of teacher training, and both the quality of the teachers' schools and their capacity for producing adequate teachers had been much discussed in the mid-1910s, and these became quite volatile issues after 1919. Jing Hengyi, a famous educator from Zhejiang, questioned the necessity of teachers' schools and suggested that regular universities and middle schools assume responsibility for preparing future teachers. Even if teachers' schools were not closed, a more consistent system would improve the quality of teaching.[8] Jing's opinion soon became gospel among his colleagues.

In October 1919, at the fifth meeting of the National Federation of Educational Associations, the Zhejiang Provincial Education Association set forth a proposal for addressing the problems with the teachers' schools – a proposal that might as well have been written by Jing. No effort was made to pass a resolution on the subject, but members of the federation were urged to consider the problems and the proposed solutions.[9] After the conference, Yun Liu, a teacher, argued that the quality of teachers' schools was inferior to that of regular middle schools and universities. He believed that teaching was a profession, much like any other, and that it did not need to be segregated from the regular educational system. Why not economize by making teachers' training one of the several vocational programs offered in the regular school system?[10]

The free tuition policy of teachers' schools was also attacked. Why was it that only future teachers were permitted to attend school free of charge? Some contended that, if one looked at the 1922 guidelines, teacher's education was basically no different than industrial, commercial, and agricultural education, none of which was offered at no cost. All vocational programs were designed for youth from modest backgrounds, all of whom could be offered the same financial aid.[11] Such ideas shaped the new policies in teachers' education.

Under the new system, teachers' schools at the secondary level maintained their nominal independence but were instructed to add regular middle school programs that corresponded to junior high school and vocational programs at the high school level. On the other hand, regular middle schools set up teacher training and other vocational programs for senior students.[12] By expanding teacher training from the junior high level to the senior high level and into regular middle schools, the reformers sought to improve the pool of future teachers; however, they ended up blurring the distinction between teachers' schools and regular middle schools. Higher teachers' colleges were upgraded to university level when they were made into four-year institutions; the scope of their curricula was enlarged to achieve parity with those of comprehensive universities. The new system also permitted any comprehensive university that so wished to open a college of education or an education department to train middle school teachers. The differences that had existed between teachers' colleges and regular universities – in the curriculum, in the time needed to acquire a degree, and even in reasons for attending school – were minimized.[13]

This design invited criticism from those who worried that the teacher training system might suffer and that there would be an inadequate source of teachers in the future. Tao Xingzhi joined the debate. He agreed that the teachers' school system, in its current form, was incapable of training enough teachers – both in terms of quantity and quality. Merging teachers' schools and middle schools struck him as wrongheaded; he believed the solution was to strengthen the schools by expanding the student body and the curriculum.[14] In a special 1922 issue of *Education Review* (*Jiaoyu zazhi*) devoted to teacher training, Chang Naide published a lengthy article that listed eight reasons commonly given for merging teachers' schools and regular middle schools. He cited, inter alia, eliminating redundancy, concentrating resources, enhancing quality, putting an end to the servile imitating of Japanese methods, and helping to expand the teaching profession. And then he criticized them one by one. He argued that, as a special profession, teaching had every right to an independent institutional existence, and he saw financial aid as compensation for teachers engaged in a non-profit enterprise.[15] Other writers responded to the mounting calls for educational consolidation by predicting that stuffing normal schools into regular high schools and universities would obstruct rather than improve teacher training. Teaching could not justly be compared to those professions because the teaching profession would yield little remuneration or political influence; therefore, free tuition could be seen as a compensation for students' piteous futures. If the free tuition policy were to be abolished, then few good students would consider entering the profession.[16]

These worries proved to be well founded. The 1922 reform had a decisively negative impact on teachers' education, precipitating a decline in teachers' schools and colleges. Local authorities and educators now initiated a campaign whose purpose was "merging teachers' schools and middle schools" (*shi zhong hebing*).[17] Many teachers' schools were converted into, or merged with regular secondary schools, the teacher training section becoming but one among several vocational programs. Zhejiang initiated the trend by merging several provincial teachers' schools into one secondary school under the name Provincial Middle School (*sheng li zhongxue*).

Immediately, Guangdong, Hubei, Fujian, Jiangsu, Anhui, Jiangxi, and several other provinces followed suit.[18] In 1922, there were 385 teachers' schools with 43,846 students; their combined budgets amounted to 4,633,919 yuan. By 1928, the number of teachers' schools had been reduced to 236. The number of students in teacher training programs fell to 29,470, and the funds allocated to teacher training decreased to 3,468,072 yuan.[19] At the same time, many provinces cancelled the special policy of providing teacher training programs tuition-free, which further discouraged students from enrolling in these programs.[20]

Teachers' colleges also declined after 1922. Most teachers' colleges were converted into comprehensive universities between 1921 and 1931. Teacher training was conducted in departments of education within the newly created universities. In 1921, Guo Bingwen, a graduate of Columbia University, led the conversion of Nanjing Teachers' College (*Nanjing gaoshi*) into Southeast University (*Dongnan daxue*). Over the next ten years, Shenyang Teachers' College (*Shenyang gaoshi*) was converted into Northeast University (*Dongbei Daxue*); Wuchang Teachers' College (*Wuchang gaoshi*) became Wuhan University (*Wuhan daxue*); and Guangdong Teachers' College (*Guangdong gaoshi*) became Guangdong University (*Guangdong daxue*). Chengdu Teachers' College (*Chengdu gaoshi*) was converted into Chengdu Teachers' University (*Chengdu shifan daxue*) in 1927 and then merged with Chengdu University (*Chengdu daxue*) in 1931, becoming Sichuan University (*Sichuan daxue*). In order to become proper universities, most teachers' colleges added new departments, and their original pedagogic mission was assigned to the department of education.[21] By 1930, the seven national teachers' colleges had been reduced to a mere two: Beiping Normal University (*Beiping shifan daxue*) and Women's Teachers' College at Beiping University (*Beiping daxue nüzi shifan xueyuan*). These two merged in 1931.[22]

Problems Facing Education and Teachers in the 1920s

The 1922 Educational Reform was inspired in part by the triumph of Wilsonism after the First World War and the spread of Progressivism in the early 1920s. China's liberal and anti-warlord reformers hoped to lay a foundation for a democratic polity by building a more flexible modern educational system. The enlightened and decentralizing trends can be heard in the movement's declared principles: "developing the personality" (*gexing fazhan*) of youth and "saving enough room for local adjustments" (*duo liu ge difang shensuo yudi*). The 1922 Educational Reform invited strong criticism and was seen as a failure.[23] Can its failure be attributed to its continuing entanglement with an undemocratic government, as many of its contemporaneous educators believed,[24] or should we blame those who mechanically copied a foreign model? The principle of "developing the personality" was manifested in the wide range of elective courses to be offered in middle schools, and it encouraged students to choose the courses in which they had some interest.[25] But the economic imbalances in China ensured that this policy benefited only a small group of urban students. The system encouraged economically and culturally advanced areas to exploit their resources and to build six-year elementary schools, which was quite unheard of in poorer areas, where the norm was a four-year school. Advanced regions could also draw from pools of highly qualified teachers to offer a wide range of elective courses, while no elective courses were offered to students – even those in secondary schools – in more backward areas.

When a delegation of European educational experts, organized by the League of Nations, visited China in 1931 to study its schools, its members echoed the criticism already articulated by those Chinese intellectuals who considered copying foreign pedagogy to be a mistake.[26] They also noted that children from well-to-do families received a good primary education and were the greatest beneficiaries of the public schools at both the elementary and the secondary levels. Reaching for positive comments, the foreign experts praised the vocational programs that gave priority to enrolling the children of the poor.[27] However, as Pepper points out, the European observers failed to note that these vocational programs would encourage class distinctions: youth from rich families would go to colleges and universities while youth from poor families would go to vocational schools that led to lower paid jobs.[28]

The visiting experts also criticized the professional orientation of students, noting that many elected to major in literature, law, or politics but that few enrolled in the sciences. Most aspired to become government officials – becoming a teacher was a secondary option. This was also true of students in secondary schools: most selected college preparatory courses and had no interest in vocational or teacher training courses.[29]

On the other hand, schools were also producing many "qualified citizens who lack the means to make a living."[30] A survey showed that a large number of Jiangsu middle school graduates had failed to find jobs: the provincial government had to set up a special committee to help those unemployed youth.[31] This became a hot story, with *Student Magazine* (*Xuesheng zazhi*) and *Education Review* devoting a number of articles to it.[32]

Qualified teachers were becoming rare. No longer obliged to teach after graduation, most graduates of middle schools set their sights on higher education. The graduates of comprehensive universities could gain lucrative positions in government and business and enjoy high social status. Although, by around 1920, the percentage of educational administrators who had been trained in teachers' schools had reached over 50 percent, the number of primary school instructors that received teacher training remained low. The scarcity of trained teachers meant that many elementary and secondary schools had to hire untrained and inexperienced faculty. The resulting pedagogy was based not on professional theory but on haphazard efforts to imitate their own teachers, as Thøgersen has shown. According to his investigation, in 1930, only one-third of Zouping's 940 teachers had graduated from teachers' schools.[33]

This trend was widespread. A 1931 survey indicates that, among the 7,119 elementary school teachers in Hubei's fifty-two counties, only 2,339 had graduated from teachers' schools, 3,900 had graduated from other types of schools, and 880 had not studied in a modern school of any kind.[34] The lack of qualified teachers was an urgent problem in Jiangsu Province. In 1933, of the province's 20,600 elementary school teachers, only 8,927 were considered qualified.[35] In the same year, officials in Zhejiang Province estimated that, out of 39,945 elementary school teachers, only 5,166 were qualified.[36] If economically and culturally advanced provinces such as Zhejiang and Jiangsu faced such a serious shortage of trained teachers, the dearth in more backward areas was even more severe. In 1933, an educational historian lamented that this result of the reform was indeed unexpected.[37]

These long-standing problems, which were exacerbated by the 1922 reform, were not the only obstacles to progress. In the 1920s, some educators – for example, Yu Jiaju – commented sadly on the pitiful situation of elementary school teachers, who faced low salaries and social isolation.[38] According to statistics published in 1933, their average monthly salary ranged from 42 yuan in Nanjing (the capital) to 4.5 yuan in Yunnan Province. The national average was 11.3 yuan. At that time, the average monthly salary for workers in China was 12.7 yuan, and each member of a working family was estimated to need an average of 7.7 yuan to meet basic expenses.[39]

In order to bring social attention to the pitiful salaries of primary schoolteachers, several surveys were published. In 1924, Qian Yizhang, a local educational administrator in Zhejiang, conducted a survey of primary schoolteachers in five counties around Shaoxing and Yuyao. Of the 95 teachers surveyed, 83 were male and 12 were female. The salary range was from 40 yuan to 360 yuan a year, with an average of 200 yuan. Qian estimated that each teacher with a family needed 350 yuan a year to meet basic expenses, but there were only two people whose salaries were over 300 yuan.[40] In 1927, another educator, Li Chucai, conducted a survey of the income of primary schoolteachers in nine counties in Jiangsu and came up with similar results: the average monthly salary varied from 11 to 22 yuan, and the average monthly salary for all counties was 17.3 yuan. According to Li's estimate, each schoolteacher needed 43 yuan per month to support his family.[41] The monthly salary for elementary schoolteachers in Fujian Province was no better than was that of their colleagues in Jiangsu and Zhejiang. A 1931 survey shows that their monthly salary varied from 2.8 yuan to 28 yuan, with an average of 12 yuan per month.[42] As I have mentioned, Jiangsu and Zhejiang were among the most economically developed areas in the country; furthermore, the counties surveyed were among the more economically advanced counties in these provinces. Teachers were not growing rich by plying their trade.

These problems were similar to those faced by teachers in the late imperial era but had been exacerbated since the establishment of the modern school system because the professionalization of teachers placed village teachers in between "modern" cities and "traditional" rural society. On the one hand, the establishment of teachers' schools not only institutionalized the separation of the bureaucracy and everything associated with education but it also marked the formation of modern teachers as a professional group. However, once these representatives of modernity entered rural society, they were stuck. They were cut off not only from any hope of promotion but also from information about the development of modern knowledge. Once these teachers had spent a few years in the countryside, the urban world viewed them as part of a "backward and traditional" society. Yu Jiaju, for instance, considered anyone who "graduated from teachers' schools fifteen years ago" to be out of step.[43]

Primary schoolteachers lived isolated existences in the villages. They had given up connections to their social networks and had no chance for intellectual exchanges with the outside world. Since student-teachers studied Western learning in an urban environment, their knowledge had nothing to do with common people's lives. Moreover, having grown accustomed to the conveniences of an urban lifestyle, they found it extremely difficult to adapt to the living and working conditions of rural communities.[44]

Elementary schoolteachers working in rural areas rarely had opportunities to improve their knowledge and social status. Many of those obliged to take a teaching position out of necessity hoped someday to work in a government office, where they might accrue material and social rewards.[45] But they rarely had a chance to continue their studies. By the time they had fulfilled the teaching obligations required by the programs they had attended, they already had families to support. Before the people of China had shaken off their feudal past, isolated village teachers who barely scraped by could still dream of passing the civil service examinations. Modern professionalization, however, destroyed these dreams without providing any avenue for upward mobility.

It was suggested that rural teachers be put in touch with urban intellectual circles in order to keep them abreast of new ideas.[46] But these kinds of alliances might only further alienate these teachers from their local communities. Villagers must have seen those who had drunk deeply of Western knowledge as representatives of an alien culture. Thomas Curran compares teachers trained in modern schools with traditional teachers, observing that, in the eyes of peasants, those who had taught in traditional schools were older and had dependable academic credentials. In contrast, modern teachers were young, and villagers viewed them with suspicion due to their alien training and pedagogy.[47] In spite of the reverence shown them by most villagers, rural teachers bitterly envied their urban counterparts, who enjoyed the conveniences of modern life, a vibrant intellectual culture, and plenty of opportunities. Feeling abandoned by the modern world, these teachers were not likely to inspire the graduates of modern schools to sign up to teach in the villages.

The Western-style schools that had been built in Chinese cities over the previous two decades had not provided solutions to these problems, and the 1922 Educational Reform, by putting more emphasis on urban areas, exacerbated them. This situation motivated a number of intellectuals to develop ideas for restructuring rural education and promoting mass education.

Women in Higher Education and the Decline of Female Teacher Training

The training of women teachers was strongly affected by the 1922 reform. The great development in female education during the late 1910s and 1920s was the opening of women's teachers' universities. During the same period, the implementation of the 1922 school system gradually reduced the importance of female teacher training at the secondary level.

Under the New Spirit: Beijing Women's Normal University

In May 1924, two years after the 1922 Educational Reform, Beijing Women's Higher Teachers' College was elevated to the status of a university, becoming Beijing Women's Normal University (*Beijing nüzi shifan daxue*). Many programs were unchanged, but, after a year of preparatory study, one's major now involved four, rather than three, years of study. New departments were added (including education and psychology), but the old departments remained virtually unchanged. From 1922 to 1925, the university generally had over 200 students.[48]

The radical changes that took place in the university in 1923 and 1924 were in keeping with the New Culture Movement and the May Fourth Movement. In the spirit of developing individuality (explicitly called for in the 1922 reform) and promoting women's equality (central to the May Fourth spirit), Beijing Women's Normal University announced new goals for women's education. Departing from Beijing Women's Higher Teachers' College's limited mission of training teachers and administrators for female secondary schools, Beijing Women's Normal University announced that it aspired to a higher standard – "to provide in-depth academic research" and "to develop women's unique and specialized talents."[49] Establishing an academic research program was a groundbreaking step for women's education. Since the establishment of women's public schools in the late Qing, the presumed "nature of motherhood" had determined the content of women's education: women were being taught to teach. The introduction of academic research into women's education broke with this trend and offered women a chance to become scholars and researchers – something that was not linked to their sexual identity. As to developing women's "unique and specialized talents," the meaning of this vague phrase is far from clear. Perhaps it signified nothing more than lip service to convention.

In other areas, convention did not fare so well. Many programs specifically designed as feminine courses were discontinued, including household management, drawing, and caring for children (music and physical education were preserved).[50] Was this a radical attack on gender segregation or was it a money-saving gesture? The lack of documentation makes it hard to be sure. The point may have been to encourage female students to strive to expand their areas of competence. The intent of this action may have been sound, but it could also have reduced the suitability of graduates for positions in secondary schools. In the 1920s, most female middle schools would readily hire male teachers, while few male middle schools would be inclined to hire women to teach traditionally "masculine" subjects such as literature, history, mathematics, physics, chemistry, and geography. At the same time, household management and handicrafts were still required subjects at girls' middle schools, and there was still a need for women to teach them.[51] Closing down these programs at Beijing Women's Normal University may have resulted in the marginalization of female teachers in secondary schools as a whole.

Under the influence of the May Fourth Movement, students of female teachers' schools became actively involved in social movements. Before 1925, students of women's teachers' schools at the secondary level formed the main body of female students. These schools, therefore, became an important force in student protests against conservative authorities. Around 1924, several student protests at female teachers' schools gained national attention. The students of Baoding Women's Normal School in Hebei, Hubei Women's Normal School, and Shandong Women's Normal School all protested against having school principals from the provincial education bureau imposed upon them. The students of Jiangxi Women's Normal School Number Two rejected the male principal appointed by the provincial bureau and insisted on having a female principal.[52] In this atmosphere, one might say that even the disastrous fate of Beijing Women's Normal University reflected the spirit of the May Fourth Movement as well as the principles of the 1922 reform.

The students of Beijing Women's Higher Teachers' College missed the first wave of strikes in the May Fourth Movement in 1919.[53] However, their successors, students of Beijing Women's Normal University, demonstrated great courage and resolution in protesting against dictatorial university and central government authorities. In the fall of 1924, students launched an appeal against the allegedly unjust punishment of three students by the university chancellor, Yang Yinyu (1884-1938), a scholar who had studied in Japan and the United States and the only female university chancellor at that time.[54] After failing to change Chancellor Yang's mind, the student government sent a petition to the Ministry of Education in January 1925, demanding that Yang be removed from her post, but it received no response.[55] A closer look at the conflict shows that, while the students had reasonable grievances – in addition to the issue of unjust punishment, they complained that fees had been unfairly imposed[56] – the clash may have had as much to do with Yang's bound feet and commitment to Confucian pedagogy as it did with more explicit complaints.[57]

When the skirmish continued, the Minister of Education, Zhang Shizhao (1882-1973), who took the position in the spring of 1925, came to support Yang. The conflict escalated when a group of faculty members, including such renowned figures as Zhou Shuren (Lu Xun), Zhou Zuoren, Qian Xuantong, and three other professors sided with the students. The students occupied the campus and would not allow Yang to enter her office. Both sides dug in their heels, and the standoff lasted for over six months. At last, the minister of education decided to dismiss Yang and close the university. When this decision was announced in early August, students refused to leave the campus and Minister Zhang called in the metropolitan police force, who dragged the resisting students off campus one by one.[58]

When the university reopened in mid-August 1925, it was as Beijing Women's University (*Beijing nüzi daxue*). A new chancellor was appointed and students previously enrolled at Beijing Women's Normal University were allowed to re-enrol at the new institution. The name change had a clear message: this was no longer a teacher training facility.[59] With the continuing struggle of the students and faculty, Beijing Women's Normal University was restored at the end of 1925. This victory lasted little more than one year; the university then merged with National Capital University (*Guoli Jingshi daxue*) to form a women's liberal arts college. In 1930, it became Beiping Women's Teacher College (*Beiping nüzi shifan xueyuan*), part of Beiping University, and then the following year it merged with Beiping Normal University, putting an end to the independent female teachers' university.[60]

Changing a teachers' university into a regular university was no accident. The 1922 reform had led to many such conversions. When the 1922 Educational Reform was first announced, the Ministry of Education had planned to make Beijing Women's Higher Teachers' College a women's university. Students and faculty expressed such fierce opposition to this change that Beijing Women's Normal University emerged as a compromise.[61] As it turned out, the protests of 1924 and 1925 provided the perfect pretext for the Ministry of Education to follow through with its original plan.

Secondary Female Teachers' Schools under the 1922 System

Secondary female education was also affected by the 1922 education reform. In order to realize the goal of an equal education for both sexes, which was encouraged by the New Culture Movement, the Ministry of Education planned to promote female education by opening coeducational schools. But resistance from the provinces ensured that there were no coeducational secondary schools until the 1930s.[62] The government turned to building regular female middle schools as well as changing and merging female teachers' schools into girls' middle schools, asserting that its goal was the development of the female personality. Like its male counterpart, female teacher training became one of many vocational programs in women's middle schools. For example, in 1926, Hubei's Bureau of Education combined a women's normal school with two women's vocational schools to create Hubei Women's Middle School Number One.[63]

At the time, regular girls' middle schools prepared students to go on to higher education, though only girls from well-to-do families could afford to do so. Very few women would be able to go to college: there simply were very few opportunities. Ending the policy of free tuition made the teacher training program in women's middle schools much less attractive to girls whose means were limited. The possibility of being unemployed after spending years in school loomed. Informally barred from most professions, girls tended to marry soon after graduating from middle school. Those who graduated from modern schools in the 1920s were sometimes called "female marriage candidates" (*nü jiehunyuan*).[64] When female education lost its goal of serving society, for many parents educating girls became merely a way to demonstrate both their open-mindedness and their wealth; they did not mind at all that their daughter's dowry was decorated by a school diploma.[65]

In the years immediately following 1922, most educators were busy adapting their programs to the reform plan, and women's education was not much discussed. When the National Federation of Educational Associations held its eleventh annual conference in Changsha in 1925, of eighty-four proposals from forty representatives (who came from all over the country) not a single one addressed women's education.[66] Though it might be said that the failure to distinguish women's from men's schooling in the reform plan implied that the goal of education was the same for women and men, this did nothing to help educated women claim new regions of social space or move into professional careers.

Emergence of the Rural Education Movement

While most educators focused their attention on improving the schools in urban areas, another movement was gradually taking shape and was determined to find educational solutions to the poverty and backwardness of rural China. Disappointed with the existing educational system, many intellectuals began to believe that China's schools needed to be rethought in the terms suggested by populist thinkers and Marxists. The rural education movement that emerged in the 1920s involved a wide variety of forms, ideas, and practices, but, in all of them, teachers' schools were expected to play a key role.

The Shift to the Countryside

In 1920, Yu Jiaju, a young graduate student at Beijing Teachers' College who later became a famous educator and scholar, pointed out that the existing educational system catered to the cities and neglected the countryside. This had created a privileged urban class and had left farmers in the dark. Yu observed that more and more rural youth moved to the city for school and never considered returning to teach in their home towns. He noted regretfully that, at the time, most teachers in rural schools were quite old, being products of either the imperial examination system or the earliest of the modern schools. Many elementary schools had not changed their curricula or pedagogy since the early Qing. These teachers had not learned anything from the waves of intellectual change that had swept repeatedly over China during the last two decades. He doubted that rural China would ever change if it had such people as teachers.[67] He also worried that, by ushering the most talented youth out of rural communities, the educational system was further impoverishing rural society and that this would eventually exhaust the human resources available to the cities as well. Therefore, improving rural schools was more than an educational issue: it could be the means to solving the rural social crisis and staving off further decline. Yu proposed a new type of rural school – one that would be integrated into rural society, accepted and supported by the villagers. The subjects taught at the school would be suitable to rural life.[68]

Yu's concerns were shared by some intellectuals who had been influenced by populism and Marxism during the May Fourth period. In February 1919, Li Dazhao, a professor at Beijing University who would soon help found the Chinese Communist Party, had appealed to educated youths to "go to villages."[69] Students in Beijing University and other schools established many "common people's schools" (*pingmin xuexiao*) around the Beijing area.[70] The capital's educated youth took up the idea of popular education with great enthusiasm.

The movement to educate the common people began to build its base in villages in 1924. In this year, the movement's most notable figure, Yan Yangchu (James Yen), turned his attention to rural education and carried out a survey in Dingxian County, Hebei, as a first step in creating a rural education program.[71] In fact, as early as 1922, Changsha had given birth to another important rural education project when Cao Dianqi and several of his fellow teachers organized the Association for Promoting Rural Extracurricular

Education (*Nongcun buxi jiaoyu she*). In addition to teaching literacy, Cao and his comrades hoped to "enrich the common sense of the rural populace and improve the life of rural society." This would be achieved largely by teaching adults who had never attended school. In addition to basic literacy, an understanding of the duties of citizenship was emphasized.[72]

While these early movements to educate the rural population achieved some success, they all suffered from a number of common problems. Few who had received a modern education in a city really wanted to live in a village among peasants. Yen decided to rely on YMCA workers, but this delayed the launching of his Dingxian program until 1929.[73] When Cao tried to persuade urban teachers and students to teach in rural communities, his pitch failed. Eventually, the movement came to rely mainly on teachers already living in villages.[74] A second problem was a lack of financial support. To reduce costs, rural education projects attempted to develop many different types of institutions, such as night schools, fall and winter schools, literacy classes, and reading rooms where little formal education would be offered. Cao believed that old-fashioned pedagogy was well suited to women students because it was private and engendered a feeling of trust in the reputation of *sishu* teachers.[75] Another teacher, Tang Jue, also suggested establishing rural secondary schools modelled after the Ming and Qing academies and *sishu* schools that would be more suitable to rural communities.[76]

Many inhabitants of rural areas viewed new schools with a measure of distrust. In the 1920s and 1930s, they embraced education only to the extent that it promised significant upward mobility.[77] Modern schooling was expensive, so "rational" peasants would only invest in the children most likely to win family prestige. To persuade peasants to accept their educational projects, reformers had to find ways to become involved in rural community life and make learning relevant to peasants' lives.

New Directions for Teachers' Schools: Training Teachers for Rural Education

A consensus on the need to develop rural education was gradually emerging in educational circles. In 1922, the Jiangsu Provincial Association for Advancing Compulsory Education (*Jiangsu yiwu jiaoyu qicheng hui*) published a series of articles advocating rural education and rural teachers' schools.[78] Between 1923 and 1924, five Jiangsu provincial teachers' schools established branches in rural areas. Several teachers' schools in other provinces, such as Shandong and Henan, followed suit. This was the beginning of a movement to establish village teachers' schools.[79] The idea was to train future teachers outside of the city so that they might grow accustomed to the austerity of rural life and come to embrace it.[80]

These village teachers' schools had significant shortcomings. First, although they were located in the countryside, they had no interaction with the local communities. Second, few concessions had been made to local conditions: the curricula of these branch schools were basically copied from those of their parent schools.[81] These institutions were essentially modern urban schools that had been dropped into a rural environment, and students never did penetrate far into rural community life.

Reforming Rural Society: Xiaozhuang Village Teachers' School, 1927-30

In the late 1920s, while teachers' schools in urban areas were declining, a new type of teachers' school appeared in rural communities – the village teachers' school. When Tao Xingzhi founded Xiaozhuang Experimental Village Teachers' School (*Xiaozhuang shiyan xiangcun shifan xuexiao* [1927-30]) in a village near Nanjing in the spring of 1927, it marked a turning point in the development of village teachers' schools. Neither a traditional school nor a Western one, it challenged the conceptions of modernity presented in the 1922 school system. The school emphasized practical and local knowledge and rejected bookish study. While new-style schools tended to be set apart from the rural community, the Xiaozhuang school was committed to reforming and leading the community. By becoming actively involved in local community affairs and in villagers' daily lives, the school attempted to establish a model for the reorganization of local communities, with the ultimate goal being the reformation of the entire society. The school's aim was to train village teachers steeped in the ways of local society to be leaders, reformers, and mediators, eventually leading the villages into the modern world.

Tao Xingzhi and his school have received scholarly attention in both China and the West. Some scholarship has highlighted the relationship between Tao's and John Dewey's educational philosophies. Kuhn believes that Tao adopted Dewey's idea but radicalized it to meet the needs of the social environment of 1920s Chinese society.[82] Keenan describes Tao's experiment as an effort to realize American democratic principles: if Dewey's pedagogic precepts were not followed to the letter, this was because of the need to modify them to suit the social conditions of 1920s China.[83] Yusheng Yao put Tao into the intellectual context of the 1920s, highlighting the influence of Marxism and anarchism on Tao's form of educational radicalism.[84] However, as the anarchist centre of the time, the National Labour University in Shanghai seemed unwilling to recognize the Xiaozhuang school as a comrade, and the two had little connection.[85] Zhixin Su spoke of "the struggle of Chinese educators in implementing Western educational ideas in Chinese educational practices."[86] Those studies have tried to fit Tao and the Xiaozhuang school into a larger framework that presents the modernization of Chinese education as a process of implementing Western educational practices and political principles. On the other hand, Brown notices how Chinese philosophy affected both Tao's attraction to Dewey's social ideas and his deviation from them.[87]

In this section, I re-examine the school not only by putting it within the historical context of the 1920s but also by reinterpreting it as an effort to create a hybridized educational model. By accentuating local traits, Tao found a remedy for both the long-standing problems of traditional education and the contradictions between the Western-style model and China's specific needs, which were quite evident in the shortcomings of the 1922 Education Reform. Although Tao, like many of his contemporaries, was excited by Dewey's ideas, the Chinese content of Tao's system has often been overlooked.[88] While Western scholars have tended to focus on Tao's educational policies, Chinese scholars have focused on the social programs organized by the Xiaozhuang school. But all too often, the importance of Chinese scholarship has suffered as the story of the school is set upon the Procrustean bed of Communist revolutionary narrative, which has tended to minimize fundamental differences between the revolutionary project of the Communist Party and Tao's rural reform project.[89]

Birth of the Xiaozhuang Village Teachers' School and Its Goals

In 1926, the Chinese National Association for the Advancement of Education (*Zhonghua jiaoyu cujin she*) created the Department of Rural Education and charged it with improving rural education. Assigned to take charge of the program, Tao Xingzhi studied several elementary schools and teachers' schools in Zhejiang, Jiangsu, and Anhui before proposing the establishment of a new and different type of village teachers' school as an experimental program.[90]

Tao Xingzhi (1891-1946) graduated from Columbia University's teachers' college in 1917 and, upon returning to China, was hired by Nanjing Teachers' College as head of instruction. He had had little exposure to progressivism before being chosen to serve as Dewey's interpreter during his tour of China in 1920.[91] He then worked for the Chinese National Association for the Advancement of Education and promoted popular education.[92]

Over time, Tao developed a two-point critique of the existing education system. First, rather than creating narrow class distinctions, modern education was creating a new urban elite.[93] Second, the existing educational system focused on book learning and led students to despise those who laboured with their hands.[94] Taking his lead from Dewey's motto "education is life," Tao advocated making education more practical. He considered it crucial to narrow the gap between study and practice, hence his idea of building teachers' schools in rural communities.[95] Rather than slavishly following Dewey's commandments, Tao said he was "turning Progressivism upside down."[96] He changed "education is life" to "life is education," while "school is society" became "society is school."[97]

As we shall see, these changes were more than rhetorical flourishes. Tao hoped the Xiaozhuang Experimental Village Teachers' School would promote "life as the center of education" by applying a "teaching method that made a unity of teaching, learning, and doing."[98] In March 1927, the Xiaozhuang school, one of the rural programs set up by the Chinese National Association for the Advancement of Education, opened its doors. Tao expounded the school's creed:

> We deeply believe that the teacher should be a friend of the people. We deeply believe that the rural school should be the center of the reform of rural life. We deeply believe that teachers in rural schools should be the soul of rural reform. We deeply believe that teachers in rural school should possess farming skills, scientific minds, and the spirit to reform society. We also deeply believe that teachers in rural schools should conquer nature using scientific methods and reform society using aesthetic concepts. And we believe that rural teachers should run the best schools in the most economical fashion.[99]

Tao and his collaborators first set up a teachers' school for elementary school teachers and, to accompany it, an elementary school where young teachers could get experience. In the following months, a village hospital, library, and meeting hall were established. The school also published a journal, *Collective Newsletter on Rural Education* (*Xiangjiao congxun*), which reported on school activities and recorded the school's program and practices. After eighteen months, a second teachers' school for training elementary teachers was opened, as were eight more elementary schools and four kindergartens. Soon the Xiaozhuang school formed a scientific society and built both a scientific and an agricultural exhibition hall. It had its own theatrical troupe and martial arts association. In time, three adult schools were opened to teach basic literacy and other skills, and the school operated two tea houses, a store, and several factories. To create strong bonds between the students and the local society, the Xiaozhuang school offered free evening classes for adults and opened a tea house staffed by students. By organizing local social programs, such as a militia and a firefighting squad, school administrators succeeded in realizing Tao's dreams of a school-centred social reform project.[100]

The democratic school administration held daily and weekly meetings that were attended by all faculty and students.[101] To promote student autonomy while constructing a close teacher-student relationship, teachers were presented not as god-like authorities but, rather, as guides. Ten students and one teacher shared a single dormitory room; they studied and ate together.[102] Students arranged their own study plans in consultation with their teachers and were encouraged to keep up a dialogue with their mentors about their studies.[103]

The precise daily schedule of Xiaozhuang students might remind some of military life and/or of monastic precision. After a brief school meeting came forty minutes of physical exercise, then breakfast, then half an hour of sweeping and cleaning. All of that took place before 8:00 AM. From 8:00 AM to 10:00 AM students studied and worked, and from 10:00 AM to 12:00 PM they carried out administrative duties. Most seminars and activities – such as music, physical training, handicrafts, and military training – were carried out in the afternoon. From 4:00 PM to 5:00 PM students and teachers worked in the fields, and from 7:00 PM to 9:00 PM they studied. At 10:00 PM students went to bed.

"Teaching-Learning-Doing in One": A New Pedagogy

One of the aims of the educators who introduced the Western educational model to China in the late Qing was to overcome the prevailing influence of examination-oriented education, which promoted book learning at the expense of practical knowledge. A few private academies had long been a haven for independent scholarship, and some led the way during this period of early reforms, but a large majority retained the old style. When the academies were transformed into new-style schools, their pedagogy remained largely conventional. Furthermore, old literati, even those who had earned proper teaching credentials, often clung to the old way of teaching, as the League of Nations' experts pointed out in their 1931 report.[104] While the original goal of Western-inspired educational reformers was to create schools that turned out practical experts capable of modernizing China, after a few years it became clear, as the social activist and philosopher Liang Shuming pointed out in 1932,[105] that China's Western-style schools had produced a parasitic class of scholars and officials. On the other hand, some argued that it was China's failed bid at industrialization that had rendered Western science irrelevant and Western-style schools useless.[106]

Tao's criticisms of book learning continued a long-standing debate among Chinese intellectuals about the origin of knowledge. This debate can be traced to ancient times. Beginning in the Song (960-1279) and Ming dynasties, two major schools of thought coalesced around opposing propositions. The Lu-Wang School (named after Lu Jiuyuan and Wang Yangming) proposed that knowledge originated from an understanding of innate human nature (*xin xing*), while the Cheng-Zhu School (named after Cheng Yi, Cheng Hao, and Zhu Xi) proposed that knowledge originated from the study of things (*ge wu*) through learning ancient classics.[107] The Cheng-Zhu School believed in the study of classical texts, while the Lu-Wang School stressed personal morality and the daily-life practices of common people.[108]

In his youth, Tao had admired Wang Yangming (1472-1528).[109] Wang's philosophy emphasized "uniting knowledge and practice into one" (*zhi xing he yi*) and regarded knowledge and practice as different aspects of the same essence, which is part of innate human nature.[110] During his study at Jinling University, Tao took the name Zhixing as a tribute to Wang Yangming's idea of *zhi xing he yi*. In 1927, however, Tao changed his name to Xingzhi, indicating that he had revised his philosophical views; he now believed that practice preceded knowledge (*xing shi zhi zhi shi*). While Tao rejected Wang's idea that practice grew out of innate consciousness, he continued to affirm Wang's idea that practice was the way to attain knowledge.[111] Tao argued that Western scientific achievement was based on gaining knowledge through practice.[112] He also believed that ancient Chinese scholars had been endowed with a scientific spirit that permitted them to learn from personal experience (i.e., practices). Confucius' knowledge, he argued, was derived from experience acquired in his youth, and Mozi and Xunzi, two other important early philosophers, valued and benefited from knowledge gained from personal experience.[113] While Tao praised the Cheng-Zhu School's tradition of "gaining knowledge through investigating things" (*zai ji wu er qiong qi li*), he rejected their bookish approach.[114] He claimed that book learning had been promoted by the ruling class of every dynasty so that they could co-opt scholars to legitimate their rule.[115] The Western school system established in China during the first two decades of the twentieth century, he claimed, maintained and revived the spirit of book learning under the guise of the irrelevant knowledge taught in Western-style schools.[116] When Liang Shuming declared that most modern schools built in China combined the worst aspects of modern Western education and traditional Chinese education, he was probably thinking of Tao's critique.[117]

If the problems teachers faced were both new and old, then solutions could draw on both innovation and tradition. The most outstanding feature of the Xiaozhuang school, and the one that most distinguished it from conventional teachers' schools, was its practical pedagogy – what was referred to as "teaching-learning-doing in one" (*jiao xue zuo he yi*). Students were to learn within a highly practical environment.[118] This approach was the reverse of traditional Chinese education: instead of learning from books, students set out to practise "arithmetic teaching-learning-doing," "natural science teaching-learning-doing," and so forth. "We do not trust any interpretation found in a book," said Yang Xiaochun, one of the school's instructors, "and we also do not need a classroom for this kind of class [that is, the teaching-learning-doing kind]. Therefore, we do not have classrooms as other schools have."[119] When they studied fish, students raised fish in ponds; when they studied farming and gardening, students invited experienced farmers to teach them in the field. Tao could be provocative: he said that it would not be bad for society if there was another book burning like the one that had occurred in the Qin Dynasty (221-206 BCE).[120] Such anti-intellectualism reeked of Wang Yangming.[121]

Like many other teachers' schools, the Xiaozhuang school sent students to its elementary school to learn by teaching. One of the most important courses at the Xiaozhuang school was entitled "teaching-learning-doing the activities of the central elementary school" (*Zhongxin xiaoxue huodong jiao xue zuo*). Students were required not only to master subjects taught in elementary schools, such as Chinese language, citizenship, arithmetic, and so on, but also to study campus design, facility management, hygiene, instruction administration, fundraising, budgeting, and accounting. To aid them in mastering all of these in the true Xiaozhuang fashion, students were put in charge of founding and running new elementary schools in the process of learning.[122] Through this process, the Xiaozhuang Experimental Village Teachers' School expanded the number of its elementary schools from one to eight.[123]

"Life Is Education": A New Type of Teacher Training

Hu Qing has shown that the combination of labour and study was an ancient tradition in rural China, a way for literati who came from families of modest means to continue their education.[124] In the late Ming, famous scholars, including Sun Qifeng, Zhang Lüxiang, and Yan Yuan, sent their students to villages to engage in physical labor.[125] Hu suggested that most scholars who followed the "tradition of ploughing and studying" (*geng du chuantong*) were from rather poor families and that their work enabled them to remain close to the common people.[126] Although the practice of ploughing and studying was not in the mainstream of traditional education, it could provide a philosophical and moral base for marginal scholars to attack elite culture and to address social problems.

The Xiaozhuang school revived this tradition. A crucial step involved eliminating the idea that educated people were superior people from other social groups. When Xiaozhuang teachers and students declared that "life is education," they were referring to the life of the common people. Students were encouraged to work, act, dress, and speak like ordinary people.[127] This meant fiercely rejecting Mengzi's adage: "Those who work with their minds rule people, and those who do physical labor are ruled by others."[128] Students built all the campus buildings, including the dormitories, the meeting hall, the library, the scientific exhibition hall, the office, the kitchen, and the lavatories with their own hands. Students were encouraged to farm on the school's lands and sell their harvest to pay for their schooling. The work-study program organized students to engage in carpentry, weaving, cooking, and printing, in addition to working at the school store and dining hall.[129]

While the school's emphasis on practical knowledge was influenced by the ideas of John Dewey, the differences between Dewey's "education is life" and Tao's "life is education" merit some attention. Dewey's idea, as summarized by Barry Keenan, was that "the subject matter of schooling was to be taken directly from daily life, so that the 'little red schoolhouse' could become a microcosm of the model life which the society outside should be like."[130] Keenan has correctly argued that Tao "dragged Dewey's theory out of the classroom and into society" and "made education a living part of village life."[131] But Tao did more than this. At his school, the point was to eliminate the boundary between education and life by requiring that students imitate the daily life of the common people, learn their language, and come to live with and for them. Despite the modern garments, here we can see Wang Yangming's spirit of "combining knowledge and action" (*zhixing he yi*).[132] Tao's rhetoric revived previous philosophical traditions to solve long-standing problems and also helped to legitimize his modernizing reforms.

By advocating the merging of life and education and the dissolution of the boundaries between school and society, Tao did not intend to eliminate education. The purpose of the village teachers' schools, after all, was to train teachers to become community leaders. To accomplish this goal, the school encouraged students to acquire practical knowledge through courses on agriculture, rural school life, daily life, and relations with peasants. Besides the conventional courses required by government regulations, the Xiaozhuang curriculum included other courses specifically useful to rural life, among them courses on village self-governance, popular education, organizing credit cooperatives, and peasant recreation.[133] To improve self-reliance, students were required to learn how to farm and cook.[134]

To make school even more like life, the Xiaozhuang school encouraged the rural student-teachers to bring their wives to the village. This was a crucial step towards ensuring that rural teaching personnel became a part of local society, and it was also conducive to promoting women's education as teachers' wives would take on some of the duties of teaching village women.[135] The school also enrolled a group of female students in its regular program and opened a female teachers' school to train kindergarten teachers.[136] Students' wives, fiancées, and female relatives were given preference with regard to gaining admission to the school.[137] Schoolmates were encouraged to marry so that they could teach together and stay in villages. Tao believed that marriage between students would make the experience of teaching in rural areas more enjoyable, increase family income, reduce turnover, help promote rural women's education and women's progress towards equality, and provide the rural community with model families.[138] He even wrote a song to promote such unions:

A male student and a female student got married and became teachers.
Where are they going to teach?
Either in the East Village or in the West Village.
They go to reform the old village and build a new one.

> The village used to have an old spirit, but now there is a new spirit.
> Each couple will be the spirit of each village.[139]

The school's leaders hoped to train female students to serve as the "leaders of the rural women's movement," but there is no documentary evidence of any special training program or activities to fulfill this goal.[140]

The teachers who graduated from village teachers' schools were expected not only to spread knowledge but also to be community mediators, organizers, and advocates. Cheng Benhai, one of the Xiaozhuang school's earliest graduates and an active promoter of Tao's pedagogy, listed a village teacher's seven duties and qualifications: (1) reforming society; (2) teaching children; (3) farming; (4) possessing scientific knowledge about the locality; (5) possessing medical knowledge; (6) possessing artistic ability; and (7) knowing how to do school chores (see appendix at the end of this chapter).[141] Some of these were generally considered part of the necessary expertise of a modern professional teacher, but most were related to the community role village teachers were expected to play, and this differed significantly from what was found in the modern job description. One might say that the Xiaozhuang school intended to deprofessionalize village teachers.

This deprofessionalization took various forms in twentieth-century China.[142] Although the Xiaozhuang school provided professional courses on education and the basic subjects taught at modern schools, what it actually did was to expand the role of the professional teacher, thus eliminating the "pure" image of professional teachers. The peculiar requirements of the school took teachers far beyond their role as mere knowledge transmitters (which was what regular modern teachers' schools required of them) and, instead, made them serve as social organizers, community leaders, caretakers, doctors, agricultural directors, legal mediators, recreational promoters, and social reformers. This was very close to the traditional role played by *sishu*-style teachers in villages, with the addition of the social and cultural responsibilities associated with rural modernization. This type of teacher was indeed needed by the rural communities, but this need undermined the professionalization of teachers.

"Society Is School": The Social Programs of the Xiaozhuang School

The Xiaozhuang School was meant to be a model of the village school as the cultural, social, and political nexus of the community. At the same time, the village school was to be a tool to reform rural society. On this point, Tao's ideas departed from Progressivism. When Dewey said "school is society," he meant that a school should be a microcosm of society, and that this should be epitomized in the school's curriculum, but the school remained separate from society in basic ways.[143] Tao spoke of the need to break the "cage" of school and to let the student-birds fly freely.[144] He eliminated the boundary between school and society, making the school an organic component penetrating into every aspect of the community.

Tao's ideas cannot be fully understood without reviewing the role of schools in premodern Chinese society. Traditionally, schools had been designed as instruments for socializing and integrating youth into local communities. Borthwick contrasted modern schools with traditional schools, arguing that the former "integrates its curriculum with the outside world, but as an institution cuts off all links with it." On the other hand, she wrote, the curricula in traditional Chinese schools were distant from daily life (especially in rural areas), but they were "organizationally integrated into the surrounding community."[145] In describing this distinction, Borthwick captures one of the fundamental reasons why, in the early twentieth century, Western-style modern schools encountered resistance from local villagers. However, she might only be partially right about traditional Chinese schools: they not only taught some basic practical skills, such as reading and writing, but their teaching of Confucian moral values and norms of social conduct also socialized students, integrated them into their communities, and set them up as moral exemplars.

Imperial schools were originally designed to "cultivate people and change [bad] customs" (*hua min yi su*).[146] An edict issued by the Kangxi emperor (r. 1661-1722) clearly states the two major purposes of Chinese schools: "educating and cultivating the community and training able men" (*xing xing jiaohua, zuoyu rencai*).[147] Other types of schools, such as community schools, charitable schools, and academies, functioned as instruments of state control in local communities, where officials and literati spread moral doctrine, lectured on imperial edicts, and set a moral example.[148] In the nineteenth century, demographic and military pressures led local governments to consider reviving community schools more as a means of maintaining local security than of selecting able men.[149] When Western-style schools were introduced, their students were intentionally segregated from the community and their curricula were largely irrelevant to Chinese society and local economic life. Cut off from the community, these modern schools did nothing to connect students to local society.

Social reform was the ultimate goal of the Xiaozhuang school. After its graduates became involved in village life, they would reform the community through education, using modern ideas. Among the tactics were "making friends [with peasants]," establishing "schools for commoners" and "village kindergartens," managing "central tea houses" and stores, opening village hospitals and clinics, assisting peasants in managing credit cooperatives, and so on. Tao and his colleagues understood that, in order to make the school the centre of social reform, the first step was to overcome local resistance to modern schools. One of the reasons that the initial establishment of the Xiaozhuang Experimental Village Teachers' School incurred little local opposition appears to have been that students and teachers were all outsiders and that the school was careful not to disturb village life. When elementary schools began to open, they stirred up opposition and even hostility among some of the villagers. Teachers and students from the school who tried to interest peasants in sending their children to the new schools were informed that it was wrong to build "foreign schools" and teach "foreign stuff." When the Xiaozhuang school was searching for a location for its primary school, parents feared that their local temples would be destroyed to make way for it.[150]

School leaders believed that they could win the trust of local people if they invited them into the school and integrated it into the community while also keeping tuition costs at the elementary schools and kindergarten low enough to make it possible for parents to send their children there. In contrast to the urban schools, which were surrounded by walls and protected by security guards, the Xiaozhuang school was built in the style of a peasant house and had no protective outer walls.[151] The main school and the elementary schools were open to all: locals were encouraged to visit, have a drink of water, and talk to students or teachers.[152] When classes were not in session, the school buildings were offered for all kinds of village activities.[153] High cost often led villagers to reject new-style schools, so at Xiaozhuang it was important to absorb the cost of establishing elementary schools in the villages and to keep expenses very low. Each new elementary school was granted forty yuan to help it open and six yuan as a regular subsidy. So successful was this approach that the Xiaozhuang school opened eight elementary schools in the area.[154]

Every Thursday afternoon, groups of three to five students and teachers went to the homes of villagers to befriend the peasants. Through this program, students came to better understand peasant life, share peasant pains and joys, and learned to speak as they did.[155] During Spring Festival, students sent peasants poetic couplets written on scrolls; at other times, they helped them write letters and read newspapers to them.[156] The school invited villagers to participate in its athletic competitions and weekend parties, and students helped villagers in their attempts to eliminate locusts.[157] Since the documentary record was created by those affiliated with the school, it is hard to know how villagers responded to these efforts. But joint school-village programs expanded over time, and the conclusion is natural. In 1930, a journalist reported that villagers considered the teachers and students to be family members. When the Xiaozhuang school was threatened with closure by the Nationalist government in 1930, a group of villagers voluntarily organized to protect the school.[158]

Xiaozhuang Experimental Village Teachers' School promoted its program of social reform through its elementary schools, which functioned as community centres. This was one reason the elementary schools were called "central schools." As Tao explains:

> The starting point of the rural education movement is to open central elementary schools. There are three meanings for the term "central elementary school." First, the center of school life is rural life. Second, the school is the center of social reform. Third, once it becomes successful, this school [Yanziji Central Elementary School, set up near Xiaozhuang] can become a center for training teachers.[159]

Most of the school's social programs utilized the sites of the central elementary schools. One such program grew out of a course devoted to "changing social conditions through teaching-learning-doing"; it included "village self-governance, popular education, organizing cooperatives, surveying the village, and peasant recreation." Later the school set up a department of social reform headed by Tao Xingzhi himself, which was composed of twelve branches: general affairs, education, public hygiene, agriculture and forestry, transportation, water control, self-defence, economy, disaster relief, women, publishing, and investigation.[160]

The second step in the Xiaozhuang school's social reform program was to pay attention to the needs of people in order to promote new knowledge and new ideas. The school opened a shelter for women and children who had fled embattled areas.[161] Responding to the poor medical conditions in the countryside, the school fostered students' medical knowledge through having them practise medicine under the direction of a physician. The school then established a hospital in the village and provided free treatment. During its first year of operation, the hospital treated over a thousand patients. When a cholera epidemic hit the city of Nanjing in 1927, students lectured in tea houses on how to prevent the disease and encouraged peasants to buy medicine from the school at cost. Students also learned how to vaccinate against smallpox, a disease that killed many infants in nearby villages.[162]

The Xiaozhuang school established several "schools for commoners" (*minzhong xuexiao*), which enrolled adult peasants, both male and female, to teach them practical skills. The school also set up a reading room in a number of nearby villages and sent students to teach there. The students compiled special textbooks for peasants, using basic Chinese characters to discuss their daily life. The students also excerpted traditional elementary textbooks such as *San zi jing* (Three character classic), *Bai jia xing* (One hundred surnames), and *Lun yu* (The analects), teaching passages with which the villagers had some familiarity. Adult students were also taught how to use an abacus, bookkeeping, how to read contracts, and how to write letters, all of which were very useful in village lives.[163] Around the country, most schools for commoners had very few female students: drawing eleven female students to one of the Xiaozhuang adult schools was considered a great success.[164]

School officials hoped to replace the villagers' old habits of gambling and opium smoking with healthier alternatives. Hence the tea houses, which would be licit establishments, lively places meant to lure people away from the old tea houses, which were used as gambling dens.[165] Every afternoon and evening, students from the teachers' school entertained those who had bought a cup of tea with stories, songs, and jokes; lectures on public health and personal hygiene; reports on national and world news; and singing. And customers could always play table tennis, go, or Chinese chess; they could read books or play the Chinese violin or flute (all equipment was provided free of charge).[166]

For Tao and his colleagues, the eventual goal of these activities was to organize the masses and to encourage them to practise democracy and reap the benefits of modern political life. To reach this goal, the organizers of the Xiaozhuang school promoted self-government in local communities. This started with the building of self-defence squads. A remote village on the outskirts of Nanjing, Xiaozhuang was occasionally raided by gangs of bandits who torched buildings and murdered those who tried to stand up to them. In 1928, bandits harassed the school and the stores in the neighbourhood, terrifying both students and peasants.[167] When Tao Xingzhi communicated what had happened to General Feng Yuxiang (1882-1948), a warlord who had given the school substantial support, Feng sent the school several dozen old rifles. A united village self-defence team (*lian cun ziwei dui*) was organized to protect both the school and the community. A total of one hundred students and young peasants from adjacent villages took responsibility for providing community security. Besides protecting the community from bandits, the self-defence squad was also in charge of maintaining order and eliminating gambling and opium smoking. After raiding more than thirty opium houses in one night, the squad organized a joint program with the village hospital to help opium addicts get off the drug.[168]

To help villagers win their political rights (*minquan*), Tao explained the need for good propaganda and indoctrination: "How can we get peasants to assert their rights? Peasants ... do not know what popular rights are. Our propaganda is the key to enlightening them. However, the most important thing is to train those who will teach young peasants ... Training peasants to assert their popular rights, teaching them how to use their power to elect, reject, legislate, and confirm – all this depends on our village teachers."[169]

To promote local self-government, the school organized a Rural Education Pioneer Team (*Xiangcun jiaoyu xianfeng tuan*). Meeting with the heads of the villages where they had opened elementary schools, school leaders preached self-government. The school drew up a program and a set of regulations regarding the qualifications for village residency, election rules, and procedures for village meetings. The self-government programs stipulated that the village chief and vice-chief – executives in charge of the village's public affairs – had to be elected by qualified village residents. Besides the self-defence squads, the self-government program also established plans to organize firefighting associations and groups to repair roads, plant trees, set up credit cooperatives, and arrange peasant handicraft exhibitions.[170]

The school also tried to train villagers to "exercise popular rights" (*lianxi minquan*).[171] A dispute over a well provided an opportunity for this. The dispute was solved through a mass meeting that was conducted democratically.[172] But the planned self-government programs rarely amounted to anything but plans, producing only a few fledgling organizations by the time the school was shut down by the Nationalist government in April 1930.

Appraising the Xiaozhuang School

Xiaozhuang Experimental Village Teachers' School combined aspects of both modern and traditional schools. From the modern educational model, it adopted the idea of teaching practical scientific knowledge. If, in urban schools, this meant studying engineering and physics, for Tao Xingzhi it meant studying the agricultural knowledge and skills needed for rural development. At the same time, the traditional educational model provided the idea of integrating the school and its students into the community.

Despite the investment of huge amounts of energy and considerable funds, Tao's experimental program achieved very little. Although most intellectuals and educators, especially those who had studied overseas, were quick to criticize the wholesale grafting of a foreign model onto the Chinese educational system, their social and educational background blinded them to the problems associated with educational modernization.[173] Modernizers of the New Culture stripe, who renounced the resources of the past, were left with no choice but to embrace the then paragon of modernity – the United States. Tao's approach was different: he wanted to create a hybrid. As Pepper points out, Tao and Yan Yangchu (James Yen) were unusual among 1920s Chinese intellectuals: "They had to set up their experiments outside the formal education system created and maintained by the returned students because there was no place for such innovations within it."[174]

There are many gaps in our understanding of the Xiaozhuang experiment. No document permits us to hear the voice of villagers, to know how village elites and others responded to the school's program of social reform.

There are no records that describe how the school reconciled its plans for new self-governing bodies with the existing village administrative system. While village schools were meant to reform and reconstruct the villages, they were not meant to replace the villages' administrative system. Even if the schools had survived, there would have been some institutional conflicts with local officials as they attempted to implement social reforms.

The Xiaozhuang experiment was launched during a period of revolutionary political upheaval and, eventually, politics spelled its doom. The school was established in 1927, shortly before the Nationalists had completed the Northern Expedition and nominally unified China. During the first several years of its rule, the Nationalist Party was weakened by quarrels between its left- and right-wing factions as it laboured to suppress its erstwhile Communist allies and deal with the demands and rebellions of local warlords. National control over local communities was quite tenuous. Tao Xingzhi and his colleagues succeeded in setting up their experimental school thanks to this power vacuum. When the school's protector, Feng Yuxiang, was defeated by the central government in 1930, the Nationalists immediately suppressed the Xiaozhuang school. Thus the school's reform project fell victim to a political struggle.

If Xiaozhuang Experimental Village Teachers' School placed heavy demands on its students, this was due to the decline of rural communities as the more talented villagers migrated to the cities. In spite of all the Xiaozhuang programs aimed at breaking down barriers, there was no getting around a basic problem: students came from outside the village and, upon graduating, they went on to other villages. As new teachers, they were outsiders and faced the problems of isolation, low income, and a harsh working and living environment – just like other village teachers. The Xiaozhuang experiment could not solve these problems: graduates were simply encouraged to keep their spirits up and to maintain a sense of moral duty. As long as the scale of the experiment could be kept small, the mission to transform and rejuvenate rural China made sense to a group of idealistic teachers and students. But it was not possible to expand this particular movement.

Appendix: Qualifications of Village Elementary Schoolteachers[175]

Type 1: Social Reform (20 percent of the entire course)

1 Be able to run a tea house;
2 Be able to open a common people's school;
3 Be able to cure light illnesses and have knowledge of hygiene;
4 Know accounting and be able to have social interaction with local people in keeping with local protocol;

5 Be able to calculate the grain tax rate, interest, to measure land and to estimate the price of land;
6 Be able to read popularized characters in pawn tickets, receipts, tax forms, contracts, and government edicts;
7 Be able to write antithetical couplets, marriage invitations, meeting notices, contracts, and letters, etc.;
8 Be able to tell jokes, and stories, and give lectures;
9 Be able to mediate quarrels, only filing a law suit when it is absolutely necessary;
10 Be able to edit, compile, and post a wall-newsletter;
11 Know several different types of martial arts, and be able to organize the masses into self-defence teams;
12 Know how to do magic tricks, perform common opera and vocal mimicry, and present a two-man comic show, etc.;
13 Be able to advise and organize a co-op and a credit union;
14 Be able to decorate school in order to create a popular park;
15 Have capacity to preside over mass assemblies;
16 Understand world affairs;
17 Understand national affairs;
18 Know local socioeconomic condition well;
19 Know local legends and current affairs well;
20 Be familiar with the social protocols of local society;
21 Understand the work of local professions and be able to introduce methods of improvement.

Type 2: Children's Education (30 percent of the entire course)

1 Be able to make friends with children;
2 Be able to tell stories and to report current affairs to children by using "national speech (Mandarin)";
3 Understand children's words;
4 Be able to answer children's questions and to spark their curiosity;
5 Be able to guide children's reading and help them search for various kinds of references;
6 Be able to preside over the anniversary week celebration and direct student's meetings;
7 Be able to help children express their opinions in writing, speech, drawings, and handicrafts;
8 Be able to notice the bad habits of children and help them to change;
9 Be able to lead children in doing physical labour, such as sweeping and cleaning;
10 Be familiar with local children's songs;
11 Be able to play children's games;

12 Understand the psychology of children over age 6;
13 Know experimental methods of education, and how to conduct educational experiments, and exams, compile statistics and make charts;
14 Be able to adopt new education methods introduced by educational magazines.

Type 3: Agricultural Labour Work (10 percent of the entire course)

1 Know how to work with a hoe. (It would be better if teachers were also able to plough since ploughing not only requires physical capacity but also technique; however, it should not be required.);
2 Know how to water land and apply fertilizer;
3 Know how to weed vegetable gardens;
4 Know how to dig a ditch;
5 Know how to repair farming implements;
6 Know how to set up a nursery garden;
7 Know how to plant local vegetables;
8 Know how to raise fruit trees, bamboo, and trees;
9 Know how to plant regular flowers and bushes;
10 Know how to raise silkworms;
11 Know how to raise bees;
12 Know how to raise chickens, ducks, and pigeons;
13 Know how to raise goats, pigs, and water-buffaloes;
14 Be able to collect wood and wild fruit;
15 Know how to raise fish;
16 Be able to understand the nature of soil;
17 Be able to understand agricultural books;
18 Make acquaintance with local agricultural institutions and elderly peasants;
19 Be familiar with local climate and important agricultural products;
20 Know important local farmers' sayings.

Type 4: Scientific Knowledge and Practice (13 percent of the entire course)

1 Be able to collect well-known local plants and preserve them as plant specimens/samples;
2 Be able to catch well-known local insects, for example, catch snakes and butterflies and preserve them as specimens;
3 Be able to catch birds;
4 Be able to prepare specimens of birds and small animals;
5 Be able to do simple dissecting of animals and preserve them as specimens;

6 Know local injurious insects and their activities;
7 Know local migratory birds and their activities;
8 Be able to prepare samples of herbs and know their origins; be able to make simple medical instruments and know how to repair them;
9 Know local minerals and geological conditions;
10 Be able to measure weather conditions and rainfall, know changes of climate and solar terms in calendar (*jieqi*);
11 Know the main stars;
12 Know the components of daily food, for example, rice, wheat, vegetables, etc.;
13 Know the manufacturing method of daily food, for example, soy sauce, oil, tea, salt, etc.;
14 Know the chemical properties of household items;
15 Know physical properties of household items;
16 Be familiar with simple machines;
17 Be able to repair common machines, for example, clocks, watches, etc.;
18 Be able to use common electronic devices, for example, the radio;
19 Be able to demonstrate and explain a curious scientific phenomenon;
20 Be able to read popular scientific magazines.

Type 5: Medical Knowledge and Practice (7.5 percent of the entire course)

1 Know the structure of the human body;
2 Maintain good hygienic habits, for example, be careful when spitting or sneezing, and clean food and utensils;
3 Be able to do physical examinations;
4 Be able to give smallpox vaccinations;
5 Be able to treat trachoma, scabies, etc.;
6 Be able to treat malaria, colds, constipation, intestinal parasites;
7 Be able to bind up a wound and stop bleeding;
8 Be able to treat simple skin diseases;
9 Know the nature and use of regular medicines, for example, quinine, aspirin, castor-oil, tincture of iodine, boric acid extract, boric acid liquid, etc.;
10 Be prepared to administer first aid for burning, drowning, heat stroke, etc.;
11 Know the basic principles of public hygiene;
12 Know children's physical development;
13 Have knowledge of nutrition;
14 Be familiar with the training methods of the Nationalist Children's Organization (*tong zi jun*);

15 Be able to practise some type of Chinese traditional martial art;
16 Be able to practise some type of physical training or play ball games;
17 Be able to hike, swim, and climb trees;
18 Be able to read popular medical books.

Type 6: Art (7.5 percent of the entire course)

1 Be able to sing harmonic songs, especially children's songs;
2 Be able to play several types of musical instruments and to use the phonograph;
3 Know how to appreciate world-famous music and understand its themes and rhymes;
4 Be able to do simple dancing;
5 Be able to paint simple paintings;
6 Be able to copy simple pictures;
7 Know how to appreciate famous paintings and understand their meaning;
8 Be able to decorate rooms and fix up a place for meetings;
9 Be able to use paper, wheat straw, beans, wild fruits, and leaves to create decorations or daily necessities;
10 Be able to repair tables, chairs, doors, and windows, etc.;
11 Be able to clean up rooms;
12 Be able to mend cloth, to sew clothing, and to knit;
13 Be able to bind books;
14 Be able to paint houses;
15 Be able to draw on walls;
16 Be able to use natural plants to design gardens;
17 Be able to do some calligraphy;
18 Be able to do simple printing;
19 Be able to cook rice or porridge;
20 Be able to cook dishes and make them tasty;
21 Be able to bake cookies and make them tasty;
22 Be able to clean up the kitchen;
23 Be able to take care of oneself: do not display the manners of wealthy people or literati;
24 Be able to train children and teach them how to keep themselves clean;
25 Know how to appreciate art works, for example, literature, engravings, photographs, embroidery, porcelain, and movies;
26 Be able to direct plays and appreciate other people's performances.

Type 7: Miscellany (10 percent of entire course)

1 Be able to do new-style bookkeeping;
2 Be able to draw up budgets and financial reports;

3 Know how to buy daily necessities and be familiar with market prices;
4 Know how to maintain school facilities;
5 Know how to conduct registration;
6 Be able to supervise and train school workers;
7 Know how to buy books and take care of libraries;
8 Be able to mail letters and goods;
9 Be able to edit reports and magazines;
10 Be able to handle guests and directors of the school district;
11 Be able to put together children's grade reports;
12 Be able to host an exhibition, a celebration, and students' parents' meetings;
13 Be able to make monthly and yearly plans;
14 Be able to preside over a conference;
15 Know how to contact other schools in the neighbourhood and cooperate in a common program;
16 Be able to deal with school documents;
17 Know recent education edicts;
18 Be able to discuss school affairs with government educational administrators.

5

Nationalizing the Local: Teachers' Schools in Rural Reconstruction, 1930-37

During the crucial decade between 1927 and 1937, the Nationalist government in Nanjing consolidated its political power, expanding its control below the county level and reshaping local communities.[1] The fledgling government had to fight with various forces for control over rural areas, including many social organizations that had launched rural reform programs since the mid-1920s. Provincial and county governments, sometimes headed by former warlords, initiated their own programs of rural reconstruction, often working closely with educational institutions.[2] In all of these rural reconstruction efforts, rural education was placed at the centre of reform.

The new Nationalist central government also launched its state-building projects, of which the reconstruction of the educational system was an important part. The reconstruction efforts focused on restoring and expanding local teachers' schools, by which I mean provincial teachers' schools (*sheng li shifan*), county teachers' schools (*xian li shifan*), village teachers' schools (*xiangcun shifan*), simplified teachers' schools (*jianyi shifan*), simplified village teachers' schools (*jianyi xiangshi*), and short-term teachers' schools (*shifan jiangxi suo*). Teachers' schools were restored to their independent position through nationalization and developed rapidly in the late 1920s and early 1930s. The government partially recognized the experience of the Xiaozhuang school with regard to education and rural reform, and it affirmed the position of village teachers' schools in the formal educational system. Local teachers' schools were unified and standardized but were put under the direct control of provincial and county authorities. In its attempt to win the competition with social organizations and previous warlords over the rural reconstruction movement, the central government used local teachers' schools as a vehicle for penetrating rural communities. These teachers' schools were assigned tasks in various rural reconstruction projects. As educational institutions, their activities in rural areas "softened" the thrust of state power, bridging the gap between state and society in rural areas.

The central government assigned the task of standardizing school curricula and social programs to teachers' schools; by thus reinforcing teacher accreditation, it buttressed its control over local society. Some village teachers' schools remained active in rural reconstruction efforts, but with the extension of the Nationalist Party and government apparatus, the social space that had been carved out by rural educational activists during the political disorder of the 1920s was retaken by government functionaries. Through standardization and formalization, village teachers' schools were gradually transformed from private, experimental, informal institutions – some of which had attempted the same radical social reforms as those on the agenda of the Xiaozhuang school – into government-run, formal, and socially and educationally moderate institutions.

Women's normal schools also underwent a transformation during this period. Under the influence of the rural reconstruction movement, educators and scholars started questioning the goals of female education described in the 1922 Educational Reform: why had no attention been paid to working and rural women? With the expansion of local teachers' schools, the government also made efforts to build more female teachers' schools in inland cities and towns, extending secondary female education both socially and geographically. Female teachers' schools not only trained teachers for local communities but also built a necessary bridge between women and society.

Nationalizing Teachers' Schools

Over the Nanjing Decade (1927-37), the national education system had three conspicuous successes: the expansion of county-level bureaucracy, a thorough administrative reorganization, and the establishment of a system of supervision.[3] Before 1927, the state's control over rural education depended largely on its work with local elite organizations such as educational associations.[4] After 1927, the Nationalist government sought to extend its power into rural communities. An important part of this effort was the nationalization and further development, under government auspices, of local teachers' schools.

State Efforts to Direct Rural Education: Recognizing Village Teachers' Schools

The effort to restore the teachers' schools system was made in the first National Conference on Education (*Di yi ci quanguo jiaoyu huiyi*), held in 1928. The conference approved a proposal made by local educational associations to promote teachers' schools, and it suggested restoring their institutional independence. It also recognized village teachers' schools, previously an experimental program, giving them a position in the formal educational system.[5] From this date, the number of village teachers' schools began to rise. Still, other political consolidations took precedence, and little happened in education until 1930.

In April 1930, the second National Conference of Education (*Di er ci quanguo jiaoyu huiyi*) was held in Nanjing, drawing educational officials from provinces, cities, and counties; presidents of national universities and colleges; and prominent education experts. Tao Xingzhi, as a revered national educator, was selected by the Ministry of Education to attend the conference, though he remained on the national "most-wanted" list because of the connection between the Xiaozhuang school and the "rebel" warlord Feng Yuxiang.[6] Obviously, Tao could not participate in the meeting. This dramatic episode shows that the Nationalist government had come to see Tao and the Xiaozhuang Experimental Village Teachers' School as both threateningly radical and as holding the secret to gaining access to rural society. The government could not ignore the issues raised by Tao: a stable and prosperous rural society was the foundation of a better China. Even in absentia, Tao exerted great influence over the conference. From 1930 on, previously experimental village teachers' schools became a part of the formal educational system.

Two decisions that were made at the conference had a significant impact on the development of teachers' education and local society. By 1935, the country was to have 1,500 new village teachers' schools, mainly at the county level.[7] The restoration of the free-tuition policy for students at teachers' schools, abolished under the 1922 educational system, was strongly advocated. At the same time, the conference members promised to establish more teachers' colleges at the provincial level to train teachers for village teachers' schools and to build more female teachers' schools.[8] Beginning with this meeting, the Chinese education system gradually shifted away from the American model adopted in 1922 and tried to develop a viable model to fit the needs of Chinese society, especially the needs of rural areas.[9] Although the ambitious plan of opening 1,500 new village teachers' schools was never realized, in many cases local governments did transform existing middle schools into teachers' schools. And the plan to reintroduce free education for those planning to become teachers was implemented nationwide.

Then, in 1932, the central government formally recognized the difference between teachers' schools and regular middle schools. Teachers' schools at all levels were to be officially built and financed by the corresponding local governments, a system similar to that in place in the early Republic. The regulations regarding teachers' schools (*shifan xuexiao guichen*) gave priority to establishing village teachers' schools in rural areas and suggested founding short-term programs in areas that urgently needed teachers. Reviving the early Republican idea, the regulations stipulated that each province be divided into a number of teachers' school districts (*shifan qu*), with at least one teachers' school per district; students would be drawn from within the district and would be trained to teach in that district. As in Xiaozhuang, students would be required to participate in the activities of the local community: they would repair roads, construct irrigation systems, promote public health and personal hygiene,[10] and engage in mass literacy projects.[11] The Nationalist government planned to yoke the students enrolled in teachers' schools to social reforms that would build public support for the state.

Development of Teachers' Schools: Expanding Secondary Education to the Countryside

Because the national government had formally acknowledged the need for an independent system of teachers' schools, local officials moved to separate teacher training programs from regular middle schools and to restore those teachers' schools that had been converted into regular middle schools. As early as 1931, the Ministry of Education ordered a freeze on new middle schools at the county level in order to devote available resources to teachers' schools.[12] Beginning in the early 1930s, recovering an independent teachers' school system became a serious concern of local education authorities. In 1931, the Jiangsu Bureau of Education decided to restore the independent position of provincial teachers' schools, which had been combined with provincial high schools in 1927. In addition, it established five village teachers' schools as branches of its provincial teachers' school. It also converted eight other middle schools, which had previously been teachers' schools, back into teachers' schools. It planned to accomplish the complete independence of the provincial teachers' school system within three years.[13] County-level teachers' schools were established in the Chinese interior, and secondary education was expanded through the establishment of teachers' schools.

Up to 1930, most middle schools had been located in provincial capitals, big cities, and, sometimes, county seats. The development of teachers' schools led to the expansion of secondary education at the county level and below, especially in inland China. In inland areas, teachers' schools made up a large part of local secondary education. In 1934, Henan provincial education inspectors spread out across the province, visiting schools in all of the province's 110 counties, evaluating personnel, facilities, and operations.[14] The resulting highly detailed reports summarize the history of education in each county and describe current educational and administrative practices.[15] According to the Henan report, most counties had at least one teachers' school. In some counties, the only secondary educational institution was a teachers' school. In others, there was only a regular middle school with a teacher training program attached. Some counties that had teachers' schools also had regular middle schools with attached (and redundant) teacher training programs. This complicated situation was the result of the 1922 reform and its undoing. In 1936, Gansu Province had only eleven regular middle schools, of which one was attached to a college, four were provincial middle schools, and six were county schools; a total of 1,570 students were enrolled. The province also had ten provincial teachers' schools and two county teachers' schools; a total of over 1,571 students were enrolled (report from one school was not included).[16] Gansu's four vocational middle schools accounted for only 337 students.[17]

Teachers' schools were also an important part of secondary education in educationally advanced areas. In Hebei, teachers' schools accounted for a large part of secondary education. In 1933, there were twenty-one provincial middle schools, of which seven had both lower and upper sections. There were only nine county middle schools, all of which were lower middle schools. Compare that with fourteen provincial teachers' schools (both upper and lower sections) and 116 county village teachers' schools (lower section only): the discrepancy is huge. Some counties had one male and one female teachers' school.[18] Shandong Province had six provincial teachers' schools, eight provincial village teachers' schools, seventeen county simplified village schools, and over forty short-term teachers' schools during this same period. Shandong's regular schools amounted to one upper middle school, four complete middle schools, nine lower middle schools, and twenty-one county lower middle schools. The thirty-one teachers' schools (I am not including the short-term teachers' schools) made up almost half of the province's secondary educational institutions.[19]

The 1932 regulations on teachers' schools encouraged the establishment of simplified teachers' schools, and, by 1933, simplified teachers' schools and simplified village teachers' schools accounted for most teachers' schools. Table 5.1 tracks the fluctuation in the number of both full-fledged and simplified teachers' schools from 1931 to 1936.

From 1931 to 1934, the number of full-fledged teachers' schools, most of which were located in urban areas, declined; in contrast, the number of simplified (village) teachers' schools, typically rural, increased. A host of causes contributed to the change. Some full-fledged teachers' schools changed to simplified or village teachers' schools and some were demoted to local teachers' schools and relocated. More simplified schools were established in rural areas to meet the demand for rural education. At the county level, teachers' schools sent their graduates to work in lower primary schools (*chuxiao*, corresponding to grades 1-4 in the United States), while most full-fledged teachers' schools were provincial, training better teachers for upper primary schools (*gaoxiao*, Grades 5 and 6).

Pepper notes that, in the 1930s, the Guomindang (Nationalist Party) government agreed with the criticism of the educational model formed in 1922 and became less dependent on foreign models in constructing its educational

Table 5.1

Teachers' schools in China, 1928-36

Year	Total number of teachers' schools	Total number of students	Full-fledged teachers' schools and village teachers' schools (six years)	Number of students	Simplified teachers' schools and simplified village teachers' schools (four years)	Number of students
1928	236	29,470				
1929	667	65,695				
1930	846	82,809				
1931	867	94,683	584	73,808	283	20,875
1932	864	99,606	518	66,477	346	33,129
1933	893	100,840	245	41,834	648	59,006
1934	876	93,675	186	30,825	690	62,850
1935	862	84,512	190	33,946	672	50,566
1936	814	87,902	198	37,785	616	50,117

Source: The Ministry of Education: *Di er ci Zhongguo jiaoyu nianjian* [The second yearbook on the education of China, 1948] (Beijing: Shangwu Yinshuguan [Commercial Press], 1948), 1428-29, 1433.

system.[20] The increasing number of simplified and village teachers' schools produced the shift from the 1922 model to a system viable in rural China (simplified and village teachers' schools would provide more teachers for rural children in lower primary schools). Through this adjustment, along with distributing provincial teachers' schools around the province, the teachers' schools formed a nationwide provincial-county hierarchical system.

The rapid increase of teachers' schools in the 1930s fuelled the development of secondary education at and below the county level, meaning that significant numbers of rural youth could for the first time attend modern secondary schools. The expansion of secondary education in rural areas would also bring about a social transformation and have a strong political impact on society (see Chapter 6).

Extending State Power: Regulating Teachers' Schools

Chinese and Western scholars who have studied Republican-era education agree that the Nationalist government expanded its control over education at all levels after 1927.[21] The purpose of this section, however, is not to present a comprehensive description of Nationalist control over education in the 1930s; it will focus mainly on issues related to teachers' schools. By legalizing village teachers' schools and expanding all types of local teachers' schools, the central government started regulating and controlling local teachers' schools. This control included the establishment of regulations on the size of schools, financial resources, and the content of curricula, as well as requirements for moral education and standards for school facilities. The strategy for controlling teachers' schools also included setting up unified comprehensive examinations for secondary education. A teacher certification system and summer in-service training programs for schoolteachers were also revived and reinforced.

Legalizing and Standardizing Teachers' Schools

The new regime leapt into curricular reform, redefining school courses and adding a course on the "partification" of education (*dang hua jiaoyu*, later *Sanmin zhuyi jiaoyu*, lit., three people's principles education) for schools of all types and all levels. Military training was also added to the curriculum, and students were barred from participating in unauthorized political activities.[22] "Party principles" (*dangyi*) became a required course in primary and secondary schools. The local Nationalist Party branch was involved in designing and teaching the party principles courses and even in determining who taught them.[23] Only members of the Nationalist Party were considered for this delicate task.[24]

Teachers' schools were placed under government supervision. When the executive central committee of the Nationalist Party met in 1932, it decided that teachers' schools had to be established and run by the government offices that appointed the school principals. There were to be no private teachers' schools, and foreign organizations were not to meddle in teacher training.[25] Although the great majority of teachers' schools had been established under government auspices since the late Qing, a small number of privately run teachers' schools had previously been tolerated. But, for the first time, the new law ruled out this option, leaving no room for future alternative experiments in teacher training (like the Xiaozhuang school).

Financial support was another means of controlling teachers' schools. The 1932 regulations decreed that every level of government had to fund the teachers' schools under its jurisdiction. If a county could not fully provide for its teachers' schools, then the provincial government would have to open its coffers.[26] Not only would tuition be free, but a new policy encouraged teachers' schools to provide housing, books, uniforms, and fee-waivers to students.[27]

This generous policy was accompanied by a stricter teaching obligation for the schools' graduates. School authorities would confer a diploma only after a young teacher had completed a long period of teaching, typically twice the number of years spent in training. Jobs were assigned by local education departments.[28] The governments also set up regulations to prevent graduates of teachers' schools from continuing on to higher levels of education before they had fulfilled their teaching duties, giving more power

Table 5.2

Curriculum of the six-year teachers' schools* in the 1922 regulations

Subject	Name of course	Credits
Subject on society	Civic education	6
	History	14
	Geography	14
	Philosophy of life	4
	Social problems	6
Language	Chinese language	54
	Foreign languages	52
Mathematics	Arithmetic	12
	Arithmetic using the abacus	
	Algebra	8
	Geometry	5
	Solid geometry	2
	Plane trigonometry	3
	Comprehensive theory of science	12
Natural science	Biology	6
	Chemistry	6
	Physics	6
Arts	Handicrafts	8
	Drawing	8
	Music	8
Physical education	Physical education	22
	Physiological hygiene	4
Education	Introduction to education theory	4
	Introduction to psychology	2
	Educational psychology	3
	Teaching methodology	8
	Primary school management	3
	Education testing and surveys	3
	Primary school textbook study	6
	Survey course on vocational education	3
	Educational theory	3
	Practicum	20
Required credits		319
Elective course credits		11
Total credits		330

* Six-year teachers' schools enrolled graduates from six-year primary schools.

Source: Liu Wenxiu, *Zhongguo shifan jiaoyu jianshi* [A brief history of Chinese teachers' education] (Beijing: People's Education Press, 1985), 48-51.

to local educational departments to control the graduates of teachers' schools.[29] Without a diploma, it was hard for a graduate to find a job and impossible to continue studying.

The government also moved to establish a standard curriculum – one that reflected its agendas – for teachers' schools. The 1922 Educational Reform had established a curriculum for teachers' schools similar to that of regular middle schools, with the addition of several elective courses on education. This curriculum stressed Western knowledge and included little that was related to rural life (see Table 5.2). In the late 1920s, a number of village teachers' schools had developed their own curricula based on the skills needed by village teachers. For example, Xiaozhuang Experimental Village Teachers' School not only added agricultural courses but also created cooking and rural society courses. The village teachers' schools in Huangdu, Huanglu, and Baiquan also created courses to train students to do agricultural work and to work on social programs (see following section).

In 1935, the Ministry of Education issued its standard curricula for village teachers' schools, notable for the inclusion of courses on agriculture, rural economics, and irrigation (see Tables 5.3.-5.6). The publication stipulated hours of study, the syllabus, and the basic content for each course.[30] Compared to the curriculum of the six-year teachers' schools outlined in the 1922 regulations, the curricula for teachers' schools in the 1935 regulations scanted mathematics and natural science, called for no English training at all, and added military training, hygiene, and physical labor.[31] The gap between teachers' schools and regular middle schools widened – a problem that echoed the criticism of teachers' schools around 1920.

In a further effort to standardize and supervise the quality of education, the Ministry of Education decided to require all graduating students to sit for a comprehensive examination (*biye huikao*) administered by the state.[32] Anyone who failed the examination would not be granted a diploma.[33] This new requirement triggered many student protests at both middle schools and teachers' schools, and it became an important issue in the 1930s student protests. A 1936 survey showed that 54 percent of lower middle school students and 62 percent of upper middle school students opposed the comprehensive examination.[34] According to a former student at a Shanxi provincial teachers' school who participated in protests against the examination, the real motive for the difficult examinations was to oblige students to spend all of their time studying so that they had no time to join the nascent political and social movements that challenged the supremacy of the Nationalists.[35] Students who were aware of the relatively poor education available in teachers' schools (see following section) may also have viewed the examination as discriminatory.

Table 5.3

Curricula of teachers' schools in the 1932 regulations: Regular teachers' school (three year)*

Course	Weekly hours 1st year (semester) 1st	2nd	2nd year (semester) 1st	2nd	3rd year (semester) 1st	2nd	Totals
Civic education**	2	2	2	2			8
Physical education	2	2	2	2	2	2	12
Military training***	3	3					6
Military nurse training***	3	3					6
Hygienic knowledge		2					2
Chinese	4	4	5	5	3	3	24
Mathematics	3	3	4	4	2		16
Geography	3	3					6
History			4	4			8
Biology	5	4					9
Chemistry			4	4			8
Physics					4	4	8
Logic					2		2
Labour (agriculture)	3	3	2	2	2		12
Labour (handicraft)	3	3	2	2	2		12
Labour (household work)***	3	3	2	2	2		12
Drawing	2	2	2	2			8
Music	2	2	2	2	1	1	10
Educational theory	4	3					7
Educational psychology			3	3			6
Study of primary school textbooks and teaching methodology			3	3	3	3	12
Primary school management					4		4
Education testing and surveys						4	4
Educational practicum					9	12	21
Total hours each week	36	36	35	35	34	29	205

* Regular teachers' schools enrolled graduates from lower middle schools or the equivalent.

** Civic education included courses on "party principles" and "three people's principles."

*** Military training was for male students. Military nurse training and household work classes were for female students.

Source: Liu Wenxiu, *Zhongguo shifan jiaoyu jianshi* [A brief history of Chinese teachers' education] (Beijing: People's Education Press, 1985), 66-73.

Table 5.4

Curricula of teachers' schools in the 1932 regulations: Regular village teachers' school (three year)*

	Weekly hours						
	1st year (semester)		2nd year (semester)		3rd year (semester)		
Course	1st	2nd	1st	2nd	1st	2nd	Totals
Civic education**	2	2	2	2			8
Physical education	2	2	2	2	2		10
Military training***	3	3					6
Military nurse training***	3	3					6
Household work training***			3	3			6
Hygienic knowledge			1	1			2
Chinese	5	5	5	5	5	3	26
Mathematics	3	3	3	3			12
Geography	3	3					6
History			4	4			8
Biology	3	4					9
Chemistry			3	4			6
Physics					6		6
Logic	2						2
Labour (handicraft)	2	2	2	2	2	2	12
Drawing	2	2	2	2	2		10
Music	2	2	2	2	2		10
Agricultural knowledge and practice	4	4	4	4	3	3	22
Rural economy and cooperatives					3		3
Irrigation					3		3
Educational theory	3	4					7
Educational psychology			3	3			6
Study on primary school textbooks and teaching methodology			3	3	3	3	12
Primary school management						4	4
Education testing and surveys					4		4
Rural education						3	3
Educational practicum					3	18	21
Total hours each week	36	36	35	35	34	29	205

* Regular teachers' schools enrolled graduates from lower middle schools or the equivalent.

** Civic education included courses on "party principles" and "three people's principles."

*** Military training was for male students. Military nurse training and household work classes were for female students.

Source: Liu Wenxiu, *Zhongguo shifan jiaoyu jianshi* [A brief history of Chinese teachers' education] (Beijing: People's Education Press, 1985), 66-73.

Table 5.5

Curricula of teachers' schools in the 1932 regulations: Simplified teachers' school (four year)*

	Weekly hours								
	1st year		2nd year		3rd year		4th year		
Course	1	2	1	2	1	2	1	2	Totals
Civic education**	2	2	2	2	2	2	2	2	16
Physical education	2	2	2	2	2	2	2	2	16
Hygienic knowledge	2	2	1	1	1	1			8
Chinese	6	6	6	6	5	5	5	3	42
Mathematics	4	4	4	4	3	3			22
Geography	3	3	3	3					12
History			3	3	3	3			12
Botany	4	4							8
Zoology	4	4							8
Chemistry			4	4					8
Physics					4	4			8
Labour (agricultural art)					3	3	3	3	12
Labour (household work)***							3	3	6
Labour (handicraft)***	2	2	2	2	2	2	2	2	16
Drawing	2	2	2	2	2	2			12
Music	2	2	2	2	2	2	2	2	16
Educational theory			3	3					6
Educational psychology					3	3			6
Rural education and popular education				3					3
Education testing and survey								3	3
Study on primary school textbooks and teaching methodology							6	6	12
Primary school management							3		
Educational practicum						3	9	12	24
Total hours each week	33	33	34	37	32	35	35	36	275
Independent study and extracurricular activities	21	21	20	20	19	19	19	18	157

* Simplified teachers' schools enrolled graduates from six-year primary schools or the equivalent.

** Civic education included courses on "party principles" and "three people's principles."

*** In the fourth year, female students took household work class, which replaced handicraft classes.

Source: Liu Wenxiu, *Zhongguo shifan jiaoyu jianshi* [A brief history of Chinese teachers' education] (Beijing: People's Education Press, 1985), 66-73.

Table 5.6

Curricula of teachers' schools in the 1932 regulations: Simplified village teachers' school (four year)*

	Weekly hours								
	1st year		2nd year		3rd year		4th year		
Course	1	2	1	2	1	2	1	2	Totals
Civic education**	2	2	2	2	2	2	2	2	16
Physical education	2	2	2	2	2	2	2		14
Hygienic knowledge	2	2	1	1	1	1			8
Chinese	6	6	6	6	6	6	4	3	43
Mathematics	4	4	3	3	2	2	2		20
Geography	3	3	3	3					12
History	3	3	3	3					12
Botany	2	2							4
Zoology	2	2							4
Chemistry			3	3					6
Physics					3	3			6
Labour (handicraft)	2	2	2	2	2	2	1		13
Drawing	2	2	2	2	2	2	1		13
Music	2	2	2	2	2	2	1		13
Agricultural knowledge and practice	5	5	5	5	5	5	5	3	38
Irrigation					2				2
Rural economy and cooperatives							4		4
Educational theory			3	3					6
Educational psychology					3	3			6
Study on primary school textbooks and teaching methodology					3	3	4		10
Educational testing and surveys								3	3
Rural education							3		3
Primary school management							3		3
Education practicum							3	24	27
Total hours each week	37	37	37	37	35	33	35	35	286
Independent study and extracurricular activities	17	17	17	17	19	21	19	21	148

* Simplified teachers' schools enrolled graduates from six-year primary schools or the equivalent.

** Civic education included courses on "party principles" and "three people's principles."

Source: Liu Wenxiu, *Zhongguo shifan jiaoyu jianshi* [A brief history of Chinese teachers' education] (Beijing: People's Education Press, 1985), 66-73.

Testing and Reforming Primary Schoolteachers

Due to the important role of elementary school teachers in villages, the Nationalist government reinforced accrediting examinations for these teachers as a way of regulating village schools. Teacher qualifications had been established as early as the Qing but were not rigorously enforced until 1928. In 1928, the Central District of the University Council (*Zhongyang da xuequ*) disseminated guidelines for teachers' licensing examinations, and some conscientious officials began to schedule tests.[36] In 1934, the Ministry of Education issued new regulations, reinforcing the qualification examination. Before 1934, the graduates of teachers' schools did not need to take an examination to be certified teachers, and only teachers in primary schools had to be examined.[37] Due to the dearth of teachers, no regulations governed teachers at middle schools and teachers' schools, and school principals were permitted to hire teachers they believed were qualified.[38] Under the new regulation, the Ministry of Education stipulated that both graduates of teachers' schools and teachers of secondary schools should take examinations, which were to be held at least once every three years. Waivers were only given to those who had some years of teaching experience.[39]

Each province implemented these regulations at a different pace. Jiangsu, for instance, started examining its primary schoolteachers in 1928, and by 1932 had held three examinations.[40] By 1933, Shandong had held two examinations (in 1931 and 1932, respectively), and over half of its primary schoolteachers had passed.[41] In 1937, the deputy director of Henan's Bureau of Education reported that, among 34,004 schoolteachers in private lower primary schools, over 20,000 were either graduates of teachers' schools or had passed the qualification examination.[42] Other provinces lagged behind. Hunan reported in 1935 that it was making plans to administer the examination for the first time.[43]

The Ministry of Education also endeavoured to create a national standard for village primary schoolteachers by introducing various training programs. In the 1910s and 1920s, local educational associations had provided short-term summer training programs for primary schoolteachers. Most of these programs were established in economically and educationally advanced regions such as Jiangsu and Zhejiang.[44] In 1930, the ministry effectively asserted its control over these programs by announcing a plan to provide in-service training for village teachers at existing educational institutions, mainly teachers' schools.[45] Finally, the government had acknowledged the isolation of village schoolteachers and accepted responsibility for training them. Summer schools were established in each provincial capital and county seat, and special textbooks were prepared.[46] The certification examination would be waived for those who finished the required courses in these summer schools.[47] Thanks to the efforts of the Ministry of Education, this type of summer program became widespread in the 1930s.[48] Village teachers who enrolled in the summer programs might make up some of the ground they had lost to their urban counterparts. Local teachers' schools ran the enrichment programs that were generally operating at the county level.[49] These programs helped to break the isolation imposed on village schoolteachers, who soon began to build professional networks. On the other hand, these programs also brought the surveying eye of the central government closer to the village.

Teachers' Schools in the Rural Reconstruction Movement: Three Cases

The Guomindang government was intent on using the newly developed teachers' schools to control rural education and to facilitate its own domination of rural communities. At the same time, government involvement in rural education and the development of village teachers' schools chipped away at the educational idealism and social radicalism advocated by the leaders of the Xiaozhuang school. While the educators in some village teachers' schools tried to maintain their educational idealism, they had to compromise with the government by reining in their social programs and reworking them to suit the Nationalists. Some schools actively facilitated the penetration of administrative power into rural communities through their social programs, but the majority of village teachers' schools probably limited their rural programs to the classroom.

Rural Education and Reconstruction in the 1930s: A Brief Review

During the late 1920s and early 1930s, most rural education and reconstruction projects were launched by social organizations. Besides the Chinese National Association for the Advancement of Education, which established Xiaozhuang Experimental Village Teachers' School, another leading group was the Chinese National Association for the Promotion of Mass Education, which established its experiment in Dingxian County, Hebei, in 1926 (see Chapter 4). That same year, the Chinese Vocational Education Association also initiated an educational program in several townships of Kunshan County, Jiangsu.[50] The brunt of the program was agricultural production, education, and village administration.

Most of these programs opened by addressing rural illiteracy, then gradually became involved in community life and introduced social reform programs. Unlike the Xiaozhuang experiment, in which the school itself functioned as an instrument to direct social reform and to train students from outside as village leaders, the Dingxian project promoted reform by recruiting local peasants into commoners' schools (*minzhong xuexiao*) and organizing the graduates from these schools to serve as local leaders in reform activities.[51] Like Dingxian, the program in Kunshan also worked by attracting peasants into reform projects by training them to participate in reform activities. Primary school principals were assigned the responsibility of promoting and directing social reform programs. The experimental regions were normally set up around the community primary schools.[52] In their early years, Dingxian, Kunshan, and Xiaozhuang were distinctive variations of school-centred rural reconstruction.

Some of China's infamous warlords, in exchange for control of their provinces, fostered important rural education projects even after they nominally surrendered to the central government after 1929. As governor of Shanxi, Yan Xishan, a former warlord, assumed responsibility for rural education projects as part of a comprehensive program to extend the provincial government into the villages.[53] Shandong's governor Han Fuqu, another former warlord general, supported Liang Shuming and, as part of broader social experiments, established schools in Zouping County. Having studied Xiaozhuang and other programs, Liang developed an innovative model of rural reconstruction in which schools carried out both governmental and pedagogical functions. "Uniting government and school" (*zheng jiao he yi*) was also adopted in other regions and influenced the way village teachers' schools developed their social activities.[54] In the above rural reconstruction programs, teachers' schools (except Xiaozhuang) generally did not play a big part; instead, local primary schools were at the centre.

During the last years of the 1920s and the early 1930s, the example set in Xiaozhuang was widely acknowledged by activists in the rural education movement, and Xiaozhuang's practices were spread by graduates and former faculty members after the school was closed. For instance, Cheng Benhai, an early graduate and disciple of Tao Xingzhi, established Longchuan Village Teachers' School in Guangdong to further the Xiaozhuang experiment, and he eventually developed his own approach to training village teachers.[55] Another former Xiaozhuang student, Cao Zhenqiu, established the Xianghu Village Teachers' School in Zhejiang after graduating in 1928.[56] A pair of former Xiaozhuang instructors, Yang Xiaochun and Zhang Zongxiang, worked for Liang Shuming in Shandong. Many of the new village teachers' schools – such as Jimei Village Teachers' School in Fujian, Huining Village Teachers' School in Guangxi, Zouping Simplified Village Teachers' School in Shandong[57] – were committed to vigorous social reform programs.

The news of these ambitious programs was not warmly received in Nanjing. Just as the Nationalists were investing great energy in fortifying their urban power base, these programs forced them to pay attention to rural society.

The Xianghu School in Zhejiang: The Turn to Moderation

When he heard that a new village teachers' school would be opened by the provincial government at a location within Xiaoshan County in Zhejiang, Tao Xingzhi recommended one of his best students, Cao Zhenqiu, to serve as principal, and a number of Xiaozhuang graduates went to Xianghu to teach. One month after it opened in 1928, Tao Xingzhi visited the school to promote his idea of teaching-learning-doing in one; a glance at the school curriculum, extracurricular programs, and outreach programs shows that it was essentially Tao's creation.[58] Soon Xianghu Village Teachers' School was being praised as "Zhejiang's Xiaozhuang" (*Zhejiang de Xiaozhuang*).[59] In 1930, when the Xiaozhuang school was closed and students and teachers associated with it faced serious political pressure, Cao Zhenqiu left Xianghu because of illness. Over the next two years, the Xianghu School went through three principals. When Jin Haiguan, a moderate educational reformer, was appointed as principal in 1932, he quickly steered the school in a less radical direction.[60]

Jin's moderate policies were, in part, a reflection of his own educational beliefs and, in part, a tactic aimed at protecting the school from suffering a fate like that of Xiaozhuang. In his inaugural speech, he declared that education should meet social needs and that the school curriculum should epitomize this need. In this sense, Jin was a true Deweyan. He emphasized that the Xianghu school, in contrast to the Xiaozhuang school, was a government institution and, therefore, should implement the official standards set for regular teachers' schools. He emphasized that the Xianghu school must learn a lesson from the radical activities of the Xiaozhuang school in order to avoid being closed down.[61]

In 1932, Jin proposed a "doing-learning-teaching work-study program" (*zuo xue jiao gong xue zhi*). The school's curriculum continued to exhibit similarities to that of the Xiaozhuang school, but, unlike at Xiaozhuang, all these programs were practised in the classroom and within the school. Agricultural knowledge and skills were included in classroom instruction, students were required to engage in physical labour, and they were trained to understand work and life in rural communities.[62]

Compared to Xiaozhuang, the Xianghu School ran a limited number of social programs. It realized that Xiaozhuang's expectation that its students would live a genuine peasant life and be village leaders was unrealistic; the school leader therefore changed this policy. The school selected a group of young peasants from nearby villages and trained them in a special program, hoping that they could perpetuate rural reform in the villages.[63] The Xianghu school's social programs concentrated on education, expanding local primary schools and common people's schools, introducing new farming skills, assisting peasants in organizing cooperatives, and improving public health and personal hygiene. The record does not show any involvement in local administration, self-governing bodies, or defence organizations.[64]

The Huangdu School in Jiangsu: A Cooperative Model

Originally a branch of the Jiangsu provincial teachers' school, Huangdu Village Teachers' School became an independent school after 1930. Modelled after the Xiaozhuang school, it launched a series of social reform programs and implemented a curriculum to match. Like the Xiaozhuang school, the goal of the school's leaders was to produce future village leaders.[65]

To foster leadership, the school offered courses such as organizing cooperatives, village education, rural society, agriculture, and handicrafts. Village education covered the process of setting up village elementary schools, peasant education halls, and mass schools. Agriculture classes introduced students to both basic agricultural knowledge and advanced farming technology. Other courses trained students to organize cooperatives, self-defence squads, village clinics, and self-governing bodies as well as to promote improved seeds, road repairs, and public health and personal hygiene. As part of a broad campaign to win the support of local peasants, the school launched a road-building project, organizing over a thousand villagers to build twenty miles of roads and seven bridges. Under the direction of the school, many villages established cooperatives in which villagers saved money, applied for loans, and jointly bought seeds, fertilizer, and large farming tools. Teachers trained and supervised the peasants who operated the cooperatives. The school, in cooperation with Jinling Agricultural College, introduced better seeds and advanced farming technology, and students were sent out to teach farmers how to use them. The school opened a clinic and a pharmacy, providing basic medical care and less expensive medicine. Self-governing organizations were also set up, with an elementary schoolteacher serving as the director of each village's organization.

But the state had its eye on these schools and soon moved to rein in certain excesses. For a period in the early 1930s, the Huangdu school fearlessly pressed on with its specially designed courses for social programs, but it then began to encounter the forces of educational standardization. As a provincial government school, it had to adopt the Ministry of Education's mandatory curriculum. This would make it impossible to continue with its own programs for training village teachers to be community leaders, the legacy of Xiaozhuang. The leaders of the school complained, but they had to yield.

On the other hand, as the Nationalist local party branch expanded its activities, the school gradually withdrew its presence in local society. When the Nationalist government extended its power into this region, the local branch of the party was given the task of building the county "centre for peasant education." The assignment of the centre was similar to that of the school's social program, including promoting literacy as well as advanced farming technology and grain seeds, helping peasants run cooperatives, improving rural hygiene, and developing self-governing organizations. But now the Huangdu school was limited to playing a subsidiary role, simply sending students periodically to assist the Guomindang county branch. As students grew increasingly busy in the classroom with the nationally mandated curriculum, the mark of the central government became increasingly visible in the fields and villages.

Baiquan Village Teachers' School in Henan: A Provincial Government Project

In 1931, a provincial teachers' school was relocated from the city of Kaifeng, then capital of Henan Province, to the town of Baiquan (*Baiquan Xiang*) in Hui County by order of the provincial government, becoming Baiquan Village Teachers' School. This was a provincial government experimental program for rural reconstruction. The Baiquan school began by establishing an adult school, an experimental elementary school, a teaching farm, and a hospital. It then expanded, with the support of the county government and its education staff, to seven more townships, creating an "experimental region" (*shiyan qu*) in 1933.[66]

A believer in "uniting government and school," the principal of the Baiquan school, Li Zhenyun, became the head of the experimental region. Radiating from the teachers' school was a network of primary schools, one in each township (*xiang*), which also carried out local administrative functions. Li reorganized the town schools into central primary schools, appointing new principals who would run them and assist Principal Li in directing student teachers from the Baiquan school, who worked in villages and carried out village reconstruction projects.[67] The principals of primary schools were in charge of both education and administration in the villages in which they were residing. The village school came to be the centre of various reconstruction programs in the community.[68]

Through the reorganized village primary schools, the Baiquan school flexed its new administrative muscle, organizing cooperatives and training village leaders. The point was to institutionalize the reformist spirit among the local people. According to the school's plan, all children in the experimental region were to receive four years of education. Over two-thirds of male adults were also to receive four years of education, and one in five was to study for six years. Of female adults, three-fifths were to receive four years of education or training in household management (*jiashi*).[69]

The school's leaders hoped to reform political, economic, and social customs. They planned to first conduct surveys that would give them a detailed picture of local population, land ownership, and social organizations. They wanted to educate the locals about their rights and the country's political system, and they scheduled the establishment of a complete self-governing organization in each township based on the will of the majority. Economic goals included persuading over 80 percent of families to use improved agricultural technology and engage in handicraft production as well as convincing 60 percent of families to join the cooperatives, which could eliminate usury and enable villagers to be economically self-reliant. Village leaders would be trained, opium use would be halted, feet would be unbound, vagrants would be educated and put to work, and healthy leisure activities would replace gambling and dissipation.[70] Unfortunately, limited sources restricted my evaluation of the results of these programs.

Besides the Henan provincial government, which used Baiquan village teachers' school to implement its rural reconstruction program, government authorities in Shandong, Jiangxi, and Hunan launched similar projects through village teachers' schools. In 1933, by government order, Jiangxi Provincial Middle School Number Four became a village teachers' school. It was relocated to a town in Jiujiang County and assigned to work with an administrative ward (*qu*), which became the formal extent of the school's reform activities. The experiment followed the "uniting government and school" model, in which the principal of the Jiujiang Village Teachers' School was also head of the ward, in charge of administrative and school affairs. The ward's functions were integrated into the school's activities, and teachers and students worked to promote these programs. The school also organized a committee to advance rural reconstruction (*Xiangcun jianshe cujin weiyuanhui*), mobilizing local elites to join the reconstruction programs.[71] A school leader announced that the teachers' school would use what had been learned from the experimental region to propel the restructuring of the countryside.[72] The school's programs focused on four aspects of rural life: administration, education, peasant livelihood, and public health and personal hygiene (*guan, jiao, yang, wei*).[73] It is evident in this case that village teachers' schools had become a means of extending government influence.

The idea that schools would be headquarters for local governance was widely adopted. In 1936, Hunan provincial authorities invited teachers and staff from Yan Yangchu's Dingxian project to duplicate it at Hengshan Village Teachers' School and several other teachers' schools.[74] In 1935, Huanglu Provincial Village Teachers' School in Anhui, located in Huanglu township in Chaoxian county, also operated a rural reconstruction program. The school established the Huanglu Rural Reconstruction Experimental Region (*Huanglu nongcun jianshe shiyan qu*), which was divided into eleven subregions. In each subregion, primary schoolteachers were designated to work as the directors of the reform projects. The teachers' school, as the leading force in the experimental region, was in charge of the reform. The school proposed a series of reform projects, including planting trees; improving farming technology; building irrigation systems; promoting citizenry education; improving public health and personal hygiene; organizing cooperatives; building commoners' schools for adult male peasants, women, and children; and banning opium and gambling. In order to involve the locals in the reform program, the school tried to integrate itself into the community, participating in village events and helping villagers. When a disastrous drought hit the region in July, the school mobilized students to work in the fields with peasants, helping the locals dig wells and ponds to relieve the situation. After the drought, the school used the village primary schools under its control to publicize the measures for drought relief as well as to train village youth to help with the reform projects.[75] By linking teachers' schools with local rural reconstruction projects, the Nationalists were able to reshape rural communities and to extend their power at the county level.

Evaluation of Village Teachers' Schools in the 1930s

In general, the extension of state power into local communities was seen as an exercise in handling subcounty administrative units and controlling the power of local elites.[76] Chauncey regards Nationalist state power as an intrusive and predatory force, harmful to local educational organizations and a profound threat to the autonomy of local elites.[77] But Curran believes that state programs sometimes benefited local communities and that elites welcomed the state's penetration into local society if it helped them to extend their influence.[78] Culp's research demonstrates that the dynamics between the state and local elites were, in fact, determined by socioeconomic conditions, and local leaders had the flexibility to change their role and to work with the state if struck by "a new impulse."[79]

In most studies of state power in local communities, the focus has been on primary schools as they were under the supervision of regional educational associations dominated by local elites. Such studies are particularly well suited to the model of state versus society, and they consistently show that the Nationalist government snatched power from the locals through power penetration. In contrast to primary schools, rural teachers' schools, being secondary schools, were under the direction of provincial and county authorities and, as outsiders, had complex relations with the state and local communities.

One important reason that teachers' schools were able to play an important role in reconstructing rural society in the 1930s had to do with their location. Previously, most provincial teachers' schools had been located either in provincial capitals or in subprovincial municipalities, which had often been prefectural centres during the imperial time. In the 1930s, decisions about where to build teachers' schools grew out of the attempt to balance educational resources and to extend state power into rural areas. Many provincial village teachers' schools – for example, Xianghu in Zhejiang; Huangdu, Jieshou, Qixiashan, and Wujiang in Jiangsu; Huanglu in Anhui; Baiquan in Henan; and Jiujiang and Nanchang in Jiangxi – were located not in county seats but in townships, and their rural education and social reform experiments were carried out in neighbouring villages. For most provinces, it was almost a rule that only the teachers' school number one was located in the capital; the rest were located in counties. When encountering regions whose county seats had their own teachers' schools, the newly emerging provincial teachers' schools or newly established village (simplified) teachers' schools had no choice but to set up outside county seats.

In the twentieth century, Chinese villages had to face state penetration, and the "cultural nexus" of the villages disintegrated under the pressure of state-building programs, as Duara's research has shown.[80] The establishment of elementary schools in villages definitely had a strong impact on the local cultural nexus. As outsiders, the faculty, staff, and students of village teachers' schools were different from those of the primary schools that had been founded by local elites. The principals of all teachers' schools, typically educators who had acquired some renown in the province, were appointed by either provincial or county authorities (depending on whether they were provincial or county schools) and then began the delicate task of reconciling the agendas of both provincial and county education bureaus and local communities. The majority of teachers and administrators in secondary teachers' schools were outsiders with no historical, economic, or genealogical involvement with local communities. Most students of teachers' schools were drawn from the provincial or county areas.[81] The financing of primary schools came from redistributing local resources, but the funding of teachers' schools came directly from provincial or county revenue. Local interests tended to determine whether the staff of local primary schools, who almost invariably came from the area, resisted or cooperated with state penetration, while the staff of teachers' schools were generally directly supervised by the government and very often carried out its agenda. At the same time, the radical educators who flocked to teachers' schools – one thinks of the veterans of the Xiaozhuang school – often tried to maintain their ideals of social reform, which sometimes conflicted with the government's agenda. Moreover, since the teachers and students had to work and live face to face with the villagers, they sometimes had to compromise with the immediate needs of local people and work hard to be welcomed in the villages in which they resided. In terms of the network of villages, it was very likely that these teachers' schools stood somewhere between being resisted by or excluded from local society, breaking down the local "cultural nexus," and joining (or using) that nexus to further their social reform agenda.[82] This would create a very complicated relationship between the state they represented and the locality in which they resided.

If we consider the extension of bureaucracy and the reinforcement of police power and fiscal control to be the "hard," or coercive, side of the Nationalist state-building project in rural areas during the Nanjing Decade, then rural education and reconstruction programs were the "soft," or constructive, side. The government attempted to expand its influence in rural areas by reshaping village teachers' schools and assigning to them an official role in reconstruction. The activities of teachers' schools seemed to be a means of bridging state and society rather than of intensifying the clash and division between the two. More detailed studies will shed light on how these schools helped push the state agenda, how they dealt with specific problems in local communities, how local people responded, and how effective these programs were.

Why did the government rural reconstruction programs that were conducted via teachers' schools seem fruitless? The reasons are manifold. The first was the length of these programs. Although rural reconstruction projects were widely and actively promoted through village teachers' schools, most of them were pursued for only a few years. In 1937, the Japanese invasion put a halt to nearly every rural reform project.

There were problems with launching the rural reconstruction program through village teachers' schools. The government-run schools, unless presided over by Tao's followers, made little effort to make modern schools fit the needs of rural society; many of the government-run village teachers' schools clung to the classic curriculum and pedagogy derived from the urban environment. This tendency was abetted by standardized examinations and school regulations. In the move from middle school to village teachers' school, the wholesale transformation required to fulfill Tao's vision was almost never attempted: the addition of a few courses on agriculture was the typical token effort. Some provincial governments only paid lip service to helping their schools. In 1931, Sichuan's provincial government relocated its urban teachers' schools to the countryside, where they were converted into village teachers' schools. The provincial government's regulations for these converted schools, however, stipulated that "besides adding a course on 'party principles,' village teachers' schools should maintain the curriculum of the regular teachers' schools."[83] These village teachers' schools were thus indistinguishable from urban-oriented teachers' schools.

Efforts to create a national network of village teachers' schools also encountered persistent problems, many of which were observed by commentators of the time. In 1936, a rural educator investigated fourteen provincial village teachers' schools in six provinces (Jiangsu, Jiangxi, Shandong, Fujian, Zhejiang, and Hubei), concluding that the curriculum of village teachers' schools did little to prepare teachers for the tasks they would face in rural China. General courses such as language, civic training, party principles, social analysis, natural science, mathematics, physical and military training, and music and drawing made up about 83 percent of the curriculum. In contrast, the critical courses for village teachers, such as rural organization, rural economy, agriculture, and so forth, made up only 8 percent to 12 percent of the curriculum. Some schools did not even have these types of courses. Among the schools surveyed, the Huangdu school was the only exception; there, courses pertaining to rural society made up about 34 percent of the curriculum.[84] In another article, Jin Zhiwen points out that the agriculture courses designed by the Ministry of Education for village teachers' schools were inadequate. In particular, village teachers needed to be able to promote advanced farming technology, but no such course was mentioned in the official curriculum.[85] Jin also points out that most agricultural textbooks emphasized theory and lacked practical instruction.[86]

Finance was another persistent problem for village teachers' schools. In 1930, there were 82,809 students in teachers' schools, and these schools received 8,419,140 yuan in annual funding, or 102 yuan per student. Regular middle schools had 396,948 students and 35,331,921 yuan in funding, or 89 yuan per student.[87] But this preliminary comparison is deeply misleading. Considering that, unlike regular middle schools, teachers' schools were all free and provided students with board and books, the cost per student to the state was much greater than it was in regular middle schools, which were all supplemented by students' tuition fees. This meant that the money that went to teacher salaries, equipment, and school facilities was pitifully inadequate, and complaints were routine. The leaders of the Huangdu school complained that a lack of money precluded a range of necessary activities.[88] Even the leader of the Baiquan school, a provincial government project, grumbled that the school's greatest problem was inadequate funding.[89] Henan's educational inspectors reported that financial shortfalls meant that many teachers' schools were comprised of shabby, dark buildings or ramshackle temples.[90] Provincial inspectors in Hebei were shocked by the conditions of the village teachers' schools they visited. While budgetary difficulties meant that hiring good teachers was challenging, many other problems plagued the schools. Due to a shortage of qualified students, schools in some places had to lower their admissions standards. Even as the number of teachers' schools increased, school facilities, teachers, and students failed to meet the standards established by the Ministry of Education. Had the Ministry of Education attempted to enforce its standards, the inspectors lamented, most village teachers' schools would have had to shut their doors.[91]

Another trend disturbed rural educators during the 1930s. The original purpose of establishing village teachers' schools in the countryside had been to train youth to serve rural communities. However, by the mid-1930s, educators found that many students regarded village teachers' schools as a route out of the village. At the second annual meeting of the Shandong Provincial Rural Education Conference, held in Jinan in 1935, participants asked whether village teachers' schools were really solving the problem of insufficient qualified teachers in rural areas. Before 1930, urban schools had drawn youth out of rural communities, never to return to their home villages; could village teachers' schools really convince bright young people to stay in their villages?[92] One educator, Lin Zhongda, pessimistically declared that no existing type of education, not even village teachers' schools, could accomplish the goal of improving rural education and furthering rural reform. He regretfully noted that the "motives of many youths who applied to village teachers' schools were determined by their economic condition. They were not really attracted by the rural reconstruction movement. Once they left the schools, they tried immediately to get to the city."[93] As the following chapter shows, this statement exaggerated the problem, but there can be no doubt that schools in remote areas were doing little to bring meaningful change to rural society.

Progress in the Hinterlands: Women's Teachers' Schools in the 1930s

While much of the education system remained a male preserve, women's education developed rapidly during the 1930s, largely in the field of teacher training. The regulations pertaining to teachers' schools issued in 1932 instructed each teachers' school district of each province to build at least one female normal school.[94] Urban intellectuals participated in a public discussion that succeeded in refashioning the concept of female education. Although the idea of training "virtuous wives and good mothers" continued to influence educational practice into the 1930s, many lashed out at that patriarchal image and proposed a new image – that of the "educated woman" (*zhishi funü*). A woman teacher could excel without ever being a wife or mother, many believed, and ideas about female independence and professionalization travelled from the urban coast to inland communities, crossing the boundary of teaching and extending to other professions.

Rethinking Women's Education

Although, under the 1922 educational system, the purpose of women's education was defined as "developing personality" – a fairly enlightened guideline that incorporated much of what we would call a liberal arts curriculum – most schools ended up emphasizing household management and other "feminine courses." These urban-centred middle schools for girls were aimed at preparing middle-class housewives for domestic duties, as though they would never emerge from the inner chamber.[95]

In the 1930s, some radical educators started questioning the purpose of women's education. A watershed was a special issue of *Women's Monthly* (*Nüzi yuekan*) that was devoted to women's education and that was published in January 1934. An article by Li Nai divided the development of modern women's education into three stages: pre-May Fourth, liberalism, and dilettantism. The first stage, for which Li proposed the label "attachmentism" (*fuyong zhuyi*), had been devoted to preparing women to be good mothers and virtuous wives: it would *attach* women to their families and to men. The second stage, liberalism (*ziyou zhuyi*), from the May Fourth Movement to the late 1920s, had witnessed women's fight for freedom and social equality but ended with the decline of the May Fourth spirit.

The third stage, typifying the present, could be called dilettantism (*langman de wu mudi zhuyi*) because most women had no sense of independence and wanted to depend on men.[96] Another article by Wei Xixun labelled the principle of virtuous wives and good mothers "feudalistic." Wei pointed out that the serious problems facing women's education turned women into consumers rather than producers. Women's schools were concentrated in cities and were completely isolated from social movements. All girls learned were the fine points of the marriage market and how to compete with each other in the consumption of luxury goods; they were, said Wei, nothing but modern "courtesans" and "socialized flowers" (*jiaoji hua*).[97]

An article that appeared two years later in another women's magazine of the day, *Women's Life* (*Funü shenghuo*), also criticized the current approach to women's education. The author, Bi Yao, divided the history of modern women's education into four periods: the first period (1844-1911) was dominated by "education for nuns" (*nigu jiaoyu*), satisfying the requirements of the early missionary schools; the second period (1911-19) was dominated by "education for wives" (*qizi jiaoyu*), satisfying the demands of the virtuous wives and good mothers period; the third period (1919-27) was dominated by "education for ladies" (*nüshi jiaoyu*), satisfying the ambitions of bourgeois women for educational and social equality; while the fourth period was dominated by "education for concubines" (*shiji jiaoyu*), satisfying those who believed that women should be taught how to please men rather provided with practical knowledge that would make them independent. Like Wei Xixun, Bi Yao bitterly complained that modern schoolgirls dreamed only of acquiring fashionable clothing and make-up, spending their time flirting and dancing so that they could be more attractive to men. This type of education, the training of concubines and courtesans, could only be despised by the people.[98]

Countless authors proposed new educational goals and methods. Under the influence of populism and socialism, writers proposed fostering women's independence, their productive capacity, and their involvement in social work. Most important, many felt that women's education should serve both urban and rural working women.[99] Agricultural schools ought to be built for rural women and industrial schools for urban women; medical schools should be opened to women; and night schools offering a variety of programs ought to be opened to women of all ages and backgrounds. At the same time, women's education was to be integrated with social reform programs that would focus on rescuing female beggars and child brides, organizing women's clubs, assisting oppressed women, and so on.[100]

The rise of the rural reconstruction movement drew the attention of intellectuals and ambitious educators to the fate of rural women. As more articles about education appeared in women's popular magazines, the subject of rural women's education came up with increasing frequency. One writer said that education should not be the exclusive privilege of the bourgeoisie: educated rural women would be more likely than would their illiterate sisters to become hard working and independent.[101] From January to June 1934, *Women's Monthly* published a series of articles on the lives of women in inland cities, towns, and villages. Reporters visited the landlocked provinces of Sichuan and Yunnan as well as Lanzhou in Gansu, Changshu and Suzhou in Jiangsu, Beijiang and Lianxian in Guangdong, Cixian in Hebei, and Pinghu in Zhejiang.[102] The articles reported on the lives of concubines, maids, women labourers, female students, teachers, and secretaries. They lingered on the lives of rural women, describing the difficulties of poverty, unending labour, patriarchy, and heavy taxation.

Women's Monthly published an article that addressed the theory and practice of educating rural women. Rural women were described as bereft of opportunities for education and work, as lacking proper recreation and social solidarity, and as ignorant of science and hygiene. But the author also praised rural women for their traditional virtues: assiduity, sincerity, strict morality, and obedience. A series of recommendations included vocational, scientific, and citizen training as well as mechanisms to encourage healthy recreation while preserving traditional virtues.[103] A subsequent article in *Women's Life* suggested that rural women's education start with basic reading skills, which could then be applied to social reform programs. These programs should be the result of a collaboration among women's organizations, local educational administrations, and popular schools; for the best results, female teachers should be hired.[104] The authors and readers of these articles were no doubt urban bourgeois intellectuals, but they reflected a changing attitude towards female education. As the Nationalist government moved to reform rural education, it is clear that such voices were not ignored.

Women's Normal Schools in Provinces and Counties

From the government's announcement of a new plan for women's education in 1930, secondary-level women's teachers' schools began to appear in rural areas. In that year, Henan had one provincial female teachers' school and seven such schools at the county level (out of forty-five counties). Altogether there were 345 students in these seven schools; young women also attended coeducational programs in two more county teachers' schools. Henan had no regular women's middle school and only one female vocational school with forty-three students.[105] This meant that virtually the only secondary schools women could attend in their local counties were female teachers' schools.

Female education was also relatively advanced in Hebei, which in 1933 had fourteen provincial teachers' schools, of which one was a women's teachers' school and four were coeducational. Among 130 counties, ninety-nine had established teachers' schools and seventeen had both male and female schools.[106] In Guangdong, the overall proportion of female students in teachers' schools in 1934 (35 percent) was much higher than it was in regular middle schools (14 percent to 17 percent) and vocational schools (27 percent). In 1931, girls made up 82 percent of the students in Fujian's eight normal schools.[107]

Coeducation began to take great strides in the 1930s, and schools opened not only in big cities but also at the county level: coeducational teachers' schools were particularly common. In Jiangsu, most secondary schools placed males and females in the same classroom, as did most provincial teachers' schools. Jiangsu had one provincial women's teachers' school, and of its six provincial teachers' schools and six provincial village teachers' schools at least ten were coeducational. The province also had forty-three county teachers' schools as well as an unknown number of county-run village teachers' schools.[108] Of Jiangsu's sixty-one counties, three had women's teachers' schools, and a number of county middle schools had female teacher training programs; at least ten county teachers' schools were coeducational.[109] At least three of Shandong's county village teachers' schools (Tancheng, Laiyang, and Shouzhang) were coeducational in 1936 and 1937, though female students were a minority.[110]

In the northwestern province of Gansu, women's normal schools were the only secondary schools open to women. As of 1936, Gansu had no women's regular middle schools and no coeducational middle schools. But it had four women's teachers' schools, one women's vocational school, and one nursing school for women. In addition, several teachers' schools also established women's teacher training programs. Of the four women's teachers' schools, one was a provincial school, and the remaining three were county schools. In the entire province, there were only 334 female secondary students.[111] Though the figures were small, it is significant that even in a remote and backward province like Gansu, female education was reaching the county level through teachers' schools.

Amid the popular education and rural reconstruction movements, schools run by provincial and county officials that prepared women to teach not only provided female teachers to local communities but also played an active role in local popular education. For instance, in 1931, Shandong Provincial Women's Normal School Number One (*Shandong shengli di yi nüzi shifan xuexiao*) had both lower and higher sections, an attached primary school, a kindergarten, and an attached commoners' school (*minzhong xuexiao*).[112] The lower section provided regular middle school courses, while the upper section comprised the teacher training program. The school also offered a special program for those who planned to teach physical education, music, or art in primary and secondary schools.

As the most prominent secondary school for women in the province, Shandong Number One had 316 boarding students, with 164 in the lower section and 152 in the teacher training program. Only thirty of these were from outside of the province, the rest being from seventy-three different counties. The school principal, Wang Baolian, stated in the preface of the school brochure that the school had graduated over 1,000 students since its foundation in the early Republican era, most of whom had gone on to teach in Shandong. Based on incomplete data, of the 601 graduates who passed through the school between 1918 and 1930, 181 went on to work in local educational institutions, nineteen worked in government, four became doctors, and one went into business. Of the twenty-seven who continued their studies beyond the secondary level, five went overseas to study and five became college professors.[113] The school had trained women who went on to serve their country and province as teachers, principals, doctors, and government agents.

Shandong Provincial Women's Normal School Number One, located in Jinan, the provincial capital, depended on the largesse of the provincial government and offered symbolic repayment by aligning itself with the dominant political party. During the warlord period, the school received limited financial support from the local government, scraping by on less than 40,000 yuan annually until 1929. After that time, the provincial government increased the funding for the school, and it received 70,000 yuan in 1931. The government got what it paid for: more than three-quarters of the students were registered members of the Nationalist Party – quite different from the case of the men's normal school, as we shall see in the following chapter. Considering the age range of the students (thirteen to thirty-four), it is possible that almost every student who could join the Nationalist Party did so.[114] In 1931, in response to the government's call for popularizing education, the school built an attached commoners' school and recruited students from poor families. As the mother school, the teachers' school raised money from its own students for the new school and also provided it with textbooks, teaching material, and equipment. In their spare time, students from the teachers' school took turns handling the commoners' school's administrative and teaching duties.

Students also participated in the training program for rural reconstruction. As part of its support for Liang Shuming's rural reform project, the provincial government required all male graduates of provincial teachers' schools to undergo special training at Liang's rural reconstruction institute before doing a stint of work for Liang. In 1935, students from two provincial female normal schools successfully appealed to the provincial authorities for the right to equal participation in Liang's program. They travelled to the countryside, where they lived with peasants while teaching women and organizing them to participate in social activities in Zouping County. Although the hardships of rural life drove half of this group back to the city within two months, about sixty completed five months of training and work.[115] Unfortunately, due to insufficient materials, I can find no further information on the activities of these students.

Women Students and Women Teachers: Opportunities and Pressures

Although female white-collar employees began to appear in Shanghai in the 1930s, in inland cities and towns and in rural communities everywhere, virtually the only modern profession available to women was teaching. Even in the wealthy city of Suzhou, the first choice of jobs for most educated women was primary schoolteacher, while the second was nurse.[116] Most people had come to regard teaching as a "respectable and decent profession" for educated women.[117]

In the 1920s and the 1930s, most students in both women's middle schools and women's teachers' schools came from middle-class families. This was the case in coastal cities and in inland areas such as Sichuan and Yunnan.[118] Among the students at Shandong Provincial Women's Normal School Number One, seventy-two were the children of farmers, seventy-one of teachers, and fifty-three of government officials, while thirty-seven were from wealthy, non-working families (*fuxian*). The rest included fifty-five from merchant families and three from philanthropic and religious families.[119] As these young women came to realize that the new world being created in urban China allowed them a great deal of freedom and independence, conflicts between their wishes and their family's became a major source of discontent.[120] Becoming teachers enabled women to escape family pressure and to begin to construct their own lives.[121] One student in a teachers' school near Shanghai told visitors that her wealthy family had wanted her to stay in their provincial home, playing the part of a cosseted female (*xiaojie*); but she refused to live such a life,[122] choosing to flee her hometown and to enter a teachers' school. During the course of her studies, she lived on the income she earned as a private tutor.[123] Schools provided one of the wedges that women drove into the antiquated system, opening up spaces that enabled them to squeeze out of social positions they could no longer bear.

Teaching not only provided financial and social independence for a group of educated women but was also a path to other fields. The experience of Lu Yin (1895-1934) suggests how some women's lives changed from the 1910s to the 1930s. Lu was the daughter of an impoverished official; after her father's death, life became very trying. She was not her mother's favourite child and felt very repressed at home. School gave her a chance to escape family pressure. She graduated from a teachers' school and worked briefly at a women's middle school. In order to save money for college, she left

Beijing and travelled alone to Anhui to take a job there; later, she worked as a teacher in Henan. She entered college in 1919. Inspired by the New Culture Movement and the new literature spilling from the presses, she began to write. Until her death in 1934, she worked as a teacher while writing essays and stories, and she served as the editor of a literary magazine.[124]

However, it was not easy for women to pursue teaching careers in the 1930s. They faced the same problems as did their male colleagues, including low pay, a heavy workload, insecure employment, and the risk of pulmonary tuberculosis – an occupational disease thought to be associated with chalk dust.[125] Many also had children and took on the large share of female domestic responsibilities that comes with patriarchy. They usually received lower pay than their male colleagues and were more likely to be fired. As education at the secondary and tertiary levels dramatically expanded in the 1930s, the competition for teaching positions in cities and towns intensified. According to a 1933 report from Sichuan, for instance, many counties had women's middle schools or teachers' schools, but graduates found it very hard to find work as primary schoolteachers (we can assume that the reference was to *urban* primary schools).[126] Even those who had work fretted about the prospect of unemployment.[127] This is a salient theme in several of the short stories that appeared in women's magazines at that time: fear of unemployment, workplace harassment, and squalid schools.[128] While women continued to turn to teaching as one of the very few ways to assert their independence and to play a part in shaping society, teachers' schools constituted a much needed bridge between women and other professions (e.g., writing, editing, journalism, the arts, and the law), carving out more space for them in the public domain.

6
Transforming the Revolution: Social and Political Aspects of Teachers' Schools, 1930-37

A remarkable success story, the Nationalist educational reforms of the Nanjing Decade (1927-37) provided children and youth with the chance to attend modern schools. However, few scholars appreciate this irony: the part many chose to play was in the ranks of the Chinese Communist Party. While the Nationalists knew that an educated mass would constitute a more easily mobilized populace, they did not anticipate that their greatest political rivals would be the ones doing the mobilizing.

During those ten years, the Nationalists saw to it that the number of tertiary and secondary schools doubled, as did the number of students, while the number of teachers' schools tripled. China's various institutions of higher learning – medical colleges, commercial colleges, engineering colleges, comprehensive universities – increased from forty-four in 1927 to eighty-five in 1930 to 108 in 1936.[1] The number of students in higher education increased from 25,198 in 1928 to 41,922 in 1936. At the same time, secondary education also grew rapidly. The number of regular middle schools more than doubled, from 954 in 1928 to 1,956 in 1936. The number of students increased from 188,700 in 1928 to 482,522 in 1936. Teachers' schools at the secondary level experienced even more rapid development, increasing from 236 schools with 29,470 students in 1928 to 814 schools with 87,902 students in 1936.[2]

The rapid growth of education in the 1930s also revealed an imbalance in the development of secondary and tertiary education, resulting in the concentration of regular middle schools and colleges in coastal and urban areas. As mentioned in the previous chapter, the Nationalist planners hoped teachers' schools would help the state to penetrate rural communities and transform a group of brilliant rural youths into state-controlled personnel. The special policy of the Nationalist government (GMD) on developing local teachers' schools extended secondary education into rural areas, and the free-tuition policy of teachers' schools attracted a large number of village teenagers from families of relatively moderate means. The appearance of rural youth in modern educational institutions led to increasing numbers of petty-intellectuals who became a new force on the political stage in 1930's China. The emergence of this group of youth redrew China's political map and led to the re-emergence of Chinese Communism. Local teachers' schools, which were attended by rural students, became ideal recruiting centres for Communist organizers. Especially in Jiangxi, teachers' schools became revolutionary training centres.

Rethinking the Relations between Modern Education and the Communist Revolution

Scholars of modern Chinese education have emphasized the role of early twentieth-century schools in producing an urban middle class and professional elite. Meanwhile, scholars of the Chinese Communist Revolution have defined the movement's self-representation as a rejection of bourgeois democracy. However, neither group has crossed into the other's territory to consider how the hundreds of thousands of educated youths from lower social strata remapped the power of social groups and changed China's political culture.

Student protests were among the most dramatic events in 1930s urban culture and were frequently reported in the news media. Using the city streets as a stage, students adopted various means to express their concerns. They strongly affected public opinion and won the support of many urbanites.[3] In the Chinese Communist narrative of modern history, student protests appear as the first steps towards more forceful resistance to feudal oppression and imperialist exploitation; however, no connection is suggested between the Communist-led student protests and the subsequent rural peasant revolution.[4] In his account of the 1930s student movement, John Israel identifies a surge of Chinese anti-imperialist nationalism as the major impulse behind the student protests. As the tide of nationalism swept higher, he argued, the Communist Party was able to establish a predominant influence among students and recruit many into its revolutionary activities.[5] While Israel has provided an important account of students' political and ideological transformation during the Nanjing Decade, his study does not differentiate between students of different social backgrounds and does not analyze how these differences affected their political inclinations. Moreover, his focus on colleges and universities in big cities has left other areas unexamined.[6]

Previous research on the student movements has overlooked secondary school students, who outnumbered college students ten to one.[7] In 1930, the total number of students in universities, colleges, and vocational schools was 37,566. In contrast, the number of students in secondary educational institutions, including middle schools, teachers' schools, and vocational schools, was 514,609.[8] Moreover, students in universities and colleges were mainly from elite urban families.[9] In contrast, it is estimated that over 50 percent of students in the regular middle schools were from rural areas, while 70 percent to 90 percent of students in teachers' schools were from rural areas. While the crucial role the student movement played in the growth of the Chinese Communist Party has been underlined, how the largely urban student protests were transformed into the subsequent peasant revolution remains lighlty documented.[10] Some Chinese scholars, much influenced by the official discourse on communist revolution, believe urban students began to assist with rural mobilization *after* the Chinese Communist Party became a strong political and military force in the Anti-Japanese War. The revolutionary centre in Yan'an attracted a large number of urban youth who, by "combining themselves with workers and peasants," transformed themselves into revolutionaries.[11] The focus of these studies is still on urban students: rural students are not mentioned and how this kind of revolutionary force was prepared has been ignored.

In the 1960s, American historians began a debate over the mid-1930s Communist resurgence. Chalmers Johnson, in proposing his famous "peasant nationalism" theory,[12] argues that the Communists used the opportunity of the Japanese invasion to successfully mobilize nationalist sentiment among peasants after 1937, developing it into a strong political and military power.[13] Mark Selden disagrees: he believes the party gained support from peasants because of the appeal of its revolutionary policies, particularly land reform.[14] Yung-fa Chen argues that the radical economic programs the Communists offered did not always fit the needs of the peasants, but the strategy developed for the Yangzi area succeeded admirably. The strategy of organizing poor peasants to struggle against the agrarian elite and destroy the existing structure of villages helped the communist mobilization of peasants.[15]

The Chinese Communist movement, it is widely believed, began as an urban intellectual movement and only developed as a rural peasant movement when the Communists were driven out of urban areas by Nationalist repression. The official Chinese Communist Party history identifies the 1927 "autumn harvest uprising" (*qiushou qiyi*) in Hunan, led by Mao Zedong, as a turning point, shifting the party's base from the city to the country. However, had the party not re-emerged over the course of the Anti-Japanese War, what is now viewed as a turning point would have been a swan song. Even party leaders do not dispute that the Japanese invasion signalled a chance for a comeback. Nonetheless, without the existence of potential grassroots forces nationwide, a comeback would have been unthinkable.

When the Long March ended in the remote northern Shaanxi town of Yan'an in 1935, the Communists had approximately 25,000 activists and Red Army soldiers.[16] How, after 1937, was a relatively small group, besieged in a barren land, able to quickly mobilize peasants to support and carry out guerrilla activity all across the country? Neither the group in Yan'an nor those operating underground in the cities seem to have been in a position to penetrate the countless villages where peasants carried out armed resistance.[17] Who were the people who went to the villages to organize the peasants? Regardless of what attracted peasants – nationalism or revolutionary policies – activists had to get to the villages.[18] These grassroots workers had to possess certain qualifications: a level of education permitting them to grasp the party's ideals and policies, strong nationalist feelings, linguistic and cultural skills that would allow them to communicate with peasants, and sympathy for peasant conditions and demands.[19] Only by possessing such traits could organizers transform a large number of rather passive peasants into a strong force of resistance. Therefore, the real question is how urban intellectuals translated imported communist ideas and nationalist ideology into language and concepts that were attractive to the peasantry. What relationship did the nationalist student movements have to the reappearance of the Chinese Communist Party as a major political and military force after 1937? It seems there is a missing link in the historical chain.

Training Rural Youths to Be Village Teachers

An important aspect of the modernization process was the transformation of the rural population into modern workers, and education was the key to accomplishing this goal. The expansion of education in the 1930s, especially of secondary education in rural areas, meant that some bright rural youths became primary schoolteachers: a few of them even went on to college.

Opening the Door for Poor Youths

Up until the early 1930s, most of China's secondary schools were in cities and most of China's people were peasants. A 1936 survey shows that, in the early 1930s, one out of every fifty people lived in one of China's eight largest cities (Shanghai, Nanjing, Beiping, Tianjin, Wuhan, Guangzhou, Fuzhou, and Xiamen), but one out of every *five* secondary students attended a school in one of those eight cities. One-seventh of all secondary schools were located in these eight cities, and they used one-fourth of the financial resources spent on secondary schools nationwide.[20] Based on the same survey in four provinces, we see that 92 percent of regular middle schools were located in cities and that 95 percent of regular middle school students attended these schools. Most of the few secondary educational institutions in rural areas were either vocational or teachers' schools. Very few peasants' sons or daughters had a chance to attend secondary school.

After the National Secondary Education Conference in 1932 the Nationalist government attempted to balance things out by building local teachers' schools. Government policy limited the expansion of regular middle schools in rural areas in favour of establishing teachers' schools and vocational schools. As a result, local teachers' schools became the main institutions of secondary education in rural areas.

In the 1930s, the most obvious change in education was the growing number of students from rural areas attending secondary schools, topping 50 percent of the total, according to Tong Runzhi. In some provinces, the proportion surpassed 80 percent. For example, in Sichuan and Shandong, all of the surveyed middle schools were located in urban areas, while 80.2 percent and 86.4 percent of the students, respectively, were from the countryside (see Table 6.1).

The author of the survey did not offer a definition of "urban" or "rural." Geography and costs would have ensured that most of those who left the countryside to seek education studied in relatively regional municipalities rather than in the big cities of Jiangnan and the coast. Students of rural origin, for instance, only made up 20 percent to 30 percent of the students in the schools surveyed in Nanjing, Shanghai, and Qingdao.[21]

Table 6.1

Origin of students in 210 secondary schools in sixteen provinces and cities, 1936

Province/City	Number of schools	Number of students	Number of students from rural areas	Rural portion (%)
Jiangsu	55	15,762	7,270	46.0
Zhejiang	24	7,581	3,845	50.7
Anhui	19	4,447	3,093	69.5
Hebei	19	5,233	3,597	68.7
Shandong	9	2,678	2,314	86.4
Sichuan	3	762	611	80.2
Jiangxi	9	2,000	1,385	69.3
Hunan	7	2,594	1,948	75.1
Hubei	3	978	591	60.4
Guangxi	3	933	634	67.5
Guangdong	8	3,866	2,375	61.2
Fujian	3	1,629	267	22.6
Nanjing	12	5,038	1,587	31.5
Shanghai	25	9,211	2,853	31.0
Beiping	9	3,147	1,647	52.4
Qingdao	2	623	152	24.4
Total	210	66,488	34,269	51.6

Source: Tong Runzhi, "Tichang xiangcun zhongdeng jiaoyu de ba da liyou" [The eight main reasons for advocating rural secondary education], *Zhonghua jiaoyu jie* 24, 2 (1936), 1-10. The order of the provinces and cities in this table follows the list of the original survey.

Another survey conducted in five Hangzhou upper middle schools in 1936 indicated that only 12 percent of the students were from the countryside. In contrast, children of merchants and government officials made up 55 percent.[22] Due to the high cost of living in cities and the high tuition charged by regular middle schools (a problem mitigated only slightly by a small number of fellowships), very few peasants could send their children to cities to study.[23] It is, therefore, likely that a large percentage of rural students in inland urban middle schools came from landlord and rich peasant families.[24] Children from prosperous rural families went to regular middle schools to prepare for college, while children from poorer families went to teachers' and vocational schools. Wan Li, who would become a Communist and eventually the leader of the Chinese People's Congress, was from a relatively rich small town family. Though he attended a lower middle school in his home county in 1931, the death of his father and the lack of financial support obliged Wan to change his plans and enter a teachers' school.[25] Of those who attended middle schools during the 1930s in regional municipalities, many, no doubt, came from backgrounds like Wan Li's.

As expected, the teachers' schools located in county seats, townships, and villages educated many peasant children. In 1933, of 804 applications to the Henan Provincial Village Teachers' School, 52 percent were children from peasant families, and, of the ninety-two admitted students, 54 percent were from villages. Among the remainder, 22 percent were from "education circles" (*xue jie*).[26] This category was most likely composed largely of the children of local teachers living in villages.[27] Thus, in 1933, 70 percent of the first-year class in the Henan Provincial Village Teachers' School may have been students of rural origin. The proportion of rural students in Hebei's provincial teachers' schools was even higher. In 1934, 92 percent of the students in the well known Hebei Provincial Teachers' School Number Seven (Daming) were from peasant families.[28] In most Jiangsu village teachers' schools, over 70 percent of the students were the children of peasants.[29]

Teachers' schools not only provided students with free tuition, they also offered them free dormitory rooms and a monthly allowance. Moreover, the location of local teachers' schools in small townships and villages reduced the cost of transportation and everyday necessities. In the 1930s, the difficulties faced by rural students were aggravated by the deterioration of the rural economy and natural and human-made disasters. When the Yangzi River flooded in 1931, many families were devastated and many students were forced to drop out of school. In the area around Beiping (the name bestowed by the Nationalist government on Beijing) and Tianjin, about 20,000 students were affected by the Japanese attack on Manchuria and Shanghai.[30] In 1934 and 1935, several provinces were affected by the flooding of the Yangzi River and the Yellow River, while thirteen other provinces were hit by drought.[31] These natural disasters dealt another blow to an already feeble rural economy and to rural students' families. Even without large-scale disasters, many students, thousands in 1935 alone, were forced to drop out of school as their families sank into poverty.[32]

Peasants also suffered from a heavy tax burden. Although there was no substantial increase in the land tax, all levels of government imposed surtaxes and irregular surcharges.[33] At the same time, the government failed to carry out promised land reform and rent reduction. The strong resistance of big landowners and the weak authority of the government over local administration limited the ability of the Guomindang government to carry out rural reforms. The constant challenge of Communists in rural areas drove the Nationalists to depend on conservative forces in local communities. Since many members of the gentry had fled the rural chaos of the 1920s and 1930s, power in local communities had often fallen into the hands of local bullies. Nationalist reconstruction of local administration often meant nothing more than legitimating the power of unscrupulous scofflaws.[34]

Under increasingly difficult economic conditions, some rural students were still able to continue their educations but only because of the opportunities offered by new teachers' schools. Yang Qiliang, for instance, entered the private Peide Middle School in Baoding City, Hebei Province, in 1929, when the economic condition of his family was comparatively good. But when his father told him the family could no longer afford his expensive education and that he had better prepare to return home to work on the land, Yang was able to continue his education only because he found a tuition-free teachers' school.[35]

In the 1930s, it was generally assumed that students in teachers' schools were from the lower strata of society, mostly from peasant families. Leaders of the Qixiashan Village Teachers' School in Jiangsu reported that their students were poor and, therefore, one would "never find luxurious living styles among the students; most students lived very simple and parsimonious lives."[36] When students from the provincial and county teachers' schools excelled over students from the regular provincial and county middle schools in the 1933 entrance examination given at Henan Provincial Teachers' School, the examiner reasoned that most students in regular middle schools were from well-to-do families and did not study very hard. In contrast, most students in teachers' schools were "poor boys" (*qiong xiaozi*) whose only chance to improve their future was to study hard and get good grades.[37]

The Social Ladder for Rural Youth

The activities of local elites in building primary schools not only boosted rural literacy rates but also intensified the competition to get into rural teachers' schools. Many young students of the period who had already finished primary school and who longed to continue their education swelled the applicant pool. For instance, in 1933, the Henan Provincial Teachers'

School planned to recruit ninety-two new students from 804 candidates.[38] The competition to get into Shandong Provincial Village Teachers' School Number Seven in 1932 was even more fierce: 1,300 took the entrance examination for eighty openings.[39] The situation in Jiangsu was not much better. Wang Ruowang (1918-2001) recalled that, when he took an entrance examination to apply to the Nanjing Qixiashan Village Teachers' School in 1932, as many as 700 candidates applied for forty-five positions.[40] The Wujiang Provincial Village Teachers' School in Jiangsu admitted forty out of 281 examinees in 1931.[41] The situation was similar in Hebei. In 1928, the rate of enrolment for the Hebei Provincial Teachers' School Number Nine was only 2 percent and, despite an increase in the number of schools, competition to get in remained fierce in the 1930s. In 1934, the Hebei Baoding Provincial Teachers' School Number Two planned to admit 100 students and there were over 2,500 examinees.[42] Overall, the passing rate for entrance examinations ranged from 2 percent to 15 percent. Although modern education served as a more effective vehicle for social mobility than had the imperial examination system, even teachers' schools were quite exclusive.

Teachers' schools trained these rural youths to be modern teachers. According to statistics from different provinces, the great majority of the graduates of teachers' schools went on to teach at the village level. In Jiangsu, Provincial Village Teachers' Schools in Jieshou, Wuxi, and Qixiashan confirmed that from 70 percent to 80 percent of their graduates worked in village primary schools.[43] A similar situation occurred in other provinces. According to 1936 data, 81 percent of those who graduated from the Henan Provincial Village Teachers' School during the five previous years taught in local educational institutions.[44] About 80 percent of the graduates of Hebei Provincial Teachers' School Number Seven also worked in the local schools.[45] While the possibility of not being accepted to the next level of education or, worse by far, not getting a job, kept graduates of regular middle schools antsy, the principal of Jiangsu's Wuxi Provincial Teachers' School stated proudly that he "had never heard of a case of a graduate of a teachers' school not finding a job."[46] Employment was a certainty, but it meant being stuck in the village, living on a pittance, and giving up any sort of lively intellectual exchange.

Many used their time in a teachers' school to prepare for further schooling. Those who graduated from the upper level of a teachers' school could either continue on to higher education or take a job as an upper-level primary schoolteacher, even possibly a lower middle schoolteacher: such jobs meant more money and improved social status. In 1933, when the Henan Provincial Teachers' School was recruiting students for its upper division, of the 804 candidates, 218 had graduated from the lower division of a teachers' school.[47] Over 10 percent of the graduates of Jieshou Provincial Village Teachers' School in Jiangsu eventually went on to the next level of education.[48] Although regulations called for strict enforcement of the teaching obligation, some local Nationalist government officials were normally more lenient with those students who were talented and who wanted to get on with their education. The Minister of Education issued an edict to education bureaus at each level of government in 1931, stipulating that, when graduates of teachers' schools applied for the next level of education, they only needed to prove that they had fulfilled at least one year of their teaching obligation.[49] For example, Liu Zhen, a graduate of Shandong Teachers' School Number One, was allowed to enrol at Shandong University after teaching primary school for one year. Xiang Kun, another graduate of Shandong Teachers' School Number One, who later became a movie star, enrolled at Nanjing College of Dramatic Arts after completing his one-year teaching duty.[50] The door was barely open, but a handful of students from lower social strata squeezed through it to attend college.

But the great majority of the students who attended local teachers' schools would return to be village teachers, with all the attendant problems. Moreover, local primary schools often encountered financial difficulties, and irregular payment of salaries sometimes drove teachers to organize protests.[51] Teaching turned out to be a less secure profession than many had assumed.

The ambitious young men studying in local teachers' schools in the 1930s proved themselves in highly competitive entrance examinations and through years of studying new and challenging subjects, only to confront the possibility that they might be locked into small-town and village jobs, with no possibility of advancement and the real possibility of an eroded standard of living. After grappling with new ideas in school, many were not content simply to return to the rural social conditions from which they had emerged. Although they were generally not from the poorest of rural families, the decline of the rural economy had brought their families great economic and social distress. The government did little to inspire confidence: its weak rural reform efforts had failed to improve the economy, and its sluggish resistance to Japanese military expansion had increased popular discontent. For many of these disillusioned students, the ideas of the Chinese Communist Party proved attractive at a time when almost any alternative would have seemed viable.

Recruiting Revolutionaries: Teachers' Schools in Shandong and Hebei

Although this was certainly not the government's intention, teachers' schools became centres of radical discussion and activities. Discontented rural students supplemented the government-stipulated curriculum with radical texts and responded enthusiastically to the encouragement they got from an older generation of leftist intellectuals who had survived the Nationalist purges of the late 1920s. Organizers won over many students in teachers' schools, recruiting them to become grassroots workers for the Communist Party.

The evidence in this section is drawn largely from a twenty-one-volume collection of biographies and autobiographies entitled *Heroic Graduates of Teachers' Schools Shine over China* (*Shifan qunying, guang yao Zhonghua*). The biographies and autobiographies in this collection were compiled in the early 1990s, and they rely on the memories of the protagonists and their comrades as well as on local archival documents.[52] As the series title indicates, the portraits amount to hagiography, and the stories are shaped by the official narrative of the victorious Communist Revolution. Time and ideology have shaped individuals' recollections of their motivations and actions, and their understanding of the events they experienced has undergone a radical transformation. Despite these problems, these stories provide us with a valuable source of information on Communist organizing in teachers' schools in the 1930s, and they provide indications of why and how teachers' schools became centres of Communist activity.[53]

I rely mostly upon Volumes 7 and 8, which include the biographies and autobiographies of important Communist leaders from Shandong and Hebei.[54] These two contiguous provinces make up an important agricultural region in northern China, and since they border Manchuria and the Pacific Ocean, they took the brunt of Japanese military expansion and were centres of anti-Japanese resistance. The Communist Party was able to turn a large part of both provinces into base areas during the Anti-Japanese War (1937-45) and the Civil War (1946-49), building resilient and effective underground village organizations that were crucial to the ultimate Communist victory in 1949. Moreover, in both Shandong and Hebei, teachers' schools accounted for a large proportion of secondary education (see Chapter 5).

Volumes 7 and 8 of the collection specifically tell the stories of Communist leaders from Shandong and Hebei who attended teachers' schools. They provide no evidence about the number of Communist leaders who studied in teachers' schools;[55] they do, however, show that teachers' schools were a key route to Communist activism.

Gathering Discontented Youth: Students in Teachers' Schools

In her study of how students in Zhejiang responded to the May Fourth Movement, Wen-hsin Yeh identifies a gap between the responses of teachers' school students from remote areas and regular middle school students in the big city of Hangzhou. She attributes the variation to different family backgrounds, different educational experiences, and different career opportunities. The

Hangzhou students largely came from urban elite families and intended to continue their education or find positions in government or business. In contrast, the teachers' school students largely came from small gentry families in inland Zhejiang and expected to teach in inland towns after graduation. Yeh reasoned that the pressure such students would have received from their conservative families, combined with the suffocating atmosphere of inland towns and backward economic areas, provoked a backlash as small-town men and women seized upon radical lessons from the May Fourth Movement.[56] After having enjoyed the openly intellectual atmosphere and advanced urban lifestyle in Hangzhou, they became increasingly resentful and vehemently attacked the patriarchal Confucian family.[57] In the following decade, as Lü Fangshang notes, students in teachers' schools launched more strikes than did any other student group. Lü attributes this to their lower social origins, their discontent with unjust and volatile social conditions, and their unhappiness at the thought of returning to the countryside.[58]

The next generation, the teachers' school students of the 1930s, was from an even lower social stratum than was their counterpart in the 1910s. While in the 1910s most teachers' schools were in provincial capitals and municipalities, by the 1930s, most teachers' schools were located at the county level and below. Since few students at teachers' schools were from rich families, their social position gave them a different perspective, and many were attracted to radical solutions.

The people in the group of Hebei and Shandong revolutionaries whose stories are told in *Heroic Graduates* were all of rural origin. Table 6A.1 contains forty-three former student activists from teachers' schools in Shandong, displaying the information on their family background, early education, and the teachers' schools in which they enrolled. Table 6A.2 covers the same group of students and lists social organizations and activities, the time and place they joined the party, their experiences and activities after they left school and during the anti-Japanese War, and the major positions they took in the party after 1949. Judging from the text summarized in Table 6A.1, most former students were from the villages' middle or lower-middle strata.[59] Many of them worked in the field at a very young age. An extreme case was Gao Junyue, who was finally able to matriculate at Shandong Pingyuan Village Teachers' School in 1931 at the age of twenty-one. He worked during much of his youth in the field and only finished his upper primary education (equivalent to Grades 5 and 6 in North America) when he was nineteen.[60]

Students in Hebei had similar experiences. Tie Ying's memoir provides what is perhaps a typical story. Tie acquired basic literacy in a *sishu*-style school, then studied Western subjects for two years in a modern elementary school, but his family could not afford to send him to an urban middle school. When a teachers' school began recruiting students – it was tuition-free and offered free living accommodations and an allowance – students were required to submit only a registration fee and a refundable security deposit. With the support of the teachers and his relatives, Tie passed the highly competitive entrance examination and entered the school.[61] Even though only a few of the Communists whose stories are included in the series were from the very poorest village families, most of them could not afford to attend any other kind of school.[62] The story becomes familiar: after primary school, students could not afford further education and had to work in the field, until teachers' schools offered them a chance to continue their education.

Students standing in line on their first day at a village teachers' school immediately discovered that they had a fair amount in common with their neighbours. Yang Qiliang recalled that, in the Hebei Baoding Provincial Teachers' School Number Two, "most students were from poor families ... Children from poor families had more to talk about. Many had similar experiences of facing financial hardship and having to fight to go to school."[63] One extreme example was Qin Hezhen's activities at Shandong's Ziyang Village Teachers' School in 1933. That year, the tensions between students from poorer families and the minority of students from richer landlord and local bureaucrat families burst into the open. The poor students, led by Qin, organized a strike and presented school authorities with a flimsy pretext for having all of the wealthier students expelled: the authorities acceded to the demand.[64] Such tensions and conflicts shored up group solidarity among students from similar backgrounds.

Passing the highly competitive entrance examinations gave the students an elite status in their rural communities. Many students developed strong feelings of social responsibility, an artefact of China's literati tradition. Qin Hezhen, a student at Shandong's Ziyang Village Teachers' School, took inspiration from a poem written by his uncle. In the poem, Qin Hezhen was described as "a piece of jade hidden deep in the mountains" (*pu cang shenshan*) (i.e., an unrecognized treasure).[65] When Tie Ying graduated from primary school with the highest marks in the county, his family received congratulations from the whole village for having such a promising child.[66] In spite of their achievements, distinguished students such as Tie Ying bitterly resented the unfairness of the Chinese class system. They had to enter second-class schools like teachers' schools, whereas, in contrast, boys from rich families who may not have been as smart would be able to go to colleges and have bright futures. Tie in Hebei and Wang Kekou in Shandong had similar experiences and were not content to pursue the ever narrower path of social mobility offered by the educational system; instead, they responded to school writing assignments by penning bitter tracts about class oppression, later graduating to more active opposition.[67]

Exiled Radicals: Teachers in Teachers' Schools

As disenchanted teachers' school students spoke out against social injustice, they encountered little resistance from faculties that included many Communists and progressive intellectuals. The first generation of Communists was baptized in the New Culture Movement of the 1910s and cut its teeth on a series of anti-imperialist movements, including the May Fourth Movement in 1919, the May Thirtieth Movement in 1925, and the anti-warlord movements. When the right wing of the Nationalist Party purged its erstwhile Communist allies in 1927, many took shelter in a political safe haven: the countryside. Some took a more active role and, hoping to resume the revolution, established revolutionary base areas in the Jinggang Mountains and other remote areas.[68] Another group of educated communists escaped to inland towns and villages, where they earned a living by the skill acquired through modern education – teaching. At the same time, other progressive intellectuals nurtured by the New Culture Movement and the May Fourth Movement exiled themselves to smaller towns, where they became teachers and continued to promote their beliefs. The expansion of rural education – and particularly teachers' schools – in the 1930s helped these disaffected activists conceal themselves in educational institutions.

Newspapers and magazines frequently labelled teachers as Communists during the 1930s.[69] Such accusations were sometimes false, but often they were not. For instance, after graduating from Beijing University in 1919, Wang Zhe studied education in the Soviet Union and joined the Chinese Communist Party in 1927. Beijing's political environment drove him from the city after 1927, and by 1931 he was serving as dean of instruction at Shandong Village Teachers' School Number Two in Laiyang. Under his direction, the school created a radical environment and recruited students based on their fondness for the Chinese Communist Party. He equipped the school library with the works of Marx, Engels, and Lenin; introductory texts on socialism and communism; and literary works by left-wing writers. Wang directed a reading group and introduced socialism and Marxism to young students. He also facilitated the activities of Communist students and shielded them from harassment on the part of the local Nationalist functionaries.[70]

Li Zhuru was a student in a Nanjing middle school who joined the Communist Party in 1927 and worked undercover for a short time at Nanjing University. When the political atmosphere became unbearable, he left Nanjing and found a teaching position at Shandong Teachers' School Number One in Ji'nan, where he continued his Communist activities.[71] Ma Shi'an joined the party in 1926 and survived the suppression of a Communist-led peasant uprising in Hubei in 1928. Three years later, he was hired to teach literature at Shandong Teachers' School Number Four in Qingzhou, and he established a base among a group of young students.[72] Ma Xiaoteng, a party member who escaped the bloody purges of Nanjing and Shanghai, became a teacher at Shandong Village Teachers' School Number Five.[73] Feng Pinyi was the interpreter for the party's Comintern advisor, Michael Borodin, during the First United Front between the Communists and Nationalists in 1924 and 1925. Escaping the anti-Communist suppression in the south, Feng was hired as a teacher at Hebei Provincial Teachers' School Number Seven. He recruited the school's principal, the teachers, and a number of students into the party and established a local party cell.[74] Hebei's Baoding Provincial Teachers' School Number Two also hired a Communist: Zhao Ruiwu. During his tenure, he was arrested by Nationalists as a suspected Communist, then released for lack of evidence after receiving glowing support from the school principal and students.[75] Wang Zhizhi, a left-wing writer and a Communist Youth League member, joined the ill-fated Communist-led uprising in Nanchang in 1927. After the uprising, he lost touch with the party and found a teaching position at Hebei's Potou Provincial Teachers' School Number Nine, where he taught literature and resumed his radical activities.[76]

At the same time, a number of older left-wing intellectuals, dissatisfied with the rightward turn of the Nationalist government after 1927, became supporters and protectors of younger Communist teachers and students. Among them were Fan Mingshu (principal of Shandong Teachers' School Number Two), Ju Simin (principal of Ji'nan Village Teachers' School in Shandong), Sun Dongge (principal of Shandong Teachers' School Number Three and the Six Counties United Village Teachers' School), Yu Yunting (principal of Wendeng Village Teachers' School in Shandong), Wang Zhuchen (principal and dean of instruction of Shandong Provincial Teachers' School), Xie Taichen (principal of Hebei Provincial Teachers' School Number Seven), Chao Zhefu (dean of instruction of Hebei Provincial Teachers' School Number Seven), Zhang Xiaoteng (principal of Hebei Teachers' School Number Two), and Meng Xianti (principal of Hebei Teachers' School Number Four).[77] The people who comprised this group of intellectuals had received their education in the late Qing and the early Republican periods, and they earned their fame in the 1911 Revolution and the Republican movements in the 1910s and 1920s. All of them hired Communists and progressive intellectuals to work at their schools, and, if the teachers or their student followers were harassed or arrested by the Nationalists, these principals used their power and influence to protect them.[78]

Teachers' schools were a convenient place to introduce socialist theories. Whether through school libraries, undercover Communist organizations, or "societies for the introduction of new books and magazines" (*shu kan jieshao she*), activists arranged for the purchase of left-wing works from Beiping and Shanghai. They then helped students to organize clubs in which the books were studied. Teachers also used special courses to introduce their students to socialist ideas. The courses specially designed for preparing students to teach in rural areas were rural economy and cooperatives, agriculture, irrigation, rural education and people's education, and so on, a wide-ranging curriculum into which teachers inserted socialist works on materialist history and class analysis. Wang Zhe not only taught Marxist social theory under the cover of required courses but, as dean of instruction, he also instructed other teachers to do so as well.[79]

To judge from the entries in *Heroic Graduates,* many of the teachers who supported alternatives to the Nationalist government approached the task of indoctrinating their students in the same way. To establish meaningful connections with their rural students, who were very concerned about their families' well-being, they began by explaining the Marxist theory of class struggle and providing the socioeconomic tools students needed in order to understand the misery of rural communities. They encouraged students to investigate their home villages during school vacations, using Marxist theory to unlock some of the evident problems. They also introduced the literary fiction of left-wing writers (*zuo yi zuojia*), relying on the sentiments evoked by such novels as Xiao Jun's *A Village in August* (*Bayue de xiangcun*) and Xiao Hong's *A Field of Life and Death* (*Sheng si hang*) to rouse students against rural misery and Japanese imperialism. They encouraged students to participate in the social movements led by the Chinese Communist Party, observed them as they socialized, and then guided them towards interschool and national organizations such as the Chinese National Liberation Vanguard ("*Minxian,*" short for *Minzu jiefang xianfeng dui*), the Great Anti-Imperialism League (*Fan di da tongmeng*), the Association for Resisting Japan and Saving the Nation (*Kang Ri jiuguo hui*), and the Association of Left-Wing Writers ("*Zuolian,*" short for *Zuoyi zuojia lianhe hui*) – all of which were connected to the Communist Party. After a period of observation, the Communist Party members in schools recruited the most promising and energetic students. Having recruited a certain number of students, the teachers then established Communist cells in the schools. With the support of progressive colleagues and their student followers, Communist teachers built up solid bases in teachers' schools.[80]

Nurturing Student Activists in Teachers' Schools

As Communist teachers and students became the most audible voices in the schools, loudly vaunting the glories of the Communist Party and denouncing the corrupt Nationalists, students and teachers who praised the ruling party in public risked being criticized. For instance, when a teacher in the Laiyang Village Teachers' School in Shandong spoke in class about "eliminating banditry" (*jiao fei*), the official term for eradicating the Communist base area in Jiangxi, students immediately protested and forced the teacher to apologize.[81] Wang Ruowang recalled that this kind of atmosphere also prevailed in his village teachers' school in Jiangsu: "Because most students of the Qixiashan Village Teachers' School were from poor families [*pin ku chushen*], they were naturally inclined toward [Communist] revolution. Among senior students, underground members of the Chinese Communist Party were very active and there were other organizations to promote various [radical] political ideas, including anarchism. But there was no one who believed in the Nationalist Party. If anybody had been a Nationalist [supporter], he or she would have had no place to stand."[82]

Students read progressive books, organized study groups and literary societies, and sometimes even published their own journals. From the entries in *Heroic Graduates,* we can glimpse their political and literary interests. Table 6.2 presents a partial list of books mentioned by these former students for this period, including the works of Marx, Engels, and Lenin; works by Chinese authors introducing and interpreting Marxist classics (including those of Ai Siqi); works by May Fourth writers; left-wing literature, including books by Lu Xun, Guo Moruo, Cao Yu, Ba Jin, Mao Dun, Xiao Jun, and Xiao Hong; and Russian and American leftist writers, including Gorky and Serafimovich. Progressive and left-wing journals were also popular; among those mentioned were *Life Weekly* edited by Zou Taofeng, *Pioneer* edited by Jiang Guangci, and *Big Dipper* edited by Ding Ling. The presence of left-wing and even Communist publications in teachers' schools is corroborated by the lists of banned publications that local governments were always sending to the schools. The Nationalist government banned not only the works of Communists but also books and magazines from other political groups, including reformist magazines and works from the left wing of the Nationalist Party.[83] Local police periodically raided teachers' schools and read mail sent to the schools, searching for radical publications.[84]

Although the Communist and activist students constituted a minority, their activities had a strong impact on the culture and political atmosphere of their schools. In his study of political activism in urban schools during the 1930s, John Israel discovered that less than 10 percent of students dominated a school's political life and that less than 1 percent controlled regional political activities and organizations.[85] Descriptions of political activities in local teachers' schools provided in Volumes 7 and 8 of *Heroic Graduates* seem to support Israel's discovery, though in Shandong and Hebei student activists made up a larger portion of the student body. For example, in Shandong Village School Number Three, there were sixty to seventy activists among 160 to 170 students in 1932.[86] In 1933, Shandong Village Teachers' School Number Seven had over thirty Communist students, about one-fifth of the entire student body; student activists must have constituted a significantly larger group.[87] An exceptional case occurred in Hebei: it was said that over 80 percent of the students of Hebei Teachers' School Number Seven were involved in various levels of Communist activities in

Table 6.2

Literature passed around among students in Shandong and Hebei teachers' schools, 1930-37[1]

Authors	Title of reading materials	Nature of book/journal[2]
Karl Marx	*Ziben lun* [Capital]	Original works of leading Marxists
Karl Marx and Friedrick Engels	*Gongchandang xuanyan* [The Communist Manifesto]	
Friedrick Engels	*Jiating, siyouzhi he guojia de qiyuan* [The Origins of the Family, Private Property and the State] *Fan Dulin lun* [Anti-Düring]	
Vladimir Lenin	*Guojia yu geming* [State and Revolution] *Weiwu zhuyi yu jingyan pipan zhuyi* [Materialism and Empirico-criticism] *Liening zhuzuo xuan* [Selected Works of Lenin] *Diguo zhuyi shi ziben zhuyi de zuigao jieduan* [Imperialism, the Highest Stage of Capitalism] *Gongchan zhuyi yundong zhong de zuopai youzhi bing* ["Left Wing" Communism: An Infantile Disorder] *Liangzhong celue* [Two Tactics of Social-Democracy in the Democratic Revolution] *Zuo shenmo* [What Is to Be Done?]	
Joseph Stalin	*Zhengzhi wenti jianghua* [Political Speeches]	
Kawakami Hajime[3]	*Zibenlun dagang* [An Outline of *Capital*] *Zhengzhi jingji xue* [Political Economy]	Introductory works on Marxism and socialism
Ai Siqi	*Dazhong zhexue* [Popular Philosophy]	
Unknown	*Weiwu zhuyi rumen* [Introduction to Materialism] *Bianzheng fa rumen* [Introduction to Dialects] *Ziben zhuyi jiepo* [Dissecting Capitalism] *Bianzheng fa qianshuo* [Elementary Introduction of Dialects]	
Unknown	*Tudi nongmin wenti zhinan* [Guide to the Problem of Peasantry and Land] *Shijie jingji dili gangyao* [Outline of World Economic Geography] *Minzhong geming yu minzhong zhengquan* [Mass Revolution and Mass Power]	Most likely Marxist or socialist books
Chen Duxiu	*Xin Qingnian* [New Youth] *Duxiu wencun* [Collected Works of Chen Duxiu]	New Culture Movement writers' works
Hu Shi	*Hu Shi wencun* [Collected Works of Hu Shi]	
Li Dazhao	No specific titles	
(Sun Fuxi and Pan Zinian)[4]	*Beixin yuekan* [New North Monthly] *Xiaoshuo yuebao* [Short Story Monthly] *Chenbao fukan* [Morning News Supplement]	

►

◄ *Table 6.2*

Authors	Title of reading materials	Nature of book/journal[2]
Guo Moruo	*Chuanzao yuekan/jikan* [Creation Monthly/Quarterly] *Fenghuang niepan* [Reincarnation of the Phoenix]	Works of left-wing writers
Lu Xun	*Yusi* [Thread of Talk] *Nahan* [Call to Arms] *Panghuang* [Wandering] *Fen* [Grave] *A Q zhengzhuan* [The True Story of Ah Q]	
Xiao Jun	*Ba yue de xiangcun* [A Village in August]	
Xiao Hong	*Sheng si chang* [A Field of Life and Death]	
Ba Jin	*Jia* [Family]	
Ding Ling Zheng Zhenduo Zhou Yang Rou Shi Mao Dun	No specific titles	
(Ding Ling)	*Beidou* [Big Dipper]	
Zou Taofen	*Shenghuo* [Life Daily Journal] *Shenghuo xingqi kan* [Life Weekly] *Dazhong shenghuo* [Mass Life]	Progressive intellectual magazines
(Li Gongpu)	*Dushu shenghuo* [Reading Life]	
(Du Zhong-yuan)	*Xinsheng* [Revitalization]	
(Jiang Guangci)	*Tuohuang zhe* [Pioneer]	
(Li Liewen)	*Zhongliu* [Midstream] *Shenbao ziyou tan* [Shanghai News/Random Talk][5] *Dongfang zazhi* [Eastern Miscellany][6]	
Unknown	*Qilu wenhua* [Shandong Culture]	Unknown; likely a local progressive magazine
Maxim Gorky	*Wo de daxue* [My University] *Muqin* [The Mother] *Zai renjian* [The World]	Soviet writers' works
(Aleksandr Fadeev)	*Huimie* [The Route][7]	

►

◄ *Table 6.2*

Authors	Title of reading materials	Nature of book/journal[2]
(Aleksandr Serafimovich)	*Tieliu* [The Iron Flood][8]	Soviet writers' works
(Dmitri Furmanov)	*Xiaboyang* [Chapajev][9]	
(Upton Sinclair)	*Tuchang* [The Jungle][10]	American writers' works
(Edgar Snow)	*Xixing manji* [Red Star over China][11]	
(Mao Zedong)	*Mao Zedong zizhuan* [The Autobiography of Mao Zedong]	CCP publications
Yun Daiying[12]	*Zhongguo qingnian* [Chinese Youth] *Xiangdao bao* [The Guide]	
CCP organizations	*Shiyue* [October] *Hongqi* [Red Flag] *Su qu ziweidui* [Soviet Red Guard] *Liu da wenxian* [Documents of the Sixth National Congress of the CCP]	CCP publications
CCP Northern District Committee	*Huoxian* [Line of Fire]	
Unknown	*Wuzhuang baodong* [Armed Uprising] *Jinghan gongren liuxue ji* [Report on the Beijing to Hankou Railway Workers' Bloody Strike in 1927] *Suweiai xianfa qianshuo* [An Elementary Introduction to the Soviet Constitution] *Mosike yinxiang ji* [Impressions of Moscow] *Su E shicha ji* [A Journal on Soviet Russia] *Mosike ribao* [Moscow Daily] *Jiefang* [Liberation]	Unknown, but most likely CCP publications

1 This table includes authors and publications mentioned in the auto/biographies in SQGZ series – *Shifan Qunying, Guangyao Zhonghu* [Heroic graduates of teachers' schools shine in Chinese history], 21 vols. (Xi'An: Shaanxi renmin jiaoyu chubanshe [Shaanxi people's education publishing house], 1992-94) – vol. 7a and b, and vol. 8. The fact that the former students remembered the names of these authors and publications many decades later indicates that the literature had a strong influence on them.

2 For information about these publications, I used the following references: Dai Zhixian, *Shinian neizhan shiqi de geming wenhua yundo*ng [The revolutionary cultural movement during the ten-year civil war period, 1927-1937] (Beijing: Chinese people's university press, 1988); Leo Ou-fan Lee, *The Romantic Generation of Modern Chinese Writers* (Cambridge, MA: Harvard University Press, 1973); Tang Yuan and Han Zhiyou (compil.), *Zhongguo xiandai wenxue qikan mulu huibian* [Compendium of the contents of modern Chinese literature magazines] (Tianjin: Tianjin peoples' press, 1988); Xu Naixiang (Chief-compiler), *Zhongguo xiandai wenxue cidian* [Encyclopedia of Chinese modern literature] (Nanning: Guangxi

►

◂ *Table 6.2*

peoples' press, 1989); Cheng Kaihua, Gong Manqun, and Zhu Zuchun (compil.), *Zhongguo xiandai wenxue cidian* [Encyclopedia of Chinese modern literature] (Xi'an: Huayue wenyi chubanshe, 1988); Beijing tushuguan shumu bianji zu , *Zhongguo xiandai zuojia zhu yi shumu* [Index of books written and translated by Chinese modern writers] (Beijing: Shumu wenxian chubanshe, 1982).

3 Kawakami Hajime (1879-1946) was a Japanese economist and Marxist. Many of his books on Marxist economics were translated into Chinese in the 1920s and 1930s.

4 Those authors' names in parentheses were not mentioned by name in the auto/biographies. I traced the authors of these books or magazines.

5 *Shanghai News* was a commercial newspaper, but its column of "Random Talk" was dominated by a group of left-wing writers.

6 *Eastern Miscellany* was regarded as a conservative bourgeois magazine, but in 1933 it published a large number of literary critiques, novels, prose, and poems by left-wing writers. See Dai Zhixian. *Shinian neizhan shiqi de geming wenhua yundo*ng [The revolutionary cultural movement during the ten-year civil war period, 1927-1937]. Beijing: Chinese People's University Press, 1988, 121-22.

7 Translated by Lu Xun in 1930.

8 Translated by Cao Jinghua in 1931.

9 The novel was translated into Chinese in 1936, but the movie based on the novel was made in 1934 by Soviet directors. There was evidence that the movie was shown in China about 1935. The protagonists did not mention whether they read the novel or watched the movie.

10 Translated by Guo Moruo in 1929.

11 The earliest version of the book was published in 1936 and it may have appeared in China in 1937. However, the Chinese version might have been published at almost the same time (at least part of it, e.g., Mao's autobiography, because the interpreters had notes in Chinese), since Snow may have provided his notes to the Communists. The former students might also have been mistaken as to when they read the book.

12 Yun Daiying was one of the first generation of Communists.

the 1930s.[88] During the late 1920s and early 1930s, the Chinese Communist Party's central organization urged its members to mobilize workers and peasants to rise up in revolt. Communist teachers responded by organizing student protests: they even mobilized nearby workers to oppose taxation and to demand wage increases.[89] Then they went further, urging students to return to their home villages to organize poor peasants to rise up against taxes and rents.[90] When the Japanese occupied Manchuria in 1931, a nationwide anti-Japanese movement attracted many students who were formerly indifferent to politics. They sent delegations to Nanjing demanding a stronger stance against Japanese aggression, a boycott of Japanese goods, and support of various anti-Japanese organizations (see Table 6A.2). Especially after the Xi'an Incident in 1936, when the Communist Party formed the Second United Front with the Nationalists against the Japanese forces, student activists pushed their anti-Japanese campaigns even more to the fore, relegating to second place their plans to bring social justice to the countryside.

The scope of student protests could be national, local, or limited to a single school, and the subject of the protests could be political or non-political (see Table 6A.2).[91] For example, most student-led political actions were protests against imperialism, Japanese aggression, or the government's accommodation of the Japanese. Most of these protests were responses to a national call but were led by regional and cross-school organizations. Such activities reached "high tide" during the span of a few months, from the Japanese attack on the city of Shenyang in Manchuria in September 1931 to the sustained bombardment and invasion of Shanghai in January 1932. The nature of local student movements was somewhat blurry. Some student protests had a less obviously political quality, such as remonstrations against the government program of military training and against comprehensive examinations for students in secondary schools. Other activities included organizing strikes, resisting taxes, and demanding the punishment of corrupt officials. Additionally, demonstrations were held to draw attention to the arrest of teachers and students for alleged Communist activities. These types of protests, which had clear political implications, were also local and were initiated by cross-school organizations. The protests within schools were mostly non-political and were often aimed at school authorities, such as corrupt principals and incompetent or unfair teachers, and at practices such as serving unappetizing food in school dining halls and summarily expelling students. At times, the activists simply wished to flex their muscle, to confront the conservative school authorities and make them suffer.

All of these actions helped student activists hone their skills. They learned how to organize and mobilize the masses, how to express their demands, how to create information channels, how to win support from outside groups, and how to form alliances. These abilities became precious when the time came to mobilize peasants to join resistance movements. Over the course of these protests, while a small group of activist students in teachers' schools in Shandong and Hebei were recruited into the party, other students joined allied organizations, such as the Chinese National Liberation Vanguard, the Association for Resisting Japan and Saving the Nation, and the other groups mentioned earlier (see Table 6A.2). And, eventually, most of them became Chinese Communist Party members in the long resistance movement.[92]

I want to end this section with a cautionary note about some of the figures presented in the previous pages. *Heroic Graduates of Teachers' Schools Shine over China* is not the result of disinterested scholarship, nor is its methodology entirely sound. But it reveals a phenomenon confirmed by other sources and gives a clear picture of the strategy that students used to gain support for the Chinese Communist Party.

From Student Activists to Guerrilla Leaders

Allow me to recapitulate, from the students' perspective this time, how students became committed revolutionaries. First, they studied socialist ideas introduced to them by their teachers and fellow students, testing these ideas by applying them to Chinese society. Second, they joined small groups, such as reading groups, to deepen their study of socialist revolution, the Chinese Communist Party, and the socialist society of the Soviet Union. Third, they became involved in protests, organizing student demonstrations against school leaders and local officials, mobilizing nearby workers and peasants, and participating in anti-Japanese campaigns. Finally, having completed their training, they returned home to disseminate the revolutionary gospel they had learned in order to help peasants ward off the unfair demands of the state and landlords, and to mobilize them to support guerrilla warfare against the Japanese invasion.

Graduates of teachers' schools were sent to villages, usually their home villages, to teach. The activists among them were thus in an excellent position to begin organizing. They spoke the peasants' language, knew how the peasants thought, and quite likely had ideas as to how they could be most effectively organized. Their personal histories and positions helped them win the trust of the peasants. After all, they were already respected as excellent students who, against great odds, had passed the entrance examinations and brought glory to the village. The increased respect owed them as teachers gave them great power.[93] After 1937, when the Japanese army marched into the areas close to their home villages, many of these activist teachers organized guerrilla squads coordinated by the Communist Party.

Table 6A.2 consists of a selective summary of the revolutionary activities of teachers' school graduates described in *Heroic Graduates*. Of the forty-three students about whom substantial information is provided, twenty-four went back to their natal villages to be teachers and later organized local guerrilla units. When the war broke out, Party organizations at teachers' schools also sent student activists to villages to organize guerrilla forces. For instance, Shandong's Huimin Village Teachers' School Number Six sent over a dozen party members to villages to mobilize peasants after July 1937.[94] Altogether, twenty-eight of the forty-three graduates, whose activities are listed in the table, organized or joined local guerrilla movements; others joined the resistance in other capacities, serving in the Red Army and in army propaganda teams.

After August 1937, when Hebei and part of Shandong fell into the hands of the Japanese, all of the schools in those areas were either closed or moved inland to areas under Chinese control. Some students returned directly to their home villages to organize resistance, while others went to the Communist headquarters in Yan'an. Some students who moved inland with relocated schools later also joined the resistance. In November 1937, Shandong's Pingyuan Village Teachers' School Number Five and Huimin Village Teachers' School Number Six jointly sent over ninety students to Yan'an.[95] Of the forty-three students included in Table 6A.2, fourteen went to Yan'an either before or after they began organizing local village resistance, while some others joined in various training programs led by the Communist Party. Training at Yan'an took place at the Resisting Japan Political and Military Academy (*Kangri junzheng daxue*) and at senior cadre schools such as the Central Party Academy (*Zhongyang dangxiao*) and the Marxist-Leninist Academy (*Ma-Lie zhuyi xueyuan*). Once their training was complete, Communists were sent back to their home regions to organize and lead guerrilla warfare.

Perhaps Wang Kekou's experience could give us a clearer picture of how a student became a guerrilla war leader. While studying at Shandong's Pengyuan Provincial Village Teachers' School Number Five, Wang joined the party, and, upon graduating in the summer of 1937 he returned to his home village to teach and to spread Communist ideas, including the need to resist the Japanese invasion. He then organized a local force by mobilizing a broad array of individuals; this included reforming a small group of bandits. By the time the Communists arrived in force to build up the revolutionary base in early 1938, Wang already had a small guerrilla team and was promptly named party secretary of his home county; later, he served as political commissioner of guerrilla teams in the region. In 1940, when a regiment of the Eight Route Army was established with his guerrilla team as its backbone, Wang was appointed the regiment's political commissioner.[96] Wang Kekou was the last cohort to graduate from local teachers' schools before the Anti-Japanese War broke out. According to the information in *Heroic Graduates,* in the late 1930s, most student leaders from local secondary schools held ward, county, and district positions. By the 1940s, most of those same people had been promoted to positions at the district and provincial levels. A minority of former student leaders lost their lives in the war, but a majority became central, provincial, regional, and city leaders after 1949 (see Table 6A.2).

The students in local teachers' schools in the 1930s can be seen as the second generation of Communists (if there is a genealogical line among Chinese Communists). Due to temporal and spatial limitations, as well as to their own educational backgrounds, their knowledge of Communism was inadequate and was mixed with nationalism. The radicalization of this group of students – unlike the first generation of Communists, who were pushed by theory and influenced by Soviet example[97] – came more from their family condition, personal experience, gloomy future, contemporary social problems, and an intense nationalism. Most of them acquired their knowledge through left-wing literature and second-hand communist/socialist readers. Although their understanding of Marxism and Communism was not as academic as was that of the first generation of Communists (e.g., Chen Duxiu, Li Dazhao, Li Da and Wang Ming, etc.), they possessed one quality that the first generation Communists did not. Perfect mediators, they not only had a basic understanding of the Communist programs but they also had the local knowledge, skills, and connections to approach and mobilize the masses of people at the bottom of society. Recognized in their communities as highly intelligent leaders, they commanded the necessary respect to organize on a massive scale. It was this group of students who became key to transforming the Communist Party into a massive peasant party based in the villages.

Communist Base Areas: Mass Education and Teachers' Schools, 1929-34

After being driven out of urban areas by the Nationalists in 1927, the Chinese Communist Party established revolutionary bases in the Jinggang Mountains of Jiangxi Province, among other areas. The central soviet government was set up in Ruijin County in Jiangxi, while in other provinces, including parts of Fujian, Hubei, Anhui, and Henan, local governments were established wherever the Red Army was able to defy the power of regional warlords and Nationalist officials. The Communist governments in these regions started administering education policies of their own design. Although aspects of their policies were inherited from the Nationalist system, they intended to create a new type of school system to educate peasants, workers, and children, while providing equal opportunities for males and females. The educational policies and practices of the Communists during the Jiangxi soviet period of the early 1930s is a huge topic and, unfortunately, access to documentary sources remains limited.[98]

Starting in 1929, the Communist governments in the revolutionary base areas began to carry out educational programs. These programs emphasized mass education in addition to training revolutionary cadres and Red Army officers. Women's education and vocational training played important parts. Although the educational policy of the soviet regional governments was both radical and ambitious, rarely did circumstances permit anything but the most rudimentary classes: the money, the teachers, and the requisite stability simply were not available. Teacher training was intensive during the early period, and eventually it expanded and emulated the Nationalist program.

Mass Education and Short-Term Teacher Training Schools

Promoting mass education was the foundation of the Communists' education policy. When the first congress of the Communist Soviet Republic in Jiangxi approved a constitution in November 1931, the declared goal of education was to provide working people with a free modern education and to ensure that male and female students had equal access to school.[99] In the following years, other regional soviet governments established various types of primary schools as well as half-day schools, night schools, and adult schools in which basic literacy classes and ideological indoctrination were emphasized.[100]

Expansion of the revolutionary army and the base areas made the production of army officers and revolutionary cadres the party's first priority; teacher training received little attention. In spite of a declared commitment to mass education, the lack of teaching personnel meant that many primary schools closed after the Communists took over a region.[101] After 1929, most regional soviet governments began to offer short-term training for teachers and educated youth so that they would be able to teach a Communist curriculum. The Fujian soviet called for the establishment of one teacher training school in each county to train teachers for the planned Lenin primary schools.[102] Between 1929 and 1933, many regions opened short-term teacher training programs, which lasted from several weeks to six months.[103]

To relieve the shortage of teachers, many local soviet governments also tried to attract teachers. The Fujian regional soviet stipulated that the salary of primary schoolteachers would be six to eight yuan a month, higher than that of government officials.[104] Additionally, teachers in Shanghang County received a higher grain ration than did government workers.[105] At the same time, the Liuan County government in the Hubei-Henan-Anhui border soviet set up an examination to recruit teachers; about fifty people participated in the examination and those deemed qualified were assigned to local Lenin primary schools.[106]

The Communists soon found that they faced many of the same problems in promoting modern education as had the Nationalists. The Lenin primary schools, largely modelled on the Nationalists' Western-style schools, encountered resistance from villagers and local teachers. In some parts of the Fujian-Anhui soviet, high truancy rates drove the soviet to mandate attendance and to establish penalties for truants and their families. Facing the same problem, the government of the Wanzai County soviet in the Hunan-Hubei-Jiangxi border region made education compulsory and threatened to punish the parents of children who failed to attend school.[107]

Schools influenced political frictions. For instance, in 1933, in the city of Tingzhou, which was under the control of the Fujian soviet, there were thirty-one *sishu*-style schools with 373 students but only one Lenin primary school with two or three students.[108] The Communists blamed the problems they encountered in this area entirely on the "feudal" and "reactionary" ideas being spread by the aged *sishu* teachers; they proposed the expulsion of incompetent teachers (*fantong jiaoshi*) and any who were reluctant to work in the new schools.[109] Due to lack of funds and teachers, the Communists had to tolerate these old schools.

After having developed education in the soviets, the Chinese Communist Party gradually developed a policy for recruiting and training new teachers, with an emphasis on political qualifications. In 1931, the Fujian soviet set up criteria for admitting students to short-term teachers' schools, stipulating that they must be of good family background (i.e., from poor and lower-middle peasant or working-class families), loyal to the revolution, and without any ties – past or present – to any counterrevolutionary organization (i.e., Nationalist organizations).[110] The government of the Liuan County soviet, in the Hubei-Henan-Anhui border area, specifically excluded certain groups of people from becoming teachers, including anyone over forty years old, anyone who had been a "gentry bully," anyone who had served the old government, and anyone who had been a sex offender or religious believer.[111] Some of these early qualifications for becoming teachers became permanently lodged in the Chinese Communist system.

Planning a Full-Fledged Soviet Teachers' School System

The government of the central soviet decided in October 1932 to establish Central Lenin Teachers' School (*Zhongyang Liening shifan xuexiao*) in Ruijin County to staff local teacher-training schools.[112] Students from poor peasant families, who were recommended by local soviet governments, were ensured admission and trained for three to six months.[113] Initially, the school had twelve full-time teachers, and it invited party leaders, including Mao Zedong, Zhang Wentian, Qu Qiubai, and Zhou Enlai, to be guest teachers. In its first year, the school recruited over 400 students, including about 100 female students – a higher ratio of females to males than was found in the Nationalist teachers' schools. From 1932 to 1934, before the Red Army retreated from the Jiangxi area and started the Long March, over 1,000 students graduated from the school.[114]

Before the central soviet government established an advanced teachers' college, local governments had already set up teachers' schools at the provincial level.[115] The Jiangxi soviet established two short-term teachers' schools in January 1932: Lenin Teachers' School Number One (*Liening di yi shifan xuexiao*) in Bosheng County and the Lenin Teachers' School Number Two (*Liening di er shifan xuexiao*) in Xingguo County.[116] The latter, considered the best provincial teachers' school in the soviet, prepared teachers to work in local Lenin primary schools.[117]

Unlike the short-term schools, which emphasized teachers' political training, Central Lenin Teachers' School and Lenin Teachers' School Number Two attempted to offer full curricula. Although the schools still had only short-term programs, they featured courses on politics, literature, natural science, mathematics, history, geography, physiology, teaching methods, teaching regulations, painting, music, handicrafts, and physical education – a set of offerings not too different from those available at the regular teachers' schools in the Nationalist regions (see Table 5.2, Chapter 5).[118] But, of course, the Communist teachers' schools also offered political courses and, from time to time, invited party leaders to deliver lectures.

Interestingly, although these schools required students to participate in physical labour, they did not follow the path blazed by Tao Xingzhi, whose example was followed by many schools opened under the Nationalists. The schools in the Communist base areas, though located in villages, were not responsible for promoting social reforms – a set of duties the soviet governments reserved for themselves.[119] In contrast to the methods of Tao Xingzhi, Liang Shuming, and others, it was the party, rather than the village schools, that directed the social reform programs. The education programs in Jiangxi and other southern soviet base areas took place in the same years as did the radical experiments carried out by Tao, Liang, and others. It seems likely that the Communists did not learn about these experiments until much later. It is also possible that other concerns outweighed the drive to set up schools that would merge with the local community: the Communists wanted to establish a centralized education system like that of their Nationalist counterparts, and, in their revolutionary experiments, they may have had little patience for a new pedagogy.

By 1934, a full-fledged teachers' training system was gradually taking shape, directed by a set of guidelines dictated by the central soviet. The first set of regulations, released in February, included "regulations on the advanced teachers' college" (*gaoji shifan xuexiao jianzhang*), "regulations on lower teachers' schools" (*chuji shifan jianzhang*), "regulations on short-term teachers' schools" (*duanqi shifan xuexiao jianzhang*), and "regulations on training programs for primary schoolteachers" (*xiaoxue jiaoyuan xunlian ban jianzhang*). At the same time, the government also promulgated a set of "rules for the special treatment of primary schoolteachers" (*xiaoxue jiaoyuan youdai tiaoli*).[120]

In courses of study lasting between six months and one year, the advanced teachers' college would train teachers to work in teachers' schools as well as senior education officials to work in government. Lower teachers' schools at the provincial level, including short-term teachers' schools, would train primary schoolteachers and local education cadres. A training course lasted from three to six months, and primary schoolteachers studied during winter and summer vacations. All that was required of applicants to the teachers' schools was basic literacy, and even this was waived for those women who applied. The new government admitted educated people who had worked for the old government to special short training programs and then placed them in schools as assistant teachers. In spite of the financial travails the soviets faced, all teachers' schools were tuition-free and students were provided with all they needed, except food and clothing. As in the Nationalist-controlled regions, all teachers and students in teachers' schools were required to join paramilitary organizations and to undergo military training.[121] Township soviet governments were also to organize the masses to assist primary schoolteachers in ploughing their land.[122] However, after fighting began in earnest in 1934, there was no chance to fully implement these regulations. All of the soviet regions in south China were abandoned in October when the Communists began the Long March.

Table 6A.1

Origins and educational backgrounds of students in Shandong teachers' schools in the 1930s who became Communist leaders

	Name	Family location (county)	Year of birth	Family background[1]	Primary education	Period in teachers' schools[2]	Reference
1	Wan Li	Dongping	1916	Military officer; impoverished local gentry	New style school	1931-33: Dongping county middle school 1933-36: Shandong No. 2 PTS in Qufu	Vol. 7a pp. 1-12
2	Lin Yueqiao	Laiyang	1909	Peasant[3]	Sishu and new school	1926-27, 1929: Laiyang county middle school 1930-33: VTS No. 2 in Laiyang	235-51
3	Liu Zhen	Ju Xian	1910	Peasant	Sishu and new school	1927-33: PTS No. 1 in Ji'nan	259-68
4	Zhang Beihua	Shanghe	1911	Upper-middle peasant	Unknown	1927-31: PTS No. 4 in Qingzhou (Yidu)	269-84
5	Li Renfeng	Linzi	1911	Lower-middle peasant	New school; education was interrupted for financial reasons	1929-32: PTS No. 4 in Qingzhou (Yidu)	285-95
6	Sheng Beiguang	Yanggu	1912	Middle peasant	Sishu and new school	1932-37: PTS No. 3 in Liaocheng	296-308
7	Zhao Zhao	Heze	1913	Lower-middle peasant	New school; education was interrupted for financial reasons	1931-32: VTS No. 3 in Linyi	310-22
8	Wang Ruojie	Zouping	1914	Unknown	New school	1933-36: Ji'nan Yuying Middle School 1936-37: PTS No. 1 in Ji'nan	323-27
9	Gu Mu	Unknown	1915?	Unknown	Unknown	1932-34: VTS No. 7 in Wendeng	328-46
10	Xiang Kun	Dexian	1915	Small merchant	Sishu (and new school?)	1929-35: PTS No. 1 in Ji'nan	347-59
11	Liu Qiren	Weihaiwei	1916	Middle peasant	New school	1933-35: VTS No. 7 in Wendeng 1935-36: PTS No. 1 in Ji'nan	360-66

12	Ma Chengzhai	Pingyuan	1916	Peasant	Sishu and new school; education was interrupted for financial reasons	1931-36: VTS No. 5 in Pingyuan	367-79
13	Wang Kekou	Yucheng	1916	Lower-middle peasant	Sishu and new school, education was interrupted for financial reasons	1933-37: VTS No. 5 in Pingyuan	380-91
14	Zhou Leting	Liaocheng	1917	Middle peasant	Sishu and new school	1933-36: PTS No. 3 in Liaocheng	392-401
15	Li Gan	Ji'ning	1918	Unknown	New school	1934-37: PTS No. 1 in Ji'nan	402-8
16	Jia Dunfang	Qihe	1918	Rich peasant[4]	Sishu and new school	1936-37: PTS No. 3 in Liaocheng	409-17
17	Li Fei	Yuncheng	1919	Impoverished rich peasant; village teacher	New school; finished his primary education through work-study	1933-35: PVTS No. 1 in Ji'nan 1935-37: PTS No. 3 in Liaocheng	418-25
18	Gao Rui	Laiyang	1919	Poor peasant	Sishu and new school	1935-37: VTS No. 2 in Laiyang[5]	426-39
19	Sun Zhongwen	Mouping	Unknown	Unknown	Unknown	1934?-37: PTS No.1 in Ji'nan	473-79
20	Tan Jingqiao	Laiyang	1920	Middle peasant	Sishu and new school	1934-37: VTS No. 2 in Laiyang	480-92
21	Gao Junyue	Pingyuan	1910	Poor peasant	Tutored by a relative with sishu background; new school; education was interrupted for financial reasons	1931-35: VTS No. 5 in Pingyuan	vol. 7b pp. 44-58
22	Li Xichen	Linzi	1912	Village doctor; peasant	Sishu and new school	1930-33: PTS No. 4 in Qingzhou (Yidu)	59-66
23	Liu Guozhu	Rongcheng	1912	Poor peasant	Sishu and new school; education was interrupted for financial reasons	1932-?: VTS No. 7 in Wendeng	67-73
24	Xie Xinhe	Boping	1912	Impoverished local gentry	New school; education was interrupted for financial reasons	1930-33: PTS No. 3 in Liaocheng	83-90
25	Qin Hezhen	Jinxiang	1913	Rich peasant, but later bankrupt	Sishu and new school, education was interrupted to work in field	1931-35: VTS No. 4 in Ziyang	98-108

▶

◄ *Table 6A.1*

	Name	Family location (county)	Year of birth	Family background[1]	Primary education	Period in teachers' schools[2]	Reference
26	Li Jinghe	Qingzhou City	1913	Unknown	New school (?)	1931-34: Qingzhou Provincial middle school 1934-37: PTS No. 4 in Qingzhou (Yidu)	109-16
27	Shi Yichen	Linzi	1914	Peasant; father was a sishu-school teacher	Sishu? and new school?; finished his primary education through work-study	1930-36: PTS No. 4 in Qingzhou (Yidu)	117-23
28	Wang Kedong	Pingyuan	1915	Poor peasant	Sishu? and new school	1932-36: PTS No. 5 in Heze	124-32
29	Lü Yiting	Guangrao	1915	Peasant[6]	New school	1934-37: PTS No. 4 in Qingzhou (Yidu)	139-45
30	Song Qiutan	Tangyi	1915	Middle peasant	Sishu and new school; schooling was interrupted due to banditry	1930-36: PTS No. 3 in Liaocheng	146-53
31	Shen Yunpu	Yanggu	1916	Poor peasant; peddler	New school	1930-31: Yanggu County Short-term TS 1931-34: PTS No. 3 in Liaocheng	161-68
32	Mu Xiang	Penglai	1916	Shop assistant	New school	1930-33: PVTS No. 2 in Laiyang	169-82
33	Li Mancun	Zhangqiu	1917	Village smith; peasant	Sishu and new school; schooling interrupted due to banditry	1932-36: VTS No. 1 in Ji'nan	183-89
34	Zhao Zhenqing	Qingping	1917	Bankrupt rich peasant	Sishu and new school; education was interrupted for financial reasons	1933-35: PVTS No. 5 in Pingyuan	190-99

35	Guo Zhuping	Guangrao	1917	Lower-middle peasant	New school; education was interrupted for financial reasons	1934-37: PVTS No. 5 in Pingyuan	200-12
36	Ding Yuan	Qingping	1917	Poor peasant	Sishu and new school; education was interrupted due to banditry	1932-36: PVTS No. 5 in Pingyuan	213-24
37	Xu Luo (Female)	Pingyuan	1918	Impoverished gentry	New school	1935-37: PVTS No. 5 in Pingyuan	225-34
38	Wu Fengxiang	Yuan'en	1918	Poor peasant	New school	1934-37: PVTS No. 5 in Pingyuan	235-48
39	Cao Yuguang	Sishui	1918	Poor peasant	Sishu and new school	1936-37: PTS No. 2 in Qufu	249-55
40	Jiang Lindong	Mouping	1918	Middle peasant	Sishu and new school	1934-37: PTS No. 2 in Qufu	256-72
41	Zhang Boda	Gaotang	1920	Lower-middle peasant; peddler	New school	1934-37: PVTS No. 5 in Pingyuan	273-81
42	Yang Side	Tengxian	1921	Middle peasant	Sishu and new school	1936-38: Tengxian County Simplified VTS	282-89
43	Yan Wu	Wendeng	1922?	Middle peasant	Unknown	1936-37: VTS No. 7 in Wendeng	290-302

TS = teachers' school, PTS = provincial TS, VTS = village TS.

1 Each autobiography describes family background, but most do not categorize families into standard Communist terms established during the land reform. I make adjustments accordingly. For example, if the protagonist says "my family was poor and we had to work in the field," I categorize his family as "middle peasant" (*zhongnong*) or "lower-middle peasant" (*xia zhongnong*). If he says "my family had almost nothing and we had to work for landlords and beg for food," I categorize the family as "poor peasant" (*pinnong*).

2 A small number of students graduated from county lower middle schools and then entered PTS for upper secondary education.

3 Based on the CCP's criteria, it is possible that his father was a rich peasant.

4 Jia's father was a student activist around 1920 and, with early Communist leader Wang Jinmei, established a radical organization in Shandong. Later, when he returned home as a teacher, he organized a Communist party cell in his village.

5 After 1934, Village Teachers' School No. 2 became Laiyang Simplified Village Teachers' School.

6 Lü's father joined the CCP in 1926.

Source: Shifan qunying, guang yao Zhonghua [Heroic graduates of teachers' schools shine in Chinese history], 21 vols. (Xi'an: Shaanxi People's Education Press, 1992-94).

Table 6A.2

Activities of students of Shandong teachers' schools in the 1930s who became Communist leaders

	Name of student	Major political activities in teachers' schools	Time and place joined CCP	Whereabouts after graduation or leaving school	Major political activities after leaving school	Major/highest/last position after 1949
1	Wan Li	Organized a reading group; mobilized students to participate in the December 9 Movement; protested against military training.	1936 in PTS No. 2	Teacher in home village	Introduced teachers in his schools to the CCP; established a party cell and a "Minxian" branch among local teachers; built up the county party organization; organized guerrilla unit after July 1937.	Chief of the Seventh Chinese People's Congress of China
2	Lin Yueqiao	Elected as president of student union; organized a strike against local warlord who arrested students in a protest against his tax levy; promoted a demonstration, demanding that the authorities create a resistance policy; led students to countryside, mobilizing peasants to join the resistance; introduced fellow students to join the party and set up a CCP party cell; mobilized a student protest against principal's corruption.	1929 in Laiyang Middle School, introduced by his primary school teacher	Village school teacher	Using his primary school as a cover, mobilized local people; organized a guerrilla team in 1934; after this team was suppressed, he engaged in a local workers' movement; joined guerrilla forces after July 1937.	Brigadier; Commander-in-Chief of the Laiyuan military sub-garrison

3	Liu Zhen	Promoted a strike demanding the resignation of incompetent teachers and corrupt principal; organized activities for strike and demonstration after 18 September 1931 incident; led a provincial petition delegation to Nanjing demanding a resistance policy.	Unknown	Entered Shandong University after teaching one year in a village teachers' school	Returned to home village to mobilize guerrilla warfare after July 1937; engaged in CCP resistance and mobilized the masses.	Deputy-Director of the Education Branch of the CCP Provincial Propaganda Department; Vice-Dean of Shandong Teachers' College
4	Zhang Beihua	Organized an anti-Christian/ anti-imperialism protest; set up a CCP party cell and introduced fellow students to the party; organized workers and peasants; initiated the anti-imperialism organization; promoted student protest against school authorities.	1930 in PTS No. 4	Professional revolutionary	Organized workers' movement in Beijing; imprisoned until 1937; returned to Shandong to organize guerrilla warfare after July 1937; in 1939 went to Yan'an and studied at Central Party Academy.	Party Secretary (PS) of Xuzhou City Comm.; PS of the Gansu Provincial Control Commission
5	Li Renfeng	Elected as president of city student union; joined literary society and organized street lectures and demonstration promoting nationalism; organized and led local "Zuolian" branch; published leftist works; set up a night school for local workers; organized a delegation to petition authorities to resist Japan.	1938 in a guerrilla team	Banished from NW Army, then returned home to be a primary schoolteacher	Organized a student propaganda team promoting resistance movement after 1937; organized a guerrilla team after Japanese occupation in 1938.	PS and Chief of the Industrial Department in East China Region Bureau; Assistant Minister of Light Industry

►

	Name of student	Major political activities in teachers' schools	Time and place joined CCP	Whereabouts after graduation or leaving school	Major political activities after leaving school	Major/highest/last position after 1949
6	Sheng Beiguang	Organized a student protest against GMD rule; initiated a peasant organization in home village during school vacation; published literary journal in school; organized anti-Japanese campaigns after 18 September 1931 Incident; protested the GMD military training program.	1932 in PTS No. 3	Returned to home village as a teacher; dean of peasant school in neighboring county	Recruited schoolteachers into CCP and established party cell in his home village; led a flood relief; organized a guerrilla team after 1937 in home area; went to Yan'an after 1940.	Chief of Guizhou Provincial Security Department; Guizhou Provincial Public Procurator-General
7	Zhao Zhao	Organized reading group; mobilized a strike promoting anti-Japanese campaign; set up a CCP party cell; organized a provincial "Anti-Imperialist Alliance"; organized an uprising against the GMD.	1927 in home village; 1931 in teachers' school[1]	Expelled by TS; exiled for a short period after the uprising; became a teacher in a village school	Used teacher's identity to mobilize peasants; organized a guerrilla team and integrated local forces into the resistance after 1937; joined the Eighth Route Army (ERA).	Commodore: Political Commissioner (PC) of East China Fleet; PC of PLA Navy Academy; Deputy-Chief of Political Dept. in Qingdao Navy Base
8	Wang Ruojie	Promoted anti-Japanese organization; mobilized a student protest supporting the December 9 Movement; used a reading group for anti-Japanese campaigns; led a party cell in school; recruited students to join the party and "Minxian."	1934 in Ji'nan Yuying Middle School	Study in TS was interrupted by Japanese invasion	Joined guerrilla army after the school was dismissed in 1937.	Major General (MG); Chief of Political Dept. of Zhejiang Garrison; Ambassador to Yemen, Vietnam; Vice-Minister of Foreign Affairs

9	Gu Mu	Set up a CCP Party cell; organized club to establish contact with peasants; promoted Marxism; organized student protests against the Japanese invasion; organized anti-Japanese organizations; published radical journals and literature.	Before entering VTS in 1932	Professional revolutionary	Worked undercover in Zhang Xueliang's army to mobilize soldiers for the war in 1936; recruited party members; assisted in the building of Jiangsu and Shandong revolutionary bases.	PS of Ji'nan; Vice-PS of Shanghai; Chief of Construction Committee in the State Department; Vice-Prime Minister
10	Xiang Kun	Participated in student reading group; joined anti-Japanese campaigns after 18 September 1931; organized workers' strike; influenced by leftist writers and wrote a novel; imprisoned for publishing leftist novel.	Unknown	Became primary teacher; entered the Nanjing Theatre College	Produced anti-Japanese theatrical works; acted in left-wing and anti-Japanese movies.	Leading actor of Shanghai Film Studio
11	Liu Qiren	Organized and joined a village uprising led by the CCP; organized a strike to expel a reactionary teacher.	1934 in VTS No. 7	Exiled to Beijing	Went to Yan'an, entered Kangda; returned to Shandong and joined the ERA, engaging in guerrilla warfare.	PLA general; Chief of Personnel Branch of the PLA General Political Department;
12	Ma Cheng-zhai	Joined reading group; recruited students to be CCP members; established a party cell in school; mobilized a student protest against the comprehensive final examination.	1934 in VTS No. 5	Returned to home village to be a village teacher	Recruited a group of youth to be Communists; organized a guerrilla team after 1937; established a short-term school for training military and political cadres for the CCP.	Director of No. 1 Automobile Factory; Director of aircraft and weaponry factories

►

	Name of student	Major political activities in teachers' schools	Time and place joined CCP	Whereabouts after graduation or leaving school	Major political activities after leaving school	Major/highest/last position after 1949
13	Wang Kekou	Founded and edited the school journal promoting anti-Japanese campaigns; joined reading group; organized student protest against the comprehensive final examination.	1936 in VTS No. 5	Returned home to be a village teacher	Recruited party members and organized a party cell; recruited youths into anti-Japanese organizations; organized protest against a reactionary principal; established a village school as a centre of resistance; organized and led a guerrilla team; died in the war in 1942.	n/a
14	Zhou Leting	Joined a demonstration supporting the December 9 Movement in 1936; protested against GMD graduate training program.	1936 in graduate training program	Teacher at a peasant school in neighbouring county	Joined and organized guerrilla groups after 1937; promoted resistance movement; recruited rural youths into guerrilla team; went to Yan'an in 1938 and entered Kangda; sent back to Shandong for establishing revolutionary base in 1939.	Vice-Commander of the PLA Qingdao Garrison Command in 1971
15	Li Gan	Joined "Minxian" and "Student Federation"; published left-wing and anti-Japanese literature; joined resistance organization; protested against authorities who arrested student activists; composed anti-Japanese songs.	1938 in Yan'an	Returned to home town (to teach?)	Organized an association among students in home area, assisting the war; joined anti-Japanese propaganda team; entered Yan'an in 1938 and studied at Lu Xun Art Academy; went back to Shandong to promote resistance movement.	Director of the Cultural Division of PLA Ji'nan Military Area Command; President of of Shandong Musicians Association

16	Jia Dunfang	Participated in the anti-Japanese campaign, including fundraising, performing street plays, giving lectures, and joining demonstrations; mobilized a protest against school authorities who attempted to prevent students from joining anti-Japanese activities.	1937 in the teachers' school (Liaocheng)	Schooling was interrupted by the war	Sent by the CCP to rural area after 1937, to mobilize the masses; recruited party members and established party organization; organized local army to prepare for guerrilla warfare; went to Yan'an in 1938 and entered Kangda.	Vice-Secretary of the Yunnan Provincial Discipline Examination Committee
17	Li Fei	Led a protest against the comprehensive final examination; organized "Minxian" local branch; promoted anti-Japanese propaganda.	1934 in PVTS No. 1	Schooling was interrupted by the war	Engaged in resistance propagation; sent to provincial party school; appointed as county leader and led the local resistance.	Vice-President of the Chinese People's Bank
18	Gao Rui	Joined a protest against the comprehensive final examination; participated in demonstration supporting the December 9 Movement 1936; mobilized peasant resistance during vacation in home village; joined in anti-Japanese campaign.	1938 in Yan'an	Schooling was interrupted by the war	Left the school for Yan'an after July 1937; sent back to Shandong after the training; was dean of local military academy that later merged with the ERA.	MG; Chief-of-staff of Lanzhou Greater Military Region; Vice-President of the PLA Military Science College
19	Sun Zhongwen	Established academic and literary societies; mobilized students to promote anti-Japanese campaigns, including fundraising, performing street plays, giving lectures, and launching strikes; published anti-Japanese literature; set up organizations to support the resistance.	1936 in PVTS No. 2	Schooling was interrupted by the war	Engaged in preparatory training for resistance until Ji'nan was occupied by the Japanese; later activities are unknown.	Chief Editor of the Journal of Literature-History-Philosophy of Shandong University

▶

	Name of student	Major political activities in teachers' schools	Time and place joined CCP	Whereabouts after graduation or leaving school	Major political activities after leaving school	Major/highest/last position after 1949
20	Tan Jingqiao	Joined the movement promoting the anti-Japanese campaign.	1938 in the ERA	Schooling was interrupted by the war	Left school to go to Yan'an but failed; then turned to Shanxi and joined the ERA in 1937.	Vice-President of the PLA Military Science College
21	Gao Junyue	Joined reading group and the school theatre to promote the anti-Japanese campaign; protested the comprehensive final examination.	1934 in PVTS No. 5	Returned to home village to be a teacher	Organized theatre for promoting resistance movement among villages; joined the ERA in 1937; went to Yan'an in 1938; sent back to Shandong base area.	PS of the Supervisory Committee at Beijing Agricultural Machinery and Chemistry College
22	Li Xichen	Joined local "Zuolian"; organized a reading group and a workers' night school; led a protest against the GMD; promoted campaign against Japanese invasion; protested against military training.	1931 in PTS No. 4	Arrested by the government in 1933 and imprisoned up to 1937	Released from prison in 1937 and returned to home county; organized a guerrilla team that merged with the ERA in 1938; died in the war in 1939.	n/a
23	Liu Guozhu	Joined activities against the Japanese; organized strike against GMD principle; joined "Broad Anti-Imperialist Alliance"; mobilized peasants resisting tax collectors during school vacation.	1937 in a guerrilla unit	Returned to home village to be a teacher	Organized local guerrilla team that later merged with the ERA.	Air Vice Marshal; Vice-Commander of PLA Air Force in the Shengyang Region

24	Xie Xinhe	Joined a reading group; mobilized peasants during school vacation; promoted the anti-Japanese campaign, including strikes, petitions, demonstrations, street lectures, boycotting Japanese goods; organized local workers' strike demanding increased wages.	1931 joined Communist Youth League in PTS No. 3; 1933 in PTS No. 3	Became a staff member at the county center for peasant education; became a village teacher	Recruited CCP members and set up a party cell; set up a reading group among village youths; established a "Minxian" branch; organized a local guerrilla team; created a local revolutionary base.	PS of Guiyang City; Vice PS of Guizhou Province; Vice-Minister of the Second Light Industry and Light Industry
25	Qin Hezhen	Joined a reading group and other social and academic organizations; petitioned against Japanese invasion; organized strikes against the GMD student agents in the school and bullied rich students; organized a "Minxian" local branch.	1933 in VTS No. 4	Returned to home village to be a teacher	Recruited colleagues to join the CCP and established the local party cell; set up a "Minxian" branch; organized a guerrilla team and created a local revolutionary base.	PS of Shandong Provincial Party Committee
26	Li Jinghe	Participated in the activities supporting the December 9 Movement; mobilized peasants against Japanese invasion during school vocation; joined "Minxian"; protested against the government's arresting progressive intellectuals.	1938 in the primary school where he was teaching	Became a teacher at a primary school in the neighbouring county	Organized anti-Japanese campaign after 1937; mobilized local youth to join guerrilla team; led the guerrilla warfare during Japanese occupation after 1938; established a local revolutionary base.	Vice-PS of Daqing Oil Field; Director of Labour Department of the Ministry of Petroleum Industry
27	Shi Yichen	Propagated communism; mobilized workers in a nearby factory; participated in anti-Japanese organization and activities.	1930 in PTS No. 4	Returned to home village to be a teacher (?)	Organized local youths into a guerrilla team; established an anti-Japanese guerrilla war base in local counties; mobilized an uprising among GMD soldiers.	MG; Vice-Commander of the PLA Fuzhou Military Region

►

	Name of student	Major political activities in teachers' schools	Time and place joined CCP	Whereabouts after graduation or leaving school	Major political activities after leaving school	Major/highest/last position after 1949
28	Wang Kedong	Led a strike against the comprehensive final examination.	1937 in a local peasant school	Became principal of local village peasant school	Recruited local youths into the party; organized a local guerrilla team; created a local revolutionary base.	Vice-Governor of Hebei Province
29	Lü Yiting	Promoted anti-Japanese campaign; joined an anti-Japanese organization in school; promoted anti-Japanese campaign among peasants during school vacation; organized a protest against local GMD educational officials.	1935 in PTS No. 4	Joined a local guerrilla team	Organized a local guerrilla team in 1937 that was later merged with the ERA; died in the war in 1939.	n/a
30	Song Qiutan	Joined a reading group; joined the student delegation demanding that the government resist the Japanese army; recruited activist students into the party.	1935 in PTS No. 3	Became dean of instruction at a local village peasant school	Established local county party organization; went to Yan'an in 1937 and studied at the Marxist-Leninist College; sent to northern Jiangsu to build a revolutionary base.	Vice-PS of the United Front Department of the Central Committee of the CCP
31	Shen Yunpu	Joined a reading group; participated in demonstrations against the Japanese invasion; mobilized factory workers to strike for higher wages.	1932 in PTS No. 3	Teacher at a local primary school	Returned to home village to organize a guerrilla team; transformed a group of bandits into a guerrilla team; recruited party members; created a local revolutionary base.	Vice-PS and Vice-Governor of Guizhou Province

32	Mu Xiang	Promoted anti-Japanese campaign, including strikes, fundraising, street lectures; joined a resistance organization; promoted anti-Japanese movement in villages and mobilized peasants; joined a student petition delegation to Nanjing; led a protest against corrupt principal.	1932 in PVTS No. 2	Teacher at local schools	Recruited CCP members among local youths and workers; organized a literary society; introduced progressive and anti-Japanese works to local youths; exiled to Tianjin; sent by the party to work in the "Ximenghui"[2] in Shanxi; led a guerrilla unit in Shanxi after 1937.	MG; PC of the Armoured Force of the Beijing Garrison; writer; PS of the PLA (August First) film studio
33	Li Mancun	Protested the GMD's concentrated training program; organized a reading group.	1938 in a guerrilla unit	Returned to home village to be a teacher	In 1937, organized a local guerrilla unit that was later merged with the ERA.	MG; Vice-PC of the National Defense University; Member of CCP Central Disciplinary Committee
34	Zhao Zhenqing	Influenced by Communist teachers.	1938 in a guerrilla unit	Returned to home village to be a teacher	Organized mass resistance; co-organized a guerrilla unit with a CCP member; mobilized the masses for warfare; recruited party members.	Vice-Director of the Personnel Department of the CCP Central Committee
35	Guo Zhuping	Participated in the campaign against Japanese invasion; joined a protest against the local government education bureau.	1937 in a guerrilla unit	Schooling was interrupted by Japanese invasion	Joined a local Communist-led guerrilla unit.	PC of the Research Department at the PLA Foreign Language Institute
36	Ding Yuan	Influenced by Communist teachers; wrote literary articles for left-wing journals.	1938 in Kangda	Became dean at a village peasant school	Went to Yan'an in 1938 and entered Kangda; later became a Communist journalist.	Vice-Minister of the Ministry of Construction Materials

▸

◄ *Table 6A.2*

	Name of student	Major political activities in teachers' schools	Time and place joined CCP	Whereabouts after graduation or leaving school	Major political activities after leaving school	Major/highest/last position after 1949
37	Xu Luo (Female)	Joined a reading group; joined the school theatre promoting the anti-Japanese movement; joined the "Minxian."	1939 in the Kangda	Schooling was interrupted by Japanese invasion	Joined a United Front propaganda team after 1937; went to Yan'an, entered Kangda and the Yan'an Medical School.	Major of PLA; medical doctor in a military hospital
38	Wu Fengxiang	Joined a reading group; joined the school theater promoting the anti-Japanese campaign; led a protest against the comprehensive final examination; edited the school magazine; organized a student group for war service	1938 in the Kangda	Schooling was interrupted by Japanese invasion	Entered a GMD military school in 1937, then escaped to Yan'an in 1938 and entered Kangda; led an Eight Route Army theatre.	Director of Personnel bureau in the Political Department of National Defence, Scientific and Engineering Committee
39	Cao Yuguang	Joined a reading group; promoted CCP influence in the local primary school; recruited schoolteachers to be CCP members; organized anti-Japanese activities; organized a protest against the conservative principal.	1936 in a teachers' school	Returned home to village after being expelled by the school in 1937 due to radical activities	Established a CCP party cell in his village and recruited villagers to be members; mobilized villagers and organized a guerrilla unit that was later merged with the ERA.	MG; Director of the Department of Mobilization of the PLA Headquarters General Staff
40	Jiang Lindong	Joined student resistance organization; participated in strikes, protests, and a team to promote anti-Japanese campaign; went to villages to mobilize peasants.	1938 in the Shaanbei Public School	Schooling was interrupted by Japanese invasion	Went to Yan'an in 1937; entered the Shaanbei Public School; sent to work in Henan-Anhui-Jiangsu Revolutionary Base Area after training.	MG; Vice-PC of the Xinjiang Military Region and Guangzhou Greater Military Region

41	Zhang Boda	Joined a reading group; participated in the protest against the comprehensive final examination; joined the "Minxian."	1938 in the ERA	Schooling was interrupted by Japanese invasion	Joined the Eight Route Army in 1937; went to Yan'an in 1938 and entered Kangda; worked in the headquarters of the ERA.	Brigadier; Vice-Dean of Instruction of the PLA Military Academy
42	Yang Side	Joined activities promoting anti-Japanese campaigns; joined the "Minxian."	1938 in the a guerrilla unit	School was closed due to the war	Joined the CCP-led guerrilla training program and a guerrilla unit after the Japanese occupation in 1938.	MG; Director of the Office of Communication of the PLA General Political Department; Director of Office of Taiwan Affairs in the CCP Central Committee
43	Yan Wu	Joined activities promoting anti-Japanese actions.	Unknown[3]	Schooling was interrupted by Japanese invasion	Joined a local theatre propagating anti-Japanese campaign; joined the ERA; became an ERA news reporter and a director of a military news agency.	Vice-Director and PS of PLA News Agency; national leading journalist

1 Zhao was recruited by the Communist Party at a very young age through his primary school teacher. Later he lost contact with the party organization and was once again recruited in the teachers' school.

2 The full name of "Ximenghui" is "Xisheng jiuguo tongmeng hui" (The alliance of sacrifice for the national salvation). The organization was established in Shanxi Province in 1936 by Yan Xishan, the governor of Shanxi. Yan formed a temporary alliance between Ximenghui and the CCP in order to prepare for fighting the Japanese Invasion. Bo Yibo, a Communist, was the top leader of the Alliance.

3 Although the biography does not mention when Yan Wu joined the party, given his official position, he must be a veteran party member.

Source: Shifan Qunying, Guangyao Zhonghu [Heroic graduates of teachers' schools shine in Chinese history], 21 vols. (Xi'An: Shaanxi renmin jiaoyu chubanshe [Shaanxi people's education publishing house], 1992-94), vol. 7a, 7b.

Conclusion

At the end of the nineteenth century, the Qing court initiated an ambitious program to build a nationwide teachers' school system – a crucial step in manufacturing the modern educational system, which was seen as an essential element of the modern nation-state. As officials and local administrators took to blending different elements of domestically cultivated educational traditions and foreign imports, China's teachers' schools became the focal point of a dynamic process. These new schools mediated between local values and Western educational practices and ideals, and brilliant schoolmasters did what they could to integrate these obtrusive institutions into local society. Governments run by the Qing court, by warlords, and by Nationalist officials used teachers' schools to shape local schools and to provide them with teaching and administrative personnel. At the same time, teachers' schools transformed old literati officials into modern educators, even as their policy of admitting students without charging tuition offered rural youths a chance to gain access to the modern world. Teaching became reason enough for women to cross the threshold of domesticity and to receive a modern, public education. Teaching provided women with the social niche they needed to begin to achieve greater freedom and independence. Teachers' schools were important venues, within which the state and society overlapped and interacted. Social organizations used these schools to test their radical social and educational reforms, while revolutionaries worked to convert them into bases for recruitment and mobilization for yet more radical projects.

The two processes I outline in the introduction and detail in the intervening chapters – "localizing the global and nationalizing the local" – continued even after the outbreak of the Anti-Japanese War in 1937. Although the role of teachers' schools has changed since the Communists took power in 1949, the schools continue to train thousands of young teachers and, even today, are considered an important part of China's modernization.

After the Japanese invasion in 1937, most colleges and universities withdrew from big cities and coastal areas and were re-established in western and southwestern China, particularly in Yunnan, Sichuan, Guizhou, and Shaanxi provinces. The relocation of modern colleges and universities brought modern education to the remote inland areas, and the process of localizing the global was repeated once again in the hinterlands. The state felt it necessary to restore teachers' colleges and to expand secondary teachers' schools in order to meet the needs of these areas. In 1938, the Ministry of Education convened a national educational meeting and issued a set of reforms to deal with wartime conditions. The teachers' colleges that had been attached to larger universities were formally permitted to strike off on their own. The reform plan also encouraged governments at all levels to build more secondary teachers' schools, both to take in refugee students and to provide refugee teachers for the localities in which they had taken up residence.[1] As a result, teachers' schools at the tertiary level were restored to the independent position that they had before the 1922 Education Reform, and teachers' education at both the tertiary and secondary levels was now carried out in independent schools. The purpose of these new teachers' colleges was to train qualified teachers for local middle schools and teachers' schools in order to promote modern education in these inland areas. After the war, the teachers' schools and colleges that had been created by several united universities (*lianhe daxue*, which were the result of the merging of city and coastal colleges and universities) remained in the inland provinces. With these schools, Shaanxi, Gansu, Guizhou, and other provinces, which previously had no tertiary educational institutions, were able to further their education systems. These schools also became the educational legacy in these inland areas, which the Communist Party continued to develop after the civil war.

The relocation of universities and colleges from coastal areas to the "Great Rear Region" (*Da houfang*) led to cultural shock and cultural transfer. The relocation of modern schools to the hinterlands, along with students' academic and social activities, also brought a new lifestyle to inland society. Many college students and teachers took part-time teaching positions at secondary schools in the places in which they resided. Students and teachers at these universities and colleges not only helped disseminate modern knowledge but also brought a new way of life to inland towns, opening remote regions to the outside world. On the other hand, students and teachers from economically and culturally advanced areas came to comprehend the poorer and less industrialized social and economic situations in the hinterlands. They were also fascinated by the diversity of local ethnic groups and the richness of their cultures.[2] Students were inspired to study Chinese society by conducting local surveys. Many scholars reoriented their research projects, shifting from following Western academic topics to discovering and studying local cultures and communities.

Teachers' schools played an even more important role in state penetration and social reform as the process of nationalizing the local continued during wartime. Under the programs of "supervising local education" (*fudao difang jiaoyu*) and "social education" (*shehui jiaoyu*), the Nationalist government assigned these teachers' colleges and schools such social tasks as directing local education and reconstructing local communities. Since the 1938 conference called for building more teachers' schools in the "Great Rear Region," the government constantly issued directives, expanding the role of teachers' schools in reforming society. The students and faculty of teachers' schools were required to assist the Guomindang government in building local self-governing bodies, promoting popular education, organizing village groups, and mobilizing masses to support the government's war effort.[3]

During the Anti-Japanese War (1937-45), education in the Communist-controlled Shaanxi-Gansu-Ningxia Border Region in northwestern China was aimed mainly at training party cadres to expand revolutionary bases and to practise guerrilla warfare against the Japanese. The Chinese Communist Party also established several teachers' schools in order to promote literacy and to mobilize the masses. Due to limited human and financial resources, during this period, the Chinese Communist Party adopted a more flexible education policy in terms of forms of schools, curricula, and pedagogy. Students were taught local knowledge and practical skills rather than Western knowledge. The schools in the Border Region became increasingly involved in community activities and were integrated into the political programs of the local government.[4] This education policy and practice, which later merged with a progressive trend from the Guomindang area represented by Tao Xingzhi, became part of the Chinese Communist Party legacy of revolutionary education. After 1949, it played an important part in shaping educational policy, educational debates, and political struggle.

Under the Communist regime after 1949, only part of the tradition of teachers' schools remained. The new Communist government rapidly expanded the entire education system. In reorganizing educational structure in the early 1950s, the national network of teachers' schools was expanded and remained separate from but parallel to the regular education system. The even geographic distribution of teachers' schools was expected to provide an equal dispensation of educational resources. As a result, almost every province or "Grand administrative district" (*da xingzheng qu*)[5] was provided with one or two teachers' colleges or universities. By 1949, there were 205 higher educational institutions, among which only twelve were independent teachers' colleges or universities. Four years later, when the program of educational reorganization was complete, the total number of higher institutions had been reduced to 182, while the number of tertiary teachers' schools had been increased to thirty-three. By 1957, the number of tertiary teachers' schools had increased to fifty-eight.[6] The number of secondary teachers' schools increased to provide more counties with at least one school to train teachers for elementary schools and kindergartens. In some rural counties, new teachers' schools established in the early 1950s were the first secondary schools in the county.

The new government reinforced its control over the teachers' schools, as it did over other educational institutions, by assigning presidents, principals, and party secretaries. All schools were under the direction of the Ministry of Education, which issued unified curricula and admissions guidelines. A national unified entrance examination was established to select students for all tertiary schools in China. All college graduates were assigned jobs according to a national plan. Since all college graduates were now recruited into the state personnel system, teachers' school graduates not only became teachers but also government cadres. The rapid growth of teachers' schools in local communities greatly assisted the expansion of basic education, especially in rural areas. On the other hand, the social role of teachers' schools in reforming local communities, except for a very brief period during 1958, was largely restrained since the Chinese Communist Party had developed its party cells and organizations to conduct the task. The significant role of teachers' schools in providing equal educational opportunity for girls and women became less important in urban areas, but teachers' schools were still the major channel by which girls in inland regions continued their education.

Like previous governments, the Communist government provided tuition, lodging, board, and a monthly allowance to all of the students in teachers' schools. By comparison, while students in polytechnic universities, colleges, and comprehensive universities also received free tuition, about 20 percent of these students (those from higher-income families) had to pay their own living costs. Tuition at regular middle schools was not free. As in the past, this policy attracted youths from rural areas and small towns, who could not afford to spend much on their education, to teachers' schools.

In the 1960s, most teachers' schools were upgraded in special training schools at the senior high school level. In the late 1970s and early 1980s these former teachers' schools were upgraded to junior colleges that focused on teacher training. Starting in the late 1980s, most of these junior colleges were upgraded to four-year colleges, and the original teachers' colleges were upgraded to teachers' universities. By the early 1990s, secondary level teachers' schools had ceased to exist.[7]

Teachers' social status and the appeal of teachers' schools appear to be related to both political and economic factors. During the Cultural Revolution, schools all across China were shuttered and teachers were treated disgracefully. When schools reopened in the late 1970s and early 1980s, many viewed teachers' schools with lingering disdain. The value of a degree from these schools, measured by the simple indices of salary upon graduation and the place of teachers' schools vis-à-vis regular colleges, did not appeal to those growing up in the post-Cultural Revolution era.

In 1992, the Ministry of Education announced that, henceforth, students at polytechnic and comprehensive colleges and universities would have to pay tuition fees and additional expenses. Teachers' schools received a brief reprieve, remaining tuition-free until 2000. During those years, more high school graduates, especially those who were disadvantaged, applied to teachers' colleges.[8] As the college entrance examination came to dominate the fates of all high schools graduates, students came to value their teachers highly and salaries began to inch up. As China's new examination culture began to affect elementary schools, the status and income of primary schoolteachers enjoyed a boost. Beginning in the new millennium, a century-long free-tuition policy for teachers' colleges and universities has been abolished, but the state still favours students who were aligned with the teacher training program, charging them only partial tuitions. Teachers' colleges and universities continue to attract students from moderate-income families.

In April 2005, a national conference on teacher training was held at Beijing Normal University, China's top teachers' university with over a hundred years of history. At the conference, the director of the Department of Teacher's Education (*shifan jiaoyu si*) in the Ministry of Education, Guan Peijun, had a presentation on the newest trend in teacher training. He revealed that the Ministry of Education's goal is to ensure that, by 2020, all teachers of both primary and secondary schools will hold college degrees. To realize this goal, the ministry will expand the teacher training program from previous teachers' schools to all types of higher educational institutions. The state will only administer the certificate examination periodically to ensure the qualification and quality of teachers.[9] This plan seems to echo the changes made in the 1922 Education Reform. Will history repeat itself?

The education policy since the 1990s has resulted in great disparity in China. A large number of students from rural areas entered urban colleges and never returned to their home villages. At the same time, village children in remote regions are still suffering from a shortage of funding and teachers. Closer to realizing the nineteenth-century modernizers' dreams of wealth and power than ever before, China is coming face to face with the same problems that have plagued it since the eighteenth century and that I mentioned at the beginning of this book. In the past 200 years, the same issues have been dealt with by the Qing state and have been addressed by both the 1922 reformers and Tao Xingzhi. The reform programs have been launched by the Qing state as well as the Nationalist and Communist governments. At the beginning of the new millennium, new voices are asking that attention be given to disadvantaged children, and various solutions have been proposed. On its march towards wealth and power, China may need to review the path taken over the past 200 years and readdress the problem of rural education and development. Whatever happens, however, the important role that teachers' schools have played in the twentieth century should not be ignored.

Notes

Abbreviations used in the notes are listed at the beginning of the bibliography on page 266.

Introduction

1 Ernest Gellner, *Nations and Nationalism* (New York: Cornell University Press, 1983), 28-38.

2 Eugen Weber, *Peasants into Frenchmen: The Modernization of Rural France, 1870-1914* (Stanford: Stanford University Press, 1976), 303-38.

3 Benedict Anderson, *Imagined Communities: Reflections on the Origin and Spread of Nationalism* (New York: Verso, 1983), 116-36.

4 Weber, *Peasants into Frenchmen*, 303.

5 Jo Burr Margadant, *Madame le Professeur: Women Educators in the Third Republic* (Princeton: Princeton University Press, 1990), 1-13.

6 Scott J. Seregny, *Russian Teachers and Peasant Revolution: The Politics of Education in 1905* (Bloomington: Indiana University Press, 1989); Mary Kay Vaughan, *Cultural Politics in Revolution: Teachers, Peasants, and Schools in Mexico, 1930-1940* (Tucson: University of Arizona Press, 1997).

7 Han Yu, "Shi shuo" [On teachers], in *Gu wen guan zhi* [A primer of classical Chinese texts], ed. Wu Chucai and Wu Diaohou, 333-35 (Beijing: Zhonghua shuju, 1959).

8 The term *shifan* first appeared in a book entitled *Fa yan* [Model sayings], written by Yang Xiong in the Western Han dynasty (206 BCE-24 CE). Yang believed that teachers should serve as role models (*shi zhe, ren zhi mofan ye*). *Ci hai* (Ocean of words), s.v., *shifan*. It was also used to praise those whose perfect conduct served as a model. The term could also be used to indicate "learning from" or "as a model." The first use of the term to refer to teachers may have occurred during the Yuan dynasty (1279-1368) or later, in the Ming dynasty (1368-1644). Wu Zhihe, *Mingdai de ruxue jiaoguan* [Education officials of the Ming dynasty] (Taipei: Taibei xuesheng shuju, 1991), 155.

9 Lydia Liu defines the term *shifan* as a "return of graphic loans," believing that it had been given a new meaning when it was re-introduced back to China from Japan. Lydia Liu, *Translingual Practice: Literature, National Culture, and Translated Modernity – China, 1900-1937* (Stanford: Stanford University Press, 1995), 327.

10 After 1949, teachers' schools remained a very important part of the Communist system. This volume addresses only the first four decades of the twentieth century, providing a foundation for further work on the Communist period.

11 Knight Biggerstaff, *The Earliest Modern Government Schools in China* (New York: Cornell University Press, 1961).

12 John Cleverley, *The Schooling of China* (Winchester: George Allen and Unwin, 1985), 3.

13 Benjamin Schwartz, "The Limits of 'Tradition versus Modernity' as Categories of Explanation: The Case of the Chinese Intellectuals," *Daedalus: Journal of the American Academy of Arts and Sciences* 101 (Spring 1972): 71-88.

14 Sally Borthwick, *Education and Social Change in China* (Stanford: Hoover Institution Press, Stanford University, 1983), 16.
15 Wen-hsin Yeh, *The Alienated Academy: Culture and Politics in Republican China, 1919-1937* (Cambridge: Harvard University Press, 1990), 92-105.
16 Ruth Hayhoe, "Cultural Tradition and Educational Modernization: Lessons from the Republican Era," in *Education and Modernization: The Chinese Experience*, ed. Ruth Hayhoe, 47-72 (Toronto: Ontario Institute for Studies in Education, 1992).
17 Ruth Hayhoe, *China's Universities, 1895-1995: A Century of Cultural Conflict* (New York: Garland Publishing, 1996), 29-63.
18 Joan Judge, "Meng Mu Meets the Modern: Female Exemplars in Early-Twentieth-Century Textbooks for Girls and Women," in *Jindai Zhongguo funü shi yanjiu* [Studies in modern Chinese women's history] 8 (Taipei: Zhongyang yanjiu yuan jindai shi yanjiusuo, 2000): 133-77.
19 Suzanne Pepper, *Radicalism and Education Reform in Twentieth-Century China* (New York: Cambridge University Press, 1996).
20 Stig Thøgersen, *A County of Culture: Twentieth-Century China Seen from the Village Schools of Zouping, Shandong* (Ann Arbor: University of Michigan Press, 2002).
21 Charles W. Hayford, *To the People: James Yen and Village China* (New York: Columbia University Press, 1990), xii.
22 Helen Chauncey, *Schoolhouse Politicians: Locality and State during the Chinese Republic* (Honolulu: University of Hawaii Press, 1992), 118.
23 Robert Culp, "Elite Association and Local Politics in Republican China: Educational Institutions in Jiashan and Lanqi Counties, Zhejiang, 1911-1937," *Modern China* 20, 4 (1994): 446-77.
24 Studies that mention teachers' schools in passing include Paul Bailey, *Reform the People: Changing Attitudes towards Popular Education in Early Twentieth-Century China* (Vancouver: UBC Press, 1990), 31-48; David Buck, "Educational Modernization in Tsinan, 1899-1937," in *The Chinese City between Two Worlds*, ed. Mark Elvin and G. William Skinner, 171-212 (Stanford: Stanford University Press, 1974); Thøgersen, *A County of Culture*, 12; Borthwick, *Education and Social Change in China*, 152-53; Keith R. Schoppa, *Chinese Elites and Political Change: Zhejiang Province in the Early Twentieth Century* (Cambridge: Harvard University Press, 1982), 70.
25 Thøgersen, *A County of Culture*, 12, 89.
26 Chuang Chai-hsuan, *Tendencies toward a Democratic System of Education in China* (Shanghai: Commercial Press, 1922), 91-131.
27 J.P. Chu, "Normal School Education in China," *Bulletin on Chinese Education* 2, 11 (1923): 1-22.
28 Theodore H. Chen, *Teacher Training in Communist China* (Washington, DC: US Department of Health, Education and Welfare, 1960).
29 Igarashi Shoichi, "Shimatsu shin kyoiku seido hogaki ni okeru kyoshi yosei kikan no sette" [The establishment of teacher training institutions during the initial period of late Qing educational reforms], in *Kindai Ajia kyoikushi kenkyu* [Studies of educational history in modern Asia], ed. Akigoro Taga, 1:61-114 (Tokyo: Iwasaki Gakujutushuppansha, 1975).
30 Kobayashi Yoshifuni, "Chugoku kindai kyoinshi kenkyu josetsu–1920-nendai no Chugoku ni okeru shoto kyoin no kumiai undo o megutte" [Prefatory remarks on the history of China's modern teachers: Primary schoolteachers and their organizations in 1920s China), *Toyoshi kenkyu* [Studies of East Asian history] 44, 4 (1986): 128-61.
31 Yu Jiaju, *Shifan jiaoyu* [Teachers' education] (Shanghai: Chung Kwa Book Co., 1926); Luo Tingguang, *Shifan jiaoyu xin lun* [A new perspective on teachers' education] (Shanghai: Nanjing shudian, 1933); Li Chaoying, *Zhongguo shifan jiaoyu lun* [On Chinese teachers' education] (Shanghai: Shangwu yinshuguan, 1939); Liu Wenxiu, *Zhongguo shifan jiaoyu jianshi* [A brief history of Chinese teachers' education] (Beijing: People's Education Press, 1985); Wu Dingchu, *Zhongguo shifan jiaoyu jianshi* [A brief history of Chinese teachers' education] (Chengdu: Sichuan jiaoyu chubanshe, 1990).
32 Lloyd Rudolph and Susanne Rudolph, *The Modernity of Tradition: Political Development in India* (Chicago: University of Chicago Press, 1967), 3.

33 Here I have followed Sally Borthwick's example, using the two terms as shorthand. See Borthwick, *Education and Social Change in China*, 16.
34 Benjamin Schwartz, *In Search of Wealth and Power: Yen Fu and the West* (Cambridge: Belknap Press of Harvard University Press, 1964), 1-5, points out that Chinese intellectuals of the late Qing dynasty did not face a monolithic West but, rather, a cultural, political, economic, and geographic mosaic.
35 Delia Davin, "Imperialism and the Diffusion of Liberal Thought: British Influences on Chinese Education," in *China's Education and the Industrialized World: Studies in Cultural Transfer*, ed. Ruth Hayhoe and Marianne Bastid, 33-56 (New York: M.E. Sharpe, 1987).
36 Thøgersen, *A County of Culture*, 8.
37 Examples of such publications include *Xue bu guan bao* [Bulletins of the Board of Education, 1904-11], *Jiaoyu gongbao* [Official Bulletin of education, 1914-27], *Da xueyuan gongbao* [Bulletins of the University Council, 1927-28], and *Jiaoyu bu gongbao* [Official Bulletin of the Ministry of Education, 1928-48].
38 Thøgersen, *A County of Culture*, 5-6, 9.
39 Richard Orb, "Chili Academies and Other Schools in the Late Ch'ing: An Institutional Survey," in *Reform in Nineteenth-Century China*, ed. Paul A. Cohen and John E. Schrecker, 231-40 (Cambridge: East Asian Research Center, Harvard University, distributed by Harvard University Press, 1976); David Buck, "Educational Modernization in Tsinan," 171-212; Chauncey, *Schoolhouse Politicians;* Thøgersen, *A County of Culture;* Culp, "Elite Association and Local Politics in Republican China," 446-77; Hayhoe, "Cultural Tradition and Educational Modernization," 47-72; Elizabeth VanderVen, "Educational Reform and Village Society in Twentieth-Century Northeast China: Haicheng, 1905-1931" (PhD dissertation, University of California at Los Angeles, 2003).

Chapter 1: The Imperial School System and Education Reform

1 Hao Chang, *Liang Ch'i-ch'ao and Intellectual Transition in China, 1890-1907* (Cambridge: Harvard University Press, 1971), 1.
2 John Chaffee, *The Thorny Gates of Learning in Sung China: A Social History of Examinations* (Cambridge: Cambridge University Press, 1985); Benjamin A. Elman, "Political, Social, and Cultural Reproduction via Civil Service Examinations in Late Imperial China," *Journal of Asian Studies* 50, 1 (1991): 7-28.
3 The Ming dynasty had two capitals: Beijing, where the imperial court and government departments actually resided, and Nanjing, which remained the nominal capital due to its importance in the founding of the dynasty.
4 *"Zhou"* is an administrative region within a province.
5 Zhang Tingyu et al., *Ming Shi* [History of the Ming dynasty] (Beijing: Zhonghua shuju, 1974) 6, 1789-90, 1834, 1851-52; see also Yang Rongchun, *Zhongguo fengjian shehui jiaoyu shi* [Educational history of feudal China] (Guangzhou: Guangdong renmin chubanshe, 1985), 364-72.
6 Ma Tai-loi, "The Local Education Officials of Ming China, 1368-1644," *Oriens Extremes* 22.1 (1975): 12; Wu Zhihe, *Mingdai de ruxue jiaoguan* [Education officials of the Ming dynasty] (Taipei: Taipei Student Press, 1991), 19-20.
7 The imperial government practised a system that set up a fixed number of students for each dynastic school. This number was decided on the basis of population and taxation in the region where the school was located. This quota system was used to decide how many students in a region would pass the examinations and receive imperial titles. Each school therefore, could only recruit students from its own jurisdiction and had strict rules on the geographic origins of its students.
8 Yang, *Zhongguo fengjian shehui jiaoyu shi*, 361-86. See also Ping-ti Ho, *The Ladder of Success in Imperial China: Aspects of Social Mobility, 1368-1911* (New York: Columbia University Press, 1962), 194-96.
9 Wu, *Mingdai de ruxue jiaoguan*, 166-73.
10 Zhao Erxun, "Xuanyu zhi" [A record of the examination system], in *Qingshi gao* [A draft of Qing history] 12 (Beijing: Zhonghua shuju, 1977), 3099-119; see also Yang, *Zhongguo fengjian shehui jiaoyu shi*, 442-46.

11 Liang Zhangju, *Tui'an suibi* [Notes from the retreat], *YZSJ*: 160; Yang, *Zhongguo fengjian shehui jiaoyu shi*, 442-46.

12 Yang, *Zhongguo fengjian shehui jiaoyu shi*, 364-72. See also Ping-ti Ho, *The Ladder of Success in Imperial China*, 194-96.

13 "Shuyuan yixue tiao shiwen" [A glossary of terms related to academies and charitable schools], *YZSJ:* 168-69; Yang, *Zhongguo fengjian shehui jiaoyu shi*, 462-66; Hsiao Kung-chuan, *Rural China: Imperial Control in the Nineteenth Century* (Seattle: University of Washington Press, 1960), 235-37.

14 Chen Yuanhui and Wang Bingzhaó, *Zhongguo gudai de shuyuan zhidu* [China's ancient academies] (Shanghai: Shanghai jiaoyu chubanshe, 1981), 91-93; Tilemann Grimm, "Academies and Urban Systems in Kwangtung," in *The City in Late Imperial China*, ed. G. William Skinner, 480-84 (Stanford: Stanford University Press, 1977).

15 Grimm, "Academies and Urban Systems," 477-78, 487-89.

16 "Shuyuan yixue tiao shiwen," *YZSJ:* 168-69; Fan Kezheng, *Zhongguo shuyuan shi* [History of Chinese academies], (Taipei: Wenjin chubanshe, 1995), 227-47; Chen Gujia and Deng Hongbo, *Zhongguo shuyuan zhidu yanjiu* [Studies of China's academies] (Nanjing: Zhejiang jiaoyu chubanshe, 1997), 55-103.

17 According to Chinese scholars, in the late Qing, there were more than 7,000 private academies in China. See Chen and Deng, *Zhongguo shuyuan zhidu yanjiu*, 460; and Liu Boji, *Guangdong shuyuan zhidu yange* [History of the academy system in Guangdong] (Shanghai: Commercial Press, 1939), 79. This scale has been confirmed by the work of a Japanese scholar who has provided statistics on newly opened academies over the course of the Qing. She showed that the greatest increase took place during the Qianlong regime (1736-95), when over 500 new institutions were established. See Okubo Hideko, *Min Shin jidai shoin no kenkyu* [A study of academies during the Ming and Qing] (Tokyo: Kokusho kankokai, 1976), 123.

18 Evelyn Sakakida Rawski, *Education and Popular Literacy in Ch'ing China* (Ann Arbor: University of Michigan Press, 1979). Before the twentieth century, there were various terms for traditional-style schools. The term *sishu* refers to those schools operated by a single teacher as opposed to those sponsored by families and clans, individuals, and the state. See Peng Deng, *Private Education in Modern China* (Westport, CT: Praeger Publishers, 1997), 6-7. The disappearance during the twentieth century of other terms for traditional schools may have been the result of the expansion of the state-controlled public educational system. Liao T'ai-ch'u has found that, while several types of traditional schools still existed in 1930s Shandong, they were all named *sishu*. See T'ai-ch'u Liao, "Rural Education in Transition: A Study of the Old-Fashioned Chinese Schools [Szu Shu] in Shantung and Szechuan," *Yanjing Journal of Social Studies* 4, 2 (1949): 1220-23. Apparently, by the twentieth century, the term *sishu* was used to distinguish different types of private schools from state schools.

19 Chen and Deng, *Zhongguo shuyuan zhidu yanjiu*, 11, 460.

20 Liu, *Guangdong shuyuan zhidu yange*, 45-46, 81-82.

21 Angela Leung, "Elementary Education in the Lower Yangtze Region in the Seventeenth and Eighteenth Centuries," in *Education and Society in Late Imperial China, 1600-1900*, ed. Benjamin A. Elman and Alexander Woodside (Berkeley: University of California Press, 1994), 387. Leung also argued that, by the Qing, the system of community schools was moribund with regard to elementary education. By contrast, Tilemann Grimm has shown that, as late as the nineteenth century, students in private Guangdong academies had often received their primary education in community schools (see Grimm, "Academies and Urban Systems," 488). It is evident that the function of community schools varied from place to place.

22 See Rawski, *Education and Popular Literacy;* Hsiao, *Rural China*; Ho, *Ladder of Success*; Alexander Woodside, "Some Mid-Qing Theorists of Popular Schools: Their Innovations, Inhibitions, and Attitudes toward the Poor," *Modern China* 9, 1 (1983): 3-35; Yang, *Zhongguo fengjian shehui jiaoyu shi*; Liu, *Guangdong shuyuan zhidu yange*; Wu Ni and Hu Yan, *Zhongguo gudai sixue yu jindai sili xuexiao yanjiu* [A study of private schools in ancient and modern China] (Ji'nan: Shandong jiaoyu chubanshe, 1997); Su Yunfeng, *Zhang Zhidong yu Hubei jiaoyu gaige* [Zhang Zhidong and educational reform in Hubei] (Taipei: Institute of Modern History Academia Sinica, 1976).

23 "Gesheng yixue" [Charitable schools in vaious provinces], *YZSJ:* 314-19.
24 According to Sarah Schneewind, the state's efforts to penetrate local communities through the promotion of education started even before the sixteenth century. At that time, local officials participated in an initiative to destroy "improper shrines" and to transform them into community schools. See Schneewind, "Competing Institutions: Community Schools and 'Improper Shrines' in Sixteenth-Century China," *Late Imperial China* 20, 1 (1999): 85-106.
25 Liu Xiangguang, "Zhongguo jinshi difang jiaoyu de fazhan – Huizhou wenren, shushi yu chuji jiaoyu, 1100-1800" [The development of local education in early modern China: Literati, schoolteachers, and elementary education in Huizhou, 1100-1800], *Jindai shi yanjiusuo jikan* [Journal of the Institute of Modern History Academic Sinica] 28 (1997): 28-39. In her essay "Competing Institutions" Schneewind argues that, although the Ming court did urge local officials to build community schools, the fate of such projects depended on the personal interest and enthusiasm of those officials. William T. Rowe's study of Chen Hongmou's activities in Yunnan during the Qing confirmed that individual officials held tremendous sway over the development of community schools. See Rowe, "Education and Empire in Southwest China: Ch'en Hung-mou in Yunnan, 1733-38," in Elman and Woodside, *Education and Society in Late Imperial China*, 417-57.
26 Woodside argued that, although literacy increased, its content, nature, and purpose were unrelated to improving the living conditions of peasants. Many bureaucrats and emperors believed that widespread literacy would encourage rebelliousness. This suggests that the relatively high rate of literacy achieved under the Qing would never have led China to form an industrial society. See Woodside, "Some Mid-Qing Theorists," 3-35; Alexander Woodside, "Real and Imagined Continuities in the Chinese Struggle for Literacy," in *Education and Modernization: The Chinese Experience*, ed. Ruth Hayhoe, 23-45 (Toronto: Ontario Institute for Studies in Education, 1992). It turned out that increasing literacy did precipitate a number of social and political problems, but they were not those anticipated by Qing alarmists, as the following section shows.
27 Leung argues that, during the seventeenth and eighteenth centuries, the state's influence on elementary educational institutions shrank as such responsibilities were taken over by local communities. But she admits that a large minority of charitable schools in Jiangnan were sponsored by the state and that the state played an active role in local elementary schools. See Leung, "Elementary Education," 386-87. It is evident that the state was still trying to penetrate local areas by establishing charitable schools. There is also evidence that, in other places, especially the frontier regions, most charitable schools were established by local officials (see "Gesheng yixue"; "Xingjian gaoshi, xiangwen" [Government edicts and documents on establishing (charitable schools)], *YZSJ:* 314-28). Local records also show that some officials, such as the governor of Xiangyang Prefecture, Zhou Kai, did make an effort to build community schools.
28 The remarkable works by Wu Zhihe and Ma Tai-loi on Ming Confucian teaching officials are brilliant exceptions. Liu Xiangguang and Sarah Schneewind also briefly mention the process of selecting teachers for family schools and community schools.
29 Wu, *Mingdai de ruxue jiaoguan;* Ma, "Local Education Officials," 11-27.
30 Zhao, *Qingshi gao*, 3099-119.
31 Wu, *Mingdai de ruxue jiaoguan.* Since they performed two distinct functions, I have used the terms "educational officials" and "teaching officials" when discussing their activities.
32 Wu, *Mingdai de ruxue jiaoguan*, 32, 48; see also Ma, "Local Education Officials."
33 Wu, *Mingdai de ruxue jiaoguan*, 19-20. Ma Tai-Loi estimated that there were about 4,200 state teaching positions at any given time during the Ming (see Ma, "Local Education Officials," 18).
34 Liu Ziyang, *Qingdai difang guan zhi kao* [A study of the Qing local bureaucratic system] (Beijing: Zijincheng chubanshe, 1988), 7.
35 Zhang, *Mingshi*, 1851-52; Wu, *Mingdai de ruxue jiaoguan*, 8-14.
36 Wu, *Mingdai de ruxue jiaoguan*, 12-19; Ma, "Local Education Officials," 16-17.
37 Zhao, *Qingshi gao*, 3358-59.
38 Ibid., 3099-119.

39 Liu, *Guangdong shuyuan zhidu yange*, 217-95; see also Fan, *Zhongguo shuyuan shi*, 171-86; Sheng Langxi, *Zhongguo shuyuan zhidu* [China's academy system] (Shanghai: Zhonghua shuju, 1934), 77-129.

40 Fan, *Zhongguo shuyuan shi*, 331-32.

41 Liu Xiangguang, "Zhongguo jinshi difang jiaoyu de fazhan," 32.

42 Liao, "Rural Education in Transition," 1221-23.

43 See Feng Menglong (1574-1646), "Su zhixian luoshan zai he" [Magistrate Su is reunited with his family through a knitted shirt] and "Zhao Chun'er chong wang Cao jia zhuang" [Zhao Chun'er revitalizes the Cao family], in *Jing shi tong yan* [Popular tales to warn the world] (reprint, Shenyang: Chunfeng wenyi chubanshe, 1994), 124-53, 467-79.

44 Liu, "Zhongguo jinshi difang jiaoyu," 28-35. See also Rawski, *Education and Popular Literacy*, 96-97; Thøgersen, *A County of Culture*: Twentieth-Century China Seen from the Village Schools of Zouping, Shandong (Ann Arbor: University of Michigan Press, 2002), 22-24.

45 Rawski, *Education and Popular Literacy*, 42-43.

46 Ibid., 192.

47 Liu, *Guangdong shuyuan*, 296-304. Chang Chung-li's estimate for the salaries of teachers at famous academies is significantly higher than this, but he noted that other teachers were paid much lower salaries. See Chang Chung-li, *The Income of the Chinese Gentry* (Seattle: University of Washington Press, 1962), 92-109.

48 Wu, *Mingdai de ruxue jiaoguan*, 9-10.

49 Rawski, *Education and Popular Literacy*, 54-61.

50 Wu, *Mingdai de ruxue jiaoguan*, 253-54; Ma, "Local Education Officials," 19-24.

51 Zhao, *Qingshi gao* 12, 3099-119.

52 Sheng, *Zhongguo shuyuan zhidu*, 133-34.

53 Alexander Woodside also noted the divorce between the political centre and education in late imperial China, but he saw this as a result of the decline of state control of education due to the expansion of private educational facilities. See Woodside, "The Divorce between the Political Center and Educational Creativity in Late Imperial China," in Elman and Woodside, eds., *Education and Society in Late Imperial China*, 458-92.

54 Benjamin A. Elman, *A Cultural History of Civil Examinations in Late Imperial China* (Berkeley: University of California Press, 2000), 125-72.

55 Ho Ping-ti, *Studies on the Population of China, 1368-1953* (Cambridge, MA: Harvard University Press, 1959), 281-82.

56 Chang Chung-li, *The Chinese Gentry: Studies on Their Role in Nineteenth-Century Chinese Society* (Seattle: University of Washington Press, 1955), 77-86.

57 Ibid., 78-89.

58 Ibid., 92.

59 Ibid., 87-91.

60 Originally, "yisheng" referred to those students who participated in ceremonial performances, but later it became a fixed title for the expanding student body during the Qing period. Therefore, I translate it as "specially appointed student" rather than "ceremonial performer."

61 See Chapter 2, Table 2.2.

62 Thøgersen, *A County of Culture*, 34-35.

63 Elman, *Cultural History*, 146-57.

64 Chang, *Chinese Gentry*, 83-90.

65 Elman, *Cultural History*, 146-57.

66 Leung, "Elementary Education," 393.

67 Wu, *Mingdai de ruxue jiaoguan*, 81-93.

68 Rawski, *Education and Popular Literacy*, 140, estimates that the literacy rate among adult males in the Qing era was about 30 percent to 45 percent of the total population. According to her definition of literacy, and considering the efforts made by both the state and local gentry with regard to elementary education, this number is likely accurate.

69 Alexander Woodside, "Real and Imagined Continuities in the Chinese Struggle for Literacy," in Hayhoe, *Education and Modernization*, 33-35.

70 Mary Clabaugh Wright, *The Last Stand of Chinese Conservatism: The T'ung-Chih Restoration, 1862-1874* (Stanford: Stanford University Press, 1975), 129-31.

71 This purpose was reiterated clearly in many school regulations at that time. See "Yixue zhangcheng" [Regulations of charitable schools], *YZSJ:* 335-55. Bailey also cites Duan Fang's proposal, which suggests establishing community schools in order to prevent mass rioting. See Paul Bailey, *Reform the People: Changing Attitudes towards Popular Education in Early Twentieth-century China* (Vancouver: UBC Press, 1990, 30). Leung, "Elementary Education in the Lower Yangtze Region," 383-84, 396-400, testifies that the only purpose of *shexue* was "moralization" (although she considers this to have been the common goal of all types of elementary schools). Even though it is difficult to separate literary study and moral training, the educational function of *shexue* should not be dismissed. In premodern China, and even in modern China, moral training was always mixed with literary learning.

72 Zhou here refers to the elementary textbooks: *Xiao'er yu* [Words for children], *Xiaoxue shizha* [Poems for elementary learning], and *Shengyu guangxun* [Amplified sacred instructions], which were published by the prefectural government.

73 Zhou Kai, "Xiangyang fu shu yixue zhangcheng" [Regulations for the charitable schools subordinated to Xiangyang Prefecture], *YZSJ:* 337.

74 Yu Zhi, ed., "De yi lu: Yue dong qimeng yishu guitiao, 1869" [Record of charitable deeds: Regulations for primary charitable schools in East Guangdong, 1869], *YZSJ:* 353.

75 Wu and Hu, *Zhongguo gudai sixue*, 72.

76 Woodside, "The Divorce between the Political Center and Educational Creativity in Late Imperial China," in Elman and Woodside, *Education and Society in Late Imperial China*, 458-62.

77 Wu and Hu, *Zhongguo gudai sixue*, 71-77; Rawski, *Education and Popular Literacy*, 30-31.

78 Woodside, "The Divorce between the Political Center and Educational Creativity," 458-62.

79 Elman, *Cultural History of Civil Examinations*, 585-94; see also Wolfgang Franke, *The Reform and Abolition of the Traditional Chinese Examination System* (East Asian Research Center, Cambridge, MA: Harvard University, 1963), 30-32.

80 Bai Xinliang, *Zhongguo gudai shuyuan* [A history of the development of ancient Chinese academies] (Tianjin: Tianjin People's Press, 1995), 236-40.

81 "Gezhe shuyuan zhao shou shengtu qi" [Announcement of admissions to the Polytechnic College], *YYSJ:* 744.

82 Barry Keenan, *Imperial China's Last Classical Academies: Social Change in the Lower Yangzi, 1864-1911* (Berkeley: Institute of East Asian Studies, University of California, Berkeley, 1994), 3-4.

83 Knight Biggerstaff, *The Earliest Modern Government Schools in China* (New York: Cornell University Press, 1961), passim.

84 Su Yunfeng, *Zhang Zhidong*; Zhou Hanguang, *Zhang Zhidong yu Guangya shuyuan* [Zhang Zhidong and the Guangya Academy] (Taibei: Zhongguo wenhua daxue chubanshe, 1983).

85 Liang Qichao, "Bianfa tongyi: Xuexiao zong lun" [A general proposal for reform: A comprehensive discussion of schools], in *Yinbingshi he ji: Wenji* [Collected works from Drinking Ice Studio: Article collections] (Shanghai: Zhonghua shuju, 1932), 1:19-29.

86 Ibid., 34-37.

87 Kang Youwei, "Qing chi ge sheng gai shuyuan yinci wei xuetang zhe" [A memorial appealing to the throne to order new schools established in each province where formerly there were academies and improper temples], *WSJ*: 52-55.

88 Guangxu emperor, "Shangyu: Shuyuan gai xuexiao" [Imperial edict: Changing academies into modern schools], *WSJ*: 55-56.

89 Dorothy Ko, "Pursuing Talent and Virtue: Education and Women's Culture in Seventeenth- and Eighteenth-Century China," *Late Imperial China* 13, 1 (1992): 9-19; see also Ko, *Teachers of the Inner Chambers: Women and Culture in Seventeenth-Century China* (Stanford: Stanford University Press, 1994); Susan Mann, "Learned Women in the Eighteenth Century," in *Engendering China: Women, Culture, and the State*, ed. Christina Gilmartin, Gail Hershatter, Lisa Rofel, and Tyrene White, 27-46 (Cambridge: Harvard University Press, 1994), 27-46; Susan Mann, "'Fuxue' (Women's Learning) by Zhang Xuecheng (1738-1801): China's First History of Women's Culture," *Late Imperial China* 13, 1 (1992): 40-62.

90 Rawski, *Education and Popular Literacy in Ch'ing China*, 6-7, 140.
91 To date, research on women's education in imperial society has concentrated on women in gentry families in the Jiangnan area. We know very little about women in northern China or women from lower gentry-official and modest literati families.
92 Susan Mann, "The Education of Daughters in the Mid-Ch'ing Period," in Elman and Woodside, *Education and Society in Late Imperial China*, 20-27.
93 Ko, *Teachers of the Inner Chamber*, 115-42.
94 Susan Mann, "The Education of Daughters," 20-27.
95 The Double Seven Festival was held by and for girls on the seventh day of the seventh lunar month. The ceremony was supposed to help them gain "spiritual assistance" in developing their household skills. According to legend, Leizu invented silk making and was regarded as the goddess of domestic skills. See Susan Mann, *Precious Records: Women in China's Long Eighteenth Century* (Stanford: Stanford University Press, 1997), 152, 170-71. More generally, see Mann, "The Education of Daughters," 20-27.
96 Harriet T. Zurndorfer, "Beyond Good Wifehood and Good Scholarship: Wang Zhaoyuan (1763-1851) and the Vanished 'Talented Women,'" in *Different Worlds of Discourse: New Views of Gender and Genre in Late Qing and Early Republican China*, ed. Richard J. Smith, Grace Fong, and Nanxiu Qian (Leiden: Brill Academic Publishers, forthcoming, 2007).
97 Mann, "Learned Women in the Eighteenth Century," 27-46; Mann, "Fuxue," 40-62.
98 Mann, "The Education of Daughters," 19-49.
99 Chen Hongmou, "Jiao *nü* yi gui" [Bequeathed guidelines for the education of women], in *Wu zhong yi gui* [Bequeathed guidelines of five kinds, preface dated 1742] (Shanghai: Jingwei shuju, 1935).
100 Paul Bailey, "'Modernising Conservatism' in Early Twentieth-Century China: The Discourse and Practice of Women's Education," *European Journal of East Asian Studies* 3, 2 (2004): 217-41.
101 Nanxiu Qian, "Revitalizing the Xianyuan (Worthy Ladies) Tradition: Women in the 1898 Reforms," *Modern China* 29, 4 (2003): 399-454.
102 Chu Ji'neng, "Nüxue xiansheng" [A pioneer of women's schooling], *DFZZ* 31, 7 (1934): 23-27; Margaret E. Burton, *The Education of Women in China* (New York: Fleming H. Revell, 1911), 35; Sun Shiyue, *Zhongguo jindai nuzi liuxue shi* [A modern history of Chinese female students studying abroad] (Beijing: Zhongguo heping chubanshe, 1995), 39-40.
103 Ida Belle Lewis, *The Education of Girls in China* (New York: Teachers' College, Columbia University, 1919), 24. Another source reports that there were 2,064 students in missionary schools in 1877. See Lei Liangbo, Chen Yangfeng, and Xiong Xianjun, *Zhongguo nüzi jiaoyu shi* [A history of Chinese women's education] (Wuhan: Wuhan chubanshe, 1993), 207. This number may not include girls in Roman Catholic missionary schools.
104 Lewis, *Education of Girls in China*, 24. Lewis did not account for Roman Catholic girls' schools during this period. According to Frank J. Rawlinsen, 74 percent of the missionary schools (for both males and females) eventually set up in China were established after 1900. See Frank. J. Rawlinsen, "Change and Progress in the Christian Movement in China during the Last Two Decades [1900-1920]," in *The Christian Occupation of China: A General Survey of the Christian Forces in China*, ed. Milton T. Stauffer (Shanghai: China Continuation Committee, 1924), 37.
105 Chu Ji'neng, "Jiawu zhan qian siwei nü liuxuesheng" [Four women who studied overseas before the first Sino-Japanese War], *YYSJ*: 369-75; see also Liang Qichao, "Ji Jiangxi Kang nüshi [On Ms. Kang from Jiangxi], *Yinbingshi heji-wenji* 1: 119-20.
106 Sun, *Zhongguo jindai nuzi liuxu shi*, 42-43.
107 Chu, "Nüxue xiansheng," 23-27. The author does not provide any information about the backgrounds of these converts.
108 Shirley Garrett, *Social Reformers in Urban China: The Chinese YMCA, 1895-1926* (Cambridge: Harvard University Press, 1970), 1-44. Garrett points out that, before the end of the nineteenth century, missionaries failed to interest China's upper classes. She summarized the content of a missionary conference held in 1877, when participants felt that "missionary relationships with China's upper classes still ranged from nonexistent to hostile. Most missionaries agreed that this lack of communication with the upper classes seriously impeded their work, but a remedy did not appear at hand" (11). Garrett concludes that, "on

political, ideological, cultural, and intellectual grounds, missionaries seemed to assault the upper classes, and the upper classes fought back" (11). At the 1877 conference, several missionaries suggested that, by teaching science, they might gain access to the upper classes, but in the 1880s, only a few missionaries attempted this experiment. It was during that decade that they began to realize there were problems with their old strategy and considered trying something new: "The best method was not to concentrate on the poor but to start as high as possible and work down" (22). According to Garrett, this change in strategy was implemented only at the end of the nineteenth century (23).

109 Chu, "Nüxue xiansheng," 23-27.

110 "Sheng Mali ya nü shuyuan xiaoshi" [The history of St. Mary's Hall for Chinese Girls], *ZJXS* 4: 306-9.

111 Walter N. Lacy, *A Hundred Years of Chinese Methodism* (New York: Abingdon-Cokesbury Press, 1948), 149. In this statement the term "regular" is crucial because the Methodist Church reported that, in the late 1880s, most institutions made attempts to become "self-reliant" by gradually encouraging students' parents to make small contributions to their daughters' education (e.g., in the form of clothing, books, small cash allowances, and so on). They even encouraged students to work in schools or sell their handicrafts in order to subsidize their own schooling. I imagine that, from the late 1880s to the early 1890s, any kind of payment was "irregular." These students differed considerably from the students in elite schools for the Chinese gentry at the end of the 1890s, who not only paid their own tuition but even brought their maids to school.

112 Li Shuren, "Li Shuren ji Fuzhou Yuying nüzi xuexiao" [Li Shuren's journal from Yuying Girls' School in Fuzhou], *ZJXS* 4: 271-74.

113 Lacy, *A Hundred Years of China Methodism*, 158.

114 Ibid.

115 *Zhonghua Jidu jiaohui nianjian* [The yearbook of Chinese Christians] 4 (1917), *ZJXS* 4: 296-97.

116 "Sheng Mali ya nü shuyuan xiaoshi," *ZJXS* 4: 307.

117 Lacy, *A Hundred Years of China Methodism*, 144.

118 Chu, "Nüxue xiansheng," 23-27; Sun, *Zhongguo jindai nüzi liuxu shi*, 42.

119 "Zhenjiang nüshu gongke jianbiao" [A brief curriculum of the Zhenjia Girls' School], ZJXS 4: 342-43. See also "Shanghai Zhongxi nüshu zhangcheng" [The regulations for the McTyeire School for Girls in Shanghai], ZJXS 4: 299-302.

120 Ibid. See also "Xue Zheng ji Shanghai Zhongxi nüshu de kecheng" [Xue Zheng's recollection on the curricula of the McTyeire School for Girls in Shanghai], *ZJXS* 4: 303-5.

121 Ye Weili, "'Nü Liuxuesheng': The Story of American-Educated Chinese Women, 1880-1920s," *Modern China* 20, 3 (1994): 315-46.

122 Chu, "Jiawu zhan qian siwei nü liuxuesheng," *YYSJ*: 369-75. See also Liang, "Ji Jiangxi Kang nüshi," 119-20.

123 Chu, "Jiawu zhan qian siwei nü liuxuesheng," *YYSJ*: 369-75. Of the four female students Chu studied, only one appears to have ever married.

124 Chu, "Nüxue xiansheng," 23-27. However, as we see in a later section, the earliest women's schools set up by Chinese elites were quite different from missionary schools in terms of motivation and curriculum.

125 Paul Bailey, "Active Citizen or Efficient Housewife? The Debate over Women's Education in Early-Twentieth-Century China," in *Education, Culture, and Identity in Twentieth-Century China*, ed. Glen Peterson, Ruth Hayhoe, and Yongling Lu (Ann Arbor: University of Michigan Press, 2001), 321.

126 Liang, "Bianfa tongyi," 37-38.

127 Qian, "Revitalizing the Xianyuan Tradition." Qian also points out that this perspective of Liang was not his own innovation but was borrowed from British missionary Timothy Richard (1845-1919) and the American Yung J. Allen (1836-1907).

128 Ibid., 37-44.

129 Liang Qichao, "Chuang she nüxuetang qi" [An announcement on the establishment of women's schools], in *Yinbingshi wenji* 2 (Shanghai: Zhonghua shuju, 1932): 19-20.

130 Ibid.
131 Liang, "Bianfa tongyi," 37-38.
132 Harriet T. Zurndorfer, "Beyond Good Wifehood and Good Scholarship."
133 See Qian, "Revitalizing Xianyuan Tradition."
134 Paul Bailey points out that it was the "modernizing conservatism" that dominated the female educational project in the early twentieth century. This "modernizing conservatism" was partially inherited from previous statecraft group thinking that considered women's education important so that women could play a critical role in the domestic domain. See Bailey, "'Modernising Conservatism.'" On the one hand, this view shrewdly points out the root of modern education for women; on the other hand, it could only partially explain the Qing court enthusiasm for building female normal schools.
135 "Si ci choubei huiyi jiyao" [Records of four preparatory meetings, 1897], *WSJ*: 192-201.
136 Ibid.
137 "Nü xuetang zhangcheng, 1897" [Women's school regulations, 1897], *WSJ*: 188-92.
138 Xia Xiaohong's remarkable work on Jingzheng Girls' School underlines the influence of missionary schools on recruiting teachers and developing curricula. The school was meant to be an ideal institution "combining Chinese and Western educational thoughts." See Xia Xiaohong *Wan Qing nüxing yu jindai Zhongguo* [Late Qing women and modern China] (Beijing: Beijing daxue chubanshe, 2004), 3-37. Nonetheless, changing opinions about female education drew on both Chinese elite and missionary ideas during this period. Chinese elites did adopt the form of missionary schools and some elements of their curricula. However, it was missionaries who were changing their original scheme in order to satisfy the demands of Chinese elites. A further study on changing curriculum and student demographics at missionary schools for girls might provide more insight into this issue. I would like to thank Chen Pingyuan for his comments and Xia Xiaohong for the gift of her book.

Chapter 2: Education and Society in Transition

1 The 1902 educational system was never put into practice.
2 Liu Dapeng, *Tuixiang zhai riji* [Diary from a retreat] (Taiyuan: Shanxi renmin chubanshe, 1990), passim. The manuscript of this diary was published in 1990.
3 Sheng was a Chinese gentry-official and then became one of the earliest entrepreneurs in Chinese modern industry. See Albert Feuerwerker, *China's Early Industrialization: Sheng Hsuan-huai (1844-1916) and Mandarin Enterprise* (Cambridge: Harvard University Press, 1958).
4 All these events occurred in Beijing. Shanghai, far from the political centre, was able to avoid such turmoil.
5 During this period, the small number of teachers' schools included Tongzhou Teachers' School set up by Zhan Jian in 1902, Zhili Teachers' College set up in 1903, and Liang Jiang Teachers' School set up in 1903. Li Youzhi, *Zhongwai shifan jiaoyu cidian* [A compendium of normal education in China and abroad] (Beijing: Zhongguo guangbo dianshi daxue chubanshe, 1994), 315, 317, 318.
6 Xue bu zongwu si [General information office of board of education], "Ge sheng xuetang li nian zeng jian bijiao biao" [A comparative table showing the increase and decrease of modern schools in every province], in *Di yi ci jiaoyu tongji tubiao, 1907* [An almanac of the first educational statistics, 1907] (Yonghe, Taipei: Wenhai chubanshe, 1987 [reprint]), 27-28. This number, which does not include any information from the capital, includes elementary schools, middle schools, vocational schools, teachers' schools, and institutions of higher education.
7 Xue bu zongwu si, "Ge sheng shifan xuetang xuesheng tongji biao" [A statistical table of teachers' schools and students in every province], in *Di yi ci jiaoyu tongji tubiao 1907*, 23-24. The teachers' school category in this table includes all levels and all types of normal schools, including institutions of higher education, secondary level institutions, and different types of short-term schools. Elementary education also expanded rapidly.
8 Including short-term training institutions, which students attended for between six months and one year before taking up teaching posts.

9 Xue bu zongwu si, "Ge sheng zhuanmen xuetang xuesheng tongji biao" [A statistical table of technical schools and students in every province], "Ge sheng shiye xuetang xuesheng tongji biao" [A statistical table of vocational schools and students in every province], and "Ge sheng putong xuetang tongji biao" [A statistical table of regular schools and students in every province], in *Di yi ci jiaoyu tongji tubiao 1907*, 19-20, 21-22, 25-26.

10 In his paper on the Guangdong academy system, Grimm points out that, in the nineteenth century, there was a hierarchy in terms of administrative region and academic renown among Guangdong academies. Lower level schools (in both senses) contributed students to higher level schools (*shuyuan*). See Tilemann Grimm, "Academies and Urban Systems in Kwantung," in *The City in Late Imperial China*, ed. G. Skinner, 475-98 (Stanford: Stanford University Press, 1977). This hierarchy became the basis of part of the regular schools in the new school system.

11 Chen Gujia and Deng Hongpo, *Zhongguo shuyuan zhidu yanjiu* [Studies of China's academies] (Nanjing: Zhejiang jiaoyu chubanshe, 1997), 462-63.

12 Xue bu (Board of Education), "Zhong xuetang zhangcheng" [Regulations for middle schools] and "Gaoden xuetang zhangcheng" [Regulations for colleges]," *XZYB*: 317-39.

13 Xue bu, "Chudeng xiao xuetang zhangcheng" [Regulations for the primary level of elementary schools], "Chuji shifan xuetang zhangcheng" [Regulations for primary teachers' schools], and "Zouding renyong jiaoyuan zhangcheng" [Imperial approved regulations on the appointment of teachers], *XZYB*: 291-306, 398-414, 428-30.

14 Xue bu, "Chuji shifan xuetang zhangcheng," *XZYB:* 398-414; Xue bu, "Youji shifan xuetang zhangcheng" [Regulations for advanced teachers' colleges], *XZYB*: 414-15.

15 Abe Hiroshi, "Borrowing from Japan: China's First Modern Educational System," in *China's Education and the Industrialized World*, ed. Ruth Hayhoe and Marianne Bastid, 57-80 (New York: M.E. Sharpe, 1987).

16 Qian Manqian and Jin Linxiang, *Zhongguo jindai xuezhi bijiao yanjiu* [Research on comparative schooling systems in modern China] (Guangzhou: Guangdong Jiaoyu chubanshe, 1996), 93-123, 100-1, 117-21.

17 Sally Borthwick, *Education and Social Change in China* (Stanford: Hoover Institute Press, Standford University, 1983), 119.

18 Zhang Zhidong, Zhang Baixi, and Rong-qing, "Xuewu gangyao" [A program for educational affairs], *JZJS:* 2, 9.

19 To institute the New Policy Reforms, the Qing court appointed three ministers of education: Zhang Zhidong, Zhang Baixi, and Rong-qing.

20 Zhang Zhidong, Zhang Baixi, and Rong-qing, "Guanxue dachen deng zou qing shiban dijian keju zhuzhong xuetang zhe" [A memorial from the ministers of education on the experiment of attenuating the civil service examinations and reinforcing new schools], *DFZZ* 1 (1904): 151-54.

21 Xue bu, "Tongxing gesheng tuiguang shifan sheng ming'e dian" [A telegram urging all of the provinces to promote enrolment in teachers' schools], *XBGB* 1 (1906): 6b.

22 Zhang et al., "Xuewu gangyao," *JZJS* 2: 10.

23 Xue bu, "Chuji shifan xuetang zhangcheng," *XZYB:* 398-414.

24 Xue bu, "Youji shifan xuetang zhangcheng," *XZYB:* 414-15.

25 Xue bu zongwusi, "Xuantong yuan nian jiaoyu tongji biao" [Tabular educational statistics for 1909], *SJSJ:* 623-25. This source lists the number of programs at each school (e.g., "wanquan ke" and "jianyi ke" might be established in one school but were often calculated as separate programs). Since some schools may have had more than one program, I calculated the number of colleges by looking at the listings under the category of geographic distribution (at the time it was rare to have more than one teachers' school in a province).

26 Xue bu zongwusi, "Xuanton yuan nian jiaoyu tongji biao," *SJSJ:* 623-25.

27 Ibid., 620-25. Frontier regions such as Qinghai, Xinjiang, and Mongolia did not have teachers' schools until later.

28 Xue bu, "Chuji shifan xuetang zhangcheng," *XZYB:* 398-414; "Bensi tongchi geshu rushu zhaojie Baoding shifan xuetang jingfei shen shao qing su chouban bi nian shicuo zha"

[Notice to all subordinate branches on the insufficient obligatory funds sent to Baoding Teachers' School: Please immediately send the balance of the funds to prevent impropriety], *SJSJ:* 644.

29 Luo Zhenyu, "Jiangsu shifan xuetang ji" [Memoir of Jiangsu Teachers' School], *SJSJ:* 645; "Sichuan zongdu Xiliang zou gaishe tongsheng shifan xuetang" [Memorial from Sichuan Governor-General Xi-liang on establishing the provincial teachers' school], *SJSJ:* 677; Zhang Zhidong, "Zha xuewuchu gai xiu Liang Hu shifan xuetang" [Memo to the provincial bureau of education on repairing the Liang Hu teachers' school], *SJSJ:* 680; "Liang Guang youji shifan xuetang zhangcheng [The regulations for Liang Guang Advanced Teachers' College]," in *Liang Guang youji shifan xuetang yi lan* [Brochure for Liang Guang Advanced Teachers' College], 1910, Shanghai Metropolitan Archives, file no. Q0-12/1086.

30 Xue bu, "Zouding chuji shifan xuetang zhangcheng," *XZYB:* 411.

31 Ibid.

32 Yuan Shikai, "Zhili zongdu Yuan Shikai zou ban Zhili shifan xuetang ji xiao xuetang zhe (fu zhangcheng)" [Memorial from governor-general of Zhili Yuan Shikai on establishing Zhili Teachers' School and Elementary School (the regulations are attached)], *SJSJ:* 628-37; "Baoding chuji shifan xuetang shuwuzhang Wang Zecheng gai tang qingxing bing" [A report from Wang Zecheng, director of admiss ions at Baoding Lower Teachers' School, on the school's situation], *SJSJ:* 738-42.

33 "Sichuan tongsheng shifan xuetang de dansheng" [The birth of Sichuan Provincial Teachers' School], *SJSJ:* 677-80; Zheng Xiaocang, "Zhejiang liangji shifan he di yi shifan xiao shi zhi yao" [Highlights from the history of Zhejiang Combined Teachers' College and the Number One Teachers' School], *SJSJ:* 696-712; "Liang Guang youji shifan xuetang zhangcheng."

34 Xue bu, "Chuji shifan xuetang zhangcheng," *XZYB:* 400; "Youji shifan xuetang zhangcheng," *XZYB:* 415.

35 Yuan Shikai, "Zhili zongdu Yuan Shikai zouban Zhili shifan xuetang ji xiao xuetang zhe (fu zhangcheng)," *SJSJ:* 628-37.

36 Yuan Shikai, "Zou wei sheli beiyang shifan xuetang yi guang jiaoyu zhe" [A memorial on establishing Beiyang Teachers' College in order to promote education], *SJSJ*: 659-61; "Beiyang shifan xuetang shiban zhangcheng" [The regulations for the trial program at Beiyang Teachers' College], *SJSJ:* 661-63.

37 Xue bu, "Youji shifan xuetang zhangcheng," *XZYB:* 425. In spite of having been recommended, this group of students was not guaranteed admission.

38 Examples include Baoding Teachers' School, Sichuan Provincial Teachers' College, Beiyang Teachers' College.

39 "Baoding chuji shifan xuetang shuwuzhang Wang Zecheng gaitang qingxing bing," *SJSJ:* 738.

40 Xue bu, "Zou ding ge xuetang jiangli zhangcheng" [Imperially approved memorial on the regulations for degrees awarded to various graduates of new schools], *XZYB*: 514-23.

41 Ibid., 517-18.

42 Ibid., 514-23.

43 During the early stages of the development of modern schools, teachers' schools, which comprised a major part of local secondary education, accepted students who either were not qualified for the entrance examination or who were not covered by government quotas, although they did charge them tuition. The status of these students was similar to that of "supplementary students" under the imperial system. See Xue bu, "Chuji shifan xuetang zhangcheng," *XZYB*: 412-13.

44 Xue bu, "Chuji shifan xuetang zhangcheng," *XZYB*: 412.

45 Xue bu, "Youji shifan xuetang zhangcheng," *XZYB*: 426.

46 Zhili xuewu chu [Education bureau of Zhili], "Benchu cheng shifan xuetang kaoxuan youji fen like wenke jiaoshou qing li'an bing, 1905" [The report from the education bureau requesting confirmation on the selection of students for the advanced program of the teachers' school and on the division of students into science and humanities for the purpose of separate teaching], *SJSJ:* 643-44.

47 According to 1909 data, there were nineteen teachers' colleges. However, I have only been able to identify fourteen that were called teachers' colleges, including the School of Teachers' Training at the Capital University.

48 This school later became an independent teachers' college, the Capital Advanced Teachers' School (*Jingshi youji shifan xuetang*).

49 Xue bu, "Zouding youji shifan xuetang zhangcheng," *XZYB*: 414-28.

50 "Jiangsu shifan xuetang xianxing zhangcheng" [The existing regulations of Jiangsu Teachers' School], *SJSJ*: 647.

51 "Zhili zongdu Yuan Shikai zouban Zhili shifan xuetang ji xiaoxuetang zhe," *SJSJ:* 629.

52 Yuan, "Zou wei sheli Beiyang shifan xuetang yi guang jiaoyu zhe," *SJSJ:* 660-61.

53 Zheng, "Zhejiang liangji shifan he Di yi shifan xiao shi zhi yao," *SJSJ:* 700-1.

54 Xue bu zongwusi, *Di yi ci jiaoyu tongji tubiao 1907*, 23-24.

55 Duan-fang and Xiao-zeng, "Sufu Duan-fang hufu Xiao-zeng zou chen Su sheng xuetang banli qingxing zhe" [Memorial from Governor Duan-fang and Assistant Governor Xiao-zeng of Jiangsu, reporting on educational affairs in the province], *SJSJ:* 644-45.

56 Yuan, "Zou wei sheli Beiyang shifan xuetang yi guang jiaoyu zhe," *SJSJ:* 660.

57 "Sichuan tongsheng shifan xuetang de dansheng," *SJSJ:* 678.

58 Xue bu, "Chuji shifan xuetang zhangcheng," *XZYB*: 398-400.

59 Xue bu zongwusi, *Di yi ci jiaoyu tongji tubiao*, 22-24. It is difficult to calculate the number of schools with any precision because some simplified programs belonged to formal teachers' schools.

60 Luo, "Jiangsu shifan xuetang ji," *SJSJ:* 645.

61 *Liang Guang youji shifan xuetang yi lan.*

62 Xue bu zongwusi, *Di yi ci jiaoyu tongji tubiao*, 22-24.

63 Xue bu, "Youji shifan xuetang zhangcheng," *XZYB*: 414-28.

64 Ibid., "Chuji shifan xuetang zhangcheng," *XZYB:* 400-2.

65 Zhang Baixi, Zhang Zhidong, and Rong-qing, "Guanxue dachen yi fu yanxuan shifan biantong xin jinshi rutang yiye pian" [Memorial from the ministers of education in response to the discussion of how to apply rigorous standards to choosing students for teachers' schools and of the need for flexibility in choosing newly advanced *jinshi* degree-holders to study in teachers' schools], *DFZZ* 1: 155-56.

66 Xue bu, "Zouding chuji shifan xuetang zhangcheng," *XZYB*: 403.

67 Xue bu, "Youji shifan xuetang zhangcheng," *XZYB*: 425.

68 "Ticao zhuanxiuke biyesheng" [Graduates of the physical education specialty program], in *Liang Guang youji shifan xuetang yi lan.*

69 Xue bu zongwusi, "Guangxu sanshi si nian gesheng shifan xuetang xuesheng tongjibiao" [1908 statistics of teachers' schools and students in each province], *ZJXS:* 2b, 466-67.

70 Xue bu, "Meng yang jia jiao he yi" [Unity of early education and family education], *XZYB*: 396.

71 The term "good mothers and virtuous wives" was imported from Japan, where it played a crucial role in educational ideology, but the idea has deep roots in Chinese tradition. As Liang Qichao said, a woman's duties were *xiangfu jiaozi* (i.e., assisting one's husband and teaching one's sons), which echoed Chen Hongmou's call for women's education. Certainly, the mother's role as the primary educator of children was universally endorsed in imperial China. But, as Joan Judge points out, when the Chinese feminist movement commandeered the Japanese phrase it expanded its implications far beyond what was embodied in Japanese nationalism. Japan's "good mothers and virtuous wives" were expected to stay at home and make an indirect contribution to the nation through being good mothers, whereas radical Chinese feminists called for Chinese women to participate in the nation's political life and make a direct contribution to the country in education and other public domains. See Joan Judge, "Talent, Virtue, and the Nation: Chinese Nationalism and Female Subjectivities in the Early Twentieth Century," *American Historical Review* 106, 2 (2001): 756-803. While Japan's highly traditional rationale for women's new role in education proved to be a drag on emancipation, the far more enlightened attitudes of China's elites, not only radical femininsts, called women to make a contribution to the nation

directly. It was this attitude that cleared the way for women to enter public education and to become politically engaged.

72 Joan Judge, "Meng Mu Meets the Modern: Female Exemplars in Early-Twentieth-Century Textbooks for Girls and Women," in *Jindai Zhongguo funü shi yanjiu* [Studies on modern Chinese women's history] 8 (Taibei: Zhongyang yanjiu yuan jindai shi yanjiusuo, 2000): 133-77.

73 Paul Bailey, "Active Citizen or Efficient Housewife? The Debate over Women's Education in Early-Twentieth-Century China," in *Education, Culture, and Identity in Twentieth-Century China*, ed. Glen Peterson, Ruth Hayhoe, and Lu Yongling, 318-47 (Ann Arbor: University of Michigan Press, 2001), 318-47.

74 "Lun nüxue yi zhuzhong deyu" [Women's education should stress moral education], *ZJXS* 2b: 584-87.

75 Dong Shou, "Xing nüxue yi" [On promoting women's education], *ZJXS* 2b: 570-72.

76 Ya Te, "Lun zhuzao guomin mu" [On forging mothers of citizens], in *ZJXS* 2b: 573-576.

77 Su Ying, "Susu nüxiao kaixue yanshuo" [Speech given at the opening ceremony of Susu Women's School], *ZJXS* 2b: 582; Ya Lu, "Ai nüjie" [Women's sorrow], *ZJXS* 2b: 577-81.

78 Xia Xiaohong, "Daodu: Wan Qing nübao de xingbie guanzhao – *Nüzi shijie* yanjiu [Readers' guide: Gender vision of women's newspapers in the late Qing – a study of *Women's world*], in Xia Xiaohong (compil.), *Nüzi shijie wenxuan* [Selected reading from *Women's world*] (Guiyang: Guizhou jiaoyu chubanshe, 2003), 1-52.

79 Zhang Jianren, "Yu chang pingdeng xian xing nüxue lun" [Promoting equality must promote women's education first], Xiao Xiaohong, *Nüzi shijie wenxuan*, 137-38.

80 Zhang Jianren, "Ji jiu jiachen nian nüzi zhi fangfa" [Urgent way to save women in the year of Jiachen 1904], Xia, *Nüzi shijie wenxuan*, 148-49.

81 "Lun nüxue yi zhuzhong deyu." For a more detailed discussion on women's education during this period, see Xiaoping Cong, "From '*Cainü*' to '*Nü jiaoxi*': Female Normal Schools and the Transformation of Women's Education in Late Qing China, 1895-1911," in *Different Worlds of Discourse: New Views of Gender and Genre in Late Qing and Early Republican China*, ed. Richard J. Smith, Grace Fong, and Nanxiu Qian (Leiden: Brill Academic Publishers, forthcoming, 2007).

82 "Ge sheng jiaoyu huizhi" [Collected news from provinces], *DFZZ* 1, 3, 5, 6, 11 (1904), 2, 9 (1905).

83 Wu Xin, "Wuben nüxue shilue" [A brief history of Wuben Women's School], *ZJXS* 2b: 589-90.

84 "Wuben nüxuexiao di er ci gailiang guize" [The second revised regulations of Wuben Women's School, 1905], *ZJXS* 2b: 590-91.

85 "Wuben nüshu zengshe chudeng, gaodeng nüzi xiaoxue guize shezhi dayi" [The regulations of the newly added lower and higher elementary school at Wuben Women's School, 1905], *ZJXS* 2b: 594-96.

86 "Beijing Yujiao nüxuetang zhangcheng" [The regulations of Yujiao Women's School in Beijing, 1905], *ZJXS* 2b: 694-96.

87 "*Shuntian shibao* ji Yujiao nüxuetang xuesheng qingkuang" [*Shuntian Times* reports on the students' situation of Yujiao women's school], in *ZJXS* 2b: 703-6.

88 Yu Ziyi, "Ji Aiguo nüxue yu Guangfuhui" [A recollection of Patriotic Women's School and the Restoration Society], *ZJXS* 2b: 627-31. See also Cai Yuanpei, "Wo zai jiaoyu jie de jingyan" [My experience in educational circles], in *Cai Yuanpei zishu* [Memoir of Cai Yuanpei] (Taibei: Zhuanji wenxue chubanshe, 1967), 39.

89 "Gedi nüxue de xingqi" [Rise of women's schools nationwide], *ZJXS* 2b: 633-48.

90 See "Shanghai nüzi Zhong Xi yi xuexiao" [Shanghai Sino-West medical school for women], "*Dongfang zazhi* ji Beijing she nü yi xuetang" [*Eastern Miscellany* reports the establishment of a female medical school in Beijing], "*Dongfang zazhi* ji Beiyang nü yi xuetang" [*Eastern Miscellany* reports Beiyang female medical school established in Tianjin], "*Dongfang zazhi* ji Hangzhou she chanke nü xuetang" [*Eastern Miscellany* reports a nurse and midwife school built in Hangzhou], in *ZJXS* 2b: 646-49.

91 "Yiyi Nü xuetang zhangcheng" [Regulations for Girls' School of Language Translation], in Yuning and Zhang Yüfa, *Jindai Zhongguo nüquan yundong shiliao, 1842-1911*, 1101-6.

92 Li Yuning and Zhang Yüfa, *Jindai Zhongguo nüquan yundong shiliao, 1842-1911* [Documents on the feminist movement in modern China, 1842-1911] (Taibei: Zhuanji wenxue chubanshe, 1975), 1038-71.

93 Sarah McElroy, "Forging a New Role for Women: Zhili First Women's Normal School and the Growth of Women's Education in China, 1901-2," in Peterson, Hayhoe, and Lu, *Education, Culture, and Identity in Twentieth-Century China*, 348-74.

94 Jiang Weiqiao, "Ji Shanghai Aiguo nüxuexiao" [Jiang Weiqiao recalls Patriotic Women's School], *ZJXS* 2b: 611.

95 Wu Ruoan, "Huiyi Shanghai Wuben nüshu" [Recollections of Nurturing Roots Women's Academy in Shanghai], *ZJXS* 2b: 608.

96 "*Shuntian shibao* ji Yujiao nüxuetang xuesheng qingkuang" (The *Shuntian Times* reports on the student background of Inculcating Doctrine Women's School), *ZJXS* 2b: 703-6.

97 Li and Zhang, *Jindai Zhongguo nüquan yundong shiliao*, 1050-51.

98 See the curricula of Nurturing Roots Women's Academy, Patriotic Women's School, and Inculcating Doctrine Women's School, *ZJXS* 2b: 591, 618, 695.

99 Ibid. See also Wu, "Huiyi Shanghai Wuben nüshu," *ZJXS* 2b: 602-9.

100 Wu Xin, "Wuben nüxue shi lue," *ZJXS* 2b: 589-90; Wu Ruoan, "Huiyi Shanghai Wuben nüshu," *ZJXS* 2b: 602-9; "Wuben nüshu zengshe chudeng, gaodeng nüzi xiaoxue guize shezhi dayi," *ZJXS* 2b: 594-97; "Aiguo nüxuexiao buding zhangcheng" [Supplementary regulations for Patriotic Women's School], *ZJXS* 2b: 619.

101 "Hubei caiche nuxue" [Banning women's schools in Hubei], *ZJXS* 2b: 653.

102 Sun Shiyue, *Zhongguo jindai nüzi liuxue shi* [A modern history of Chinese female students studying abroad] (Beijing: Zhongguo heping chubanshe, 1995), 66-69.

103 "Beiyang nüzi shifan xuetang kai xiao ji sheng" [Grand opening ceremony of Beiyang Women's Normal School], *ZJXS* 2b: 689-90.

104 "Gesheng jiaoyu zhi [1906]" [Collected education news in the provinces], *DFZZ* 3, 6 (1906).

105 "Guangdong she nüxuetang zhi fengbo" [The dispute and conflict surrounding the establishment of women's schools in Guangdong], *ZJXS* 2b: 650-51.

106 "Hunan nüxue feibi zhi yuanyin" [Reasons for closing the women's schools in Hunan], *ZJXS* 2b: 652-53.

107 "Hubei caiche nüxue," *ZJXS* 2b: 653.

108 "Jiangsu xuewuchu pi nüxue bu neng yan nan jiaoxi" [The instructions of Jiangsu's education bureau regarding women's schools: Male teachers not to be hired, 1906], *ZJXS* 2b: 653-54.

109 "Gesheng jiaoyu huizhi," [Collected education news in the provinces], *DFZZ* 1, 2 (1904): 41-42.

110 "Guangxu sanshi san nian quanguo nuzi xuetang tongji biao" [1907 statistics for women's schools nationwide], *ZJXS* 2b: 649-50.

111 Liu Xun, "Xuewu yaoduan zhe" [A memorial on the important issues related to education], *ZJXS* 2b: 587-88.

112 Xue bu, "Xue bu zou yi nüzi shifan xuetang zhangcheng zhe [fu zhangcheng]" [Memorial from the Education Bureau on women's normal school regulations (regulations attached)], *SJSJ:* 573.

113 "Jiangsu xuewuchu pi nüxue bu neng yan nan jiaoxi," *ZJXS* 2b: 653-54. Some exceptions were made: male teachers over the age of fifty, for instance, were allowed to teach at female schools. Conservatives complained. See "Changzhou nüxue zhi zuli" [Obstacles to women's schooling in Changzhou], *ZJXS* 2b: 654-55; "Ping Su xuewuchu yu Ning xuewuchu zhi pishi" [Criticism of the instructions from the Jiangsu and Nanjing Education Bureaus], *ZJXS* 2b: 654-57.

114 "Zhili Tianjin xian xiang song shiban nüxuetang zhangcheng" [Attentative regulations on girls' schools submitted by Tianjin county, Zhili province], in Li and Zhang, *Jindai Zhongguo nüquan yundong* 2, 1023-24.

115 "Nüxue jishi: Bokuan xingxue" [News on female schooling: (Provincial authorities) allocated fund for girls' school], in Li and Zhang, *Jindai Zhongguo nüquan yundong* 2, 1130.

116 For all these schools, see Zhou Jianfan, "Zhounan nüzi shifan xuexiao jingying zhuangkuang" [The management of Zhounan Women's Normal School], *SJSJ:* 976-77;

"Hunan nüxue zhi diaocha" [A study of Hunan women's schooling], in Li and Zhang, *Jindai Zhongguo nüquan yundong* 2, 1038; "Gesheng jiaoyu huizhi," *DFZZ* 3, 5 (1906): 97-98.

117 "Yi ding nüxue zhangcheng" [A discussion of how to regulate women's schooling], in Li and Zhang, *Jindai Zhongguo nüquan yundong* 2, 1117.

118 Xue bu, "Zouding nüzi shifan xuetang ji nüzi xiaoxuetang zhangcheng" [Imperially approved regulations for women's normal schools and girls' elementary schools], *JZJS* 2: 169-73.

119 "Cuimin nüxue shifan sheng zuye" [Graduating from the teacher training program at Cuimin Women's School], in Li and Zhang, *Jindai Zhongguo nüquan yundong* 2, 1189.

120 Li and Zhang, *Jindai Zhongguo nüquan yundong* 2, 1179, 1208, 1231, 1236, 1237.

121 Xue bu, "Zouding nüzhi shifan xuetang ji nüzi xiaoxuetang zhangcheng," *JZJS* 2: 169-73.

122 Ibid.

123 Xue bu, "Zouding nüzi xiaoxuetang zhangcheng" [Imperially approved regulations for women's elementary schools], *XZYB*: 593-94; and "Zou zun ni nüxue fuse zhangcheng" [Board of education established regulations on the colours and style of clothing for female students (10 January 1910)], *ZJXS* 2b: 675-76.

124 Xue bu, "Zouding nüzi shifan xuetang ji nüzi xiaoxuetang zhangcheng," *JZJS* 2: 169-73.

125 Xue bu, "Zouding mengyang yuan zhangcheng ji jiating jiaoyu fa zhangcheng" [Imperially approved regulations for kindergartens and family education methods], *XZYB*: 393-96.

126 Xue bu, "Zou yi nüzi shifan xuetang zhangcheng zhe," *XZYB*: 576-77.

127 Xue bu, "Zouding nüzi xiao xuetang zhangcheng," *XZYB*: 584.

128 McElroy, "Forging a New Role for Women," 348.

129 "Yan'ge lue" [A brief history of Liang Guang Advanced Teachers' College], in *Liang Guang youji shifan xuetang yi lan*.

130 Ibid.

131 *Liang Guang youji shifan xuetang yi lan*.

132 I did not include three Japanese teachers.

133 "Liang Hu shifan xuetang zhiyuan diaocha biao" [A comprehensive survey of Liang Hu Teachers' School faculty], *SJSJ*: 685-93.

134 "Zhe fu Zhang Zengyang zou ban quan Zhe shifan xuetang zhe" [A memorial from Zhejiang Governor Zhang Zengyang on establishing Zhejiang Teachers' School], *SJSJ*: 694-95.

135 "Liangjiang shifan jiao zhi yuan lüli biao ji Ri ji jiaoyuan lüli biao, 1909" [Table on students at Liang Jiang Teachers' College and CVs of faculty and Japanese teachers at Liang Jiang Teachers' College], *SJSJ*: 720-21.

136 Among 145 graduates, 3 were listed as dead, 71 provided no information, 7 were continuing their studies either at a higher level of education or overseas. See "Xuetang guanliyuan lianxisuo biyesheng" [List of graduates from the school administrator training program], in *Liang Guang youji shifan xuetang yi lan*.

137 "Ben xiao xianzai xuesheng xingming biao" [List of enrolled students at this school], *Liang Guang youji shifan xuetang yi lan*.

138 Thøgersen, *A County of Culture: Twentieth-Century China Seen from the Village Schools of Zouping, Shanong* (Ann Arbor: Universiy of Michigan Press, 2002), 65.

139 Zheng, "Zhejiang liangji shifan he Di yi shifan xiao shi zhi yao," *SJSJ*: 711.

140 Xue bu, "Zouding xuetang zhangcheng," *XZYB*: 399.

141 Xue bu zongwusi, "Guangxu san shi si nanfen di er ci jiaoyu tongji tubiao" [The second compilation of educational statistics, 1908], *SJSJ*: 620-21.

142 Xue bu zongwusi, "Xuantong yuan nian fen di san ci jiaoyu tongji tubiao" [The third compilation of educational statistics, 1909], *SJSJ*: 624-25.

143 Helen Chauncey, *Schoolhouse Politicians: Locality and State during the Chinese Republic* (Honolulu: University of Hawaii Press, 1992), 88-89.

144 See Chapter 3.

145 Xue bu zongwusi (compil.), *Di yi ci jiaoyu tongji tubiao*, 25-26. I do not have the statistics for 1909, so I use 1907 data. This number does not include schools in the capital.

146 Xue bu zongwusi, *Di yi ci jiaoyu tongji tubiao*, 50-51.

147 Xue bu zongwusi (compil.), "Xuantong yuan nianfen di san ci jiaoyu tongji tubiao," *SJSJ*: 624-25.

148 Some influential literati successfully transformed themselves into modern politicians in the local constitutional movement, as is shown in Joseph Esherick, *Reform and Revolution in China: The 1911 Revolution in Hu'nan and Hubei* (Berkeley: University of California Press, 1976); and Mary Rankin, *Elite Activism and Political Transformation in China, Zhejiang Province, 1865-1911* (Ann Arbor: University of Michigan Press, 1979).

149 See Liu Dapeng, *Tuixiang zhai riji.*

Chapter 3: Pursuing Modernization in Trying Times

1 Ernest Young, *The Presidency of Yuan Shih-k'ai: Liberalism and Dictatorship in Early Republican China* (Ann Arbor: University of Michigan Press, 1977), 2-4, 6-19, 83-98.

2 Cyrus Peake, *Nationalism and Education in Modern China* (New York: Howard Fertig, 1932), 72-119; Theodore Hsi-en Chen, "Education in China, 1927-1937," in *The Strenuous Decade: China's Nation-Building Efforts, 1927-1937*, ed. Paul K.T. Sih, 289-314 (Baltimore: St. John's University Press, 1970).

3 Political instability created administrative chaos, and the documentary record is sparse. Until 1917, the Ministry of Education still managed to collect information from provinces and to publish yearly education statistics. From 1918 to 1927, however, political disintegration made any data collection impossible. The only data available for this period are two incomplete surveys conducted by the Chinese Vocational Education Association in 1923 and 1925, *DYCZJNJ* 3: 16.

4 Jiaoyu bu (Ministry of Education), "Dian ge sheng banfa putong jiaoyu zhanxing banfa" [Telegram from the Ministry of Education to every province regarding provisional solutions for regular education], *XZYB*: 596-97. In official documents, other terms were also changed, e.g., female teachers became *nü jiaoyuan instead of nü jiaoxi,* although no official instruction ordered these changes.

5 Ibid. Note that Yuan Shikai briefly revived the study of Confucian texts.

6 This document was written in March 1914. It is not clear who was minister of education at the time. Yan Xiu had been appointed on 20 February 1914. Before Yan actually assumed his responsibilities, Cai Rukai was appointed acting minister of education. The record does not indicate when Yan arrived to take over. "Jiaoyu zongzhang xingming ji renzhi shijian, 1912-1922" [Names and time in office of the ministers of education, 1912-22], *DYCZJNJ* 5: 205-6.

7 Jiaoyu bu, "Jiaoyu zongzhang ju cheng da zongtong ni zhan she gaodeng shifan liu xiao wei tongyi jiaoyu banfa" [A program to establish provisionally six advanced teachers' colleges, submitted by the minister of education as a means of unifying education (1914)], *SJSJ:* 798-99.

8 The previous "advanced teachers' colleges" had now become "higher teachers' colleges." In what follows, I sometimes refer to these as "teachers' colleges."

9 Jiaoyu bu, "Jiaoyu zongzhang ju cheng da zongtong ni zhan she gaodeng shifan liu xiao wei tongyi jiaoyu banfa."

10 Between 1918 and 1927, the number of public universities increased ten times and the number of private universities doubled. By 1927, there were twenty-one national universities and nine provincial universities. During the same period, the number of registered private universities increased to ten, *DYCZJNJ* 3: 15-16.

11 Jiaoyu bu, "Jiaoyu zongzhang ju cheng da zongtong," 798-99.

12 Li Youzhi, *Zhong wai shifan jiaoyu cidian* [The compendium of teachers' education in China and the World] (Beijing: China Broadcasting and Television Press, 1994), 320-21. See also Jiaoyu bu, "Ge sheng gaodeng shifan xuexiao yi lan biao" [Table of provincial higher teachers' colleges (1915)], *JYGB*, yr. 3 (1915), 8, "Zhuanjian" [Special documents]: 13-15.

13 For instance, provincial teachers' colleges in Shandong, Fujian, Hunan, Henan, and Zhejiang were closed. Li, *Zhong wai shifan jiaoyu cidian*, 316-17. Jiangxi Provincial Higher Teachers' College was demoted, becoming a provincial teachers' school; Hunan Provincial Higher Teachers' College was closed. See also Ding Zhipin, ed., "Zhongguo jin qishi nian lai jiaoyu jishi" [Events commemorating Chinese education during the last seventy years], *Minguo congshu*, 2, 45 (Shanghai: Shanghai shudian, 1933): 66.

14 Jiaoyu bu, "Quanguo jiaoyu jihua shu" [Plan for national education], *SJSS*: 813-14.

15 Jiaoyu bu, "Quanguo gaodeng shifan xuexiao xiaozhang huiyi yijue an: Gaodeng shifan xuexiao ruhe zhaokao xuesheng ge sheng xuansong ming'e ying ruhe fenpei an" [Proposals made at the meeting of presidents of national higher teachers' colleges: Admissions policies of teachers' colleges and how each province should draw up quotas], *SJSJ:* 835-36.
16 Jiaoyu bu, "Jiaoyu bu gongbu shifan jiaoyu ling" [The Ministry of Education's order on teachers' schools (1912)], *XZYB*: 660-61.
17 Jiaoyu bu,"Jiaoyu bu gongbu shifan jiaoyu ling," 660-61. According to the records, sixteen teachers' schools were run by missionaries in 1920-21. Zhonghua Jidujiao jiaoyu diaochahui, *Zhonghua Jidujiao jiaoyu shiye* [The educational cause of the Chinese Christian] (Shanghai: Commercial Press, 1922), 20-23.
18 Jiaoyu bu, "Minguo liu nian quanguo shifan xuexiao yi lan biao" [Table of teachers' schools nationwide (1917)], Chinese Historical Archives Number Two in Nanjing, file no. 1057-68.
19 Jiaoyu bu, "Zi Jingzhaoyin gesheng xun'anshi ge dutong Zhili zengshe shifan er bu ying zhuoliang qingxing fangzhao banli wen" [Consultative document suggesting that governors of the capital region and the provinces consider following Zhili's example in establishing secondary departments in teachers' schools], *SJSJ:* 800.
20 Ding, *Zhongguo jin qishi nian lai jiaoyu jishi*, 66-67.
21 Xinjiang sheng, "Xinjiang quan sheng jiaoyu jinxing jihua shu" [Report: Education plan for Xinjiang province], *JYGB*, yr. 4 (1917), 8, "baogao" [reports]: 1-10.
22 Ding, *Zhongguo jin qishi nian lai jiaoyu jishi*, 90.
23 Jiaoyu bu, "Jiaoyu bu gongbu shifan xuexiao guicheng" [Regulations for teachers' schools issued by the Ministry of Education (1912)], *XZYB*: 676-90.
24 "Jiaoyu gangyao" [Educational program], *JYZZ* 7, 9-10 (1915) "zhuanjian" [special documents], 9-14, 15-20. Northwest China was not included because it was supposed to be under the direction of Shaanxi Higher Teachers' College.
25 "Di wu jie quanguo jiaoyu hui lianhe hui dahui jueyi an: Gaodeng shifan xiaozhang huo zhuren jiaoyuan shicha fujin sheng qu jiaoyuan zhuangkuang banfa an" [Resolutions of the fifth National Federation of Educational associations conference: A proposal that the presidents or deans of higher teachers' schools inspect educational affairs in nearby provinces (October 1916)], *SJSJ:* 837-38; Liu Wenxiu, *Zhongguo shifan jiaoyu jianshi* [A brief history of Chinese teachers' education] (Beijing: Renmin Chubanshe, 1985), 41.
26 Yun Liu, "Xianxing shifan xuezhi de liubi jiqi gaige fa" [The drawbacks to the current system of teachers' schools and how to reform it], *SJSJ*: 856-59.
27 "Quanguo shifan xuexiao xiaozhang huiyi yijue an: Guanyu zhengdun quanguo shifan xuexiao jiaoyu zhi yijian shu" [Proposals from the meeting of presidents of teachers' schools nationwide: Recommendations for rectifying teachers' schools nationwide (August 1915)], *SJSJ:* 819-21. The program of teachers' school districts was reaffirmed by the Ministry of Education in early 1916, just before Yuan Shikai resigned. There were to be eight districts and, for the first time, Mongolia, Tibet, Qinghai, and Xinjiang would be included. Jiaoyu bu, "Jiaoyu quyu zhi huading" [Mapping educational districts], *JYZZ* 8, 2 (1916): 11-12.
28 Jiaoyu bu, "Zi Sichuan xunanshi kaiban ji gaizu zhongxue shifan deng xiao ying zhun beian wen" [Approval for Sichuan governor's plan to establish and reorganize provincial middle schools and teachers' schools], *JYGB*, yr. 1 (1914), 2, "Gongdu" [Official files]: 27-28.
29 See *JYGB*, yr. 5 (1918), "Fengtian shengzhang bao huafen gaisheng shifan quyu dagai qingxing wen" [Fengtian governor reporting the situation on setting up the province's teachers' schools districts], "Shanxi jiaoyuting cheng fusong Shanxi shixiao xuequ biao wen" [Shanxi provincial bureau of education submitting the table of the province's teachers' school districts] 3: 69, 109-119; "Anhui shengzhang zi song shifan xuequ suoshu xian fen yi lan biao qing chazhao wen" [Anhui governor submitting the table of teachers' school districts and the counties under their charge], "Shaanxi jiaoyuting chengsong di yi, er shifan xuequ suoshuo xian fen biao qing jian he wen" [Shaanxi provincial bureau of education submitting the first and second teachers' school districts and the counties under their charge], "Jiangxi jiaoyuting chengsong ge dao qu shifan xuexiao suoshu xian fen biao wen" [Jiangxi provincial bureau of education submitting the list of teachers' school districts and the counties under their charge], "Jilin jiaoyuting chengsong ge shifan qu suoshu

xian fen yi lan biao qing he bei wen" [Jilin provincial bureau of education submitting the list of teachers' school districts and the counties under their charge], 4: 64, 93-94, 94-95, 95-96; "Guangxi shengzhang zi song gai sheng ge shifan xuexiao qu nei suoshu xian fen biao qing he xingwen" [Guangxi governor submitting the province's teachers' schools, the districts, and the counties under their charge], "Jiangsu jiaoyuting cheng zunling guafen shifan xuequ qing he bei wen" [Jiangsu provincial bureau of education submitting a document showing the province having set up the teachers' school districts as instructed], "Henan jiaoyuting chengsong ge shifan xuexiao xianzai didian ji xuequ huafen qingxing qingzhe qing jian he wen" [Henan provincial bureau of education submitting the list of the locations of the provincial teachers' schools and the arrangement of the teachers' school district], "Zhejiang jiaoyuting chengsong shengli ge shifan xuequ nei suoshu ge xian qingdan qing he wen" [Zhejiang provincial bureau of education submitting the list for province's teachers' school districts and the counties they cover], and "Zhili jiaoyuting chengsong shengli ge shifan xuequ shangdai gengding wen" [Zhili provincial bureau of education responding to (Ministry of Education) on the program of teachers' school district in revision], 5: 31-32, 48-49, 96-97, 97-98, 99-100 (all in "gongdu" section).

30 Jiaoyu bu, "Zhiling Heilongjian jiaoyu ting shifan xuequ zhan nan huafen suo ding xiaozhang shicha ge jie ying zhaozhun wen" [An instructive document approving its plan that when Heilongjian has a difficulty establishing their teachers' schools district, the principals (of teachers' schools) would inspect (local schools)], *JYGB*, yr. 5 (1918), 6, "Gongdu" [Official files]: 45-46.

31 Jiaoyu bu, "Jiaoyu bu ling Jiangxi sheng zhengdun xuewu" [The Ministry of Education directs Jiangxi Province to rectify provincial education], *JYZZ* 9, 10 (1917): 73-74.

32 "Baogao: Henan jiaoyu ting zhengdun Henan jiaoyu jihua shu" [Report: Henan's Bureau of Education on its plan to rectify Henan's educational system], *JYGB*, yr. 8 (1921), 8, "Baogao" [report section]: 6-10.

33 "Jiaoyu jie xiaoxi: Jiangsu ba shi qu xiaoxue jiaoyu yanjiuhui jiyao" [Education news: On the Association for Research on Primary Education under the Jiangsu Number Eight Teachers' School District], *JYZZ* 17, 2 (1925): 15-16.

34 Ruth Hayhoe, "Cultural Tradition and Educational Modernization: Lessons from the Republican Era," in *Education and Modernization: The Chinese Experience*, ed. R. Hayhoe (Toronto: Ontario Institute for Studies in Education, 1992), 60.

35 Scholars maintain that people throughout much of northern China were long able to communicate using Mandarin (*guanhua*), an oral language based on the Beijing dialect. Wang Zhao, a pioneer researcher of late Qing popular language, contends that, contrary to popular belief, the term *guanhua* did not originally mean "official language"; rather, it meant "common language." Li Jinxi, *Guoyu yundong shigang* [Outline history of the movement for a national language], Minguo congshu, ser. 2, 52, (Shanghai: Shangwu yinshuguan, 1934, reprint, Shanghai: Shanghai shudian, 1990), 1-117.

36 Jiaoyu bu, "Shicha di qi qu xuewu zong baogao" [Report on the inspection of educational district number seven], *JYGB*, yr. 2 (1914), 6, "Baogao" [Reports]: 8-26.

37 "Fu Gaodeng shifan xuexiao xiaozhang huiyi yijue jiaoyu bu zixun an di yi xiang" [The decision made to the consulting proposal number one from the Ministry of Education at the meeting of the presidents of national teachers' colleges], *JYGB*, yr. 5 (1918), 10, "Mingling" [Orders]: 4-5.

38 Wo Yi, "Linshi jiaoyu huiyi riji" [A journal from the Provisional Conference on Education (July 1912)], in *YZYB*: 640.

39 Li, *Guoyu yundong shigang* 2, 50-52.

40 The *zhuyin* system included borrowing from the Japanese language's Hiragana alphabet and from Chinese characters. A modified version of this system, known as *zhuyin fuhao*, is still in use in Taiwan today.

41 Li, *Guoyu yundong shigang* 2, 50-52.

42 Jiaoyu bu, "Jiaoyu bu guoyu jiaoyu jinxing gaikuang" [The Ministry of Education's report on the implementation of the national language], *JYGB*, yr. 9 (1922), 6, "Baogao": 12-19.

43 Li, *Guoyu yundong shigan* 1, 66-67.

44 Hu Shi, "Guoyu yundong de lishi" [History of the movement for a national language], *JXJJT*: 387-89; Li, *Guoyu yundong shigan* 1, 70-72.
45 Jiaoyu bu, "Xunling" [Directive] 235, *JYGB*, yr. 5 (1918), 10, "Mingling": 5-6.
46 Li, *Guoyu yundong shigang* 1, 71-72.
47 "Ni qing jiaoyu bu tuixing guoyu jiaoyu banfa wu tiao" [Five measures suggested to the Ministry of Education for promoting the national language], *JYGB*, yr. 6 (1919), 10, "Gongdu"; see also *JXJJT*: 386-87.
48 Jiaoyu bu, "Jiaoyu bu guoyu jiaoyu jinxing gaikuang," 12-19.
49 Ibid.
50 "Fu gaodeng shifan xuexiao fu she guoyu jiangxi ke yijue an" [Attachment: Proposal that higher teachers' colleges establish national-language programs], *JYGB*, yr. 5 (1918), 10, "Mingling": 7-8.
51 Jiaoyu bu, "Zhiling Chendu gaodeng shifan xuexiao: Jingshi xian she you zhuyin zimu chuanxisuo gai xiao ke su pai yuan xuexi wen" [A directive to Chengdu Higher Teachers' College: Immediately send people to the short-term school in Beijing to learn the *zhuyin* system], *JYGB*, yr. 5 (1918), 14, "Gongdu": 21-22.
52 Jiaoyu bu, "Zhiling 357 hao" [Instructive order no. 357] *JYGB*, yr. 6 (1919), 5, "Mingling": 19-21; see also "Jiaoyu jie xiaoxi" [News in educational circles], *Zhonghua jiaoyu jie* 8, 2 (1919): 4.
53 Jiaoyu bu, "Ge shifan xuexiao ying ban guoyu jiangxi ke yi yu shizi wen" [All teachers' schools ought to establish national language programs in order to train more teachers], *JYGB*, yr. 7 (1920), 8, "Gongdu": 2-3.
54 Jiaoyu bu, "Zi ge sheng qu guomin xuexiao yi er nianji zi ben nian qiuji qi xian gai guowen wei yutiwen yi wei guoyu jiaoyu zhi yubei wen" [Instruction to provinces and districts to change the Chinese literature class of the first and second grades of citizens' schools to a class in vernacular literature beginning in the fall in order to prepare for teaching the national language], *JYGB*, yr. 7 (1920), 2, "Gongdu": 12.
55 Jiaoyu bu, "Zi ge sheng qu zi ding bennian xia xueqi qi fan shifan xuexiao ji gaodeng shifan xuexiao jun ying zhuo jian guowen zhongdian jia shou guoyu qing chazhao banli wen" [Recommendation to every province and district: All teachers' schools and higher teachers' colleges ought to reduce the time devoted to classical Chinese in order to add (a course devoted to) the national language next semester], *JYGB*, yr. 8 (1921), 4, "Gongdu": 17.
56 Jiaoyu bu, "Zi Fujian shengzhang gai sheng di er shifan xue xiao kechengbiao ying zhun bei an wen" [Notice to Fujian governor: The curriculum of Fujian Provincial Teachers' School number two has been approved], *JYGB*, yr. 5 (1918), 8, "Gongdu": 5-8.
57 "Hubei sheng di er shifan xue xiao benke (1-4 nianji) jiaoshou yong shu qi zhi biao" [The textbooks used in Hubei Provincial Teachers' School Number Two for the courses from one to four years], *JYGB*, yr. 8 (1921), 7, "Jizai" [Records]: 28-33.
58 *JXJJT*: 289-90.
59 Ding, *Zhongguo jin qishi nian lai jiaoyu jishi*, 90.
60 "Jiaoyu jie xiaoxi: Juban jiaqi guoyu jiangxi hui" [Education news: Vacation national-language training program opens], *Zhonghua jiaoyu jie* 8, 2 (1919): 4.
61 Jiaoyu bu, "Zi ge sheng qu chaofa Anhui sheng choubei guoyu tongyi weiyuanhui tuiguang guoyu banfa caoan yong bei cankao wen" [Recommendation to all provinces and districts by distributing the proposal from Anhui Preparatory Committee for National Language Unification on the measures of promoting national language for your reference], *JYGB*, yr. 9 (1922), 1, "Gongdu": 1-3; "Zhiling di 272 hao" [Directive order no. 272], JYGB, yr. 10 (1922), 2, "Mingling": 26 (see its attachment).
62 Ding, *Zhongguo jin qishi nian lai jiaoyu jishi*, 100. The national-language movement appeared to diverge after 1924, when a group of intellectuals started pushing to Romanize Chinese characters. See Li, *Guoyu yundong shigang* 3: 127-71. This movement also advocated federalism and strong local governments. Due to its political program, this movement did not win the support of the Nationalist government. See John DeFrancis, *Nationalism and Language Reform in China* (Princeton: Princeton University Press, 1950). This is one reason that the Romanization movement faded away after the 1930s. But the major problem the

movement faced was the practical difficulties involved in making sense of Romanized Chinese.

63 Young, *The Presidency of Yuan Shih-k'ai*, 83. See also Sun Liping, "Cong minzhu zhengzhi dao quanwei zhengzhi" [From democratic politics to authoritarian politics], in *Zhongguo xiandaihua shi* [A history of modernization in China], ed. Xu Jilin and Chen Dakai, 270-92 (Shanghai: Sanlian shudian, 1995).

64 "Zhongyao jiaoyu xingzheng renyuan yi lan" [List of major educational personnel], *DYCZJNJ* 5: 205-6.

65 Ka-che Yip, "Warlordism and Educational Finances, 1916-1927," in *Perspectives on a Changing China*, ed. Joshua Fogel and William Rowe, 183-95 (Colorado: Westview Press, 1979).

66 *DYCZJNJ* 3: 193, 423. Although these figures are likely to be incomplete and inaccurate, they convey something of the trends in educational development.

67 Ibid.

68 *DYCZJNJ* 3: 16. We should not exclude the possibility that many universities grew after 1922, when a new school system was established; however, such a large number of universities needed a certain amount of lead time before opening. Indeed, the large number of colleges and universities that opened from 1915 to 1925 proves that educational development was not entirely stagnant during the warlord period.

69 David Buck, "Educational Modernization in Tsinan, 1899-1937," in *The Chinese City between Two Worlds*, ed. Mark Elvin and G. William Skinner, 192-98 (Stanford: Stanford University Press, 1974).

70 Paul Bailey, *Reform the People: Changing Attitudes towards Popular Education in Early Twentieth-Century China* (Vancouver: UBC Press, 1990), 157-58.

71 Stig Thøgersen, *A County of Culture: Twentieth-Century China Seen from the Village Schools of Zouping, Shandong* (Ann Arbor: University of Michigan Press, 2002), 57-90.

72 Keith Schoppa, *Chinese Elites and Political Change: Zhejiang Province in the Early Twentieth Century* (Cambridge, MA: Harvard University Press, 1982), 38; Helen Chauncey, *Schoolhouse Politicians: Locality and State during the Chinese Republic* (Honolulu: University of Hawaii Press, 1992), 118; Thøgersen, *A County of Culture*, 40-43; Hayhoe, "Cultural Tradition and Educational Modernization," 47-72; Robert Culp, "Elite Association and Local Politics in Republican China: Educational Institutions in Jiashan and Lanqi Counties, Zhejiang, 1911-1937," *Modern China* 20, 4 (1994): 446-77; Thomas Curran, "Educational Reform and the Paradigm of State-Society Conflict in Republican China," *Republican China* 18, 2 (1993): 26-63.

73 "Gesheng jiaoyu zonghui lianhe hui jiyao" [Record of the United Association of Provincial Educational associations], *JXJJT*: 184; "Quanguo jiaoyu hui lianhe hui di yi ci kaihui ji lue" [A brief record of the first meeting of the National Federation of Educational Associations], *JXJJT*: 200-5.

74 Jiaoyu bu, "Xunling di 255 hao" [Directive order no. 255], *JYGB*, yr. 5 (1918), 11, "Mingling": 3-5.

75 "Quanguo jiaoyu hui lianhe hui di liu ci huiyi jiyao" [Record of the sixth meeting of the National Federation of Educational Associations (1920)], *JXJJT*: 227-34. See also Ding, *Zhongguo jin qishi nian lai jiaoyu jishi*, 86, 89.

76 "Di qi jie quanguo jiaoyu hui lianhe hui jilue" [Records of the seventh annual meeting of the National Federation of Educational Associations], *XZYB*: 848-64; Hu Shi, "Ji di ba jie quanguo jiaoyu hui lianhe hui taolun xin xuezhi de jingguo" [A recall on the discussion on the new school system at the eighth meeting of the National Federation of Educational Associations], *XZYB*: 985-89.

77 "Jiaoyu jie xiaoxi: Jiaoyu dangju fugu sixiang zhi shixian" [Education news: The educational authorities carry a policy of restoring old ideology], *JYZZ* 17, 12 (1925): 1-3.

78 Yip, "Warlordism and Education Finance," 183. Yip provides a detailed discussion of the movement.

79 "Quanguo jiaoyu hui lianhe hui yijue an: Difang jiaoyu jingfei guihua an" [National Federation of Educational Associations proposals: Proposal on planning local education budgets], *JYGB*, yr. 4 (1917), 7 "Zhuanjian": 1-2.

80 "Quanguo jiaoyu hui lianhe hui di liu ci huiyi jiyao" [Records of the sixth meeting of the National Federation of Educational Associations (1920, Shanghai)], *JXJJT:* 227-34.

81 Suzanne Pepper, *Radicalism and Education Reform in Twentieth-Century China* (New York: Cambridge University Press, 1996), 72-75.

82 "Da zongtong ling ge sheng xingzheng gongshu nei she jiaoyu si, 1913" [President orders establishment of bureau of education in provincial government], *JXJJT:* 122; Jiaoyu bu, "Gongbu jiaoyu ting zhanxing tiaoli" [Provisional regulations of the provincial bureau of education] and "Jiaoyu bu hezhun jiaoyu ting shu zuzhi dagang" [Ministry of Education approved organizational outline of provincial bureaus of educations], *JXJJT:* 132-33; Jiaoyu bu, "Jiaoyu bu guiding jiaoyu tingzhang zhiquan" [The Ministry of Education spelled out the powers of the commissioners of the bureaus of educations], *JXJJT:* 133-34.

83 Ding, *Zhongguo jin qishi nian lai jiaoyu jishi,* 70. For example, Huang Yanpei, the former leader of the Jiangsu Education Association and the leader of the NFEA, was appointed the education commissioner of Zhili; other commissioners with similar backgrounds include Jiang Weiqiao (Jiangsu, Zhejiang), Ma Xulun (Zhejiang), Xu Shoushang (Fengtian, Jiangxi), Shen Enfu (Hunan), and Fu Dingsheng (Jiangsu, Guangdong). See "Ge sheng jiaoyu tingzhang xingming ji renzhi shijian" [Names and tenures of commissioners of provincial bureaus of education], *JXJJT:* 138-40; for the names of leaders of the provincial educational associations and the National Federation of Educational associations see "Li jie huiyi yijue an" [NFEA propositions for all annual meetings], *JXJJT:* 200-35.

84 "Jiaoyu bu fu Qian dujun zhi dianwen" [The Ministry of Education's reply to the telegram of the Guizhou governor], *JYZZ* 9 (1917), 11 "Jishi" [Events]: 81-82.

85 See *DYCZJNJ* 1: 38-41.

86 Buck, "Educational Modernization in Tsinan," 192-98, also noted the rise of educational professionalism in the early Republican period. My definition of professional educators, however, is much narrower than is Buck's. His definition includes everyone involved in educational activities, while mine includes only those individuals who were specially trained in teachers' schools and who worked as either teachers or educational administrators.

87 For example, most evaluations were written in the following format: "judging the person's education background, the length and the experience in educational circle, he is qualified for the current position." "(Ge sheng) jiaoyu ting/shengzhang chengsong gai ting zhiyuan mingdan lüli ce qing he bei wen (Heilongjiang, Chahar, Hunan, Hubei, Shanxi, Zhejiang, Henan, Jiangxi, Xinjiang, Jiangsu, Zhili, Jilin, Anhui, Shaanxi, deng sheng) [Bureaus of education (in provinces)/provincial governors submitting the staff lists and their CVs for examination and approval (including Heilongjiang, Chahar, Hunan, Hubei, Shanxi, Zhejiang, Henan, Jiangxi, Xinjiang, Jiangsu, Zhili, Jilin, Anhui, Shaanxi, etc)]," *JYGB*, yr. 4 (1917), 6: 14-15; 24-25; no. 7: 32; yr. 5 (1918), no. 3: 102-8, 112-14; no. 4: 100-1; no. 5: 33-36; no. 7: 38-39; no. 6: 39-41; 62-64; no. 8: 9-12; no. 11:36-38; no. 13: 25-26, 44-45; no. 14: 9; no. 15: 24, 36-37, 39-42, 52-59; no. 16: 27, 33-36, 44 (all in "gongdu" section); "Banli jiaoyu xingzheng hezhun beian renyuan yi lan biao" [Table(s) listing the educational administrative officials], *JYGB*, yr. 6 (1919), 1: 32-35; 2: 132-35; 3: 44-55; 4: 44-45; 5: 30-31; 6: 25-29; 7: 22; 8: 6-7; 9: 8-10; 9: 8-10; 10: 4-5; yr. 7 (1920), 1: 3-4; 2: 11-12; 3: 2-3; 4: 4-6; 5: 4-8; 6: 3-4; 7: 4-9; 8: 11-12; 9: 3-4; 10: 4; 11: 6-10; 12: 3-5; yr. 8 (1921), 1: 3-5; 2: 10-11; 3: 16-18; 4: 2-5; 5: 2-3; 6: 7-8; 7: 18-20; 8: 12-18; 9: 5-7; 10: 4-8; 11: 1-3; yr. 9 (1922), 1: 1-2; 2: 1-3; 3: 10-14; 4: 12-17; 5: 12-13; 6: 16-18; 7: 12-15; 8: 1-2; 9: 13-15; 10: 11-12; 12: 13-14; yr. 10 (1923), 1: 1-3; 2: 2-4; 3: 9-10; 4: 8-10; 5: 10-12; 6: 3-5 (all in "jizai" section).

88 Ibid.

89 Duara's excellent study on northern Chinese villages provides us with a way of observing the dynamics of local society, especially at the village and inter-village levels, and its response to state penetration. See Prasenjit Duara, *Culture, Power, and the State: Rural North China,* 1900-1942 (Stanford: Stanford University Press, 1988). However, I hesitate to use his term "cultural nexus" because it refers to much more than the educational elite that I am describing. Their cultural and social connections with the environment may differ from those that Duara describes at the village level.

90 See Chauncey, *Schoolhouse Politicians*, 64-71; Culp, "Elite Association and Local Politics in Republican China," 446-77; Curran, "Educational Reform and the Paradigm of State-Society Conflict in Republican China," 26-63. An exceptional case is Schoppa's study of Zhejing elites, in which he notes that county educational administrators played a major role in the activities of local associations during the warlord period. But his hypothesis is not detailed. See Keith Schoppa, *Chinese Elites and Political Change: Zhejiang Province in the Early Twentieth Century* (Cambridge, MA: Harvard University Press, 1982), 38.

91 Chauncey, *Schoolhouse Politicians*, 86.

92 Thøgersen, *A County of Culture*, 72.

93 Jiaoyu bu, "Gongbu jiaoyu hui guicheng" [Regulations on educational associations], *JXJJT:* 252-53.

94 Jiaoyu bu, "Xiuding jiaoyu hui guicheng" [Revised regulations on educational associations], *JXJJT:* 253-55.

95 "Henan jiaoyuting chengsong tin shu zhiyuan lüli biao qing bei wen" [Henan provincial bureau of education submitting the list of its staff and their CVs for examination and records], *JYGB*, yr. 5 (1918), 3, "Gongdu": 106-8.

96 See data from CVs listed in note 87 above.

97 See *JYGB*, yr. 7 (1920), 7 "Jizai": 4-9.

98 Jiaoyu bu, "Putong jiaoyu zhanxing banfa" [Provisional regulations on regular education (January 1912)], *XZYB*: 596-97.

99 Paul Bailey, "Active Citizen or Efficient Housewife? The Debate over Women's Education in Early-Twentieth-Century China," in *Education, Culture, and Identity in Twentieth-Century China*, ed. Glen Peterson, Ruth Hayhoe, and Lu Yongling (Ann Arbor: University of Michigan Press, 2001), 327.

100 Sally Borthwick, "Changing Concepts of the Role of Women from the Late Qing to the May Fourth Period," in *Ideal and Reality: Social and Political Change in Modern China, 1860-1949*, ed. David Pong and Edmund S.K. Fung, 81-87 (New York: University Press of America, 1985).

101 Jiaoyu bu, "Zhengli jiaoyu fang'an" [Plan for educational rectification (1914)], *XZYB*: 743.

102 Elizabeth VanderVen, "Educational Reform and Village Society in Twentieth-Century Northeast China: Haicheng, 1905-1931" (PhD dissertation, University of California, Los Angeles, 2003), 248-54, 274-77.

103 See Xia Xiaohong, *Wan Qing nüxing yu jindai Zhongguo* [Late Qing women and modern China] (Beijing: Beijing daxue chubanshe, 2004), 223-56, 257-85.

104 Liu Sheng, "Fakanci er" [Foreword number two], *Funü zazhi* [Women's magazine] 1, 1 (1915): 2-4.

105 Zhang Zhu Hanfen, "Tuiguang nüzi chudeng xiaoxue siyi" [A personal opinion on promoting lower primary schools for girls], *Funü zazh* 1, 6 (1915): 4-5.

106 Ding Fengzhu, "Zhenxing nüxue zhi gongxiao" [The efficacy of advocating women's education], *Funü zazhi* 1, 7 (1915): 4-6.

107 Bailey, "Active Citizen or Efficient Housewife?" 329-31.

108 Zhan Lu, "Duiyu zhuchi nüxue zhe zhi zhi yan" [Frank words to those who are running women's education], *Funü zazhi* 1, 6 (1915): 1-2.

109 Chen Qitian, *Jindai Zhongguo jiaoyu shi* [A history of modern Chinese education] (Taibei: Zhonghua shuju, 1969), 252-55. See also "Jiaoyu bu gongbu zhong xuexiao ling shishi guize" [Implementing regulations for middle schools issued by the Ministry of Education (September 1912)], *XZYB*: 669-76.

110 Tian Shiqian, "Kaocha Jiangsu zhongdeng jiaoyu baogao" [An examination of secondary education in Jiangsu], *JYGB*, yr. 6 (1919), 3 "Baogao": 19-20.

111 Hou Diao, "Jiangsu jiaoyu zhi tese" [Special characteristics of education in Jiangsu], *Zhonghua jiaoyu jie* 5, 6 (1916): 1-8.

112 On this event, see Borthwick, "Changing Concepts of the Role of Women," 63-91.

113 Gao Guiqiao, "Letter to Mr. Tsai Yuan-pei, Minister of the Board of Education, June 1912," Chinese Historical Archives Number Two in Nanjing, file 1057-584. The original letter was written in English.

114 Bai Yun, "Nüzi zhiye tan" [A discussion of women's professions], *Funü zazhi* 1, 9 (1915): 6-8.

115 Hou Hongjian, "Lun nüzi zhiye jiaoyu zhi shiji" [On the reality of women's vocational education], *Zhonghua jiaoyu jie* [Chinese Educational Circle] 6, 3 (1917), "Lun shuo" [Discussion section]: 1-5.

116 "E jiaoyu si zhi jiaoyu xingzheng" [Hubei Provincial Bureau of Education and its educational management], *JYZZ* 5, 10 (1914): 86-87.

117 Jiaoyu bu, "Zi Hunan shengzhang Pingjiang sili Qiming nüxiao cheng ni biangeng xuenian kaishi yibian xu ban shifan benke shishu tebie zhun zhaoban wen" [Approval of the special request of the private Qiming Women's School to change its semester schedule in order to continue its teacher training program], *JYGB*, yr. 3 (1916), 12, 32-33.

118 *Henan difang jiaoyu shicha baogao* [Report on local educational inspection in Henan] 1 (1934).

119 Huang Xinxian, *Zhongguo jinxiandai nüzi jiaoyu* [Women's education in modern China] (Fuzhou: Fujian jiaoyu chubanshe, 1992), 43.

120 Jiaoyu bu, "Minguo liu nian quanguo shifan xuexiao yi lan biao." Another source indicates that a total of sixty-one female normal schools existed in 1917. Chai-hsuan Chuang, *Tendencies toward a Democratic System of Education in China* (Shanghai: Commercial Press, 1922), 105.

121 Jiaoyu bu, "Zi ge sheng qu ying shefa chouban nüzi zhongxuexiao wen" [Consultative document advising all provinces and regions to establish women's middle schools], *JYGB*, yr. 6 (1919), 7, "Gongdu": 21.

122 Tang Chindon Yiu, "Women's Education in China," *Bulletins on Chinese Education* (Shanghai: The Commercial Press, 1925), vol. 2, bulletin 9, 15-19.

123 According to Wang Zheng's remarkable work on Chinese women in the New Cultural and May Fourth Period, Lu Lihua once considered going to female normal schools if she had no other choice, while Zhu Su'e and her sister did indeed go to teachers' schools. See Wang Zheng, *Women in the Chinese Enlightenment: Oral and Textual Histories* (Berkeley: University of California Press, 1999): 149, 188-9.

124 If not specifically noted, all information on Beijing Women's Normal School comes from Fang Huan, "Beijing nüzi shifan xuexiao yilan" [Beijing Women's Normal School: A brochure (1918)]. Fang Huan was the principal of this school from 1917 to the time the brochure was written.

125 Jiaoyu bu, "Pi nüzi shifan xuexiao: Nüzi gaodeng shifan wei she yiqian zhanzhun gaixiao fushe zhuanxiu ke" [Approval of the request of the (Beijing) Women's Teachers' School to establish a temporary college-level program before the establishment of a women's higher teachers' college], *JYGB*, yr. 2 (1914), 2, "Gongdu": 57-58.

126 Jiaoyu bu, "Jiaoyu bu zhiling, 522 hao" [Ministry of Education: The instructional order no. 522], *SJSJ*: 1035-36.

127 "Quanguo jiaoyu hui lianhe hui yijue an: Qing she nüzi gaodeng shifan xuexiao an" [The National Federation of Educational Associations' proposals: Proposal to establish a women's higher teachers' college], *JYGB,* yr. 4 (1917). 7, "Zhuanjian": 3-4.

128 Early universities founded by Christian missionaries included Lingnan University in Guangzhou (1905), Beijing Xiehe Women's University (1909), Huangnan University in Fuzhou (1914), and Jinling Women's University in Nanjing (1915). Chen Dongyuan, *Zhong funü shenghuo shi* [A history of the life of Chinese women] (Shanghai: Shangwu yinshu guan, 1937, reprint: 1998), 388.

129 Jiaoyu bu, "Jiaoyu bu xunling di 239 hao, minguo ba nian liu yue" [The Ministry of Education: The order number 239, June 1919], *SJSJ*: 1036-42.

130 Sun Jixu, "Beijing nüzi gaodeng shifan" [Beijing Women's Higher Teachers' College], *SJSJ:* 1028-35. See also Yen-chu Sun, "Chinese National Higher Education for Women in the Context of Social Reform, 1919-1929: A Case Study" (PhD diss., New York University, 1985), 78-117.

131 See Meng Guofang, "Meng Guofang ji Deng Chunlan ru Beida de jingguo" [Meng Guofang's recollection of Deng Chunlan's experience on entering Beijing University], *ZJXS* 3b: 82-87.

132 Li, *Minguo jiaoyu shi*, 723-26.

133 Thøgersen, *A County of Culture*, 58; Bailey, "Active Citizen," 327-30.

134 Sarah McElroy, "Forging a New Role for Women: Zhili First Women's Normal School and the Growth of Women's Education in China, 1901-2," in Peterson, Hayhoe, and Lu, *Education, Culture, and Identity in Twentieth-Century China*, 359-61.

135 Jiaoyu bu, "Pi nüzi shifan xuexiao nüzi gaodeng shifan wei she yiqian zhan zhun gaixiao fu she zhuanxiu ke," JYGB, yr. 2 (1914), 2, "Gongdu": 57-58. However, this program did not enroll students until 1916 due to political and financial problems.

136 Jiang Weiqiao, "Lun nü xuexiao zhi jiashi shixi" [On the hands-on practice of household management in girls' schools], *JYZZ* 9, 6 (1917): 105-11. Paul Bailey believes that Jiang's inconsistency on the issue led him to support the study of household management in girls' schools, which probably simplified the issue. See also Bailey, "Active Citizen," 324, 330.

137 Tang, "Women's Education in China," 18.

Chapter 4: Modernity and the Village

1 Suzanne Pepper, *Radicalism and Education Reform in Twentieth-Century China* (New York: Cambridge University Press, 1996), 88-109.

2 Barry Keenan, *The Dewey Experiment in China: Educational Reform and Political Power in the Early Republic* (Cambridge: Harvard University Press, 1977), 55-79.

3 Barry Keenan has explained the growing influence of American education and Dewey's educational philosophy after 1919 as a result of the enhancement of America's global position after the First World War. See Keenan, *Dewey Experiment in China*, 35.

4 Qian Manqian and Jin Linxiang, *Zhongguo jiandai xuezhi bijiao yanjiu* [Research on comparative schooling system in modern China] (Guangzhou: Guangdong jiaoyu chubanshe, 1996), 227-28.

5 "Di qi jie Quanguo jiaoyuhui lianhehui ji lue" [Record of the seventh conference of the National Federation of Educational Associations], *XZYB*: 853-54.

6 Qian Manqian and Jin Linxiang argued that the 1922 Educational Reform did not simply imitate the American system but, rather, stitched together a program from examples in many foreign countries. Qian and Jin, *Zhongguo jiandai xuezhi bijiao yanjiu*, 276-77.

7 "Xuezhi xitong caoan" [A draft proposal for the school system], *XZYB*: 860-64.

8 Jing Hengyi, "Gaige shifan jiaoyu de yijian" [My thoughts on reforming teachers' education], *Jiaoyu chao* [Educational tide] 1, 4 (1919): 53-63.

9 "Di wu jie quanguo jiaoyu hui lianhe hui dahui yijue an, fujian: Gaige shifan jiaoyu yi'an" [Proposals from the fifth conference of the National Federation of Educational Associations, with attached proposal: A proposal for reforming teachers' education], *SJSJ*: 838-47.

10 Yun Liu, "Xianxing shifan xuezhi de liubi jiqi gaige fa," *SJSJ*: 856-61.

11 "Jiaoyu jie xiaoxi: Zhonghua zhiye she ben jie nianhui zhi tiyian" [Educational news: Proposals from the 1925 annual conference of the Chinese Vocational Society], *JYZZ* 17, 7 (1925): 10-11.

12 Jiaoyu bu, "Xuexiao xitong gaige ling di 23 hao, 1922 nian 11 yue 1 ri" [The order for reforming school system, 1 November 1922], *ZJSJZ* 2: 264-68.

13 Ibid.

14 Tao Xingzhi, "Shifan jiaoyu zhi xin qushi" [The new direction of teacher's education], *Shishi xinbao* [The new current affairs daily], 22 October 1921.

15 Chang Naide, "Shifan jiaoyu gaizao wenti" [The issue of reforming the teachers'-school system], *JYZZ* 14 (1922): 1-30.

16 Wang Maozu, "Shifan jiaoyu san da wenti" [Three great problems facing teachers' education], *Jiaoyu huikan* [The chronicle of education] 2, 1 (1924): 1-9

17 "Zhe sheng shixing xin xue zhi zhi zhunbei" [Zhejiang province is preparing for the implementation of new school system], *Xin jiaoyu* [New education] 6, 1: 120-21. "Anhui sheng zhi xuezhi gaige" [Reform of school system in Anhui province], *Xin jiaoyu* 6, 1 (1923): 4-16.

18 Zhang Zhongyuan, "Zhongguo shifan jiaoyu de zong jiantao" [An overall self-criticism on Chinese teachers' schools], *JYZZ* 25, 7 (1935): 45-84.

19 *DYCZJNJ* 3: 311.

20 Luo Tingguang, *Shifan jiaoyu xin lun* [A new perspective on teachers' education] (Shanghai: Nanjing shudian, 1933), 40.

21 Liu Wenxiu, *Zhongguo shifan jiaoyu jian shi* [A brief history of teachers' education in China] (Beijing: Renmin jiaoyu chubanshe, 1984), 55.

22 Beijing shifan daxue xiaoshi bianxie zu, *Beijing shifan daxue xiao shi* [A brief history of Beijing Normal University] (Beijing: Beijing shifan daxue chubanshe, 1982), 84.

23 According to Pepper, in the 1920s, most Chinese intellectuals, including leftists, conservatives, and bureaucrats, at the very least acknowledged the problems with the 1922 reform. Such criticism emerged even before the European experts' visit in 1931. But unravelling the varied motives for voicing criticism is tricky, and while nationalism may be the thread that connects them, there are certainly many shades of nationalism. Pepper, *Radicalism and Education Reform*, 86-109.

24 Keenan, *Dewey Experiment in China*, 111-25; Pepper, *Radicalism and Education Reform*, 90-110.

25 Jiaoyu bu, "Xuexiao xitong gaige ling di 23 hao, 1922 nian 11 yue 1 ri," *ZJSJZ* 2: 264-68.

26 Carl. H. Becker, M. Falski, P. Langevin, and R.H. Tawney, *The Reorganization of Education in China* (Report of the League of Nations' Mission of Educational Experts) (Paris: League of Nations' Institute of Intellectual Co-operation, 1932), 19-29. While these European experts correctly identified the problems of inefficiency in China's educational system, they did not realize that a key political motive behind the 1922 Educational Reform was to establish a democratic polity through the decentralization of educational systems. Keenan, *Dewey Experiment in China*, 55-79.

27 Becker, *Reorganization of Education*, 65-67, 98-138.

28 Pepper, *Radicalism and Educational Reform*, 41.

29 Becker, *Reorganization of Education*, 58-61, 98-117, 139-89.

30 Xia Chengfeng, "Gaizhi hou zhongdeng jiaoyu zhengce shangque" [A discussion of the secondary education system after the reform], *JYZZ* 17, 7 (1925): 1-5.

31 Sheng Langxi, "Shi nian lai Jiangsu zhongdeng xuexiao biyesheng chulu tongji" [Statistics on the number of graduates of secondary schools in Jiangsu over the past ten years], *JYZZ* 17, 4 (1925): 1-30; "Jiaoyu xiaoxi: Jiangsu biyesheng jiuye zhidao weiyuanhui zhi chengli" [Education news: The establishment of the career guidance committee for the graduates of middle schools in Jiangsu], *JYZZ* 18, 10 (1926): 4-5.

32 Based on her study of student magazines, Ling Xiao proposed that one of the causes of student unrest in the 1920s and 1930s was the anxiety that regular middle school students felt about continuing their education and/or getting a job. See Ling Xiao, "Reading and Revolution: The Political Economy of Youth Anxiety in the Republican Era," paper presented at the Association for Asian Studies West Conference, Long Beach, California, October 2000. Reporting on the persistent student protests and unrest all over the country at a government meeting in 1930, an official named Qian Changzhao offered the same diagnosis. Qian called on the government to offer more help to students. "Jiaoyu jie xiaoxi: Ji dai jiejue zhi qingnian wenti" (Education news: The problems of young people in desperate need of resolution), *JYZZ* 22, 9 (1930): 119.

33 Stig Thøgersen, "Learning in Lijiazhuang: Education, Skills, and Careers in Twentieth-Century Rural China," in *Education, Culture, and Identity in Twentieth-Century China*, ed. Glen Peterson, Ruth Hayhoe, and Yonglin Lu, 241-46 (Ann Arbor: University of Michigan Press, 2001). See also Stig Thøgersen, *A County of Culture: Twentieth-Century China Seen from the Village Schools of Zouping, Shandong* (Ann Arbor: University of Michigan Press, 2002), 85.

34 Li Ruian, "Xiangcun jiaoyu fudao zhi xingzheng zuzhi wenti" [Issues of administration and organization in rural education], *Xiangcun jiaoyu* (Rural education) 29 (July 1935): 1-13.

35 Ibid. The article does not indicate how a teacher's qualifications were determined. The government considered qualified those who graduated from either a teachers' school or a regular secondary school and who passed a teaching certifying examination. The qualifying examination is discussed in the next chapter.

36 Li, "Xiangcun jiaoyu fudao."

37 Luo Tingguang, *Shifan jiaoyu xin lun*, 37-38.

38 Yu Jiaju, "Xiangcun jiaoyu de weiji" [The crisis in rural education], *Zhonghua jiaoyu jie* 10, 1 (July 1920): 83-86.

39 *Er shi er nian du quanguo gaodeng jiaoyu tongji* (1933 national higher education statistics [1936]), cited in Liu Laiquan, Guan Peijun, and Lan Shibin, "Wo guo jiaoshi gongzi daiyu de lishi kaocha, 1909-1949" [A historical examination of teachers' salary and conditions in China, 1909-1949], *Jiaoyu yanjiu* [Studies in education] 4 (1993): 30-35.
40 Qian Yizhang, "Xiaoxue jiaoyuan shiji shenghuo diaocha" [A study of the actual lives of elementary schoolteachers], *Zhonghua jiaoyu jie* 13, 12 (1924): 1-13.
41 Li Chucai, "Xiaoxue jiaoshi de shenghuo wenti" [The livelihood of elementary schoolteachers], *Zhonghua jiaoyu jie* 17, 6 (1928): 1-12.
42 Li Xizhen, "Ti ji hao han zhi shenghuo" [A life of tears thanks to hunger and cold], *Zhonghua jiaoyu jie* 20, 8 (1933): 13-27.
43 Yu, "Xiangcun jiaoyu de weiji."
44 Yang Xiaochun, "Xiangcun xiaoxue jiaoshi wenti" [The problems faced by rural elementary schoolteachers], *Jiaoyu huikan* 2, 1921: 1-8.
45 Ibid.
46 Tian Guangsheng, "Xiaoxue jiaoyu zhi weiji" [The crisis of primary education], *Xin jiaoyu* [New education] 3, 1 (1921): 110-15.
47 Thomas Curran, "Educational Reform and the Paradigm of State-Society Conflict in Republican China," *Republican China* (Min kuo) 18, 2 (1993): 42-43.
48 Sarah McElroy, "Forging a New Role for Women: Zhili First Women's Normal School and the Growth of Women's Education in China, 1901-2," in *Education, Culture, and Identity in Twentieth-Century China*, ed. Glen Peterson, Ruth Hayhoe, and Lu Yongling (Ann Arbor: University of Michigan Press, 2001), 367; Sun Yen-chu, "Chinese National Higher Education for Women in the Context of Social Reform, 1919-1929: A Case Study" (PhD diss., New York University, 1985), 128.
49 Sun, "Chinese National Higher Education for Women," 119.
50 Ibid., 119-20.
51 "Jiaoyu jie xiaoxi: Jiaobu duiyu nüzi jiaoyu zhi tongling" [Education news: Instructions about female education from the Ministry of Education], *JYZZ* 17, 11 (1925): 6.
52 *Funü zhou bao* [Women's Weekly] 35 (23 April 1924), 40 (28 May 1924), 50 (13 August 1924), 52 (27 August 1924), 53 (3 September 1924).
53 The students of Beijing Women's Teachers' College did not participate in the May Fourth demonstration because their parents kept them at home and prevented them from being involved in the movement. See Sally Borthwick, "Changing Concepts of the Role of Women from the Late Qing to the May Fourth Period," in *Ideal and Reality: Social and Political Change in Modern China, 1860-1949*, ed. David Pong and Edmund S.K. Fung (New York: University Press of America, 1985), 85.
54 Three students were two months late for the fall semester because a war among warlords had led to the railroad's being barricaded. Chancellor Yang expelled them, refusing to accept their explanation. See "Jiaoyu jie xiaoxi: Beijing nüzi shifan daxue" (Education news: Beijing Women's Normal University), *JYZZ* 17, 3 (1925): 9-10.
55 "Jiaoyu jie xiaoxi: Beijing nüzi shifan daxue."
56 Ibid.
57 Lu Xun strongly criticized Yang's thoughts and her managing of the school. See "Fen, guafu zhuyi" [Graves and widowhood], in *Lu Xun quanji* [Complete works of Lu Xun] 1 (Beijing: Renmin wenxue chubanshe, 1981), 266. See also Sun, "Chinese National Higher Education for Women," 126-27.
58 "Jiaoyu jie xiaoxi: Beijing nüzi shifan daxue zhi jiesan yu tingban" [Education news: The end of Beijing Women's Normal University), *JYZZ* 17, 9 (1925): 1-3; "Jiaoyu jie xiaoxi: Dongda yu nüshida fengchao zhi weisheng" [Education news: The epilogue to the student protests at Southeast University and Beijing Women's Normal University), *JYZZ* 17, 10 (1925): 10.
59 "Jiaoyu jie xiaoxi: Dongda yu nüshida fengchao zhi weisheng."
60 Beijing shifan daxue xiaoshi bianxie zu, *Beijing shifan daxue xiaoshi*, 1902-1982 [History of Beijing normal university, 1902-1982] (Beijing shifan daxue chubanshe, 1982), 75-84.

61 Ibid., 74.
62 "Jiaoyu jie xiaoxi: Jiangnan jiaoyu zhi fandong de qingxiang" [Education news: Reactionary trend of education in Jiangnan], *JYZZ* 18, 10 (1926): 3-4; "Jiaoyu jie xiaoxi: Shanxi nannü tongxue qingyuan zhi jieguo" (Education news: The result of a petition for coeducation in Shanxi), *JYZZ* 17, 11 (1925): 6.
63 "Jiaoyu jie xiaoxi: Guomin zhengfu xia zhi E sheng jiaoyu" [Education news: Education in Hubei under the Nationalist government], *JYZZ* 18, 12 (1926): 3-4.
64 Luo Suwen, *Nüxing yu jindai Zhongguo shehui* [Woman and modern Chinese society] (Shanghai: Shanghai renmin chubanshe, 1996), 249.
65 In one of her stories, "Liuli wa" (Glazed tiles), Zhang Ailing, a writer in the 1930s, satirized these parents as makers of "glazed tiles." Zhang, *Zhang Ailing wenji* [A collection of Zhang Ailing's works] 1 (Hefei: Anhui wenyi chubanshe, 1992): 111-23. Traditionally, giving birth to a girl was called "producing a tile" (*nong wa*), while giving birth to a boy was called "producing jade" (*nong zhang*). Modern education would make the girls from rich families "glazed tiles" as, with their schooling, they would fetch a better price in the marriage market.
66 "Jiaoyu jie xiaoxi: Di shiyi jie quan guo sheng jiaoyu hui lianhe hui zhi genggai" [Education news: A summary of the eleventh conference of the National Federation of Educational Associations), *JYZZ* 17, 12 (1925): 4-8.
67 Yu, "Xiangcun jiaoyu de weiji."
68 Yu Jiaju, "Xiangcun jiaoyu yundong de hanyi he fangxiang" [The meaning and direction of the rural education movement], *Zhonghua jiaoyu jie* 10, 10 (1921); 11-25.
69 Li Dazhao, "Qingnian yu nongcun" [Youth and rural villages], in *Li Dazhao xuanji* [Selected works of Li Dazhao] (Beijing: Beijing renmin chubanshe, 1962), 146-50.
70 Du Yuanzai, "Wu si yihou Zhongguo de pingmin jiaoyu yundong" [China's popular education movement after the May Fourth Movement], *Pingmin jiaoyu* [Popular education] 68/69 (October 1923); 34-47. See also Pepper, *Radicalism and Education Reform*, 96.
71 Wu Xiangxiang, *Yan Yangchu zhuan: Wei quanqiu xiangcun gaizao fendou liushi nian* [A biography of James Yen: Sixty years of struggle for global rural reform) (Taibei: Shibao chubanshe, 1981), 70, 179-81. On James Yen's work as a populist in promoting mass education, see Charles Hayford's excellent *To the People: James Yen and Village China* (New York: Columbia University Press, 1990).
72 Cao Dianqi, "Changsha zhi nongcun buxi jiaoyu yundong" [The rural education movement in Changsha], *Zhonghua jiaoyu jie* 13, 12 (1924): 1-20.
73 The problem lasted until 1929, when Yen's program began to train local staff to promote the movement. Wu, *Yan Yangchu zhuan*, 70, 179-81.
74 Cao, "Changsha zhi nongcun buxi jiaoyu yundong."
75 Ibid.
76 Tang Jue, "Xiangxiang zhong de xiangcun zhongxue" [How I imagine rural middle schools], *Xin jiaoyu* 9, 4 (1924): 733-39.
77 Thøgersen, *County of Culture*, 36-37.
78 Gu Mei, *Xiangcun shifan gaiyao* [The essentials of village teachers' schools] (Shanghai: Shangwu yinshuguan, 1936), 29-30.
79 In 1919, Shanxi established the Teachers' School for Citizens' Elementary Education (*Guomin shifan*) to train teachers for citizens' elementary schools (*Guomin xiaoxue*). This school was regarded by some educators as the first rural teachers' school. Jin Haiguan, "Lun woguo zhi xiangcun shifan" [On our country's rural teachers' schools], in *Xiaozhuang piban* [Critique of Xiaozhuang], ed. Sun Mingxun and Dai Zian, 139-58 (Shanghai: Ertong shuju, 1934). The problems with this conclusion were pointed out by Gu Mei: the Teachers' School for Citizens' Elementary Education was located in Taiyuan, the capital of Shanxi, and training teachers for rural schools was not mentioned as one of its goals. See Gu, *Xiangcun shifan gaiyao*, 31.
80 Gu, *Xiangcun shifan gaiyao*, 31.
81 Ibid., 32.

82 Philip Kuhn, "T'ao Hsing-chih, 1981-1946: An Educational Reformer," *Harvard Papers on China* 13 (1959): 163-95.
83 Keenan, *Dewey Experiment in China*, 82-109.
84 Yao Yusheng, "National Salvation through Education: Tao Xingzhi's Educational Radicalism" (PhD diss., University of Minnesota, 1999), 11-12.
85 The faculty and students of Labour University paid a brief visit to the Xiaozhuang school in 1929 but strongly disagreed with the school's practice. See Chan Ming K. and Arif Dirlik, eds., *Schools into Fields and Factories: Anarchist, the Guomindang, and the National Labor University in Shanghai, 1927-1932* (Durham: Duke University Press, 1991), 101.
86 Zhixin Su, "Teaching, Learning, and Reflective Acting: A Dewey Experiment in Chinese Teacher Education," *Teachers College Record* 98, 1 (Fall 1996): 128.
87 Hubert Brown, "American Progressivism in Chinese Education: The Case of Tao Xingzhi," in *China's Education and the Industrialized World: Studies in Cultural Transfer*, ed. Ruth Hayhoe and Mariannne Bastid, 120-38 (New York: M.E. Sharpe, 1987).
88 Keenan acknowledged the differences between Tao's attitude towards Dewey and that of other educators, such as Jiang Menglin and Hu Shi. However, since Keenan ignored the local sources of Tao's ideas, he maintained that Tao's practice was an extension or variation of Dewey's ideas. See Keenan, *Dewey Experiment in China*, 86, 92-106.
89 Xin Yuan and Xie Fang, eds., *Tao Xingzhi yu Xiaozhuang shifan* [Tao Xingzhi and Xiaozhuang Teachers' School] (Nanjing: Jiangsu jiaoyu chubanshe, 1986), 68-70.
90 Ibid., 4-6.
91 Brown, "American Progressivism in Chinese Education," 126.
92 "Tao Xingzhi xiansheng nianpu" [A chronicle of Tao Xingzhi's life], in *Tao Xingzhi wenji* [Collected works of Tao Xingzhi], ed. Jiangsu sheng Tao Xingzhi jiaoyu sixiang yanjiu hui and Nanjing Xiaozhuang shifan Tao Xingzhi yanjiu shi (Nanjing: Jiangsu renmin chubanshe, 1981), 879-81.
93 Tao Xingzhi, "'Wei zhishi' jieji" [A class for "bogus knowledge"], in *Tao Xingzhi wenji*: 191-201.
94 Tao Xingzhi, "Shifan jiaoyu zhi chedi gaige" [The thorough reform of teachers' education], in *Tao Xingzhi wenji*: 167-68.
95 Tao Xingzhi, "Zhonghua jiaoyu gaijin she gaizao quanguo xiangcun jiaoyu xuanyan" [A manifesto from the Chinese National Association for the Advancement of Education on reforming rural education], in *Tao Xingzhi wenji*: 142.
96 Tao Xingzhi, "Shenghuo ji jiaoyu" [Life is education], in *Tao Xingzhi wenji*: 243-50. In a forum on rural teacher training held in Xiaozhuang Village in the winter of 1929, Tao gave a speech (reproduced in the previous citation) entitled "Life Is Education." He said, "The phrase 'Education is life' comes from Mr. Dewey and we used it a lot in the past. But we never thought about the genuine meaning of this phrase. Now, I will turn it a half-somersault [*fan le ban ge jindou*], changing it into 'Life is education'" (234).
97 Tao, "Shenghuo ji jiaoyu," in *Tao Xingzhi wenji*: 244-45.
98 Tao, "Jiao xue zuo he yi" [Teaching, learning, and doing in one], *Tao Xingzhi wenji*: 184-86.
99 Tao Xingzhi, "Women de xintiao" [Our new creed], in *Zhongguo jiaoyu gaizao* [The reform of Chinese education] (Beijing: Dongfang chubanshe, 1996), 73-74.
100 "Zhonghua jiaoyu gaizao she Xiaozhuang xuexiao baogao shu" [A report on the Xiaozhuang school by the Chinese National Association for the Advancement of Education], *Xiangjiao congxun* [Collective newsletter on rural education] 2, 11 (16 June 1928): 1-2.
101 Xin and Xie, *Tao Xingzhi yu Xiaozhuang shifan*, 61-63. The Xiaozhuang administrative style was likely influenced by the Chinese anarchist movement of the 1910s and 1920s.
102 Tao Xingzhi, "Shiyan xiangcun shifan xuexiao da ke wen" [Answering questions from visitors regarding (Xiaozhuang) Experimental Village Teachers' School], in *Tao Xingzhi wenji*: 149-54.
103 Yang Xiaochun, "Xing jiang yi sui de Nanjing shiyan xiangcun shifan" [Approaching the end of the first year of the Nanjing Experimental Village Teachers' School], *Zhonghua jiaoyu jie* 17, 5 (1928): 1-20.

104 Becker et al., *Reorganization of Education in China*, 95-96.
105 Liang Shuming, "Danmai de jiaoyu yu women de jiaoyu" [Education in Denmark and China], *Liang Shuming jiaoyu lunzhu xuan* [Liang Shuming: Selected essays on education] (Beijing: Beijing renmin chubanshe, 1994), 78-79.
106 David Buck, "Educational Modernization in Tsinan, 1899-1937," in *The Chinese City between Two Worlds*, ed. Mark Elvin and G. William Skinner (Stanford: Stanford University Press, 1974), 197-98. See also Thøgersen, *A County of Culture*, 90.
107 Yu Ying-shih, "Some Preliminary Observations on the Rise of Ch'ing Confucian Intellectualism," *Tsing Hua Journal of Chinese Studies* 11 (1975): 105-43.
108 Ibid.
109 "Tao Xingzhi xiansheng nianpu," 879.
110 Miawfen Lü, "Practice as Knowledge: Yang-ming Learning and *Chiang-hui* in Sixteenth-Century China" (PhD diss., University of California at Los Angeles, 1997), 3.
111 Tao Xingzhi, "Xing shi zhi zhi shi" [Practice is the beginning of knowledge], in *Tao Xingzhi wenji*: 182-83.
112 Tao Xingzhi, "Shenghuo gongju zhuyi zhi jiaoyu" [On instrumentalist education for life], in *Tao Xingzhi wenji*: 172-73; Tao Xingzhi, "Xing shi zhi zhi shi," 182-83.
113 Tao Xingzhi, "Da Zhu Duanyan zhi wen" [Responding to Zhu Duanyan's questions], in *Tao Xingzhi wenji* (1981): 226-31.
114 Tao Xingzhi, "Zai lao li shang lao xin" [Improving one's mind through physical labour], in *Tao Xingzhi wenji*: 187-88.
115 Ibid., 196-97.
116 Ibid., 198-99.
117 Liang Shuming, "Baoqian, tongku, yijian you xingwei de shi" [Regret, pain, and an interesting thing], in *Liang Shuming jiaoyu lunzhu xuan* (Beijing: Beijing renmin chubanshe, 1994), 21-27.
118 Tao, "Jiao xue zuo he yi," in *Tao Xingzhi wenji*: 184-86.
119 Yang, "Xing jiang yi sui de Nanjing shiyan xiangcun shifan."
120 Tao, "Jiao xue zuo he yi xia zhi jiao ke shu" [Textbooks in teaching-learning-doing-in-one], in *Tao Xingzhi wenji*: 294-305.
121 Hubert Brown found the same type of anti-intellectualism in Dewey's thought, but I doubt that Tao had spotted it. Brown, "American Progressivism in Chinese Education," 129. On Wang Yangming's anti-intellectualism, see Yu, "Some Preliminary Observations," 105-43.
122 Tao Xingzhi, "Zhongguo xiangcun jiaoyu yundong zhi yi ban" [A glimpse into China's rural education movement], in *Tao Xingzhi wenji* (1981): 203-13.
123 Xin and Xie, *Tao Xingzhi yu Xiaozhuang shifan*, 29.
124 Hu Qing found traces of this tradition in historical records from many periods, including the ancient *Book of Documents* and *Zhuangzi*, in the practices of private schools during the Han Dynasty, and in Song academies. Hu, *Shuyuan de shehui gongneng jiqi wenhua tese* [Social functions and cultural characteristics of academies] (Hankou: Hubei jiaoyu chubanshe, 1996), 166-72. Yuan (1206-1368 AD) and Ming scholars inherited this tradition of physical labour and self-support. Gao Shiliang, ed., *Mingdai jiaoyu lunzhu xuan* [Selected articles on education in the Ming Dynasty] (Beijing: Renmin chubanshe, 1990), 90-91.
125 Hu, *Shuyuan de shehui gongneng*, 166-72.
126 Ibid.
127 Xin and Xie, *Tao Xingzhi yu Xiaozhuang shifan*, 43.
128 *Mengzi yi zhu* [Mengzi translated and annotated], trans. Yang Bojun (Beijing: Zhonghua shuju, 1981), 124.
129 Tao, "Shiyan xiangcun shifan xuexiao da ke wen," in *Tao Xingzhi wenji*: 153; Yang, "Xing jiang yi sui de Nanjing shiyan xiangcun shifan."
130 Keenan, *Dewey Experiment in China*, 89. Hubert Brown was perceptive in pointing out that Tao's sympathy with Dewey's ideas was rooted in their resemblance to those of his beloved Lu-Wang School, but he failed to look outside of philosophical traditions in accounting for Tao's thinking. Brown, "American Progressivism in Chinese Education," 120-38.

131 Keenan, *Dewey Experiment in China*, 99.

132 It was well known that Tao admired Wang Yangming and often used the Wangian terms *zhi* and *xing* in his writings. Though he initially endorsed Wang's ideal of "combining knowledge and action," he later gave one of Wang's mottoes a "half-somersault": "knowledge is the starting point of action" (*zhi shi xing zhi shi*) became "action is the starting point of knowledge." Tao, "Xing shi zhi zhi shi," in *Tao Xingzhi wenji*: 182.

133 Tao Xingzhi, "Shiyan xiangcun shifan di yi yuan jianzhang caoan" [Drafted regulations for Department Number One of the (Xiaozhuang) Experimental Village Teachers' School], *in Tao Xingzhi wenji*: 145-47; Tao, "Zhongguo xiangcun jiaoyu yundong zhi yi ban," in *Tao Xingzhi wenji*: 203-13.

134 Tao, "Shiyan xiangcun shifan xuexiao da ke wen," in *Tao Xingzhi wenji*: 152.

135 Bai Qixiang, "Guan yu xiangcun danji xiaoxue jiaoshi de yi ge wenti" [On a problem faced by teachers in rural elementary schools], *Xiangjiao congxun* 2, 9 (15 May 1928): 1-2.

136 Yang, "Xing jiang yi sui de Nanjing shiyan xiangcun shifan."

137 Tao, "Zhongguo xiangcun jiaoyu yundong zhi yi ban," in *Tao Xingzhi wenji*: 211.

138 Ibid., 211-12.

139 Tao Xingzhi, "Cun hun ge" [Song of village spirit], in *Tao Xingzhi wenji*: 265.

140 Yang, "Xingjiang yi sui de Nanjing shiyan xiangcun shifan."

141 Cheng Benhai, *Xiangcun shifan jingyan tan* [On the experience of village teachers' schools] (Kunming: Zhonghua shuju, 1939).

142 In his study of Zouping County, Stig Thøgersen used the term "deprofessionalization" to refer to an increase in the number of nonprofessionals in the teaching corps. Thøgersen, "Learning in Lijiazhuang," 244. While Thøgersen points to the Cultural Revolution as a rare period of deprofessionalization in twentieth-century China, the drop in the number of teachers' schools in the 1920s meant that a large number of schoolteachers came from nonprofessional schools. In this book, I define deprofessionalization according to a functionalist perspective: when professionally trained teachers are asked to perform services unrelated to their profession, I refer to this as deprofessionalization.

143 Keenan points out that John Dewey had later revised his idea of "school is society" to reflect the idea that the school is open to the society; but he also admits that Tao did not read Dewey's revision until 1929. See Keenan, *The Dewey Experiment in China*, 106.

144 Tao, "Shenghuo ji jiaoyu," in *Tai Xingzhi wenji*: 244-45.

145 Borthwick, *Education and Social Change in China*, 31.

146 *Li ji: Xue ji* [Book of rites: School].

147 Kangxi emperor, "Kangxi sishi yi nian yu chi shizi wen" [Imperial edict on teaching, 1701], *YZSJ:* 120.

148 Hsiao Kung-chuan, *Rural China*, 235-44.

149 Mary Clabaugh Wright underlined the importance of the restoration of local academies after the Taiping Rebellion. She ascribed the measure to the need to identify able men who could reinforce local stability. See Wright, *The Last Stand of Chinese Conservatism: The T'ung-Chih Restoration, 1862-1874* (Stanford: Stanford University Press, 1975), 130. Of course, the role of the schools in imperial society was not limited to this function.

150 Yang, "Xing jiang yi sui de Nanjing shiyan xiangcun shifan." The suspicions of Xiaozhuang villagers resemble those that peasants exhibited towards new-style schools, as reported by Mao Zedong in his famous report on the Hunan peasant movement. See Mao, "Hunan nongmin yundong kaocha baogao" [Report on an investigation of the Hunan peasant movement], in *Mao Zedong xuanji* [Selected works of Mao Zedong] 1 (Beijing: Beijing renmin chubanshe, 1968): 39-40.

151 Editor, "Zhe yi qi" [This issue], *Xiangjiao congxun* 2, 22 (1928): 1.

152 Lu Jingshan, "Gei xiangcun xiaoxue jiaoshi de xin" [A letter to village elementary schoolteachers], *Xiangjiao congxun* 2, 17 (1928): 2-4.

153 Tao, "Zhongguo xiangcun jiaoyu yundong zhi yi ban," *Tao Xingzhi wenji*: 207-8.

154 Yang, "Xing jiang yi sui de Nanjing shiyan xiangcun shifan."

155 Li Chucai, *Po Xiao* [To the dawn] (Shanghai: ertong shuju, 1932), 55-58.

156 Cheng Benhai, *Zai Xiaozhuang* [In Xiaozhuang village] (Shanghai: Zhonghua shuju, 1930), 37-39.

157 Li, *Po Xiao*, 102; "Xiao wen yi shu" [School news briefs], *Xiangjiao congxun* 2, 18 (1 October 1928): 4.
158 Xie Bao, "Lun Xiaozhuang shifan bei feng shi" [On the closing of the Xiaozhuang teachers' school], in *Xiaozhuang pipan* [Critique of Xiaozhuang], ed. Sun Mingxun and Dai Zian (Shanghai: Ertong shuju, 1934), 137.
159 Tao, "Zhongguo xiangcun jiaoyu yundong zhi yi ban," *Tao Xingzhi wenji*: 204.
160 *Xiangjiao congxun* 2, 20 (1928); Xin and Xie, *Tao Xingzhi yu Xiaozhuang shifan*, 39-40.
161 Xin and Xie, *Tao Xingzhi yu Xiaozhuang shifan*, 15-16.
162 Yang, "Xing jiang yi sui de Nanjing shiyan xiangcun shifan."
163 Xin and Xie, *Tao Xingzhi yu Xiaozhuang shifan*, 45-46.
164 Bai Qixiang, "Chu chuang de Shencemen minzhong xuexiao" [The initial stage of Shencemen School for Commoners], *Xiangjiao congxun* 2, 11 (1928): 2.
165 Shao Chongxiang, "Heimoyuan zhongxin chayuan" [Heimoyuan central tea house], *Xiangjiao congxun* 2, 9 (1928): 3-4; Li Chucai, *Poxiao*, 58.
166 Yang, "Xing jiang yi sui de Nanjing shiyan xiangcun shifan"; Min Keqin, "Zhongyang daxue di yi shiyan minzhong xuexiao baogao shu" [Report on Central University's Experimental School for Commoners Number One], *Xiangjiao congxun* 2, 10 (1928): 1-2.
167 Cheng, *Zai Xiaozhuang*, 32-36.
168 "Gei Feng Huanzhang xiansheng de xin" [A letter to Mr. Feng Huanzhang (Yuxiang)]; "Xiaozhuang liancun ziwei xintiao" [The self-defence creed of the united villages of Xiaozhuang]; "Xiaozhuang liancun ziweituan zuzhi dagang" [An organizational outline of the self-defence squad of the united villages of Xiaozhuang]; "Liancun ziweituan di yi hao bugao" [The first proclamation of the united villages self-defence squad]; "Liancun jinyan weiyuanhui zhangcheng" [Regulations of the united villages committee to ban opium smoking]; "Ju du yundong dagang" [Outline of the campaign to ban opium smoking]. The preceding works, all by Tao Xingzhi, published in *Xiangjiao congxun* 2, 22 (30 November 1928): 1-4.
169 Tao Xingzhi, "Ruhe jiao nongmin chu tou" [How can we teach peasants to free themselves?], in *Tao Xingzhi wenji* (1981): 177.
170 Zhang Zonglin, "Man le yi sui ban yihou de Xiaozhuang" [Xiaozhuang one and a half years later], *Xiangjiao congxun* 2, 20 (30 October 1928): 1-3.
171 *Xiangjiao congxun* 2, 11 (16 June 1928): 2.
172 Tao, "Shenghuo ji jiaoyu,"in *Tao Xingzhi wenji*, 248-49.
173 Pepper, *Radicalism and Education Reform*, 88-109.
174 Ibid., 110-11.
175 Cheng Benhai, *Xiangcun shifan jingyan tan* [On the experience of village teachers' schools] (Kunming: Zhonghua shuju, 1939). Cheng was one of the first group of students enrolled in the Xiaozhuang School in March 1927, and he was also a close friend of Tao Xingzhi. He was hired by the Education Bureau of Longchuang County, Guangdong Province, as the principal of Longchuan County Village Teachers' School in 1930. His practice in the Longchuan School was derived directly from that of the Xiaozhuang School. This book is a collection of Cheng's articles on his ideas and practices in the Longchuan School during the early 1930s.

Chapter 5: Nationalizing the Local

1 Robert Bedeski, *State-Building in Modern China: The Kuomintang in the Prewar Period* (Berkeley: University of California Berkeley Institute of East Asian Studies, 1981); Philip Kuhn, "Local Self-Government under the Republic: Problems of Control, Autonomy, and Mobilization," in *Conflict and Control in Late Imperial China*, ed. Frederic Wakeman and Carolyn Grant, 257-99 (Berkeley: University of California Press, 1975).
2 An example is Yan Xishan's programs in Shanxi. See Kuhn, "Local Self-Government," 257-99.
3 Theodore Hsi-en Chen, "Education in China 1927-1937," in *The Strenuous Decade: China's Nation-Building Efforts 1927-1937*, ed. Paul T.K. Sih, 289-314 (Baltimore: St. John's University Press, 1970); Kuhn, "Local Self-Government under the Republic" 257-99; Robert Culp, "Elite Association and Local Politics in Republican China," *Modern China* 20, 4 (1994): 446-77.

4 Culp, "Elite Association and Local Politics," 446-77; Chauncey, *Schoolhouse Politicians: Locality and State during the Chinese Republic* (Honolulu: University of Hawaii Press, 1992), 19-20; Curran, "Educational Reform and the Paradigm of State-Society Conflict in Republican China," Republican China 18 (1993): 26-63.

5 Da xueyuan [university council], "Zhengdun shifan jiaoyu zhidu an" [Proposal for rectifying the teacher education system], Da Xueyuan, *Quanguo jiaoyu huiyi baogao 1928* [Report of the National Conference on Education, 1928] (reprint) (Taibei: Wenhai chubanshe, 1977), 139-50; Gu Mei, *Xiangcun shifan gaiyao* [The essentials of village teachers' schools] (Shanghai: Shangwu yin shuguang, 1936), 48; Li Huaxing, ed., *Minguo jiaoyu shi* [A history of education in Republican China] (Shanghai: Shanghai jiaoyu chubanshe, 1997), 664; Xiong Ming'an, *Zhonghua minguo jiaoyu shi* [A history of education in the Republic of China] (Chongqing: Chongqing chubanshe, 1990), 108.

6 Wu Xiangxiang and Liu Shaotang (compil.), *Di er ci quanguo jiaoyu huiyi shi mo ji, 1930* [Records of the second National Conference of Education, 1930] (Taibei: Zhuangji wenxu chubanshe, 1971, reprint), 25.

7 At the time, China had 1,915 counties.

8 Wu and Liu, *Di er ci quanguo jiaoyu huiyi*, 143-47.

9 Gu, *Xiangcun shifan gaiyao*, 42-46.

10 The term "weisheng," or simply "wei," in rural reconstruction documents refers to both public health and personal hygiene. In some cases, it also refers to "self-defense" in the short term.

11 Jiaoyu bu, "Shifan xuexiao fa" [Law regarding teachers' schools], *ZJSJZ*: 324-26; Jiaoyu bu, "Shifan xuexiao guicheng" [Regulations regarding teachers' schools], *ZJSJZ*: 326-48.

12 Jiaoyu bu, "Wei tong ling xianzhi sheli putong zhongxue zengshe zhiye xuexiao zai putong zhongxue tian she zhiye ke huo zhiye kemu, xianli chuzhong ying fushe huo gai she xiangcun shifan ji zhiye ke you" [Summary of instructions for limiting the establishment of regular middle schools, increasing vocational courses and programs in regular middle schools, and establishing village teacher training and vocational programs at county lower middle schools or converting them into village teachers' schools), *JYBGB* (1931): 3, 13, "Mingling": 7-10.

13 Jiangsu sheng jiaoyu ting bian shen shi, *Jiangsu jiaoyu gailan, minguo er shi yi nian* [A general review of education in Jiangsu, 1932) 1, (Taibei: Zhuanji wenxue chubanshe, reprint 1971), 82.

14 I have only been able to locate the reports for a total of forty-five counties.

15 Henan Province Bureau of Education, *Henan difang jiaoyu shicha baogao* [Reports on local educational inspection in Henan] 1 (1934).

16 The author did not receive the data for Provincial Tianshui Teachers' School for his report.

17 Zhuang Zexuan, "Gansu jiaoyu xianzhuang yi pie" [A glimpse of education in Gansu Province today], *Zhonghua jiaoyu jie* 24, 7 (1937): 157-63. See also Ruth Hayhoe, "Cultural Tradition and Educational Modernization: Lessons from the Republican Era," in *Education and Modernization: The Chinese Experience*, ed. Ruth Hayhoe, 47-72 (Toronto: Ontario Institute for Studies in Education, 1992).

18 Jiaoyu bu, "Hebei sheng jiaoyu shicha baogao" [Report on educational inspection in Hebei], in *Jiaoyu bu shicha yuan shicha ge sheng shi jiaoyu baogao huibian* [A collection of reports from the Ministry of Education's inspectors on educational conditions in each province and city] (Ministry of Education print, 1933).

19 Zhang Shufeng, *Shandong jiaoyu tongshi: Jinxiandai juan* [A comprehensive history of education in Shandong: Modern section] (Jinan: Shandong renmin chubanshe, 2001), 199-208.

20 Suzanne Pepper, *Radicalism and Education Reform*, in *Twentieth-Century China*, 64 (New York: Cambridge University Press, 1996).

21 Chen Qingzhi, *Zhongguo jiaoyu shi* [History of Chinese education] (Shanghai: Shanghai Shangwu yinshu guan, 1936 [Minguo congshu, bian 1, juan 48, reprint, 1989]), 792-93; see also Ye Jianxin, *Kangzhan qian Zhongguo zhongdeng jiaoyu zhi yanjiu, 1928-1937* [A study of Chinese secondary education before the Sino-Japanese War, 1928-37] (Taipei: Wenshezhe chubanshe, 1982); Xiong, *Zhonghua minguo jiaoyu shi*, 108.; Yeh, *The Alienated Academy*; Chen, "Education in China," 289-314; Chauncey, *Schoolhouse Politicians*, 20-21.

22 Xiong, *Zhonghua mingguo jiaoyu shi*, 157-61.
23 Chen, *Zhongguo jiaoyu shi*, 6, 792-93. See also Jiaoyu bu, "Jiaoyu fagui: Shencha dangyi jiaoshi zige tiaoli" [Educational regulations: Criteria for examining qualifications for teaching party principles], *JYZZ* 23, 2 (1931): 119.
24 Jiaoyu bu, "Jiaoyu fagui: Shencha dangyi jiaoshi zige tiaoli" [Educational laws and regulations: Criteria for examining qualifications for teaching party principles], *JYZZ* 23, 2 (1931): 119.
25 Xiong, *Zhonghua mingguo jiaoyu shi*, 101. See also Jiaoyu bu, "Shifan xuexiao fa," *ZJSJZ*: 324-25.
26 Jiaoyu bu, "Shifan xuexiao guicheng," 329.
27 Ibid., 339.
28 Ibid., 339-40; See also Xiong, *Zhonghua mingguo jiaoyu shi*, 146-47.
29 Jiaoyu bu, "Shifan xuexiao guicheng," 339-40.
30 Jiaoyu bu, *Xiangcun shifan xuexiao kecheng biaozhun* [Standard curricula for village teachers' schools] (Shanghai: Zhonghua shuju, 1935).
31 Students were required to engage in field, factory, or school chores.
32 Xiong, *Zhonghua mingguo jiaoyu shi*, 161-62.
33 Chen, "Education in China, 1927-1937," 295.
34 Li Jianxun, "Zong lun" [General discussion], *JYZZ* 26, 4 (1936): 104. This was a special issue of *Jiaoyu zazhi* entitled "Biye huikao wenti yanjiu zhuanhao" [A special issue on the comprehensive examinations].
35 Luo Yi (number one secretary of Zhejiang provincial party committee, 1970s; student at Shanxi Teachers' School Number One, 1935), in interview with the author (Shanghai, 1 January 1998).
36 "Zhongyang da xuequ jianding xiaoxue jiaoyuan zhanxing guicheng" [Central District of the University Council: Provisional regulations on examining primary schoolteachers], *DXYGB* (1928): 122-27.
37 "Da jishi" [Important events], *JYZZ*, 8, 12 (1916), "Jishi": 75-78; "Shanxi jiaoyuting cheng bao bennian jianding xiaoxue jiaoyuan qingxing qing he wen" [Shanxi provincial bureau of education reporting this result of the examination of primary school teachers in the year], *JYGB*, yr. 5 (1918), 12, "Gongdu": 78; Jiaoyu bu, "Zhiling di 357 hao" [Instructive order no. 357], *JYGB*, yr. 6 (1919), 5, "Mingling": 17-19.
38 "Xiaoxue fa" [Primary school law], *Zhongyang minguo zhengfu gonggao* [Central republican government bulletin], *KJKHJ* (Republican period) 3: 182.
39 Jiaoyu bu, "Xiaoxue jiaoyuan jianding zhanxing guichen," 5, 21 (1934). [Provisional regulations on examining primary schoolteachers 21 May 1934], *ZJSJZ*: 376-79; Jiaoyu bu, "Zhongxue ji shifan xuexiao jiaoyuan jianding zhanxing guicheng" 5, 21 (1934). [Provisional regulations on examining teachers of middle schools and teachers' schools, 21 May 1934], *ZJSJZ*: 371-74.
40 Jiangsu sheng jiaoyu ting bian shen shi, *Jiangsu jiaoyu gailan*, 30-31.
41 Jiaoyu bu, "Shandong sheng jiaoyu shicha baogao," in *Jiaoyu bu shicha yuan shicha ge sheng jiaoyu*.
42 Ye Zonglin, "You ben sheng xiaoxue jiaoshi shang lai toushi 'He'nan jiaoyu'" [A review of the primary schoolteachers based on *Henan Educational Review*], *Xiangcun gaizao* [Rural reform] 6, 6 (1937): 1-8.
43 Hunan sheng zhengfu (Hunan provincial government), "Hu'nan sheng zhengfu jin nian de jiaoyu sheshi" [The education programs carried out by the Hunan government in recent years], *JYZZ* 25, 2 (1935): 5-16.
44 "Juban xiaoxue jiaoshoufa jiangxi hui ji xiaoxue jiaoyuan shuqi jiangxi hui" [Organizing training meetings on the primary education pedagogy and summer training classes for primary schoolteachers], *JXJJT:* 289; "Baoshan xian jiaoyu hui" [Baoshan County Educational Association], *JXJJT:* 346.
45 Jiaoyu bu, "Chou she geji gezhong shizi xunlian jiguan jihua (8): Zhong xiao xue jiao zhi yuan jinxiu banfa" [Plan for establishing various types of teacher training institutions: How to accomplish this at all levels of education], *DECZJNJ* 3 (1930): 19-20.
46 Ibid.

47 Jiaoyu bu, "Xiaoxue jiaoyuan jianding zhanxing guichen," *ZJSJZ*: 371-79.

48 Jiaoyu bu, "Jiaoyu bu xunling, 4395 hao" [Ministry of Education, directive no. 4395], *JYBGB* 7, 15/16 (1935); Jiaoyu bu, "Jiaoyu bu xunling, 6922 hao," in *JYBGB* 7, 21/22 (1935); Hunan sheng zhengfu, "Hu'nan sheng zhengfu jinnian de jiaoyu sheshi," 11; Fujian sheng jiaoyu ting, "Fujian sheng jiaoyu ting di san jie shuqi xuexiao jihua dagang" [Fujian's Bureau of Education outlines a teaching plan for the third year of summer school], in *JYBGB* 3 (1931), 15, "Fuzai" [Attachment]: 36-38; Shaanxi sheng jiaoyu ting [Shaanxi provincial bureau of education], "Ben ting guanyu di si qu xuexiao juban xiaoxue jiaoyuan jiaqi jiangxi hui banfa deng cailiao, (minguo) 25 nian, 6 yue" [On the regulations and other materials regarding the summer training program of primary schoolteachers in the fourth district, June 1936], Shaanxi Provincial archives, file no. 8-1-57.

49 "Henan shengli xiangcun shifan xuexiao shuqi xiangcun jiaoyu jiangxi hui jianzhang" [A brief description of the summer program of the Henan provincial village teachers' schools], *Xiangcun gaizao* 1, 6 (1932).

50 Huang Yanpei, "Yu Anting qingnian hezuoshe tan xiangcun shiye" [Discussing rural improvement with the Anting Youth Cooperative], *Huang Yanpei jiaoyu lunzhu xuan* [Huang Yanpei: Selected essays on education] (Beijing: Renmin jiaoyu chubanshe, 1993), 216.

51 Yan Yangchu, "Zhonghua pingmin jiaoyu cujin hui Dingxian gongzuo dagai" [Report on the Chinese National Association for the Promotion of Mass Education program in Dingxian] 1 of *Xiangcun jianshe shiyan*, in *Minguo congshu* 4, 16: 53-61.

52 Jiang Hengyuan, "Zhonghua zhiye jiaoyu she zhi nongcun gongzuo" [The rural programs of the Chinese Vocational Education Association] 1 of *Xiangcun jianshe shiyan*, in *Minguo congshu* 4, 16: 39-51.

53 Kuhn, "Local Self-Government under the Republic."

54 Liang Shuming, "Baoqian–tongku–yijian you xingwei de shi" [Regret, pain, and an interesting thing], *Liang Shuming jiaoyu lunzhu xuan* [Liang Shuming: Selected essays on education] (Beijing: Renmin jiaoyu chubanshe, 1994), 16-27; Liang Shuming, "Shandong xiangcun jianshe yanjiu yuan gongzuo baogao" [Report on the work of the Shandong Rural Reconstruction Institute]; "Shandong xiangcun jianshe yanjiu yuan ji Zouping shiyan xian gongzuo baogao" [Work report on the Shandong rural reconstruction institute and the Zouping experimental county], all in Zhang Yuanshan and Xu Shilian, eds., *Xiangcun jianshe shiyan* [Rural reconstruction experiment] (Shanghai: Zhonghua shuju, 1934) 1, 31-38, 177-78; see also Guy Alitto, *The Last Confucian: Liang Shuming and the Chinese Dilemma of Modernity* (Berkeley: University of California Press, 1986).

55 Fang Yuyan, "Xuyan" [Preface], in Cheng, *Xiangcun shifan jingyan tan* [On the experience of village teachers' schools] (Kunming: Zhongua shuju, 1939).

56 Cao Zhenqiu, "Chu fa hou" [After setting off], *Xiang jiao cong xun* 2, 15 (1928): 2-4.

57 Zhang Zonglin, "Xueyuan zhi de xiangcun shifan" [Village teachers' schools in school field], *Zhonghua jiaoyu jie* 23, 11 (1936): 25-32.

58 Wu Guangsong, "Xianghu shifan xuexiao: Zhejiang de Xiaozhuang" [Xianghu Village Teachers' School: Zhejiang's Xiaozhuang], *SQGZ* 18: 255-62.

59 Wang Chuncai, "Cao Zhenqiu: Shuang zhong ye geng hong, huanghua wan jie xiang" [Cao Zhenqiu: Frost makes maple leaves redder and yellow flowers become more aromatic at the end – an educator's biography], *SQGZ* 4: 100-9; Zhang Bin, *Cong Zhejiang kan Zhongguo jiaoyu jindai hua* [Education modernization in Zhejiang] (Guangzhou: Guangdong Education Press, 1996), 293-99.

60 Zhang, *Cong Zhejiang kan Zhongguo jiaoyu*, 293-99. Jin Haiguan was a student in the Department of Education at Nanjing Teachers' College in 1918, when Tao Xingzhi was departmental chair. Jin only stayed at Nanjing Teachers' College very briefly, and it seems that he was not influenced by Tao's radical ideas.

61 Zhang, *Cong Zhejiang kan Zhongguo jiaoyu*, 293-99.

62 Ibid.

63 Zhejiang sheng, "Zhejiang shengli Xianghu xiangcun shifan de xiangcun tuiguang jiaoyu" [Zhejiang's Xianghu Provincial Village Teachers' Schools' promotion of rural education], in *Xiangcun jianshe shiyan* 3: 491-512.

64 Ibid.; Wu, "Xianghu shifan xuexiao," *SQGZ* 18: 255-62.
65 Jiangsu Huangdu xiangcun shifan xuexiao, *Yige xinxing de shifan xuexiao* [A newly emerged teachers' school] (Huangdu xiangcun shifan xuexiao print, 1936), all information on Huangdu village teachers' schools comes from this text unless specifically noted.
66 Tong Jupu and Shang Zhensheng, "Henan shengli xiangshi shiyanqu tuiguang gaikuang ji jihua caohan" [Draft plan and general situation of the experimental region associated with Henan Provincial Village Teachers' School], *Xiangcun gaizao* [Rural reform] 2, 11 (1933), 17-24.
67 Ibid.
68 Ibid.
69 Ibid.
70 Ibid.
71 Jiang He, "Shengli Jiujiang xiangcun shifan shiyan qu yi ge ban yue zhi zhuangkuang" [The situation of experiment region operated by Jiujiang Provincial Village Teachers' School: After one month and a half], *Xiang xiao jikan (chuan kan hao)* [Village schools quarterly], 1 (first issue special) (1934): 63-83.
72 Miu Zheng, "Women de shiyan qu" [Our experimental region], *Xiang xiao jikan* 1, 4 (1935): 55-60.
73 Ibid.
74 Gao, *Zhongguo jiaoyu shi yanjiu*, 214.
75 Yang Xiaochun, "Huanglu shifan yu Huanglu hanzai kangzhan" [Huanglu teachers' school and Huanglu's drought-relief], *Zhonghua jiaoyu jie* 23, 10 (1936): 69-73.
76 Kuhn, "Local Self-Government under the Republic," 283.
77 Chauncey, *Schoolhouse Politicians* 3-6, 146-54.
78 Curran, "Educational Reform," 28-29.
79 Culp, "Elite Association," 472.
80 Prasenjit Duara, *Culture, Power, and the State: Rural North China 1900-1942* (New York: Stanford University Press, 1988).
81 In Chauncey's study, local primary schools were sometimes involved in disputes with other local forces over money. See Chauncey, *Schoolhouse Politicians*, 128-37. In Culp's study, the local elites either worked with county administration or lineages to promote modern primary schooling. See Culp, "Elite Association."
82 Since my study ends at 1937, and most of the local programs associated with these teachers' schools were initiated in the mid-1930s, unfortunately, there is not enough evidence to evaluate the development of these programs and the interaction between the teachers' school and the local "cultural nexus."
83 "Jiaoyu fagui" [Educational regulations], *DYCZJNJ* 2: 177.
84 Chen Youduan, "Woguo xianxing xiangcun shifan kecheng de jiantao" [A reexamination of the curriculum of existing village teachers' schools in China], *Zhonghua jiaoyu jie* 24, 2 (1936): 47-54.
85 Jin Zhiwen, "Xiangshi nongye jiaoxue wenti zhi jiantao" [A re-examination of the pedagogy of agricultural courses in village teachers' schools], *Zhonghua jiaoyu jie* 24, 3 (1936): 25-31.
86 Ibid.
87 Jiaoyu bu, "Min yuan yilai quanguo zhongdeng jiaoyu ge lei xuexiao xiaoshu xuesheng ji jingfei shu bijiao biao" [A comparative table of the schools, students, and finances of secondary education since 1912], *DYCZJNJ* 4: 133.
88 Jiangsu Huangdu xiangcun shifan xuexiao, *Yige xinxing de shifan xuexiao*, 48-166.
89 Li Zhenyun, "Shengli Baiquan xiangcun shifan xuexiao gongzuo baogao" [Working report on Baiquan Provincial Village Teachers' School], *Xiangcun jianshe shiyan* 3: 387-92.
90 Henan Province Bureau of Education, *He'nan difang jiaoyu shicha baogao*, 1.
91 Jiaoyu bu, "Hebei sheng jiaoyu shicha baogao."
92 "Xiangjiao yanjiu hui di yi jie nianhui jilu" [The records of the first annual meeting of the Association for Rural Education], *Xiangcun jiaoyu* 26/27 (June 1935): 49.
93 Lin Zhongda, "Xiangcun jiaoyu neng gaizao Zhongguo xiangcun shehui ma?" [Can rural education reform rural Chinese society?], *Zhonghua jiaoyu jie* 23, 9 (1936): 1-8.

94 Jiaoyu bu, "Shifan xuexiao guicheng," 326-47.
95 Li Nai, "Zhongguo nüzi jiaoyu de shibai jiqi bujiu" [The failure of Chinese women's education and its remedy], *Nüzi yuekan* (Women's monthly) 2, 1 (1934): 1758-61.
96 Ibid.
97 Wei Xixun, "Zhongguo nüzi jiaoyu zhi genben gaizao" [Making a fundamental change to women's education in China], *Nüzi yuekan* 2, 1 (1934): 1739-48.
98 Bi Yao, "Lue tang nüzi Zhongguo jiaoyu shi" [A brief review of the history of female education in China], *Funü shenghuo* (Women's life) 3, 7 (1936): 25-29.
99 Li, "Zhongguo nüzi jiaoyu de shibai"; Wei, "Zhongguo nüzi jiaoyu zhi genben gaizao"; Liang Fusheng, "Nüzi jiaoyu zhi xunlian hua" [Women's education moving towards training skills], *Nüzi yuekan* 2, 1 (1934): 1748-50; Li Zhengfu, "Nüzi jiaoyu zhi pingmin hua" [Popularization of female education], *Nüzi yuekan* 2, 1 (1934): 1750-54.
100 Cao Yunjiao, "Zhongguo funü jiaoyu de zhongyao jiqi shishi" [The importance of Chinese women's education and its implementation], *Nüzi yuekan* 2, 1 (1934): 1762-66.
101 Li Zhengfu, "Nüzi jiaoyu zhi pingmin hua," *Nüzi yuekan* 2, 1 (1934): 1750-54.
102 *Nüzi yuekan* vol. 2, no. 1 (1934), vol. 4 (1934), vol. 7 (1934).
103 Wei Ruichi and Ma Zhenfu, "Nongcun funü jiaoyu de lilun yu shiji" [The theory and practice of rural women's education], *Nüzi yuekan* 2, 7 (1934): 2509-16.
104 Shi Sheng, "Zenyang shishi nongcun funü jiaoyu?" [How shall we implement rural women's education?], *Funü shenghuo* 3, 5 (1936): 3-5.
105 Henan Province Bureau of Education, *Henan difang jiaoyu shicha baogao* 1 (1934).
106 Jiaoyu bu, "Hebei sheng jiaoyu shicha baogao," in *Jiaoyu bu shicha yuan shicha ge sheng shi jiaoyu baogao huibian*, Ministry of Education print, 1933.
107 Hayhoe, "Cultural Tradition and Educational Modernization," 62-63.
108 Jiangsu sheng jiaoyu ting bian shen shi, *Jiangsu jiaoyu gailan,* 1 and 2: 150, 316-444. The two other schools were not mentioned.
109 Ibid., 617-939. No indication was given as to whether the other county teachers' schools were coeducational.
110 Shandong Provincial Archives, file nos. J101-12-0296, J101-12-431, and J101-12-0435.
111 Zhuang, "Gansu jiaoyu xianzhuang."
112 Wang Baolian, *Shandong shengli di yi nüzi shifan xuexiao yi lan* [Shandong Provincial Women's Normal School Number One: A brochure], Shandong Provincial Archives, file no. J101-14-30. Wang was the school principal at the time the brochure was printed. All information regarding the school is from this document.
113 Besides 170 graduates who were untraceable, fifty-one had died and 139 had stayed home. The data only provide the status quo of the graduates. Those who stayed home may also have taken jobs until they had families.
114 I assume that the minimum age for party membership was eighteen.
115 Xiu Sheng, "Nü tongxue shou xun lue shu" [A brief report on the training of female students], *Funü shenghuo* 3, 2 (1936): 22-24.
116 Gao Xuehui, "Suzhou chengshi funü de gaikuang" [The general situation of city women in Suzhou], *Nüzi yuekan* 2, 2 (1934): 1995-2010.
117 Gao Yuexin, "Pinghu de funü zhuangkuang" [Women's condition in Pinghu], *Nüzi yuekan* 1, 7 (1934): 2579-83.
118 Yang Jiayu, "Sichuan funü shenghuo gaiguan" [The general situation of women's lives in Sichuan], *Nüzi yuekan* 2, 1 (1934): 1819-26; Zong Shunhua, "Changshu funü de weiji" [Women's crisis in Changshu], *Nüzi yuekan* 2, 1 (1934): 1829-31; Gao, "Suzhou chengshi funü de gaikuang"; Gao, "Pinghu de funü zhuangkuang"; Xin Wu, "Yunnan funü gaiguan" [The general situation of women in Yunnan], *Nüzi yuekan* 1, 10 (1933): 57-60.
119 Wang, *Shandong shengli di yi nüzi shifan.*
120 See Yang Jiayu, "Sichuan funü shenghuo gaiguan," *Nüzi yuekan* 2, 1 (1934): 1819-26; Zong Shunhua, "Changshu funü de weiji," *Nüzi yuekan* 2, 1 (1934): 1829-31; Gao Xuehui, "Suzhou chengshi funü de gaikuang," *Nüzi yuekan* 2, 2 (1934): 1995-2010; Gao Yuexin, "Pinghu de funü zhuangkuang," *Nüzi yuekan* 1, 7 (1934): 2579-83; Xin Wu, "Yunnan funü gaiguan," *Nüzi yuekan* 1, 10 (1933): 57-60.
121 As described in Ba Jin's famous novel, *Family*.

122 Prior to 1949, the term *xiaojie* was used to describe rich girls who lived lives of leisure.

123 Qian, "Nü xuesheng tan pian–zuotanhui jilue" [The record from female student's speeches in a forum], *Funü shenghuo* 1, 4 (1934): 68-79.

124 Lu Yin, *Lu Yin zizhuan* [Autobiography of Lu Yin] (Shanghai: Di yi chubanshe, 1934). Lu Yin was the penname of Huang Ying, a famous female writer of the 1930s.

125 Xu Bing, "Yi ge xiaoxue jiaoshi de husheng" [The voice of a primary schoolteacher], *Funü shenghuo* 3, 4 (1936): 31-33. It is a widespread belief in China that one of the causes of tuberculosis is long-time exposure to dust (e.g., chalk dust). Tuberculosis was still considered a serious occupational disease among schoolteachers after 1949.

126 Wang Jiliang, "Sichuan de funü" [Women in Sichuan], *Nüzi yuekan* 1, 4 (1933): 46-52.

127 Yang, "Sichuan funü shenghuo gaiguan."

128 Qiao Qiao, "Nü jiaoyuan" [The female teacher], *Nüzi yuekan* 2, 12: 3289-95; Jiang Ping "Nü jiaoyuan de beiai" [The sorrow of the female teacher], *Nüzi yuekan* 2 (1934), 2: 2001-2; Zhi Xian, "Nü jiaoshi" [The female teacher], *Jiaoshi zhi you* [Teachers' friend] 1, 10 (1935): 1612-14.

Chapter 6: Transforming the Revolution

1 These figures are drawn from official documents. Conflicts over registration between some private and missionary universities and the government may have led to the underreporting of enrolment totals.

2 *DECZJNJ* 1400: 1429; *DYCZJNJ* 4: 133. By 1931, China had only one teacher's university. The large-scale rebuilding of teachers' schools at the tertiary level occurred after 1949 under the Communist regime.

3 Jeffrey Wasserstrom, *Student Protests in Twentieth-Century China*: *The View from Shanghai* (Stanford: Stanford University, 1991), 1-5.

4 Shanghai qingyun shi yanjiu hui and Gongqingtuan Shanghai shiwei qingyun shi yanjiu shi, eds., *Shanghai xuesheng yundong shi* [A history of student movements in Shanghai] (Shanghai: Xuelin chubanshe, 1995); Zhang Jihe, ed., *Dan xin bi xue–jiu Zhongguo lici xue chao shilu* [Crimson hearts and cherry blood: Historical records of student movements in old China] (Shijiazhuang: Hebei daxue chubanshe, 1996); Sun Sibai, ed., *Beijing daxue yi er jiu yundong huiyi lu* [The students of Beijing University collectively recall the December Ninth Movement] (Beijing: Beijing daxue chubanshe, 1988); Qinghua daxue, ed., *Zhandou zai yi er jiu yundong de qianlie* [Fighting on the front lines of the December Ninth Movement] (Beijing: Qinghua daxue chubanshe, 1985).

5 John Israel, *Student Nationalism in China, 1927-1937* (Stanford: Stanford University Press, 1966), 85-86.

6 This criticism also applies to Wasserstrom's *Student Protests in Twentieth-Century China.*

7 In his study of Jinan, Shandong, David Buck notes that students from secondary schools were very active in the 1930s student movements. See Buck, "Educational Modernization in Tsinan, 1899-1937," in *The Chinese between Two Worlds,* ed. Mark Elvin and G. William Skinner, 200 (Stanford: Stanford University Press, 1974). Unfortunately, his comment has been ignored for decades.

8 *DECZJNJ*: 1400; *DYCZJNJ* 4: 132.

9 As John Israel observes, in 1931 the number of college students was 44,167, accounting for 0.01 percent of the population. Most came from urban elite families; only 20 percent came from rural families. See Israel, *Student Nationalism in China,* 5-7. Taking into account the high tuition costs of the day and the expenses involved in living far from home in a big city, it is safe to assume that every college student from a rural area was the son or daughter of a rich peasant or landlord.

10 Wasserstrom, *Student Protests in Twentieth-Century China,* 5-6.

11 Yu Xueren, *Zhongguo xiandai xuesheng yundong shi changbian* [A detailed history of modern student movements in China] (Changchun: Dongbei daxue chubanshe, 1988), 522-50.

12 Chalmers Johnson, *Peasant Nationalism and Communist Power* (Stanford: Stanford University Press, 1962).

13 In a recent retrospective article on this debate, Suzanne Pepper points out that the intellectual debate brought about by Johnson's book was fuelled by the Cold War question: "Who

lost China?" In Pepper's opinion, Johnson's "peasant nationalism" did not provide a convincing explanation for the reemergence of the Chinese Communist Party in the 1930s, much less for its final victory in 1949. She thinks that the studies that followed, which took into account a variety of factors (such as rural society, military activities, and how peasants responded to different approaches), have advanced our knowledge of the topic. Pepper emphasizes the long labours necessary to provide a clear understanding of the Communist revival. See Suzanne Pepper, "The Political Odyssey of an Intellectual Construct: Peasant Nationalism and the Study of China's Revolutionary History – A Review Essay," *Journal of Asian Studies* 63, 1 (2004): 105-25.

14 Mark Selden, *The Yenan Way in Revolutionary China* (Cambridge: Harvard University Press, 1971). Joseph Esherick's study of the local cadres in Gulin County shows that over 50 percent of local cadres joined the Revolution between 1934 and 1936, the period when the Communists were pitching their radical policies in that area. See Joseph Esherick, "Deconstructing the Construction of the Party-State: Gulin County in the Shaan-Gan-Ning Border Region," *China Quarterly* 140 (1994): 1052-79. This study supports Selden's thesis.

15 Chen Yung-fa, *Making Revolution: The Communist Movement in Eastern and Central China, 1937-1945* (Berkeley: University of California Press, 1986), 3-16.

16 Ibid., 2-3.

17 Although, in the 1930s, urban students did participate in activities referred to as "going to the people," they were not successful. A former student activist recalled that villagers could not understand what students said and were, in any case, quite indifferent to their appeals. See Sun, *Beijing daxue yi er jiu yundong*, 28-31.

18 In separate studies, Pauline Keating and Joseph Esherick show that, in order to win the support of the peasantry, Communist policies had to be adapted to local conditions. This meant relying on local cadres to make policy decisions. See Pauline Keating, "The Yan'an Way of Co-operation," *China Quarterly* 140 (1994): 1025-51; Esherick, "Deconstructing the Construction of the Party-State," 1052-79.

19 In his study of the Taihang base area, Ralph Thaxton spoke of the importance of connections between local revolutionary leaders and outside resources in achieving the Communist Party's revolutionary goals. According to Thaxton, most local leaders were migrant workers and labourers in urban sweatshops. He also notes that students of normal schools from the villages were one source for local leaders. See Ralph Thaxton, *China Turned Rightside Up: Revolutionary Legitimacy in the Peasant World* (New Haven: Yale University Press, 1983), 93-95. Unfortunately, he did not go further to explore the process of becoming a local leader. Several accounts of Communist organizing in villages have also documented the important role of village teachers. See, for instance, Edward Friedman, Paul G. Pickowicz, and Mark Selden, eds., *Chinese Village, Socialist State* (New Haven: Yale University Press, 1991); Odoric Wou, *Mobilizing the Masses: Building Revolution in Henan* (Stanford: Stanford University Press, 1994). In contrast, Steven Levine, in his study of Manchuria, suggests that the "urban nucleus" of Communists sojourning in the countryside "had learned to speak the language of the peasants" (13, 243). See Steven Levine, *Anvil of Victory: The Communist Revolution in Manchuria, 1945-1948* (New York: Columbia University Press, 1987). However, Esherick's work on Gulin County does not support this point of view (Esherick, "Deconstructing the Construction of the Party-State," 1052-79). My research does not support it either.

20 Tong Runzhi, "Tichang xiangcun zhongdeng jiaoyu de ba da liyou" [The eight main reasons for advocating rural secondary education], *Zhonghua jiaoyu jie* 24, 2 (1936): 1-10.

21 Ibid.

22 Zhang Wenchang, "Qingnian wenti yanjiu–Hang shi 577 gaozhong xuesheng diaocha tongji jieguo" [A study of youth problems: A survey of 577 students from Hangzhou's upper middle schools], *Jiaoyu zazhi* 26, 1 (1936): 94.

23 According to the "amended regulations for middle schools" (*xiuzheng zhongxue xuexiao guicheng*) issued by the Ministry of Education in 1935, the tuition fees for middle schools varied from seven to ten yuan per semester for lower middle school students to ten to sixteen yuan for upper middle school students. Tuition fees for private middle schools

might be twice as high, on top of the cost of board. See Jiaoyu bu, "Amended Regulations for Middle Schools" [*Xiuzheng zhongxue xuexiao guicheng*] *Jiaoyu zazhi* 25, 8 (1935): 128-34.

24 In the 1930s, virtually no rural teacher could afford to send his children to an urban school. Data show that, in 1933, the average salary of a primary schoolteacher was between two and fifteen yuan per month. See Chapter 5 for the living conditions of primary schoolteachers.

25 Liu Zhenjia, "Wan Li: Qing er shi zhi qizhi, xian geming zhi da bo" [Wan Li: Bearing the flag of the second provincial teachers' school, advocating a great wave of revolution], in *Shifan qun ying, guang yao Zhonghua* [Heroic graduates of teachers' schools shine over China] 7A (Xi'an: Shaanxi remin jiaoyu chubanshe), 1-12.

26 Pei Zhi, "Ben xiao er shi er niandu ruxue shiyan de yanjiu" [A study of entrance examinations to this school in 1933], *Xiancun gaizao* [Rural reform] 2, 13/14 (1933): 3-10.

27 Ibid.

28 "Xuesheng jiating zhiye tongji tu" [Chart of students' families' occupations], in *Hebei shengli Daming shifan yi lan* [General information on Hebei's Daming Provincial Teachers' School], Hebei Provincial Archives, file no. 645-1-36.

29 Jiangsu sheng jiaoyuting bianshen shi [Jiangsu Provincial Bureau of Education, Records Office] (compil.), *Jiangsu jiaoyu gailan* [Almanac of education in Jiangsu, 1932] (Taibei: Zhuanji wenxue chubanshe, reprint, 1971), 368-422.

30 Israel, *Student Nationalism in China*, 87-88.

31 Lloyd Eastman, *Abortive Revolution: China under Nationalist Rule, 1927-1937* (Cambridge: Harvard University Press, 1990), 188-90. On natural disasters during the Republican period, see Xia Mingfang, *Minguo shiqi de ziran zaihai yu xiangcun shehui* [Natural disasters and rural society in Republican China] (Beijing: Zhonghua shuju, 2000).

32 Israel, *Student Nationalism in China*, 87-88.

33 Eastman, *Abortive Revolution*, 195-212.

34 Zhang Yimin, "Xiandai hua bianqian zhong de tudi gaige" [Land reform in the course of modernization], in *Zhongguo xiandai hua shi* [A history of modernization in China] 1, ed. Xu Jilin and Chen Dakai, 452-77 (Shanghai: Sanlian shuju, 1995).

35 Yang Qiliang, "Xiang wo de muxiao Baoding ershi huibao" [A report to my alma mater, Baoding Teachers' School Number Two], *SQGZ* 8: 124-37. Yang later joined the Chinese Communist Party and, after 1949, served as a diplomat for the People's Republic of China. Thøgersen's study of Zouping also reports that peasants had no motive to send their children to costly secondary schools unless this education could offer upward social mobility. Thøgersen, *A County of Culture: Twentieth-Century China Seen from the Village Schools of Zouping, Shandong* (Ann Arbor: University of Michigan Press, 2002), 63-64. In another study of the same region, Thøgersen discovered that teachers' schools were attractive to local people both because teaching was a respected occupation and because the free-tuition policy was very helpful to them. See Stig Thøgersen, "Learning in Lijiazhuang: Education Skills and Careers in Twentieth-Century Rural China," in *Education, Culture, and Identity in Twentieth-Century China*, ed. Glen Peterson, Ruth Hayhoe, and Lu Yonling, 241-46 (Ann Arbor: University of Michigan Press, 2001).

36 Jiangsu sheng jiaoyuting bianshen shi, *Jiangsu jiaoyu gailan*, 398.

37 Pei, "Ben xiao er shi er niandu ruxue shiyan de yanjiu."

38 Ibid.

39 *SQGZ* 7b: 68.

40 Wang Ruowang, *Wang Ruowang zizhuan* [Autobiography of Wang Ruowang] (Hong Kong: Mingbao chubanshe, 1991), 53.

41 Jiangsu sheng jiaoyuting bianshen shi, *Jiangsu jiaoyu gailan*, 441.

42 *SQGZ* 8: 85.

43 Jiangsu sheng jiaoyuting bianshen shi, *Jiangsu jiaoyu gailan*, 332, 398, 419.

44 Li Ruian, "Cong 1931 nian gai wei xiangshi hou wu nian lai biyesheng tongji" [Statistics on the graduates for the five years since the school became a village teachers' school in 1931], *Xiangcun gaizao* 5, 11/12 (1936): 32.

45 "Biye xuesheng fuwu zhuangkuang tongji tu, 1934" [Chart of the positions taken by graduates, 1934], in *Hebei shengli Daming shifan yi lan*.

46 Jiangsu sheng jiaoyuting bianshen shi, *Jiangsu jiaoyu gailan*, 332. For complaints of unemployment from the graduates of regular middle schools, see Chapter 4.

47 Pei, "Ben xiao er shi er niandu ruxue shiyan de yanjiu." There is a discrepancy in Pei Zhi's figures: 804 is the total number of candidates if one adds up the individual figures listed by county of origin, whereas the total given elsewhere is 794.

48 Jiangsu sheng jiaoyuting bianshen shi, *Jiangsu jiaoyu gailan*, 398, 419. Because Jieshou Village Teachers' School was a lower-level school, the 10 percent of graduates who continued their education might have done so by going to the upper level of a provincial teachers' school. Jiangsu's Taicang Teachers' School stated that about 10 percent of its graduates went on to the next level of education (345).

49 "Jiaoyu jie xiaoxi: Jiaobu zuijin zhi liang tongling" [Educational news: Two recent directives from the Ministry of Education], *JYZZ* 23, 9 (1931): 137. Other provinces also imposed this rule. For instance, in his unpublished memoir, Cong Yiping, my father, who in 1935 graduated from the teaching program of a high school in Anqing, then capital of Anhui Province, recalled that he was allowed to enrol at Shandong University after fulfilling his one-year teaching duty.

50 *SQGZ* 7a, 264: 353.

51 "Henan xiaoxue jiaoyuan bake chao" [The wave of strikes by primary schoolteachers in He'nan], *JYZZ* 22, 2 (1930): 130; "Nan bei jiaoshi suo xin yundong zhi fen qi" [The rise of a movement of teachers in the south and the north demanding payment of back salaries], *JYZZ* 22, 10 (1930): 125-26; "Xiaoxue jiaoyuan zhi suo xin yundong" [A movement among primary schoolteachers demanding payment of back salaries], *JYZZ* 23, 3 (1931): 129.

52 According to the preface to the collection, the compilation was conducted by a group of college professors, middle schoolteachers, archivists, and staff members of local historical offices as part of a local history project. Most of the biographies were based on interviews with the subjects and their contemporaries. All information was checked against local historical documents, archival materials, and school records. To assist with the writing of autobiographies, the compilers provided authors with documents to compare with their recollections.

53 The information about these former students of teachers' schools that I have judged most reliable is that regarding their family backgrounds, education, the times and places of their political activities, the social organizations they joined, facts surrounding their Communist Party membership, and the positions they took in the party. The credibility of such information is relatively high because, from the 1940s to the 1980s, Communist cadres had to return to these details again and again as they presented their life stories in party meetings. Throughout that period, the Communist Party checked every story carefully. Telling these stories repeatedly served different purposes. For example, the 1940s rectification in Yan'an and the designation of official ranks in the 1950s both depended on such narratives. Probably the most thorough investigation of party members' stories that ever took place was that carried out by the Red Guards during the Cultural Revolution. During this period, any slight deviation from the outcome of the Red Guards' investigation could have been fatal. In the 1980s, these aging party members had to tell their stories once again, providing witnesses for each stage of their revolutionary experience, in order to receive retirement benefits. Their pensions and medical insurance were raised or lowered based on the length of their commitment to the Revolution and the positions they had held in the party. In my opinion, the less reliable sections of the biographies are those devoted to revolutionary achievements, social critiques, historical perspective, second-hand reports of the praise they received from local people, and so on.

54 *SQGZ* 7a, 7b, 8. The collection is roughly divided by province; Volume 7 is devoted to students, teachers, and schools in Shandong Province, and volume 8 is devoted to those in Hebei.

55 Light may be shed on this question when the personnel files of the Chinese Communist Party are opened to the public.

56 A Chinese movie in the 1960s, "Early Spring" [*Zao chun er yue*], captures the conservative and insulated atmosphere of the inland towns during the 1930s.

57 Ye Wenxin, "Baoshou yu jijin–shi lun wusi yundong zai Hangzhou" [Conservative and radical: The May Fourth Movement in Hangzhou], in *Zhongguo xiandai hua wenti–yi ge duo fangwei de lishi tansuo* [China's quest for modernization: A historical perspective], ed. Wang Xi and Frederic Wakeman, Jr., 200-15 (Shanghai: Fudan daxue chubanshe, 1994). See also Wen-hsin Yeh, *Provincial Passages: Culture, Space, and the Origins of Chinese Communism* (Berkeley: University of California Press, 1996).

58 Lü Fangshang, *Cong xuesheng yundong dao yundong xuesheng: Minguo ba nian zhi shiba nian* [From student movement to mobilizing students, 1919-29] (Taibei: Institute of Modern History, Academic Sinica, 1994), 75-89.

59 In forty-three cases, information was provided about the economic conditions of the families of biographical subjects (see Table 6A.1). Of these, twenty-four might be grouped as middle class and eight as poor. Seven biographies used terms associated with wealth: three of these were said to come from "impoverished gentry" and one from an "impoverished rich peasant" family. These biographies were compiled in the early 1990s, when family background was no longer attached to political advantages or disadvantages, as it had been in the first decades after the 1949 revolution. It was no longer necessary for people to try to cover up or exaggerate their family backgrounds, though they may have continued to do so out of habit.

60 Wang Chaoxi, "Gao Junyue: Wei le dadi de mingtian" [Gao Junyue: For the sake of this land's future], *SQGZ* 7b: 44-58. (This biography is based on Gao's own memoirs.) Similar stories were told by a long list of revolutionaries in Shandong Province: Wan Li, Liu Guozhu, Xie Xinhe, Qin Hezhen, Wang Kedong, Song Qiutan, Shen Yufu, Li Mancun, Zhao Zhenqing, Guo Zhuping, Ding Yuan, Wu Fengxiang, Cao Yuguang, and so on. See *SQGZ* 7b: 67, 83, 98, 124, 146, 161, 183, 190, 200, 213, 235, 249.

61 Tie Ying, "Baoding ershi qiuxue jishi" [Recollections of Baoding Provincial Teachers' School Number Two], *SQGZ* 8: 89-101. Tie Ying was the chief secretary of the Chinese Communist Party's Zhejiang Provincial Committee and a member of the party's Central Committee in the 1970s and 1980s.

62 *SQGZ* 7b: 67, 83, 98, 124, 146, 161, 183, 190, 200, 213, 235, 249.

63 Yang, "Xiang wo de muxiao baogao."

64 Li Maoru, "Qin Hezhen: Ziyang xiangshi zou chu de geming jia" [Qin Hezhen: A revolutionary from the Ziyang Village Teachers' School], *SQGZ* 7b: 98-108. (This biography was based on an interview with Qin.)

65 *SQGZ* 7b: 98-100.

66 Tie Ying, in *SQGZ* 8: 89-101.

67 Ibid., 97; 7a: 381.

68 Philip Huang, "The Jiangxi Period: An Introduction," in *Chinese Communists and Rural Society, 1927-1934*, ed. Philip Huang, Lynda Bell, and Kathy Walker (Berkeley: University of California Press, 1978), 1.

69 *Education Review* [*Jiaoyu zazhi*] reported many arrests of suspected Communist teachers. "Jiaoyu jie dang yu zhi manyan" [The spreading terror: Communists in educational circles arrested], *JYZZ* 22, 11 (1930): 126-27; "Xuexiao dang yu zhi manyan" [The spreading terror: Communists in schools arrested], *JYZZ* 22, 11, 12 (1930): 126-27; "Jiaoyu jie dang yu zhi yu bo" [A last wave: Communists in educational circles arrested], *JYZZ* 23, 2, 3 (1931): 117, 128-29.

70 Jia Xuchun, "Wang Zhe zai Laiyang xiang shi de geming huodong" [Wang Zhe's revolutionary activities in Laiyang Village Teachers' School], *SQGZ* 7a: 99-115.

71 Wang Chaoxi, "Li Zhuru: Juanjuan bixue xie chunqiu" [Li Zhuru: Making history by sacrificing his life], *SQGZ* 7a: 170-82.

72 *SQGZ* 7a: 270.

73 *SQGZ* 7a: 142-53.

74 *SQGZ* 8: 15.

75 *SQGZ* 8: 99-100.

76 Ibid.

77 *SQGZ* 7a: 13-19, 20-29, 43-50, 25, 51-59; 8, 10-20, 21-26, 193-94, 205.

78 Ibid.
79 Jia, "Wang Zhe zai Laiyang," 99-115.
80 *SQGZ* 7a: 170-82, 270, 142-53; *SQGZ* 8: 15, 99-100.
81 *SQGZ* 7a: 107.
82 Wang, *Wang Ruowang zizhuan*, 60-61. Wang studied at Qixiashan Village Teachers' School for a year (1932-33), only to be expelled for his radical activities. During this period, he read a range of Marxist and socialist works. After leaving school, he participated in the workers' movement in Shanghai and joined the Chinese Communist Party in 1937. In time he came to be involved in literary activities and worked as the chief editor of a national literary journal after 1949. In 1957, he was accused of being a rightist and was removed from his editorial position. In the 1980s, his criticism of the Chinese Communist Party earned him the label "bourgeois liberal." After 1989, he emigrated to the United States and started working with the overseas community to promote democratic reforms in China. It seems reasonable to assume that his testimony would not exaggerate the influence of revolutionary thinking in the teachers' schools.
83 The local government provided Hebei Teachers' School Number Seven with several lengthy lists of banned publications: "Prohibited Reactionary Propaganda, 1930" [Yanjin fandong xuanchuan, 1930], "Prohibited Reactionary Publications, 1932" [Yanjin fandong kanwu, 1932], "Prohibiting Reactionary Propaganda" [Chajin fandong xuanchuan, 1933]. Although most banned publications were Communist, included in these lists were books and magazines published by moderate organizations. See Hebei Provincial Archives, files no. 645-1-7, 645-1-1, 645-1-2.
84 "Baoding shi jingchaju chachao shifan xuexiao youjian suo faxian de dixia kanwu" [Underground publications found by the Baoding City Police Department by intercepting mail to several teachers' schools, 1930-31], Hebei Provincial Archives, files no. 645-1-1, 645-1-7, 645-1-2.
85 Israel, *Student Nationalism in China*, 7.
86 *SQGZ* 7a: 315,
87 *SQGZ* 7a: 330.
88 *SQGZ* 8: 29.
89 *SQGZ* 7a: 59-66, 83-90, 269-84, 347-59.
90 *SQGZ* 7a: 67-73, 296-308, 328-46.
91 John Israel divided student protests into two types, "student tides" (*xuechao*) and "student movements" (*xueyun*). The former were "local school disorders provoked by dissatisfaction with educational conditions and personalities," while the latter were "nationwide reactions to major domestic and foreign problems." See Israel, *Student Nationalism in China*, 89. However, such definitions are of limited utility when discussing the nature of student activities: some protests were nationwide but non-political, while others were local and political.
92 *Heroic Graduates*, Volume 7, does not present an exhaustive list of the student activists in the teachers' schools of 1930s Shandong. Some activists, for example, are only mentioned in others' biographies. A few examples are Zhao Jianmin (served as governor of Shandong), Jing Xiaocun (served as minister of Machinery Industry Number Seven), Yu Yiquan (served as first secretary of the Chinese Communist Party Disciplinary Committee), Pan Fusheng (served as party secretary of the Henan and Heilongjiang Party Committees), Gao Qiyun (served as party secretary of the Shandong Party Committee), and Wang Yiping (served as party secretary of the Shanghai Municipal Party Committee). Besides the students recorded in *Heroic Graduates*, Volume 7 (Shandong Province), about seventy names of student activists were mentioned, but these biographies did not give details of their activities and whereabouts.
93 When the ratio of passing the entrance examination for teachers' schools was between 2 percent and 15 percent, many rural literate youths lost their chance for secondary education. Their educations would have enabled them to read Communist primers and to understand nationalist ideas, and they were certainly capable of communicating with local teachers in villages. Many of them might be friends, relatives, former classmates, or neighbours of

those local teachers. Although no research has been conducted on this group of people, they could have played a part in the mass movement.

94 *SQGZ* 7a: 148.

95 Pingyuan Village Teachers' School Number Five enrolled a total of 400 students over the course of its existence. One-fourth of them joined the Communist Revolution during this period. See *SQGZ* 7a: 148-49.

96 *SQGZ* 7a: 380-91. Wang died in a battle several years later.

97 The study on the first Communist general, by Arif Dirlik, provides a very complex, multifacted picture. However, this group of Communists had a much clearer understanding of Marxism and Communism as theories and ideologies. Moreover, their activities were more closely connected and were accompanied by a cultural movement that included a lot of studies and discussions, as Dirlik shows. See Arif Dirlik, *The Origins of Chinese Communism* (New York: Oxford University Press, 1989). It was no coincidence that Mao Zedong became the leader of the Chinese Communist revolution in the 1930s. Mao's personal background, education, and experience more closely resembles that of the second generation of Communists than that of the first.

98 Many records from this period are held in the Chinese Communist Party Historical Archives, and while a few have been published, the records are not open to non-party members. This section is based on published documents and secondary materials.

99 Huangfu Shuyu, Song Jian'ge, and Gong Shoujing, *Zhongguo geming genjudi jiaoyu jishi: 1927.8-1949.9* [Educational events in Chinese revolutionary base areas, August 1927-September 1949] (Beijing: Jiaoyu kexue chubanshe, 1989), 50. Gao Qi, *Zhongguo jiaoyu shi yanjiu (xiandai fen juan)* [A study of the history of Chinese education: The Modern period] (Shanghai: Huadong shifan daxue chubanshe, 1994), 176.

100 Huangfu, Song, and Gong, *Zhongguo geming genjudi jiaoyu*, 26-83.

101 Ibid., 33.

102 The Chinese soviet government named all Western-style primary schools "Lenin primary schools" (Liening xiaoxue) as a memorial to Lenin.

103 Huangfu, Song, and Gong, *Zhongguo geming genjudi jiaoyu*, 50.

104 Ibid., 25.

105 Ibid., 66.

106 Ibid., 44.

107 Ibid., 67.

108 Ibid., 28, 50-51, 76.

109 Ibid., 33, 62.

110 Ibid., 44.

111 Huangfu, Song, and Gong, *Zhongguo geming genjudi jiaoyu*, 49. The term "gentry bully" (*lieshen*) was not defined. It is likely that it referred to abusive landlords.

112 Zhu Jiading and Chen Guanglian, "Hongse tudi shang de baochun xinya–zhongyang suqu Liening shifan" [Buds predicting spring in the red earth: Central soviet Lenin teachers' schools], *SQGZ* 5: 219-31.

113 Huangfu, Song, and Gong, *Zhongguo geming genjudi jiaoyu*, 66. However, the actual study period was only four months. See Zhu and Chen, "Hongse tudi shang de baochun xinya," 221-22.

114 Zhu and Chen, "Hongse tudi shang de baochun xinya," 221-22.

115 Set up as experimental administrative regions by the Communists, the soviets governed remote parts of several provinces.

116 Zhu and Chen, "Hongse tudi shang de baochun xinya," 221-22; Huangfu, Song, and Gong, *Zhongguo geming genjudi jiaoyu*, 93.

117 Zhu and Chen, "Hongse tudi shang de baochun xinya," 221-22.

118 Huangfu, Song, and Gong, *Zhongguo geming genjudi jiaoyu*, 66, 93.

119 Central Lenin Teachers' School was located in Yangxi Township, outside of the Ruijin County seat. Lenin Teachers' School Number Two was located in Fenghuazhuang Village in Xingguo County. Zhu and Chen, "Hongse tudi shang de baochun xinya," 221, 223.

120 *ZJSJZ*: 819-26.

121 Ibid., 823-26.
122 Ibid.

Conclusion

1 Liu Wenxiu, *Zhongguo shifan jiaoyu jianshi* [A brief history of Chinese teachers' education] (Beijing: Renmin jiaoyu chubanshe, 1985), 143-53.

2 Yunnan sheng zhengxie wenshi ziliao yanjiu weiyuanhui [Historical and cultural documents research committee of the Yunnan Provincial Political Consultative Conference], Xi'nan lianghe daxue Beijing Kunming xiaoyouhui [The alumni associations in Beijing and Yunnan of the Southwest United University], and Yunnan shifan daxue [Yunnan teachers' university] (compilation), *Yunnan wenshi ziliao xuanji* [Selection on Yunnan historical and cultural documents 34]: *Xi'nan lianhe daxue jianxiao wushi zhounian jinan zhuanji* [A special collection in commemoration of the fiftieth anniversary of the establishment of the Southwest United University] (Kunming: Yunnan Remin chubanshe, 1988); Xi'nan lianda chuxi fukan, ed. [Editorial group for the supplementary edition of the Southwest United University Journal, ed.], *Lianda ba nian* [Eight years in the Southwest United University] (Kunming: Xi'nan lianda xuesheng chubanshe, 1946).

3 Jiaoyu bu, "Ge shengshi shifan xuexiao fudao difang jiaoyu banfa, 1939" [The method for directing local education in teachers' schools in each province and city, 1939], and "Shifan xuexiao fudao difang jiaoyu banfa, 1943" [The method for directing local education in teachers' schools, 1943], the Second Historical Archives: file no. 10844-5.

4 Liu Xianzeng and Liu Duanfen, chief eds., *Shan-Gan-Ning bianqu jiaoyu shi* [History of education in the Shaanxi-Gansu-Ningxia Board Region] (Xi'an: Shaanxi remin chubanshe, 1994).

5 "Grand administrative district" refers to a type of special administrative institution that existed from the 1950s to the late 1960s. It normally included several provinces, with divisions based on geographical regions. Rather than having a concrete administrative duty, these "districts" played a mediating and coordinating role between provincial and central governments.

6 Zhongyang jiaoyu kexue yanjiu suo [Central research institute of educational science], (compilation), *Zhonghua renmin gongheguo jiaoyu dashiji, 1949-1982* [Chronology of education in the People's Republic of China, 1949-1982] (Beijing: Jiaoyu kexue chubanshe, 1983); and Zhongguo jiaoyu nianjian bianjibu [Editorial department for the Chinese education yearbook], *Zhongguo jiaoyu nianjian, 1949-1981* [Chinese education yearbook, 1949-1981] (Beijing: Zhongguo dabaikequanshu chubanshe, 1984).

7 Zheng Chao, "Jiaoyu bu yunniang quxiao shifan sheng, jiaoshi zige jiang dingqi renzheng" [The Ministry of Education is brewing a plan to abolish teachers' schools while periodically examining teachers for certificates]. See http://www.wforum.com/newspool/articles/culedu/55668.html.

8 Yang Kaimin and Yang Xuepeng, "Xiri men qian lengluo, jinri zheng ru jiaotan: Jiangsu zhongduo kaosheng shouxuan shifan" [Teaching was formerly an unpopular major, and now everyone fights to get in: Many who took the college entrance examination in Jiangsu selected teachers' colleges as their first choice], *Guangming ribao* [Guangming daily], 29 August 1996; Li Xin, "Shifan yuanxiao xi shou shengyuan" [Teachers' colleges pleased to have more applicants], *Beijing qingnian bao* [Beijing youth daily], 11 September 1996; Liu Guanquan, "Shandong shifan yuanxiao re qilai le" [Teachers' colleges in Shandong have become hot], *Renmin ribao* [People's daily], 13 August 1996.

9 Zheng Chao, "Jiaoyu bu yunniang quxiao shifan sheng, jiaoshi zige jiang dingqi renzheng" See http://www.wforum.com/newspool/articles/culedu/55668.html. See also Guan Peijun, "Guanyu jiaoshi jiaoyu gaige fazhan de shi ge guandian" [Ten points of view on the reform and development of teachers' education], *Xinhua wen zhai* [Digests of Chinese journals] 9 (2004): 102-5.

Glossary of Chinese Names and Terms

People

Ai Siqi 艾思奇
Ba Jin 巴金
Bi Yao 碧遙
Bo Yibo 薄一波
Cai Rukai 蔡儒楷
Cai Yuanpei 蔡元培
Cao Dianqi 曹典琦
Cao Jinghua 曹靖華
Cao Yuguang 曹宇光
Cao Yu 曹禺
Cao Zhenqiu 操震球
Cen Chunxuan 岑春[火宣]
Chang Naide 常乃德
Chao Zhefu 晁哲甫
Chen Duxiu 陳獨秀
Chen Hongmou 陳宏謀
Cheng Benhai 程本海
Cheng Hao 程灝
Cheng Yi 程頤
Cong Yiping 叢一平
Deng Chunlan 鄧春蘭
Ding Fengzhu 丁鳳珠
Ding Ling 丁玲
Ding Yuan 丁原
Du Zhongyuan 杜重遠
Duan-fang 端方
Fan Mingshu 范明樞
Fan Zizhan 範子瞻
Feng Guifen 馮桂芬
Feng Pinyi 馮品毅
Feng Yuxiang 馮玉祥
Fu Dingsheng 傅鼎勝
Fu Zengxiang 傅增湘
Gao Guiqiao 高桂喬
Gao Junyue 高峻岳
Gao Qiyun 高奇云
Gao Rui 高銳
Gu Mu 谷牧
Guan Peijun 管培俊
Guo Bingwen 郭秉文
Guo Moruo 郭沫若
Guo Zhuping 郭祝平
Han Fuqu 韓复渠
Han Yu 韓愈
Hou Hongjian 侯鴻鑒
Hu Shi 胡適
Huang Yanpei 黄炎培
Huang Ying 黄英
Jia Dunfang 賈敦芳
Jiang Guangzi 蔣光慈
Jiang Lindong 姜林東
Jiang Menglin 蔣夢麟
Jiang Weiqiao 蔣維喬
Jin Haiguan 金海觀
Jin Zhiwen 金志文
Jing Hengyi 經亨頤

Jing Xiaocun 景曉村
Ju Simin 鞠思敏
Kang Youwei 康有為
Kawakami Hajime 河上肇
Leizu 嫘祖
Li Chucai 李楚才
Li Da 李達
Li Dazhao 李大釗
Li Duanfen 李端棻
Li Fei 李飛
Li Gan 李淦
Li Gongpu 李公朴
Li Jinghe 李荊和
Li Liewen 黎烈文
Li Mancun 李曼村
Li Nai 李耐
Li Renfeng 李人鳳
Li Xichen 李曦晨
Li Yujie 李豫杰
Li Zhenyun 李振雲
Li Zhuru 李竹如
Liang Qichao 梁啟超
Liang Shuming 梁漱溟
Lin Yueqiao 林月樵
Lin Zhongda 林仲達
Liu Dapeng 劉大鵬
Liu Guozhu 劉國柱
Liu Qiren 劉其人
Liu Sheng 劉[王盛]
Liu Xun 劉撏
Liu Zhen 劉震
Lu Guixing 陸桂星
Lu Jiuyuan 陸九淵
Lu Xun 魯迅
Lu Yin 盧隱
Lü Yiting 呂乙亭
Luo Yi 羅毅
Ma Chengzhai 馬誠齋
Ma Shi'an 馬石安
Ma Xiaoteng 馬霄騰
Ma Xulun 馬敘倫
Mao Dun 茅盾
Mao Zedong 毛澤東
Meng Guofang 孟國芳
Meng Xianti 孟憲禔
Mu Xiang 慕湘
Pan Fusheng 潘复生
Pan Zinian 潘梓年
Qian Changzhao 錢昌照
Qian Xuantong 錢玄同
Qian Yizhang 錢義璋
Qin Hezhen 秦和珍
Qu Qiubai 瞿秋白
Rong-qing 榮慶
Rou Shi 柔石
Shen Enfu 沈恩孚
Shen Yunpu 申雲甫
Sheng Beiguang 盛北光
Sheng Xuanhuai 盛宣懷
Shi Yichen 石一宸
Song Qiutan 宋秋潭
Sun Dongge 孫東閣
Sun Fuxi 孫福熙
Sun Qifeng 孫奇峰
Sun Zhongwen 孫衷文
Tan Gao Junyue 高峻岳
Tang Jue 唐玨
Tang Qunying 唐群英
Tao Xingzhi 陶行知
Tie Ying 鐵瑛
Tong Runzhi 童潤之
Wan Li 萬里
Wang Baolian 王葆廉
Wang Jinmei 王盡美
Wang Kedong 王克東
Wang Kekou 王克寇
Wang Ming 王明
Wang Ruojie 王若杰
Wang Ruowang 王若望
Wang Xianqian 王先謙
Wang Yangming 王陽明
Wang Yiping 王一平
Wang Zhe 王哲
Wang Zhouyao 王舟瑤
Wang Zhizhi 王志之
Wang Zhuchen 王祝晨
Wei Xixun 魏錫勛
Wu Chucai 吳楚材
Wu Diaohou 吳調侯
Wu Fengxiang 吳風翔
Xiang Kun 項[方方土]
Xiao Hong 蕭紅
Xiao Jun 蕭軍
Xie Taichen 謝台臣

Xie Xinhe 謝鑫鶴
Xingzhi 行知
Xu Luo 徐珞
Xu Shoushang 許壽裳
Xue Fucheng 薛福成
Ya Te 亞特
Yan Wu 閻吾
Yan Xishan 閻錫山
Yan Xiu 嚴修
Yan Yangchu 晏陽初
Yan Yuan 顏元
Yang Qiliang 楊琪良
Yang Side 楊斯德
Yang Xiaochun 楊效春
Yang Xiong 楊雄
Yang Yinyu 楊蔭榆
Yu Jiaju 余家菊
Yu Yiquan 于毅全
Yu Yunting 于雲亭
Yuan Shikai 袁世凱
Yun Daiying 惲代英
Yun Liu 雲六
Zhan Lu 瞻盧
Zhang Ailing 張愛玲
Zhang Baixi 張百熙
Zhang Beihua 張北華
Zhang Boda 張伯達
Zhang Jianren 張肩任
Zhang Luxiang 張履祥
Zhang Shizhao 章士釗
Zhang Wentian 張聞天
Zhang Xiaoteng 張霄騰
Zhang Xueliang 張學良
Zhang Zengyang 張增[易文],
Zhang Zhidong 張之洞
Zhang Zongxiang 張宗祥
Zhao Jianmin 趙健民
Zhao Ruiwu 趙瑞五
Zhao Zhao 趙昭
Zhao Zhenqing 趙振清
Zheng Guanying 鄭觀應
Zheng Zhenduo 鄭振鐸
Zhixing 知行
Zhou Enlai 周恩來
Zhou Kai 周凱
Zhou Leting 周樂亭
Zhou Shuren 周樹人
Zhou Yang 周揚
Zhou Zuoren 周作人
Zhu Xi 朱熹
Zou Taofeng 鄒韜奮

Places

Baiquan 百泉
Baoding 保定
Beijiang 北江
Beiping 北平
Boping 博平
Chahar 察哈爾
Changshu 常熟
Chaoxian 巢縣
Chengdu 成都
Daming 大名
Dangshan 碭山
Dexian 德縣
Dingxian 定縣
Dongping 東平
Fengtian 奉天
Fuzhou 福州
Gaotang 高唐
Guangrao 廣饒
Guangzhou 廣州
Gulin 固臨
Hangzhou 杭州
Heze 荷澤
Huangdu 黃渡
Huanglu 黃麓
Huimin 惠民
Huixian 輝縣
Ji'nan 濟南
Ji'ning 濟寧
Jieshou 界首
Jingzhao 京兆
Jinxiang 金鄉
Jiujiang 九江
Ju Xian 莒县
Kunshan 昆山
Laiyang 萊陽
Lanzhou 蘭州
Liaocheng 聊城
Linyi 臨沂

Linzi 臨淄
Liuan 六安
Longchuan 龍川
Mouping 牟平
Nanchang 南昌
Nanjing 南京
Ningbo 寧波
Penglai 蓬萊
Pinghu 平湖
Pingjiang 平江
Pingyuan 平原
Potou 泊頭
Qihe 齊河
Qingdao 青島
Qingping 清平
Qingzhou 青州
Qixiashan 棲霞山
Qufu 曲阜
Rehe 熱河
Rongcheng 榮城
Ruijin 瑞金
Runan 汝南
Shanghang 上杭
Shanghe 商河
Shaoxing 紹興
Shenyang 沈陽
Shouzhang 壽張
Sishui 泗水
Suzhou 蘇州
Taihang 太行
Suiyuan 綏遠
Taiyuan 太原
Tangyi 堂邑
Tengxian 滕縣
Tingzhou 汀州
Wanzai 萬載
Weihaiwei 威海衛
Wendeng 文登
Wuchang 武昌
Wuhan 武漢
Wujiang 吳江
Wuxi 無錫
Xi'an 西安
Xiamen 廈門
Xiangyang 襄陽府
Xiaoshan 蕭山
Xingguo 興國
Yan'an 延安
Yanggu 陽谷
Yidu 益都
Yuan'en 原恩
Yucheng 禹城
Yuncheng 惲城
Yuyao 余姚
Zhangqiu 章丘
Zhengyang 正陽
Zhili 直隸
Ziyang 滋陽
Zouping 鄒平

Schools, Organizations, and School Regulations

Aiguo nüxue 愛國女學
Baoding chuji shifan xuetang 保定初級師範學堂
Beijing nü yi xuetang 北京女醫學堂
Beijing nüzi daxue 北京女子大學
Beijing nüzi gaodeng shifan xuexiao 北京女子高等師範學校
Beijing nüzi shifan daxue 北京女子師範大學
Beijing nüzi shifan xuexiao 北京女子師範學校
Beiping daxue nüzi shifan xueyuan 北平大學女子師範學院
Beiping nüzi shifan xueyuan 北平女子師範學院
Beiping shifan daxue 北平師範大學
Beiyang nü yi xuetang 北洋女醫學堂
Beiyang nüzi shifan xuetang 北洋女子師範學堂
Beiyang youji shifan xuetang 北洋優級師範學堂
Chengdu daxue 成都大學
Chengdu gaoshi 成都高師

Chengdu shifan daxue 成都師範大學
Chongshi shuyuan 崇實書院
Chudeng xiao xuetang zhangcheng 初等小學堂章程
Chuji shifan jianzhang 初級師範學校簡章
Chuji shifan xuetang zhangcheng 初級師範學堂章程
Cuihua nüxue 粹化女學
Cuimin nüxue 粹敏女學
Dongbei Daxue 東北大學
Dongnan daxue 東南大學
Duanqi shifan xuexiao jianzhang 短期師範學校簡章
Duyin tongyi hui 讀音統一會
Fan di da tongmeng 反帝大同盟
Fujian Chuanzheng Xuetang 福建船政學堂
gaoden xuetang zhangcheng 高等學堂章程
Gaoji shifan xuexiao jianzhang 高級師範學校簡章
Gezhi Shuyuan 格致書院
Guang Fangyan Guan 廣方言館
Guangdong daxue 廣東大學
Guangdong gaoshi 廣東高師
Guoli Jingshi daxue 國立京師大學
Guomin shifan 國民師範
Guomin xiaoxue 國民小學
Guoyu tongyi choubei hui 國語統一籌備會
Guoyu yanjiu hui 國語研究會
Guozijian 國子監
Hangzhou chanke nü xuetang 杭州產科女學堂
Hengshan xiangcun shifan 衡山鄉村師範
Huanan daxue 華南大學
Huanglu nongcun jianshe shiyan qu 黃麓農村建設實驗區
Huanglu xiangcun shifan xuexiao 黃麓鄉村師範學校
Jianding xiaoxue jiaoyuan weiyuan hui 檢定小學教員委員會
Jiangsu shifan xuetang 江蘇師範學堂
Jiangsu xuewu chu 江蘇學務處
Jiangsu yiwu jiaoyu qicheng hui 江蘇義務教育期成會
Jiaoyu bu 教育部
Jieshou xiangcun shifan 界首鄉村師範
Jingshi da xuetang youji shifan ke 京師大學堂師範科
Jingshi da xuetang 京師大學堂
Jingshi nüzi shifan xuetang 京師女子師範學堂
Jingshi nüzi shifan xuexiao 京師女子師範學校
Jingshi Tongwen Guan 京師同文館
Jingzheng nüxue 經正女學
Jingzhu nüxuexiao 景珠女學校
Jinling nüzi daxue 金陵女子大學
Jiujiang xiancun shifan xuexiao 九江鄉村師範學校
Kang Ri jiuguo hui 抗日救國會
Kangda 抗大

Kangri junzheng daxue 抗日軍政大學
Liang Guang sucheng shifan guan 兩廣速成師範館
Liang Guang xuewu chu 兩廣學務處
Liang Guang youji shifan xuetang yi lan 兩廣優級師範學堂一覽
Liang Guang youji shifan xuetang 兩廣优級師範學堂
Liang Hu shifan xuetang 兩湖師範學堂
Liang Hu youji shifan xuetang 兩湖优級師範學堂
Liang Jiang youji shifan xuetang 兩江優級師範學堂
Lianhe daxue 聯合大學
Liening di er shifan xuexiao 列寧第二師範學校
Liening di yi shifan xuexiao 列寧第一師範學校
Liening xiaoxue 列寧小學
Lingnan daxue 嶺南大學
Lize nüzi shifan xuexiao 麗則女子師範學校
Longchuan xiancun shifan xuexiao 龍川鄉村師範學校
Longmen shuyuan 龍門書院
Ma-Lie zhuyi xueyuan 馬列主義學院
Minxian 民先
Minzu jiefang xianfeng dui 民族解放先鋒隊
Nanjing gaoshi 南京高師
Nanjing shuyuan 南菁書院
Nanyang gongxue 南洋公學
Nongcun bixi jiaoyu she 農村補習教育社
Peide zhongxue 培德中學
Qiming nüzi xuexiao 啟明女子學校
Qinding xuetang zhangcheng 欽定學堂章程
Qixiashan xiangcun shifan 棲霞山鄉村師範
Shandong shengli di yi nüzi shifan xuexiao 山東省立第一女子師範學校
Shanghai nüzi Zhong Xi yi xuexiao 上海女子中西醫學堂
Sheng ma li ya nü shuyuan 圣瑪利亞女書院
Shenyang gaoshi 沈陽高師
Shifan xuexiao guicheng 師範學校規程
Sichuan daxue 四川大學
Sichuan tongsheng youji shifan xuetang 四川通省師範學堂
Taicang xiangcun shifa 太倉鄉村師範
Weijing shuyuan 味經書院
Wuben nüshu 務本女塾
Wuhan daxue 武漢大學
Wuhan gaoshi 武漢高師
Xiangcun jianshe cujin weiyuanhui 鄉村建設促進委員會
Xiangcun jiaoyu xianfeng tuan 聯村教育先鋒團
Xianghu xiancun shifan xuexiao 湘湖鄉村師範學校
Xiaoxue jiaoyuan xunlian ban jianzhang 小學教員訓練班簡章
Xiaoxue jiaoyuan youdai tiaoli 小學教員優待條例
Xiaozhuang shiyan xiangcun shifan xuexiao 曉莊實驗鄉村師範學校
Xiaozhuang xiangcun shifan xuexiao 曉莊鄉村師範學校
Xiehe nüzi daxue 協和女子大學

Ximenghui 犧盟會
Xinan lianhe daxue 西南聯合大學
Xisheng jiuguo tongmeng hui 犧牲救國同盟會
Xue bu 學部
Yiyi Nü xuetang 譯藝女學堂
Youji shifan xuetang zhangcheng 优級師範學堂章程
Yujiao nüxuetang 豫教女學堂
Zhengmeng shuyuan 正蒙書院
Zhenjiang nüshu 鎮江女塾
Zhili shifan xuetang 直隸師範學堂
Zhong xuetang zhangcheng 中學堂章程
Zhonghua jiaoyu cujin she 中華教育促進社
Zhongxi Nüshu 中西女塾
Zhongyang da xuequ 中央大學區
Zhongyang dangxiao 中央黨校
Zhongyang Liening shifan xuexiao 中央列寧師範學校
Zhounan nüzi shifan xuexiao 周南女子師範學校
Zou ding ge xuetang jiangli zhangcheng 奏定各學堂獎勵章程
Zouding nüzi shifan xuetang ji nüzi xiaoxuetang zhangcheng 奏定女子師範學堂暨女子小學堂章程
Zouding renyong jiaoyuan zhangcheng 奏定任用教員章程
Zouding xuetang zhangcheng 奏定學堂章程
Zouping jianyi xiangcun shifan 鄒平簡易鄉村師範
Zunjing shuyuan 尊經書院
Zuolian 左聯
Zuoyi zuojia lianhe hui 左翼作家聯合會

General Terms and Educational Programs

anfen zhi liangmin 安分之良民
bagong 拔貢
baogao 報告
baomu jiangxi ke 保姆講習科
baosong 保送
basheng 拔生
ben ke 本科
biye huikao 畢業會考
bowu 博物
buyong 補用
cainü 才女
chuan Dao, shou ye, jie huo 傳道授業解惑
chuanxi suo 傳習所
chuji bu 初級部
chuji shifan xuetang 初級師範學堂
chuxiao 初小
chuzhong 初中
cong jiupin 從九品
congjiu 從九
da houfang 大後方
da xingzheng qu 大行政區
dajia fengfan 大家風範
dang hua jiaoyu 黨化教育
dangyi 黨義
danji jiaoshou lianxi suo 單級教授練習所
Di er ci quanguo jiaoyu huiyi 第二次全國教育會議
Di yi ci quanguo jiaoyu huiyi 第一次全國教育會議
di yi yaowu 第一要務
dujing 讀經
duo liu ge difang shensuo yudi 多留各地方伸縮余地
duxuedao 督學道
e shen 惡紳
fan le ban ge jindou 翻了半個筋斗

fantong jiaoshi 飯桶教師
fenlei ke 分類科
fu huizhang 副會長
fu 府
fubang jinshi 副榜進士
fudao difang jiaoyu 輔導地方教育
fugong 副貢
fugong 附貢
fusheng 附生
fuxian 賦閑
fuxue 府學
fuyong zhuyi 附庸主義
fuzai 附載
gaodeng ke 高等科
gaodeng shifan xuexiao 高等師範學校
gaodeng xuexiao 高等學校
gaoshang 高尚
gaoxiao 高小
gaozhong 高中
ge wu 格物
genben zhi genben 根本之根本
geng du chuantong 耕讀傳統
gexing fazhan 個性發展
gezhi 格致
gongbu zhushi 工部主事
gongdu 公牘
gonggong ke 公共科
gongsheng 貢生
gongyuan 貢院
guan, jiao, yang, wei 管、教、養、衛
guanhua 官話
guanliyuan lianxi suo 管理員訓練所
guanxue dachen 管學大臣
guanxue 官學
guomin jiaoyu zhi pitai 國民教育之胚胎
guomin 國民
guowen 國文
guoyin 國音
guoyu ke 國語科
guoyu yundong 國語運動
guoyu 國語
hong shizi 宏師資
houbu zhifu 候補知府
houbu 候補
hua min yi su 化民易俗
huizhang 會長
jia shi 家事
jiangxi suo 講習所
jianju 薦舉
jiansheng 監生
jianyi bu 簡易部
jianyi ke 簡易科
jianyi shifan 簡易師範
jianyi xiangshi 簡易鄉師
jiao fei 剿匪
jiao xue zuo he yi 教學做合一
jiaoguan 教官
jiaoji hua 交際花
jiaoshou lianxi suo 教授練習所
jiaoshou 教授
Jiaoyu ju 教育局
Jiaoyu ting 教育廳
jiaoyu 教諭
jiaoyuan jiangxi suo 教員講習所
jiashi jiyi zhuanxiu ke 家事技藝專修科
jiashi yuanyi 家事園藝
jiashi 家事
jiashu 家塾
jiaxi ke 加習科
jieqi 節氣
jingli 經歷
jingshi 經史
jingshi 經師
jinshi 進士
jishi 記事
jizai 記載
juanna 捐納
juren 舉人
keyuan 科員
kezhang 科長
langman de wu mudi zhuyi 浪漫的無目的主義
lian cun ziwei dui 聯村自衛隊
liang qi xian bu zhuyi 良妻賢母主義
liangfu, liangqi, liangmu 良婦良妻良母
liangji shifan xuetang 兩級師範學堂

liangjia guixiu 良家閨秀
lianxi minquan 練習民權
lieshen 劣紳
lingong 廩貢
linsheng 廩生
long mu jiao 隆母教
lunshuo 論說
mengshi 蒙師
mengxue 蒙學
mengyang ... wei guomin jiaoy zhi di yi jizhi 蒙養..為國民教育之第一基址
mingling 命令
minquan 民權
minzhong xuexiao 民眾學校
nigu jiaoyu 尼姑教育
nong wa 弄瓦
nong zhang 弄璋
nü jiaoshi 女教師
nü jiaoxi 女教習
nü jiaoyuan 女教員
nü jiehunyuan 女結婚員
nüshi jiaoyu 女士教育
Nüzi jiaoyu wei guomin jiaoyu zhi genji 女子教育為國民教育之根基
pin ku chushen 貧苦出身
pinnong 貧農
pingmin xuexiao 平民學校
pu cang shenshan 璞藏深山
putong zhong xuetang 普通中學堂
qiong xiaozi 窮小子
qiushou qiyi 秋收起義
qizi jiaoyu 妻子教育
qu 區
quanxue suo 勸學所
ruxue jiaoguan 儒學教官
Sanmin zhuyi jiaoyu 三民主義教育
shanzhang 山長
shehui jiaoyu 社會教育
sheng li shifan 省立師範
sheng li zhongxue 省立中學
sheng shixue 省視學
shengyuan 生員
shexue 社學
shi que 實缺
shi wei guojia genben zhiji 實為國家根本至計
shi zhe, ren zhi mofan ye 師者，人 之模範也
shi zhong hebing 師中合併
shifan guan 師範館
shifan jiangxi suo 師範講習所
shifan jiaoyu si 師範教育司
shifan qu 師範區
shifan yuan 師範院
shifan 師範
shiji jiaoyu 侍姬教育
shixi Qidouwei 世襲騎都尉
shixue yuan 視學員
shixue 視學
shiyan qu 實驗區
shiye xuetang 實業學堂
shiyong 試用
shiyuan 試院
shougong 手工
shu kan jieshao she 書刊介紹社
shuyuan 書院
sishu 私塾
sucheng ke 速成科
suigong 歲貢
suozhang 所長
tianxia 天下
ting qi zi ying sheng ye 聽其自營生業
tong ... xian 同...銜
tong zi jun 童子軍
tongyangxi 童養媳
tu long shu 屠龍術
wanquan ke 完全科
wei ren shibiao 為人師表
wei 衛
weisheng 衛生
weixue 衛學
weiyuan 委員
wen yan tongyi 文言統一
wen yan wen 文言文
wenguan kaoyan 文官考驗
wu pinji 無品級
wubin jungong 五品軍功
wubin zhixian 五品職銜
wuju 武舉
xi guanhua 習官話
xia zhongnong 下中農

xian jiaoyu hui huizhang 縣教育會
xian li shifan 縣立師範
xian 縣
xiancheng 縣丞
xiang 鄉
xiangcun shifan 鄉村師範
xiangcun shuyuan 鄉村書院
xiangfu jiaozi, yijia shanzhong 相夫教子, 宜家善種
xiangjian laosheng hanru 鄉間老生寒儒
xianmu liangfu 賢母良婦
xianmu, liangqi, shunu 賢母良妻淑女
xianxue 縣學
xianyuan 賢媛
xiaojie 小姐
xin xing 心性
xing shi zhi zhi shi 行是知之始
xing xing jiaohua, zuoyu rencai 興行教化，作育人材
xiushi 秀士
xizi 習字
xuan ke 選科
xue jie 學界
xue'e 學額
xuechao 學潮
xuetang 學堂
xuexiao 學校
xueyun 學運
xuezheng 學政
xuezheng 學正
xundao 訓導
xunjian 巡檢
yi wei yangshi fuyu zhi zi 以為仰事俯育之資
yiban 一般
yinci 淫祠
yisheng 佾生
yishu 義塾
yixue 義學
yougong 優貢
youji shifan xuetang 優級師範學堂
youxi 遊戲
yu ke 預科
yuanzhang 院長
yuti wen 語體文
zai ji wu er qiong qi li 在即物而窮其理
zaliu 雜流
zengsheng 增生
Zhejiang de Xiaozhuang 浙江的曉莊
zhen guojiao 振國教
zheng jiao he yi 政教合一
zheng jiazheng 整家政
zheng qipin 正七品
zhi shi xing zhi shi 知是行之始
zhi xing he yi 知行合一
zhishi funü 知識婦女
zhixian 職銜
zhongnong 中農
zhongxin xiaoxue huodong jiao xue zuo 中心學校活動教學做
zhou 州
zhoutong 州同
zhouxue 州學
zhuanjian 專件
zhuanmen ke 專門科
zhuanmen xuetang 專門學堂
zhuanxiu ke 專修科
zhujiao 助教
zhuren 主任
zhuyin fuhao 注音符號
zhuyin zimu 注音字母
zhuyin 注音
ziyou zhuyi 自由主義
zuo xue jiao gong xue zhi 做學教工學制
zuo yi zuojia 左翼作家
zushu 族塾平

Printing Terms

A Q zhengzhuan 阿 Q 正傳
Bai jia xing 百家姓
Bayue de xiangcun 八月的鄉村

Beidou 北斗
Beifang hongqi 北方紅旗
Beixin yuekan 北新月刊
Bianfa tongyi 變法通議
Bianzheng fa qianshuo 辯證法淺說
Bianzheng fa rumen 辯證法入門
Chenbao fukan 晨報副刊
Chuanzao yuekan/jikan 創造月刊/季刊
Ci hai 辭海
Dagong bao 大公報
Dazhong shenghuo 大眾生活
Dazhong zhexue 大眾哲學
Diguo zhuyi shi ziben zhuyi de zuigao jieduan 帝國主義是資本主義的最高階段
Dongfang ribao 東方日報
Dongfang zazhi 東方雜誌
Dushu shenghuo 讀書生活
Duxiu wencun 獨秀文存
Fa yan 法言
Fan Dulin lun 反杜林論
Fandui baise kongbu 反對白色恐怖
Fen 墳
Fenghuang niepan 鳳凰涅盤
Funü shenghuo 婦女生活
Funü zazhi 婦女雜誌
Gongchan zhuyi yundong zhong de zuopai youzhi bing 共產主義運動中的左派幼稚病
Gongchandang xuanyan 共產黨宣言
Guojia yu geming 國家與革命
Hongqi ribao 紅旗日報
Hongqi 紅旗
Hu Shi wencun 胡適文存
Huimie 毀滅
Huoxian 火線
Jia 家
Jiaoyu bu gongbao 教育部公報
Jiaoyu gongbao 教育公報
Jiaoyu zazhi 教育雜誌
Jiating, siyouzhi he guojia de qiyuan 家庭、私有制和國家的起源
Jiefang 解放
Jinghan gongren liuxue ji 京漢工人流血記
Liangzhong celue 兩種策略
Liening zhuzuo xuan 列寧著作選
Liu da wenxian 六大文獻
Liuli wa 琉璃瓦
Lun nüxue 論女學
Lun yu 論語

Mao Zedong zizhuan 毛澤東自傳
Minzhong geming yu minzhong zhengquan 民眾革命與民眾政權
Mosike ribao 莫斯科日報
Mosike yinxiang ji 莫斯科印象記
Muqin 母親
Nahan 吶喊
Nü bao 女報
Nüzi shijie wenxuan 女子世界
Nüzi yuekan 女子月刊
Panghuang 徬徨
Qilu wenhua 齊魯文化
Quanguo Suweiai quyu daibiao dahui laodong baohu fa 全國蘇維埃區域代表大會勞動保護法
Quanguo Suweiai quyu daibiao dahui muqian xuanyan 全國蘇維埃區域代表大會目前時局宣言
Quanguo Suweiai quyu daibiao dahui xuanyan 全國蘇維埃區域代表大會宣言
San zi jing 三字經
Shenbao ziyou tan 申報自由談
Sheng si hang 生死場
Shenghuo xingqi kan 生活星期刊
Shenghuo 生活
Shenhui zhoukan 《社會周刊》
Shi shuo 師說
Shifan qunying, guang yao Zhonghua 師範群英，光耀中華
Shijie jingji dili gangyao 世界經濟地理綱要
shiwubao 時務報
Shiyue 十月
Su E shicha ji 蘇俄視察記
Su qu chiweidui 蘇區赤衛隊
Suweiai xianfa qianshuo 蘇維埃憲法淺說
Tieliu 鐵流
Tuchang 屠場
Tudi nongmin wenti zhinan 土地農民問題指南
Tuixiang zhai riji 退想齋日記
Tuohuang zhe《拓荒者》
Weiwu zhuyi rumen 唯物主義入門
Weiwu zhuyi yu jingyan piban zhuyi 唯物主義與經驗批判主義
Wo de daxue 我的大學
Wuzhuang baodong 武裝暴動
Xiaboyang 夏伯陽
Xiangdao bao 向導報
Xiangjiao congxun 鄉教叢迅
Xiaoshuo yuebao 小說月報
Xin Qingnian 新青年
Xinsheng 新生
Xixing manji 西行漫記

Xue bu guan bao 學部官報
Xuesheng zazhi 學生雜誌
Xuewu gangyao 學務綱要
Yusi 語絲
Zai renjian 在人間
Zao chun er yue 早春二月
Zhengzhi jingji xue 政治經濟學
Zhengzhi wenti jianghua 政治問題講話
Zhinan hongqi 直南紅旗
Zhongguo Gongchandang zhongyang weiyuanhui gao minzhong shu 中國共產黨中央委員會告民眾書
Zhongguo qingnian 中國青年
Zhongliu 中流
Ziben lun 資本論
Ziben zhuyi jiepo 資本主義解剖
Zibenlun dagang 資本論大綱
Zuo shenmo 作什麼？

Bibliography

Abbreviations Used in the Notes and Bibliography

DECZJNJ The Ministry of Education: *Di er ci Zhongguo jiaoyu nianjian* [The second yearbook on the education of China, 1948] (Beijing: Shangwu yinshuguan [Commercial Press], 1948).

DFZZ *Dong fang za zhi* [Eastern Miscellany, 1904-48].

DXYGB The University Council: *Daxueyuan gongbao* [Official Bulletin of the University Council, 1927-28].

DYCZJNJ The Ministry of Education: *Di yi ci Zhongguo jiaoyu nianjian* [The first yearbook on the education of China, 1932] (Shanghai: Kaiming Shudian, 1934. Taipei: Zhuanji Wnxue Chubanshe, reprint, 1971).

JYBGB The Ministry of Education: *Jiaoyubu gongbao* [Official Bulletin of the Ministry of Education, 1928-48].

JYGB The Ministry of Education: *Jiaoyu gongbao* [Official Bulletin of Education, 1914-27].

JYZZ *Jiaoyu zazhi* [Educational review, 1909-48]

JXJJT Zhu Youhuan, Qi Mingxiu, Qian Manqian, and Huo Yiping (compil.), *Jiaoyu xingzheng jigou ji jiaoyu tuanti* [Education administrations and organizations] (Shanghai: Shanghai jiaoyu chubanshe [Shanghai Education Press], 1993). One of the *ZJJZH* series.

JZJS Shu Xincheng, *Jindai Zhongguo jiaoyu shiliao* [Historical materials on the education of modern China] (Shanghai: Shangwu yinshuguan [Commercial Press], 1927).

KJKHJ Akigoro Taga (compil.), *Kindai Chugoku kyoikushi shiroyo* [Historical materials on the education of modern China] (Tokyo: Nihon Gakujutsu Shinkokai [Association for academic revival in Japan], 1975).

SJSJ Ju Xingui, Tong Fuyong, and Zhang Shouzhi (compil.), *Shiye jiaoyu, shifan jiaoyu* [Vocational education and teacher training] (Shanghai: Shanghai jiaoyu chubanshe [Shanghai Education Press], 1994). One of *ZJJZH* series.

SQGZ *Shifan qunying, guangyao Zhonghu* [Heroic graduates of teachers' schools shine in Chinese history], 21 vols. (Xi'An: Shaanxi renmin jiaoyu chubanshe [Shaanxi people's education publishing house], 1992-94).

WSJ Tang Zhijun and Chen Zu'en (compil.), *Wuxu shiqi jiaoyu* [Education in China during the 1898 Reform period] (Shanghai: Shanghai jiaoyu chubanshe [Shanghai Education Press], 1993). One of *ZJJZH* series.

XBGB The Board of Education, *Xue bu guanbao* [Official Bulletin of the Board of Education, 1904-11].

XZYB Ju Xingui and Tang Liangyan (compil.), *Xuezhi yanbian* [Evolution of school systems] (Shanghai: Shanghai jiaoyu chubanshe [Shanghai Education Press], 1991). One of *ZJJZH* series.

YYSJ Gao Shiliang (compil.), *Yangwu yundong shiqi jiaoyu* [Education in China during the period of the Self-Strengthening Movement] (Shanghai: Shanghai jiaoyu chubanshe [Shanghai Education Press], 1992). One of *ZJJZH* series.

YZSJ Ju Xingui (compil.), *Yapian zhanzheng shiqi jiaoyu* [Chinese education prior to and during the period of the Opium War] (Shanghai: Shanghai jiaoyu chubanshe [Shanghai Education Press], 1990). One of *ZJJZH* series.

ZJJSZL Shu Xincheng, *Zhongguo jindai jiaoyu shi ziliao* [Source materials related to the modern education history of China], 3 vols. (Beijing: Remin jiaoyu chubanshe [People's education publishing house], 1963).

ZJJZH Chen Yuanhui (chief compiler), *Zhongguo jindai jiaoyu shi ziliao huibian* [Compilation of source materials on the modern education of China] (Shanghai: Shanghai jiaoyu chubanshe [Shanghai Education Press], 1990-96).

ZJSJZ Li Youzhi, Li Chunnian, Liu Chuanxin, and Ge Jiaxun (compil.), *Zhongguo jinxiandai shifan jiaoyu shi ziliao* [Source materials related to the history of teachers' education in modern and contemporary China], 4 vols. (n.p., 1983).

ZJXS Zhu Youhuan (compil.) *Zhongguo jindai xuezhi shiliao* [Historical materials on the school system of modern China], 4 vols. (Shanghai: Huadong shida chubanshe [East China Normal University Press], 1989).

Abe Hiroshi. "Borrowing from Japan: China's First Modern Educational System." In Hayhoe and Bastid, *China's Education and the Industrialized World*, 57-80.

–. "Shinmotsu no kaigaku bodo" [Anti-Modern School Revolts in Early Twentieth Century China]. In Taga, *Kindai Ajia kyoikushi kenkyu* [Study of educational history in modern Asia), 69-142.

"Aiguo nüxuexiao buding zhangcheng" [Supplementary regulations for Patriotic Women's School]. *ZJXS*, 2b: 618-20.

Akigoro Taga, ed. *Kindai Ajia kyoikushi kenkyu* [Studies of educational history in modern Asia]. Tokyo: Iwasaki Gakujutu shuppansha, 1975.

– (compil.). *Kindai Chugoku kyoikushi shiroyo* [Historical documents on modern Chinese education]. Nihon Gakujutsu Shinkokai, 1975.

Alitto, Guy. *The Last Confucian: Liang Shuming and the Chinese Dilemma of Modernity*. Berkeley: University of California Press, 1986 [1979].

Anderson, Benedict. *Imagined Communities: Reflections on the Origin and Spread of Nationalism*. New York: Verso, 1983.

"Anhui sheng zhi xuezhi gaige" [Reform of school system in Anhui province]. *Xin jiaoyu* 6, 1 (1923): 114-16.

"Anhui shengzhang zi song shifan xuequ suoshu xian fen yi lan biao qing chazhao wen" [Anhui governor submitting the table of teachers' school districts and the counties under their charge]. *JYGB*, yr. 5 (1918), 4, "Gongdu": 64.

Bai Qixiang. "Chu chuang de Shencemen minzhong xuexiao" [The initial stage of Shencemen School for Commoners). *Xiangjiao congxun* 2, 11 (1928): 2-3.

–. "Guan yu xiangcun danji xiaoxue jiaoshi de yi ge wenti" [On a problem faced by teachers in rural elementary schools]. *Xiangjiao congxun*, 2, 9 (1928): 1-2.

Bai Xinliang. *Zhongguo gudai shuyuan fazhan shi* [A history of the development of ancient Chinese academies]. Tianjin: Tianjin People's Press, 1995.

Bai Yun. "Nüzi zhiye tan" [A discussion of women's professions]. *Funü zazhi* 1, 9 (1915): 6-8.

Bailey, Paul. "Active Citizen or Efficient Housewife? The Debate over Women's Education in Early-Twentieth-Century China." In Peterson, Hayhoe, and Lu, *Education, Culture, and Identity in Twentieth-Century China*, 318-47.

–. "'Modernising Conservatism' in Early Twentieth-Century China: The Discourse and Practice of Women's Education," *European Journal of East Asian Studies* 3, 2 (2004): 217-41.

–. *Reform the People: Changing Attitudes towards Popular Education in Early Twentieth-Century China*. Vancouver: UBC Press, 1990.

"Baoding chuji shifan xuetang shuwuzhang Wang Zecheng gai tang qingxing bing" [A report from Wang Zecheng, director of admissions at Baoding Lower Teachers' School, on the school's situation]. *SJSJ*: 738-42.

"Baoding shi jingchaju chachao shifan xuexiao youjian suo faxian de dixia kanwu, 1930-31" [Underground publications found by the Baoding City Police Department by intercepting mail to several teachers' schools, 1930-31]. Hebei Provincial Archives, files 645-1-1, 645-1-7, 645-1-2.

"Baoshan xian jiaoyu hui" [Baoshan County Educational Association]. *JXJJT:* 342-48.

Bastid, Marianne. *Educational Reform in Early Twentieth-Century China.* Trans. Paul Bailey. Ann Arbor: University of Michigan, 1988.

Becker, Carl. H., M. Falski, P. Langevin, and R.H. Tawney. *The Reorganization of Education in China* [Report of the League of Nations' Mission of Educational Experts]. Paris: League of Nations' Institute of Intellectual Co-operation, 1932.

Bedeski, Robert. *State-Building in Modern China: The Kuomintang in the Prewar Period.* Berkeley: University of California Berkeley Institute of East Asian Studies, 1981.

"Bei ji" [Records on tablets]. *YZSJ:* 329-34.

Beijing qingnian bao [Beijing youth daily].

Beijing shifan daxue xiaoshi bianxie zu. *Beijing shifan daxue xiaoshi* 1902-1982 [History of Beijing normal university, 1902-1982]. Beijing shifan daxue chubanshe, 1982.

Beijing tushughuan shumu bianji zu. *Zhongguo xiandai zuojia zhu yi shumu* [Index of books written and translated by Chinese modern writers]. Beijing: Shumu wenxian chubanshe, 1982.

"Beijing Yujiao nüxuetang zhangcheng" [The regulations of Yujiao Women's School in Beijing] (1905). *ZJXS* 2b: 694-98.

"Beiyang nüzi shifan xuetang kai xiao ji sheng" [Grand opening ceremony of Beiyang Women's Normal School]. *ZJXS* 2b: 689-90.

"Beiyang shifan xuetang shiban zhangcheng" [The regulations for the trial program at Beiyang Teachers' College]. *SJSJ:* 661-72.

"Bensi tongchi geshu rushu zhaojie Baoding shifan xuetang jingfei shen shao qing su chouban bi nian shicuo zha" [Notice to all subordinate branches on the insufficient obligatory funds sent to Baoding Teachers' School: Please immediately send the balance of the funds to prevent impropriety]. *SJSJ:* 644.

Bi Yao. "Lue tan nüzi Zhongguo jiaoyu shi" [A brief review of the history of female education in China]. *Funü shenghuo* [Women's life] 3, 7 (1936): 25-29.

Biggerstaff, Knight. *The Earliest Modern Government Schools in China.* New York: Cornell University Press, 1961.

Borthwick, Sally. "Changing Concepts of the Role of Women from the Late Qing to the May Fourth Period." In Pong and Fung, *Ideal and Reality*, 63-91.

–. *Education and Social Change in China.* Stanford: Hoover Institution Press, Stanford University, 1983.

Brown, Hubert. "American Progressivism in Chinese Education: The Case of Tao Xingzhi." In Hayhoe and Bastid, *China's Education and the Industrialized World,* 120-38.

Buck, David. "Educational Modernization in Tsinan, 1899-1937." In Elvin and Skinner, *The Chinese City between Two Worlds,* 171-212.

Bulletins on Chinese Education, 1923. Issued by the Chinese National Association for the Advancement of Education. Shanghai: The Commercial Press, 1925.

Burton, Margaret E. *The Education of Women in China.* New York: Fleming H. Revell Company, 1911.

Cai Yuanpei. *Cai Yuanpei zishu* [Memoir of Cai Yuanpei]. Taibei: Zhuanji wenxue chubanshe, 1967.

–. "Duiyu jiaoyu fangzhen zhi yijian" [My opinion on the goals of education]. *XZYB*, 608-614.

–. "Wo zai jiaoyu jie de jingyan" [My experience in educational circles]. In *Cai Yuanpei zishu*, 35-48.

Cao Dianqi. "Changsha zhi nongcun buxi jiaoyu yundong" [The rural education movement in Changsha]. *Zhonghua jiaoyu jie* 13, 12 (1924): 1-20.

Cao Yunjiao. "Zhongguo funü jiaoyu de zhongyao jiqi shishi" [The importance of Chinese women's education and its implementation]. *Nüzi yuekan* 2, 1 (1934): 1762-66.

Cao Zhenqiu. "Chu fa hou" [After setting off]. *Xiang jiao cong xun* 2, 15 (1928): 2-4.

Chaffee, John. *The Thorny Gates of Learning in Sung China: A Social History of Examinations*. Cambridge: Cambridge University Press, 1985.
"Chajin fandong xuanchuan, 1933" [Prohibiting reactionary propaganda, 1933]. In Hebei Provincial Archives, files 645-1-2.
Chan, Ming K., and Arif Dirlik, *Schools into Fields and Factories: Anarchist, the Guomindang, and the National Labor University in Shanghai, 1927-1932*. Durham: Duke University Press, 1991.
Chang Chung-li. *The Chinese Gentry: Studies on Their Role in Nineteenth-Century Chinese Society*. Seattle: University of Washington Press, 1955.
–. *The Income of the Chinese Gentry*. Seattle: University of Washington Press, 1962.
Chang Hao. *Liang Ch'i-ch'ao and Intellectual Transition in China, 1890-1907*. Cambridge: Harvard University Press, 1971.
Chang Naide. "Shifan jiaoyu gaizao wenti" [The issue of reforming the teachers'-school system]. *JYZZ* 14 (1922): 1-30.
"Changzhou nüxue zhi zuli" [Obstacles to women's schooling in Changzhou]. *ZJXS* 2b: 654-55.
Chauncey, Helen. *Schoolhouse Politicians: Locality and State during the Chinese Republic*. Honolulu: University of Hawaii Press, 1992.
Chen Dongyuan. *Zhongguo funü shenghuo shi* [A history of the life of Chinese women]. Shanghai: Shangwu yinshu guan [Commercial Press], 1937 (1998 reprint).
Chen Gujia, and Deng Hongbo. *Zhongguo shuyuan zhidu yanjiu* [Studies of China's academies]. Nanjing: Zhejiang jiaoyu chubanshe [Zhejiang education press], 1997.
Chen Hongmou. "Jiao nü yi gui" [Bequeathed guidelines for the education of women]. In Chen, *Wu zhong yi gui*, [Bequeathed guidelines of five kinds, 1742], preface (1742).
–. *Wu zhong yi gui* [Bequeathed guidelines of five kinds, 1742]. Shanghai: Jingwei shuju [Jingwei press], 1935 (reprint).
Chen Qingzhi. *Zhongguo jiaoyu shi* [History of Chinese education]. Shanghai: Shanghai Shangwu yinshu guan, 1936 (1989 reprint).
Chen Qitian. *Jindai Zhongguo jiaoyu shi* [A history of modern Chinese education]. Taipei: Zhonghua shuju, 1969.
Chen, Theodore Hsi-en. "Education in China, 1927-1937." In Sih, *The Strenuous Decade*, 289-314.
–. *Teacher Training in Communist China*. Washington, DC: US Department of Health, Education and Welfare, 1960.
Chen Youduan. "Woguo xianxing xiangcun shifan kecheng de jiantao" [A reexamination of the curriculum of existing village teachers' schools in China]. *Zhonghua jiaoyu jie* 24, 2 (1936): 47-54.
Chen Yuanhui (chief compiler). *Zhongguo jindai jiaoyu shi ziliao huibian* [Compilation of the source materials on the modern education of China], 1990-1996.
–, Yin Dexin, and Wang Bingzhao. *Zhongguo gudai de shuyuan zhidu* [China's ancient academies]. Shanghai: Shanghai jiaoyu chubanshe [Shanghai education press], 1981.
Chen Yung-fa. *Making Revolution: The Communist Movement in Eastern and Central China, 1937-1945*. Berkeley: University of California Press, 1986.
Cheng Benhai. *Xiangcun shifan jingyan tan* [On the experience of village teachers' schools]. Kunming: Zhonghua shuju, 1939.
–. *Zai Xiaozhuang* [In Xiaozhuang village]. Shanghai: Zhonghua shuju, 1930.
Cheng Kaihua, Gong Manqun, and Zhu Zuchun (compil.). *Zhongguo xiandai wenxue cidian* [Encyclopedia of Chinese modern literature]. Xi'an: Huayue wenyi chubanshe, 1988.
Chu, J.P. "Normal School Education in China." *Bulletin on Chinese Education* 2, 11 (1923): 1-22.
Chu Ji'neng. "Jiawu zhan qian siwei nü liuxuesheng" [Four women who studied overseas before the first Sino-Japanese War]. *YYSJ*: 369-75.
–. "Nüxue xiansheng" [A pioneer of women's schooling]. *DFZZ* 31, 7 (1934): 23-27.
Chuang Chai-hsuan, *Tendencies toward a Democratic System of Education in China* (Shanghai: Commercial Press, 1922).
Ci hai [Ocean of words]. Shanghai cishu chubanshe, 1982.

Cleverley, John. *The Schooling of China: Tradition and Modernity in Chinese Education*. Winchester: George Allen and Unwin, 1985.

Cohen, Paul A., and John E. Schrecker, eds. *Reform in Nineteenth-Century China*. Cambridge: East Asian Research Center, Harvard University, dist. by Harvard University Press, 1976.

Commercial Press, ed. *Zuijin san shi wu nian zhi Zhongguo jiaoyu* [Chinese education in the past thirty-five years]. Shanghai: Shangwu yinshu guan [Commercial Press], 1931.

Cong, Xiaoping, "From *'Cainü'* to *'Nü jiaoxi'*: Female Normal Schools and the Transformation of Women's Education in Late Qing China, 1895-1911." In *Different Worlds of Discourse: New Views of Gender and Genre in Late Qing and Early Republican China,* ed. Smith, Fong, and Qian.

"Cuimin nüxue shifan sheng zuye" [Graduating from the teacher training program at Cuimin Women's School]. In Li and Zhang, *Jindai Zhongguo nüquan yundong* 2, 1189.

Culp, Robert. "Elite Association and Local Politics in Republican China: Educational Institutions in Jiashan and Lanqi Counties, Zhejiang, 1911-1937." *Modern China* 20, 4 (1994): 446-77.

Curran, Thomas. "Educational Reform and the Paradigm of State-Society Conflict in Republican China." *Republican China* 18, 2 (1993): 26-63.

"Da jishi" [Important events], *JYZZ* 8, 12 (1916), "Jishi": 75-78.

Da xueyuan (university council). "Dahui wei yi da xueyuan renwei ke gong cankao ge an" [The proposals that did not get discussed in the conference but that the University Council regards as having value for reference]. *Quanguo jiaoyu huiyi baogao*, 1928 [Report on national education conference, 1928]. Taipei: Wenhai Press (reprint), 50-58.

–. (compil.). *Quanguo jiaoyu huiyi baogao, 1928* [Report of the National Conference on Education, 1928]. Taipei: Wenhai chubanshe, 1977 (reprint).

–. "Zhengdun shifan jiaoyu zhidu an" [Proposal for rectifying the teacher education system]. *Quanguo jiaoyu huiyi baogao 1928*: 139-50.

Da xueyuan gongbao [Official Bulletin of the University Council, 1927-28].

"Da zongtong ling ge sheng xingzheng gongshu nei she jiaoyu si, 1913" [President orders establishment of education bureau in provincial government]. *JXJJT*: 122.

Dai Zhixian. *Shinian neizhan shiqi de geming wenhua yundo*ng [The revolutionary cultural movement during the ten-year civil war period, 1927-1937]. Beijing: Chinese People's University Press, 1988.

Davin, Delia. "Imperialism and the Diffusion of Liberal Thought: British Influences on Chinese Education." In Hayhoe and Bastid, *China's Education and the Industrialized World,* 33-56.

DeFrancis, John. *Nationalism and Language Reform in China*. Princeton: Princeton University Press, 1950.

Deng, Peng. *Private Education in Modern China*. Westport, CT: Praeger Publishers, 1997.

"Di qi jie quanguo jiaoyu hui lianhe hui jilue" [Record of the seventh annual meeting of the National Federation of Educational Associations]. *XZYB:* 848-64.

"Di wu jie quanguo jiaoyu hui lianhe hui dahui jueyi an: Gaodeng shifan xiaozhang huo zhuren jiaoyuan shicha fujin sheng qu jiaoyuan zhuangkuang banfa an" [Resolutions of the fifth National Federation of Educational associations conference: A proposal that the presidents or deans of higher teachers' schools inspect educational affairs in nearby provinces (October 1916)]. *SJSJ:* 837-38.

"Di wu jie quanguo jiaoyu hui lianhe hui dahui yijue an, fujian: Gaige shifan jiaoyu yi'an" [Proposals from the fifth conference of the National Federation of Educational Associations, with attached proposal: A proposal for reforming teachers' education]. *SJSJ:* 838-47.

"Di yi er jie quanguo jiaoyu hui lianhe hui dahui yijue an zhiyi: Qi su she ge sheng qu jiaoyuting an" [One of the propositions of the NFEA: The proposal to request immediately to construct provincial and regional education bureaus]. *JXJJT*: 130-32.

Dirlik, Arif. *The Origins of Chinese Communism*. New York: Oxford University Press, 1989.

–, and Chan Ming. *Schools into Fields and Factories: Anarchist, the Guomindang, and the National Labor University in Shanghai, 1927-1932*. Durham: Duke University Press, 1991.

Ding Fengzhu. "Zhenxing nüxue zhi gongxiao" [The efficacy of advocating women's education]. *Funü zazhi* 1, 7 (1915): 4-6.

Ding Zhipin, ed. *Zhongguo jin qishi nian lai jiaoyu jishi* [Events commemorating Chinese education during the last seventy years]. Shanghai: Shanghai shudian, 1933.

Dong Shou. "Xing nüxue yi" [On promoting women's education] (1902). *ZJXS* 2b: 570-72.

"*Dongfang zazhi* ji Beijing she nü yi xuetang" [*Eastern Miscellany* reports the establishment of a female medical school in Beijing], ZJXS 2b: 648.

"*Dongfang zazhi* ji Beiyang nü yi xuetang" [*Eastern Miscellany* reports Beijyang female medical school established in Tianjin], ZJXS 2b: 648.

"*Dongfang zazhi* ji Hangzhou she chanke nü xuetang" [*Eastern Miscellany* reports a nurse and midwife school built in Hangzhou], ZJXS 2b: 648.

Du Yuanzai. "Wu si yihou Zhongguo de pingmin jiaoyu yundong" [China's popular education movement after the May Fourth Movement]. *Pingmin jiaoyu* [Popular education] 68/69 (October 1923): 34-47.

Duan-fang, and Xiao-zeng. "Sufu Duan-fang Hufu Xiao-zeng zou chen Su sheng xuetang banli qingxing zhe" [Memorial from Governor Duan-fang and Assistant Governor Xiao-zeng of Jiangsu, reporting on educational affairs in the province]. *SJSJ:* 644-45.

"Duanqi shifan xuexiao jianzhang" [Regulations on short-term teachers' schools]. *ZJSJZ*: 825-26.

Duara, Prasenjit. *Culture, Power, and the State: Rural North China,* 1900-1942. New York: Stanford University Press, 1988.

Duiker, William. *Ts'ai Yuan-pei: Educator of Modern China*. University Park: Pennsylvania State University Press, 1977.

"E jiaoyu si zhi jiaoyu xingzheng" [Hubei Provincial Bureau of Education and its educational management]. *JYZZ* 5, 10 (1914): "Jishi [Events]," 86-87.

Eastman, Lloyd. *Abortive Revolution: China under Nationalist Rule, 1927-1937*. Cambridge: Harvard University Press, 1990 [1974].

Elman, Benjamin A., and Alexander Woodside, eds. *Education and Society in Late Imperial China, 1600-1900*. Berkeley: University of California Press, 1994.

–. "Political, Social, and Cultural Reproduction via Civil Service Examinations in Late Imperial China." *Journal of Asian Studies* 50, 1 (1991): 7-28.

–. *A Cultural History of Civil Examinations in Late Imperial China*. Berkeley: University of California Press, 2000.

Elvin, Mark, and G. William Skinner, eds. *The Chinese City between Two Worlds*. Stanford: Stanford University Press, 1974.

Esherick, Joseph. "Deconstructing the Construction of the Party-State: Gulin County in the Shaan-Gan-Ning Border Region." *China Quarterly* 140 (1994): 1052-79.

–. *Reform and Revolution in China: The 1911 Revolution in Hu'nan and Hubei*. Berkeley: University of California Press, 1976.

–, and Ye Wa. *Chinese Archives: An Introductory Guide*. Berkeley and Los Angeles: University of California Press, 1996.

Fan Kezheng. *Zhongguo shuyuan shi* [History of Chinese academies]. Taipei: Wenjin chubanshe [Wenjin press], 1995.

Fang Huan. "Beijing nüzi shifan xuexiao yilan" [Beijing Women's Normal School: A brochure (1918)].

Fang Yuyan. "Xuyan" [Preface]. In Cheng, *Xiangcun shifan jingyan tan*.

Feng Menglong. *Jing shi tong yan* [Popular tales to warn the world]. Shenyang: Chunfeng wenyi chubanshe [Chunfeng literature and art press], 1994 (reprint).

–. "Su zhixian luoshan zai he" [Magistrate Su is reunited with his family through a knitted shirt]. In *Jing shi tong yan*: 467-79.

–. "Zhao Chun'er chong wang Cao jia zhuang" [Zhao Chun'er revitalizes the Cao family]. In *Jing shi tong yan*: 124-53.

"Fengtian shengzhang bao huafen gaisheng shifan quyu dagai qingxing wen" [Fengtian governor report the situation on setting up the province's teachers' schools districts]. *JYGB*, yr. 5 (1918), 3, "Gongdu": 69.

Feuerwerker, Albert. *China's Early Industrialization: Sheng Hsuan-huai (1844-1916) and Mandarin Enterprise*. Cambridge: Harvard University Press, 1958.

Fogel, Joshua, and William Rowe, eds. *Perspectives on a Changing China*. Boulder, CO: Westview Press, 1979.

Franke, Wolfgang. *The Reform and Abolition of the Traditional Chinese Examination System*. East Asian Research Center, Cambridge, MA: Harvard University, 1963.

Friedman, Edward, Paul G. Pickowicz, and Mark Selden. *Chinese Village, Socialist State*. New Haven: Yale University Press, 1991.

"Fu Gaodeng shifan xuexiao xiaozhang huiyi yijue jiaoyu bu zixun an di yi xiang" [The decision made to consulting proposal number one from the Ministry of Education at the meeting of the presidents of national teachers' colleges]. *JYGB* yr. 5 (1918), 10, "Mingling": 4-5.

Fujian sheng jiaoyu ting, "Fujian sheng jiaoyu ting di san jie shuqi xuexiao jihua dagang" [Fujian's Bureau of Education outlines a teaching plan for the third year of summer school]. *JYBGB* 3 (1931), 15, "Fuzai" [Attachments]: 36-38.

Gao Guiqiao. "Letter to Mr. Tsai Yuan-pei, Minister of the Board of Education, June 1912." Chinese Historical Archives Number Two in Nanjing, file 1057-584.

Gao Qi, ed. *Zhongguo jiaoyu shi yanjiu: Xiandai fenjuan* [A study of the history of Chinese education: The modern period). Shanghai: Huadong shida chubanshe [East China Normal University Press], 1994.

Gao Shiliang, ed. *Mingdai jiaoyu lunzhu xuan* [Selected articles on education in the Ming Dynasty]. Beijing: Renmin jiaoyu chubanshe [People's Education Press], 1990.

– (compil.). *Yangwu yundong shiqi jiaoyu* [Education in China during the period of the Self-Strengthening Movement]. Shanghai: Shanghai Education Press, 1992. One of *ZJJZH* series.

Gao Xuehui. "Suzhou chengshi funü de gaikuang" [The general situation of city women in Suzhou]. *Nüzi yuekan* 2, 2 (1934): 1995-2010.

Gao Yuexin. "Pinghu de funü zhuangkuang" [Women's condition in Pinghu]. *Nüzi yuekan* 2, 7 (1934): 2579-83.

"Gaoji shifan xuexiao jianzhang" [Regulations on the advanced teachers' college]. *ZJSJZ*: 822-23.

Garrett, Shirley. *Social Reformers in Urban China: The Chinese YMCA, 1895-1926*. Cambridge: Harvard University Press, 1970.

"Ge sheng jiaoyu huizhi" [A collected news from provinces]. *DFZZ* 1, 1, 3, 5, 6, 11 (1904), and 2, 9 (1905).

"Ge sheng jiaoyu tingzhang xingming ji renzhi shijian" [Names and tenures of commissioners of provincial bureaus of education]. *JXJJT:* 138-40.

"Ge sheng jiaoyu zonghui lianhe hui jiyao" [Record of the United Association of Provincial Educational associations]. *JXJJT:* 184.

"Ge sheng putong xuetang tongji biao" [A statistical table of regular schools and students in every province]. In *Di yi ci jiaoyu tongji tubiao 1907:* 25-26.

"Ge sheng shiye xuetang xuesheng tongji biao" [A statistical table of vocational schools and students in every province]. In *Di yi ci jiaoyu tongji tubiao 1907:* 21-22.

"Ge sheng yixue" [Charitable schools in vaious provinces]. *YZSJ:* 314-19.

"Gedi nüxue de xingqi" [Rise of women's schools nationwide]. *ZJXS* 2b: 633-48.

Gellner, Ernest. *Nations and Nationalism*. New York: Cornell University Press, 1983.

"Gezhi shuyuan zhao shou shengtu qi" [Announcement of admissions to the Polytechnic College]. *YYSJ:* 744.

Gillin, Donald. *Warlord: Yen Hsi-shan in Shansi Province, 1911-1949*. Princeton: Princeton University Press, 1967.

Gilmartin, Christina, Gail Hershatter, Lisa Rofel, and Tyrene White, eds. *Engendering China: Women, Culture, and the State*. Cambridge MA: Harvard University Press, 1994.

Grimm, Tilemann. "Academies and Urban Systems in Kwangtung." In Skinner, *The City in Late Imperial China,* 475-98.

Gu Mei. *Xiangcun shifan gaiyao* [The essentials of village teachers' schools]. Shanghai: Shangwu yinshuguan, 1936.

Guan Peijun. "Guanyu jiaoshi jiaoyu gaige fazhan de shi ge guandian" [Ten points of view on the reform and development of teachers' education]. *Xinhua wen zhai* [Chinese news digests] 9 (2004): 102-5.

Guan Xiaohong. "Wan Qing Xue bu chengli qian de zhongyang jiaoyu xingzheng jigou yan'ge" [Changes in central educational administrative institutions prior to the Board of Education in the late Qing. *Jindai shi yanjiu* 4 (1998): 89-111.

–. *Wan Qing Xue bu yanjiu* [A study on the board of education in late Qing]. Guangzhou: Guangdong Education Press, 2000.

"Guangdong she nüxuetang zhi fengbo" [The dispute and conflict surrounding the establishment of women's schools in Guangdong]. *ZJXS:* 650-51.

"Guangdong shenli di yi zhongxuexiao nüsheng zhuangkuang" [Conditions of female students in the number one provincial middle school in Guangdong]. *ZJXS* 3-A: 520-21.

"Guangxi shengzhang zi song gai sheng ge shifan xuexiao qu nei suoshu xian fen biao qing he xingwen" [Guangxi governor submitting the province's teachers' schools, the districts, and the counties under their charge]. *JYGB*, yr. 5 (1918), 5, "Gongdu": 31-32.

Guangxu (Emperor). "Shangyu: shuyuan gai xuexiao" [Imperial order: Changing academies to new schools]. *WSJ*: 55-56.

–. "Yu ge sheng, fu, zhili zhou ji ge zhou, xian fen bie jiang shuyuan gai she da, zhong, xiao xuetang" [An imperial edict to each province, prefecture, directly subordinate district, district, and county on changing academies into colleges, middle schools, and elementary schools respectively, 1901]. *XZYB*: 5-6.

"Gesheng jiaoyu huizhi." *DFZZ* 3, 5 (1906): 23-28.

"Guangxu sanshi san nian quanguo nüzi xuetang tongji biao" [1907 statistics for women's schools nationwide]. *ZJXS* 2b: 649-50.

Han Yu. "Shi shuo" [On teachers]. In Wu and Wu, *Gu wen guan zhi* [A primer of classical Chinese texts], 333-35.

Hayford, Charles W. *To the People: James Yen and Village China*. New York: Columbia University Press, 1990.

Hayhoe, Ruth, ed. *China's Universities, 1895-1995: A Century of Cultural Conflict*. New York: Garland Publishing, 1996.

–. "Cultural Tradition and Educational Modernization: Lessons from the Republican Era." In Hayhoe, *Education and Modernization,* 47-72.

–. *Education and Modernization: The Chinese Experience*. Toronto: Ontario Institute for Studies in Education, 1992.

–, and Mariannne Bastid, eds. *China's Education and the Industrialized World: Studies in Cultural Transfer*. New York: M.E. Sharpe, 1987.

Hebei sheng li Daming shifan. "Biye xuesheng fuwu zhuangkuang tongji tu, 1934" [Chart of the positions taken by graduates, 1934]. In *Hebei shengli Daming shifan yi lan.*

–. "Xuesheng jiating zhiye tongji tu" [Chart of students' families' occupations]. In *Hebei shengli Daming shifan yi lan.* Hebei Provincial Archives, file 645-1-36.

–. *Hebei shengli Daming shifan yi lan* [General information on Hebei's Daming Provincial Teachers' School]. Hebei Provincial Archives, file 645-1-36.

"Henan jiaoyuting chengsong ge shifan xuexiao xianzai didian ji xuequ huafen qingxing qingzhe qing jian he wen" [Henan provincial bureau of education submitting the list of the locations of the provincial teachers' schools and the arrangement of the teachers' school district]. *JYGB*, yr. 5 (1918), 5, "Gongdu": 96-97.

"Henan Jiaoyuting chengsong ting shu zhiyuan lüli biao qing bei wen" [Henan Provincial bureau of education submitting the list of its staff and their CVs for examination and records]. *JYGB*, yr. 5 (1918), 3 "Gongdu": 106-8.

"Henan quan sheng jiaoyu zonghui zhangcheng, 1907" [Regulations of the He'nan provincial education association]. *JXJJT:* 310-12.

Henan sheng jiaoyu ting. "Henan jiaoyu ting zhengdun Henan jiaoyu jihua shu" [Henan's Bureau of Education on its plan to rectify Henan's educational system]. *JYGB* yr. 8 (1921), 8, "Baogao" [Reports]: 6-10.

–. *Henan difang jiaoyu shicha baogao* [Reports on local educational inspection in Henan], 1 (1934).

"Henan shengli xiangcun shifan xuexiao shuqi xiangcun jiaoyu jiangxi hui jianzhang" [A brief description of the summer program of the Henan provincial village teachers' schools]. *Xiangcun gaizao* 1, 6 (1932): 1-2.

"Henan xiaoxue jiaoyuan bake chao" [The wave of strikes by primary schoolteachers' in He'nan]. *JYZZ* 22, 2 (1930): 130.

Ho Ping-ti. *The Ladder of Success in Imperial China: Aspects of Social Mobility, 1368-1911*. New York: Columbia University Press, 1962.

–. *Studies on the Population of China, 1368-1953*. Cambridge, MA: Harvard University Press, 1959.

Hou Diao. "Jiangsu jiaoyu zhi tese" [Special characteristics of education in Jiangsu]. *Zhonghua jiaoyu jie* 5, 6 (1916): 1-8.

Hou Hongjian. "Lun nüzi zhiye jiaoyu zhi shiji" [On the reality of women's vocational education]. *Zhonghua jiaoyu jie* [*Chinese Educational Circle*] 6, 3 (1917): "Lun Shuo" [Discussion], 1-5.

Hsiao Kung-chuan. *Rural China: Imperial Control in the Nineteenth Century*. Seattle: University of Washington Press, 1960.

Hu Hanmin. "Jiesan Xiaozhuang shifan xuexiao de yuanyin he jingguo" [The causes and processes of the closure of the Xiaozhuang Teachers' School (on 14 April 1930)]. In *Xiaozhuang piban*: 129-35.

Hu Qing. *Shuyuan de shehui gongneng jiqi wenhua tese* [Social functions and cultural characteristics of academies]. Hankou: Hubei jiaoyu chubanshe, 1996.

Hu Shi. "Guoyu yundong de lishi" [History of the movement for a national language]. *JXJJT:* 387-89.

–. "Ji di ba jie quanguo jiaoyu hui lianhe hui taolun xin xuezhi de jingguo" [A recall on the discussion on the new school system at the eighth meeting of the National Federation of Educational Associations]. *XZYB:* 985-89.

Huang Jingsi. "Si nian lai Zhongguo zhi xiangcun jiaoyu – yi bufen shiliao" [China's rural education in the last four years – some documents]. *JYZZ* 23, 7 (1931): 85-100.

Huang, Philip. "The Jiangxi Period: An Introduction." In Huang, Bell, and Walker, *Chinese Communists and Rural Society,* 1-4.

–, Lynda Bell, and Kathy Walker, eds. *Chinese Communists and Rural Society, 1927-1934.* Berkeley: University of California Press, 1978.

Huang Xinxian. *Zhongguo jinxiandai nüzi jiaoyu* [Women's education in modern China]. Fuzhou: Fujian jiaoyu chubanshe, 1992.

Huang Yanpei. *Huang Yanpei jiaoyu lunzhu xuan* [Huang Yanpei: Selected essays on education]. Beijing: Renmin jiaoyu chubanshe, 1993.

–. "Yu Anting qingnian hezuoshe tan xiangcun shiye" [Discussing rural improvement with the Anting Youth Cooperative]. *Huang Yanpei jiaoyu lunzhu xuan*, 216.

Huangfu Shuyu, Song Jian'ge, and Gong Shoujing. *Zhongguo geming genjudi jiaoyu jishi: 1927.8-1949.9* [Educational events in Chinese revolutionary base areas, August 1927-September 1949]. Beijing: jiaoyu kexue chubanshe, 1989.

"Hubei caiche nuxue" [Banning women's schools in Hubei]. *ZJXS* 2b, 653.

"Hubei sheng di er shifan xuexiao benke (1-4 nianji) jiaoshu yong shu qi zhi bioa" [The textbooks use in Hubei Provincial Teacher's Schools Number Two for the courses (from 1-4 years)]. *JYGBI,* yr. 8 (1921), 7, "Jizai" [Records]: 28-33.

"Hunan nüxue feibi zhi yuanyin" [Reasons for closing the women's schools in Hunan]. *ZJXS* 2b*:* 652-53.

"Hunan nüxue zhi diaocha" [A study of Hunan women's schooling]. In Li Yuning and Zhang Yüfa, *Jindai Zhongguo nüquan yundong* 2, 1038.

Hunan sheng. "Hunan sheng li mingzhong jiaoyu guang jinxing gaikuang" [A survey of the Hunan provincial centre for common people's education]. *Xiangcun jianshe shiyan* 3: 547-50.

Hunan sheng zhengfu [Hunan provincial government]. "Hunan sheng zhengfu jin nian de jiaoyu sheshi" [The education programs carried out by the Hunan government in recent years]. *JYZZ* 25, 2 (1935): 5-16.

Igarashi Shoichi. "Shimatsu shin kyoiku seido hogaki ni okeru kyoshi yosei kikan no sette" [The establishment of teacher training institutions during the initial period of late Qing educational reforms]. In Taga, *Kindai Ajia kyoikushi kenkyu*, 1: 61-114.

Israel, John. *Student Nationalism in China, 1927-1937*. Stanford: Stanford University Press, 1966.

Jia Fengzhen. "Minguo si nian jiaoyu zhi huigu" [Education retrospectus in 1915]. *JYZZ* 8, 1 (1916): 22-25.

Jia Xuchun "Wang Zhe zai Laiyang xiang shi de geming huodong" [Wang Zhe's revolutionary activities in Laiyang Village Teachers' School]. *SQGZ* 7A: 99-115.

Jiang He. "Shengli Jiujiang xiangcun shifan shiyan qu yi ge ban yue zhi zhuangkuang" [The situation of experiment region operated by Jiujiang Provincial Village Teachers' School: After one month and a half]. *Xiang xiao jikan (chuan kan hao)* [Village schools quarterly] 1 (1st issue special) (October 1934): 63-83.

Jiang Hengyuan. "Zhonghua zhiye jiaoyu she zhi nongcun gongzuo" [The rural programs of the Chinese Vocational Education Association]. In Zhang and Xu, *Xiangcun jianshe shiyan* 1: 39-51.

Jiang Ping. "Nü jiaoyuan de bei ai" [The sorrow of the female teacher]. *Nüzi yuekan* 2 (1934), 2: 2001-2.

Jiang Weiqiao. "Ji Shanghai Aiguo nüxuexiao" [Jiang Weiqiao recalls Patriotic Women's School]. *ZJXS* 2b: 610-13.

–. "Lun nü xuexiao zhi jiashi shixi" [On the hands-on practice of household management in girls' schools]. *JYZZ* 9, 6 (1917): 105-11.

Jiangsu Huangdu xiangcun shifan xuexiao. *Yige xinxing de shifan xuexiao* [A newly emerged teachers' school]. Huangdu xiangcun shifan xuexiao print, 1936.

"Jiangsu jiaoyu hui zhangcheng, 1908" [Regulations of the Jiangsu education association]. *JXJJT*: 271-73.

"Jiangsu jiaoyu hui zhangcheng, 1912" [Regulation of the Jiangsu education association]. *JXJJT*: 281-82.

"Jiangsu jiaoyuting cheng zunling huafen shifan xuequ qing he bei wen" [Jiangsu Provincial Bureau of Education submitting a document showing the province having set up the teachers' school districts as instructed]. *JYGB*, yr. 5 (1918), 5, "Gongdu": 48-49.

Jiangsu sheng jiaoyu ting bian shen shi [Jiangsu Provincial Bureau of Education Records Office], *Jiangsu jiaoyu gailan, minguo er shi yi nian* [Almanac of education in Jiangsu, 1932], Vol. 1-2. Taipei: Zhuanji wenxue chubanshe, 1971(reprint).

Jiangsu sheng Tao Xingzhi jiaoyu sixiang yanjiu hui and Nanjing Xiaozhuang shifan Tao Xingzhi yanjiu shi, eds. "Tao Xingzhi xiansheng nianpu" [A chronicle of Tao Xingzhi's life]. In *Tao Xingzhi wenji*: 879-81.

"Jiangsu shifan xuetang xianxing zhangcheng" [The existing regulations of Jiangsu Teachers' School]. *SJSJ*: 647-59.

"Jiangsu xuewuchu pi nüxue bu neng yan nan jiaoxi" [The instructions of Jiangsu's education bureau regarding women's schools: Male teachers not to be hired, 1906]. *ZJXS* 2b: 653-54.

"Jiangxi jiaoyuting chengsong ge dao qu shifan xuexiao suoshu xian fen biao wen" [Jiangxi provincial bureau of education submitting the list of teachers' school districts and the counties under their charge]. *JYGB*, yr. 5 (1918), 4, "Gongdu": 94-95.

Jiaoshi zhi you [Teachers' friend].

Jiaoyu bu [Ministry of Education]. "Amended Regulations for Middle Schools" [*xiuzheng zhongxue xuexiao guicheng*]. *JYZZ* 25, 8 (1935): 128-34.

–. "Chou she geji gezhong shizi xunlian jiguan jihua (8): Zhong xiao xue jiao zhi yuan jinxiu banfa" [Plan for establishing various types of teacher training institutions: How to accomplish this at all levels of education]. *DECZJNJ* 3 (1930): 19-20.

–. "Dian ge sheng banfa putong jiaoyu zhanxing banfa" [Telegram from the Ministry of Education to every province regarding provisional solutions for regular education]. *XZYB*: 596-97.

–. "Fu gaodeng shifan xuexiao fu she guoyu jiangxi ke yijue an" [Attachment: Proposal that higher teachers' colleges establish national-language programs]. *JYGB*, yr. 5 (1918), 10, "Mingling" [Orders]: 7-8.

–. "Ge sheng gaodeng shifan yi lan biao" [Table for provincial higher teachers' colleges, 1915]. *JYGB*, yr. 3 (1916), 8, "Zhuanjian" [Special documents]: 13-15.
–. "Ge shengshi shifan xuexiao fudao difang jiaoyu banfa, 1939" [The method for directing local education by teachers' schools in each province and city, 1939], Nanjing: Second Historical Archives: file 10844-5.
–. "Shifan xuexiao fudao difang jiaoyu banfa, 1943" [The method for directing local education by teachers' schools, 1943], Nanjing: Second Historical Archives: file 10844-5.
–. "Ge shifan xuexiao ying ban guoyu jiangxi ke yi yu shizi wen" [All teachers' schools ought to establish national language programs in order to train more teachers]. *JYGB*, yr. 7 (1920), 8, "Gongdu" [Official files]: 2-3.
–. "Gongbu jiaoyu hui guicheng" [Regulations on educational associations]. *JXJJT:* 252-53.
–. "Gongbu jiaoyu ting zhanxing tiaoli" [Provisional regulations of the provincial bureau of education]. *JXJJT:* 132-33.
–. "Hebei sheng jiaoyu shicha baogao" [Report on educational inspection in Hebei]. In Jiaoyu bu, *Jiaoyu bu shicha yuan shicha ge sheng shi jiaoyu baogao huibian* [A collection of reports from the Ministry of Education's inspectors on educational conditions in each province and city].
–. "Jiaobu ling Jiangxi sheng zhengdun xuewu" [The Ministry of Education directs Jiangxi Province to rectify provincial education]. *JYZZ* 9, 10 (1917): 73-74.
–. "Jiaoyu bu fú Qian dujun zhi dianwen" [The Ministry of Education's telegram to reply to the Guizhou governor]. *JYZZ* 9 (1917), 11, "Jishi" [Events]: 81-82.
–. *Jiaoyu bu gongbao* [Official bulletins of the Ministry of Education, 1914-27].
–. "Jiaoyu bu gongbu shifan jiaoyu ling" [The Ministry of Education's order on teachers' schools (1912)]. *XZYB:* 660-61.
–. "Jiaoyu bu gongbu shifan xuexiao guicheng" [Regulations for teachers' schools issued by the Ministry of Education (1912)]. In *XZYB:* 676-90.
–. "Jiaoyu bu gongbu zhong xuexiao ling shishi guize" [Implementing regulations for middle schools issued by the Ministry of Education (September 1912)]. In *XZYB:* 669-76.
–. "Jiaoyu bu guoyu jiaoyu jinxing gaikuang" [The Ministry of Education's report on the implementation of the national language]. *JYGB*, yr. 9 (1922), 6, "Baogao": 12-19.
–. "Jiaoyu bu guiding jiaoyu tingzhang zhiquan" [The Ministry of Education spelled-out the powers of the commissioners of the bureaus of educations]. *JXJJT*: 133-34.
–. "Jiaoyu bu hezhun jiaoyu ting shu zuzhi dagang" [Ministry of Education approved organizational outline of provincial bureaus of educations]. *JXJJT:* 132-33.
–. *Jiaoyu bu shicha yuan shicha ge sheng shi jiaoyu baogao huibian* [A collection of reports from the Ministry of Education's inspectors on educational conditions in each province and city]. Ministry of Education print, 1933.
–. "Jiaoyu bu xunling, 4395 hao" [Ministry of Education, directive order no. 4395]. *JYBGB* 7, 15/16 (April 1935).
–. "Jiaoyu bu xunling, 6922 hao" [Ministry of Education, directive order no. 6922], *JYBGB* 7, 21/22 (June 1935).
–. "Jiaoyu bu xunling di 239 hao, minguo ba nian liu yue" [The Ministry of Education: Order no. 239, June 1919). *SJSJ*: 1036-42.
–. "Jiaoyu bu zhiling, 522 hao" [Ministry of Education: The instructional order no. 522]. *SJSJ:* 1035-36.
–. "Jiaoyu fagui" [Educational acts and regulations]. *DYCZJNJ* 2: 177.
–. "Jiaoyu fagui: Shencha dangyi jiaoshi zige tiaoli" [Educational acts and regulations: Criteria for examining qualifications for teaching party principles]. *JYZZ* 23, 2 (1931): 119.
–. "Jiaoyu quyu zhi huading" [Mapping educational districts]. *JYZZ* 8, 2 (February 1916): 11-12.
–. "Jiaoyu zongzhang ju cheng da zongtong ni zhan she gaodeng shifan liu xiao wei tongyi jiaoyu banfa" [A program to establish provisionally six advanced teachers' colleges, submitted by the minister of education as a means of unifying education (1914)]. *SJSJ:* 798-99.
–. "Jiaoyu zongzhang xingming ji renzhi shijian, 1912-22" [Names and time in office of the ministers of education, 1912-22]. *DYCZJNJ* 5: 205-6.

–. "Min yuan yilai quanguo zhongdeng jiaoyu ge lei xuexiao xiaoshu xuesheng ji jingfei shu bijiao biao" [A comparative table of the schools, students, and finances of secondary education since 1912]. *DYCZJNJ* 4: 133.
–. "Minguo liu nian quanguo shifan xuexiao yi lan biao" [Table of teachers' schools nationwide, 1917]. Chinese Historical Archives Number Two in Nanjing, file 1057-68.
–. "Pi nüzi shifan xuexiao: Nüzi gaodeng shifan wei she yiqian zhanzhun gaixiao fushe zhuanxiu ke" [Approval of the request of the (Beijing) Women's Teachers' School to establish a temporary college-level program before the establishment of a women's higher teachers' college]. *JYGB*, yr. 2 (1914), 2, "Gongdu": 57-58.
–. "Putong jiaoyu zhanxing banfa" [Provisional regulations on regular education, January 1912]. *XZYB*: 596-97.
–. "Quanguo gaodeng shifan xuexiao xiaozhang huiyi yijue an: Gaodeng shifan xuexiao ruhe zhaokao xuesheng ge sheng xuansong ming'e ying ruhe fenpei" [Proposals made at the meeting of presidents of national higher teachers' colleges: Admissions policies of teachers' colleges and how each province should draw up quotas]. *SJSJ:* 835-36.
–. "Quanguo jiaoyu jihua shu" [Plan for national education]. *SJSJ*: 813-14.
–. "Shicha di qi qu xuewu zong baogao" [Report on the inspection of educational district number seven]. *JYGB*, yr. 2 (1914), 6, "Baogao": 8-26.
–. "Shifan xuexiao fa" [Law regarding teachers' schools]. *ZJSJZ:* 324-26.
–. "Shifan xuexiao guicheng" [Regulations regarding teachers' schools]. *ZJSJZ:* 326-48.
–. "Wei tong ling xianzhi sheli putong zhongxue zengshe zhiye xuexiao zai putong zhongxue tian she zhiye ke huo zhiye kemu, xianli chuzhong ying fushe huo gai she xiangcun shifan ji zhiye ke you" [Summary of instruction for limiting the establishment of regular middle schools, increasing vocational courses and programs in regular middle schools, and establishing village teacher training and vocational programs at county lower middle schools or converting them into village teachers' schools]. *JYBGB* (1931): 3, 13, "Mingling": 7-10.
–. *Xiangcun shifan xuexiao kecheng biaozhun* [Standard curricula for village teachers' schools]. Shanghai: Zhonghua shuju, 1935.
–. "Xiaoxue jiaoyuan jianding zhanxing guichen" [Provisional regulations on examining primary schoolteachers (21 May 1934)]. *ZJSJZ:* 376-79;
–. "Xiuding jiaoyu hui guicheng" [Revised regulations on educational associations]. *JXJJT:* 253-55.
–. "Xuexiao xitong gaige ling di 23 hao, 1922 nian 11 yue 1 ri" [The order for reforming school system, 1 November 1922]. *ZJSJZ* 2: 264-68.
–. "Xunling di 235 hao" [Directive order no. 235]. *JYGB*, yr. 5 (1918), 10, "Mingling": 5-6.
–. "Xunling di 255 hao" [Directive order no. 255]. *JYGB*, yr. 5 (1918), 11, "Mingling": 3-5.
–. "Zhengli jiaoyu fang'an" [Plan for educational rectification (1914)]. *XZYB:* 743.
–. "Zhiling 357 hao" [Instructive order no. 357]. *JYGB,* yr. 6 (1919), 5, "Mingling": 19-21.
–. "Zhiling Chendu gaodeng shifan xuexiao: Jingshi xian she you zhuyin zimu chuanxisuo gai xiao ke su pai yuan xuexi wen" [A directive to Chengdu Higher Teachers' College: Immediately send people to the short-term school in Beijing to learn the *zhuyin* system]. *JYGB,* yr. 5 (1918), 14: "Gongdu": 21-22.
–. "Zhiling di 357 hao" [Instructive order no. 357], *JYGB*, yr. 6 (1919), 5, "Mingling": 17-19.
–. "Zhiling Heilongjian jiaoyu ting shifan xuequ zhan nan huafen suo ding xiaozhang shicha ge jie ying zhaozhun wen" [An instructive document approving its plan that when Heilongjian has a difficulty establishing their teachers' schools district, the principals (of teachers' schools) would inspect (local schools)]. *JYGB*, yr. 5 (1918), 6, "Gongdu": 45-46.
–. "Zhongxue ji shifan xuexiao jiaoyuan jianding zhanxing guicheng" [Provisional regulations on examining teachers of middle schools and teachers' schools (21 May 1934)]. *ZJSJZ:* 371-74.
–. "Zi Fujian shengzhang gai sheng di er shifan xuexiao kecheng biao ying zhun bei an wen" [Notice to Fujian governor: the curriculum of Fujian Provincial Teachers' School Number Two has been approved]. *JYBG,* yr. 5 (1918), 8, "Gongdu": 5-8.
–. "Zi ge sheng qu guomin xuexiao yi er nianji zi ben nian qiuji qi xian gai guowen wei yutiwen yi wei guoyu jiaoyu zhi yubei wen" [Instruction to provinces and districts to

change the Chinese literature class of the first and second grades of citizens' schools to a class in vernacular literature beginning in the fall in order to prepare for teaching the national language]. *JYGB*, yr. 7 (1920), 2, "Gongdu": 12.

–. "Zi ge sheng qu ying shefa chouban nüzi zhongxuexiao wen" [Consultative document advising all provinces and regions to establish women's middle schools]. *JYGB*, yr. 6 (1919), 7, "Gongdu": 21.

–. "Zi ge sheng qu zi ding bennian xia xueqi qi fan shifan xuexiao ji gaodeng shifan xuexiao jun ying zhuo jian guowen zhongdian jia shou guoyu qing chazhao banli wen" [Recommendation to every province and district: All teachers' schools and higher teachers' colleges ought to reduce the time devoted to classical Chinese in order to add (a course devoted to] the national language next semester)]. *JYGB*, yr. 8 (1921), 4, "Gongdu": 17.

–. "Zi Hunan shengzhang Pingjiang sili Qiming nüxiao cheng ni biangeng xuenian kaishi yibian xu ban shifan benke shi shu tebie zhun zhaoban wen" [Document to Hunan government in approval of the special request of the private Qiming Women's School to change its semester schedule in order to continue its teacher training program]. *JYGB*, yr. 3 (1916), 12, "Gongdu": 32-33.

–. "Zi Jingzhaoyin ge sheng xun'anshi ge dutong Zhili zengshe shifan er bu ying zhuoliang qingxing fangzhao banli wen" [Consultative document suggesting that governors of the capital region and the provinces consider following Zhili's example in establishing secondary departments in teachers' schools]. *SJSJ:* 800.

–. "Zi Sichuan xunanshi kaiban ji gaizu zhongxue shifan deng xiao ying zhun beian wen" [Approval for Sichuan governor's plan to establish and reorganize provincial middle schools and teachers' schools]. *JYGB*, yr. 1 (1914), 2, "Gongdu": 27-28.

"Jiaoyu gangyao" [Educational program]. *JYZZ* 7, 9-10 (1915), "Zhuanjian" [Special document]: 9-14, 15-20.

"Jiaoyu jie dang yu zhi manyan" [The spreading terror: Communists in educational circles arrested]. *JYZZ* 22, 11 (1930): 126-27.

"Jiaoyu jie dang yu zhi yu bo" [A last wave: Communists in educational circles arrested]. *JYZZ* 23, 2, 3 (1931): 117, 128-29.

"Jiaoyu jie xiaoxi: Beijing nüzi shifan daxue" [Education news: Beijing Women's Normal University). *JYZZ* 17, 3 (1925): 9-10.

"Jiaoyu jie xiaoxi: Beijing nüzi shifan daxue zhi jiesan yu tingban" [Education news: The end of Beijing Women's Normal University]. *JYZZ* 17, 9 (1925): 1-3.

"Jiaoyu jie xiaoxi: Di shiyi jie quan guo sheng jiaoyu hui lianhe hui zhi genggai" [Education news: A summary of the eleventh conference of the National Federation of Educational Associations]. *JYZZ* 17, 12 (1925): 4-8.

"Jiaoyu jie xiaoxi: Dongda yu nüshida fengchao zhi weisheng" [Education news: The epilogue to the student protests at Southeast University and Beijing Women's Normal University]. *JYZZ* 17, 10 (1925): 10.

"Jiaoyu jie xiaoxi: Guomin zhengfu xia zhi E sheng jiaoyu" [Education news: Education in Hubei under the Nationalist government]. *JYZZ* 18, 12 (1926): 3-4.

"Jiaoyu jie xiaoxi: Ji dai jiejue zhi qingnian wenti" [Education news: The problems of young people in desperate need of resolution]. *JYZZ* 22, 9 (1930): 119.

"Jiaoyu jie xiaoxi: Jiangsu ba shi qu xiaoxue jiaoyu yanjiuhui jiyao" [Education news: On the Association for Research on Primary Education under the Jiangsu Number Eight Teachers' School District]. *JYZZ* 17, 2 (1925): 15-16.

"Jiaoyu jie xiaoxi: Jiangnan jiaoyu zhi fandong de qingxiang" [Education news: reactionary trend of education in Jiangnan]. *JYZZ* 18, 10 (1926): 3-4.

"Jiaoyu jie xiaoxi: Jiangsu biyesheng jiuye zhidao weiyuanhui zhi chengli" [Education news: The establishment of the career guidance committee for the graduates of middle schools in Jiangsu]. *JYZZ* 18, 10 (1926): 4-5.

"Jiaoyu jie xiaoxi: Jiaobu duiyu nüzi jiaoyu zhi tongling" [Education news: Instructions about female education from the Ministry of Education]. *JYZZ* 17, 11 (1925): 6.

"Jiaoyu jie xiaoxi: Jiaobu zuijin zhi liang tongling" [Educational news: Two recent directives from the Ministry of Education]. *JYZZ* 23, 9 (1931): 137.

"Jiaoyu jie xiaoxi: Jiaoyu dangju fugu sixiang zhi shixian" [Education news: The educational authorities carry a policy of restoring old ideology]. *JYZZ* 17, 12 (1925): 1-3.

"Jiaoyu jie xiaoxi: Juban jiaqi guoyu jiangxi hui" [Education news: Vacation national-language training program opens]. *Zhonghua jiaoyu jie* 8, 2 (1919): 4.

"Jiaoyu jie xiaoxi: Shanxi nannü tongxue qingyuan zhi jieguo" [Education news: The result of a petition for coeducation in Shanxi]. *JYZZ* 17, 11 (1925): 6.

"Jiaoyu jie xiaoxi: Zhonghua zhiye she ben jie nianhui zhi tiyian" [Educational news: Proposals from the 1925 annual conference of the Chinese Vocational Society]. *JYZZ* 17, 7 (1925): 10-11.

"Jiaoyu quyu zhi huading" [Mapping educational districts]. *JYZZ* 8, 2 (1916), "Jishi," 11-12.

Jin Haiguan. "Lun woguo zhi xiangcun shifan" [On our country's rural teachers' schools]. In Sun and Dai, *Xiaozhuang piban* [Critique of Xiaozhuang], 139-58.

Jin Zhiwen. "Xiangshi nongye jiaoxue wenti zhi jiantao" [A reexamination of the pedagogy of agricultural courses in village teachers' schools]. *Zhonghua jiaoyu jie* 24, 3 (1936): 25-31.

Jing Hengyi. "Gaige shifan jiaoyu de yijian" [My thoughts on reforming teachers' education]. *Jiaoyu chao* [Educational tide] 1, 4 (1919): 53-63.

Johnson, Chalmers. *Peasant Nationalism and Communist Power*. Stanford: Stanford University Press, 1962.

Ju Xingui (compil.). *Yapian zhanzheng shiqi jiaoyu* [Chinese education prior to and during the period of the opium war]. Shanghai Education Press, 1990. One of *ZJJZH* series.

–, and Tang Liangyan (compil.). *Xuezhi yanbian* [Evolution of the school system]. Shanghai Education Press, 1991. One of *ZJJZH* series.

–, Tong Fuyong, and Zhang Shouzhi (compil.). *Shiye jiaoyu, shifan jiaoyu* [Vocational education and teacher training]. Shanghai: Shanghai Education Press, 1994. One of *ZJJZH* series.

"Juban xiaoxue jiaoshoufa jiangxi hui ji xiaoxue jiaoyuan shuqi jiangxi hui" [Organizing training meetings on the primary education pedagogy and summer training classes for primary schoolteachers]. *JXJJT*: 289.

Judge, Joan. "Meng Mu Meets the Modern: Female Exemplars in Early-Twentieth-Century Textbooks for Girls and Women." In *Jindai Zhongguo funü shi yanjiu* [Studies in modern Chinese women's history] 8: 133-77. Taipei: Zhongyang yanjiu yuan jindai shi yanjiusuo, 2000.

–. "Talent, Virtue, and the Nation: Chinese Nationalism and Female Subjectivities in the Early Twentieth Century," *American Historical Review* 106, 2 (2001): 756-803.

Kang Youwei. "Qing chi ge sheng gai shuyuan yinci wei xuetang zhe" [A memorial appealing to the throne to order new schools established in each province where formerly there were academies and improper temples]. *WSJ*: 52-55.

Kangxi (Emperor). "Kangxi sishi yi nian yu chi shizi wen" [Imperial edict on teaching students in year 41 of the Kangxi regime]. *YZSJ*: 120.

Keating, Pauline. "The Yan'an Way of Co-operation." *China Quarterly* 140 (1994): 1025-51.

Keenan, Barry. *The Dewey Experiment in China: Educational Reform and Political Power in the Early Republic*. Cambridge: Harvard University Press, 1977.

–. "Educational Reform and Politics in Early Republican China." *Journal of Asian Studies* 33, 2 (1974): 225-37.

– *Imperial China's Last Classical Academies: Social Change in the Lower Yangzi, 1864-1911*. Berkeley: Institute of East Asian Studies, University of California, Berkeley, 1994.

–. "The Lung-men Academy in Shanghai and the Expansion of Kiangsu's Educated Elite, 1865-1911." In Elman and Woodside, *Education and Society in Late Imperial China*, 493-524.

Ko, Dorothy. "Pursuing Talent and Virtue: Education and Women's Culture in Seventeenth- and Eighteenth-Century China." *Late Imperial China* 13, 1 (1992): 9-39.

–. *Teachers of the Inner Chambers: Women and Culture in Seventeenth-Century China*. Stanford: Stanford University Press, 1994.

Kobayashi Yoshifuni. "Chugoku kindai kyoinshi kenkyu josetsu: 1920 nendai no Chugoku ni okeru shoto kyoin no kumiai undo o megutte" [Prefatory remarks on the history of

China's modern teachers: Primary schoolteachers and their organizations in 1920s China]. *Toyoshi kenkyu* [Studies of East Asian history] 44, 4 (1986): 128-61.

Kuhn, Philip. "Local Self-Government under the Republic: Problems of Control, Autonomy, and Mobilization." In Wakeman and Grant, *Conflict and Control In Late Imperial China*, 257-99.

–. "T'ao Hsing-chih, 1981-1946, An Educational Reformer." *Harvard Papers on China* 13 (1959): 163-95.

Lacy, Walter N. *A Hundred Years of China Methodism*. New York: Abingdon-Cokesbury Press, 1948.

Lee, Leo Ou-fan. *The Romantic Generation of Modern Chinese Writers*, Cambridge, MA: Harvard University Press, 1973.

Lee, Thomas. "The Discovery of Childhood: Childhood Education in Sung China (960-1279)." In Paul, *Kultur: Begrif und Wort in China und Japan*, 159-89.

Lei Liangbo, Chen Yangfeng, and Xiong Xianjun. *Zhongguo nüzi jiaoyu shi* [A history of Chinese women's education]. Wuhan: Wuhan chubanshe [Wuhan press], 1993.

Leung, Angela. "Elementary Education in the Lower Yangtze Region in the Seventeenth and Eighteenth Centuries." In Elman and Woodside, *Education and Society in Late Imperial China*, 381-416.

Levine, Steven. *Anvil of Victory: The Communist Revolution in Manchuria, 1945-1948*. New York: Columbia University Press, 1987.

Lewis, Ida Belle. *The Education of Girls in China*. New York: Teachers' College, Columbia University, 1919.

Li Chaoying. *Zhongguo shifan jiaoyu lun* [On Chinese teachers' education]. Shanghai: Shangwu yinshuguan [Commercial press], 1939.

Li Chucai. *Po Xiao* [To the dawn]. Shanghai: Ertong shuju, 1932.

–. "Xiaoxue jiaoshi de shenghuo wenti" [The livelihood of elementary school teachers]. *Zhonghua jiaoyu jie* 17, 6 (1928): 1-12.

Li Dazhao. *Li Dazhao xuanji* [Selected works of Li Dazhao]. Beijing: Beijing renmin chubanshe, 1962.

–. "Qingnian yu nongcun" [Youth and rural villages]. In *Li Dazhao xuanji*: 146-50.

Li Huaxing. *Minguo jiaoyu shi* [A history of education in Republican China]. Shanghai: Shanghai jiaoyu chubanshe, 1997.

Li Jianxun. "Zong lun" [General discussion]. In "Biye huikao wenti yanjiu zhuanhao" [A special issue on the comprehensive examinations]. *JYZZ* 26, 4 (1936): 93-105.

"Li jie huiyi yijue an" [NFEA propositions for all annual meetings]. *JXJJT*: 200-35.

Li Jinxi. *Guoyu yundong shigang* [Outline history of the movement for a national language]. Shanghai: Shangwu yinshuguan, 1934 [Shanghai: Shanghai shudian 1990 (reprint): 1-117].

Li, Lincoln. *Student Nationalism in China, 1924-1949*. New York: State University of New York, 1994.

Li Maoru. "Qin Hezhen: Ziyang xiangshi zou chu de geming jia" [Qin Hezhen: A revolutionary from the Ziyang Village Teachers' School]. *SQGZ* 7B: 98-108.

Li Nai. "Zhongguo nüzi jiaoyu de shibai jiqi bujiu" [The failure of Chinese women's education and its remedy]. *Nüzi yuekan* [Women's monthly] 2, 1 (1934): 1758-61.

Li Rui'an. "Cong 1931 nian gai wei xiangshi hou wu nian lai biyesheng tongji" [Statistics on the graduates for the five years since the school became a village teachers' school in 1931]. *Xiangcun gaizao* 5, 11/12 (1936): 2-35.

–. "Xiangcun jiaoyu fudao zhi xingzheng zuzhi wenti" [Issues of administration and organization in rural education]. *Xiangcun jiaoyu* [Rural education] 29 (1935): 1-13.

Li Shuren. "Li Shuren ji Fuzhou Yuying nüzi xuexiao [Li Shuren's journal from Yuying Girls' School in Fuzhou]." *ZJXS* 4: 271-74.

Li Xin. "Shifan yuanxiao xi shou shengyuan" [Teachers' colleges pleased to have more applicants]. *Beijing qingnian bao* [Beijing youth daily], 11 September 1996, 1.

Li Xizhen. "Ti ji hao han zhi shenghuo" [A life of tears thanks to hunger and cold]. *Zhonghua jiaoyu jie* 20, 8 (1933): 13-27.

Li Youzhi, Li Chunnian, Liu Chuanxin, and Ge Jiaxun (compil.). *Zhongguo jin xiandai shifan jiaoyu shi ziliao* [The source materials related to the history of teachers' education in modern and contemporary China]. 4 vols. Publisher unknown, 1983.

–. *Zhongwai shifan jiaoyu cidian* [The compendium of teachers' education in China and the world]. Beijing: China Broadcasting and Television Press, 1994.

Li Yuning, and Zhang Yüfa. *Jindai Zhongguo nüquan yundong shiliao, 1842-1911* [Documents on the feminist movement in modern China, 1842-1911]. Taipei: Zhuanji wenxue chubanshe, 1975.

Li Zhengfu. "Nüzi jiaoyu zhi pingmin hua" [Popularization of female education]. *Nüzi yuekan* 2, 1 (1934): 1750-54.

Li Zhenyun. "Shengli Baiquan xiangcun shifan xuexiao gongzuo baogao" [Working report on Baiquan Provincial Village Teachers' School]. *Xiangcun jianshe shiyan* 3: 387-92.

"Liancun jinyan weiyuanhui zhangcheng" [Regulations of the united villages committee of anti-opium smoking]. *Xiang jiao cong xun* 2, 22 (1928): 4.

"Liancun ziweituan di yi hao bugao" [The proclamation of the united villages self-defence team, number one]. *Xiang jiao cong xun* 2, 22 (1928): 4.

Liang Fusheng. "Nüzi jiaoyu zhi xunlian hua" [Women's education moving towards training skills]. *Nüzi yuekan* 2, 1 (1934): 1748-50.

Liang Guang youji shifan xuetang. "Ben xiao xianzai xuesheng xingming biao" [List of enrolled students at this school]. In *Liang Guang youji shifan xuetang yi lan.*

–. *Liang Guang youji shifan xuetang yi lan* [Brochure for Liang Guang Advanced Teachers' College (1910)]. Shanghai Metropolitan Archives, file Q0-12/1086.

–. "Liang Guang youji shifan xuetang zhangcheng" [The regulations for Liang Guang Advanced Teachers' College]. In *Liang Guang youji shifan xuetang yi lan.*

–. "Ticao zhuanxiuke biyesheng" [Graduates of the physical education specialty program]. In *Liang Guang youji shifan xuetang yi lan.*

–. "Xuetang guanliyuan lianxisuo biyesheng" [List of graduates from the school administrator training program]. In *Liang Guang youji shifan xuetang yi lan.*

–. "Yan'ge lue" [A brief history of Liang Guang Advanced Teachers' College]. In *Liang Guang youji shifan xuetang yi lan.*

"Liang Hu shifan xuetang zhiyuan diaocha biao" [A comprehensive survey of Liang Hu Teachers' School faculty]. *SJSJ:* 685-93.

"Liang Jiang shifan jiao zhi yuan lüli biao ji Ri ji jiaoyuan lüli biao, 1909" [Table on students at Liang Jiang Teachers' College and CVs of faculty and Japanese teachers at Liang Jiang Teachers' College]. *SJSJ:* 720-25.

Liang Qichao. "Bianfa tongyi: Xuexiao zong lun" [A general proposal for reform]. In *Yinbingshi he ji: wenji* [Collected works from drinking ice studio: article collections]. Shanghai: Zhongua shuju, 1932, 1: 1-64.

–. "Chuang she nüxuetang qi" [An announcement on the establishment of women's schools]. In *Yinbingshi wenji* 2: 19-20.

–. "Ji Jiangxi Kang nüshi [On Ms. Kang from Jiangxi]. In *Yinbingshi heji-wenji* 1: 119-20.

–. *Yinbingshi he ji* [Collected works from drinking ice studio]. Shanghai: Zhonghua shuju [Zhonghua press], 1932.

Liang Shuming. "Baoqian, tongku, yijian you xingwei de shi" [Regret, pain, and an interesting thing]. *Liang Shuming jiaoyu lunzhu xuan*: 16-27.

–. "Danmai de jiaoyu yu women de jiaoyu" [Education in Denmark and China]. *Liang Shuming jiaoyu lunzhu xuan*: 56-84.

–. *Liang Shuming jiaoyu lunzhu xuan* [Liang Shuming: Selected essays on education]. Beijing: Beijing renmin chubanshe, 1994.

–. "Shandong xiangcun jianshe yanjiu yuan gongzuo baogao" [Report on the work of the Shandong Rural Reconstruction Institute]. In Zhang and Xu, *Xiangcun jianshe shiyan,* 1:31-38.

–. "Shandong xiangcun jianshe yanjiu yuan ji Zouping shiyan xian gongzuo baogao" [Work report on the Shandong Rural Reconstruction Institute and the Zouping Experimental County]. In Zhang and Xu *Xiangcun jianshe shiyan,* 1:177-78.

Liang Zhangju. *Tui'an suibi* [Notes from the retreat]. *YZSJ*: 160.

Liao, T'ai-ch'u. "Rural Education in Transition: A Study of the Old-Fashioned Chinese Schools [Szu Shu] in Shantung and Szechuan." *Yanjing Journal of Social Studies* 4, 2 (1949): 19-67.

Lin Zhongda. "Xiangcun jiaoyu neng gaizao Zhongguo xiangcun shehui ma?" [Can rural education reform rural Chinese society?]. *Zhonghua jiaoyu jie* 23, 9 (1936): 1-8.

Linden, Allen. "Politics and Education in Nationalist China: The Case of the University Council, 1927-1928." *Journal of Asian Studies*, 27, 4 (1968): 763-76.

Ling Xiao. "Reading and Revolution: The Political Economy of Youth Anxiety in the Republican Era." Paper presented at the Association for Asian Studies West Conference. Long Beach, California, October 2000.

Liu Boji. *Guangdong shuyuan zhidu yange* [History of the academy system in Guangdong]. Shanghai: Commercial Press, 1939.

Liu Dapeng. *Tuixiang zhai riji* [Diary from a retreat]. Taiyuan: Shanxi renmin chubanshe [Shanxi people's press], 1990.

Liu Guanquan. "Shandong shifan yuanxiao re qilai le" [Teachers' colleges in Shandong have become hot]. *Renmin ribao* [People's daily], 13 August 1996.

Liu Laiquan, Guan Peijun, and Lan Shibin. "Wo guo jiaoshi gongzi daiyu de lishi kaocha, 1909-1949" [A historical examination of teachers' salary and conditions in China, 1909-1949]. *Jiaoyu yanjiu* [Studies in education] 4 (1993): 30-35.

Liu, Lydia. *Translingual Practice: Literature, National Culture, and Translated Modernity – China, 1900-1937*. Stanford: Stanford University Press, 1995.

Liu Sheng. "Fakanci er" [Foreword number two]. *Funü zazhi* 1, 1 (1915): 2-4.

Liu Wenxiu. *Zhongguo shifan jiaoyu jianshi* [A brief history of Chinese teachers' education]. Beijing: Remin jiaoyu chubanshe [People's Education Press], 1985.

Liu Xiangguang. "Zhongguo jinshi difang jiaoyu de fazhan: Huizhou wenren, shushi yu chuji jiaoyu, 1100-1800" [The development of local education in early modern China: Literati, schoolteachers, and elementary education in Huizhou, 1100-1800]. *Jindai shi yanjiusuo jikan* 28 (1997): 1-45.

Liu Xianzeng, and Liu Duanfen (chief editors). *Shan-Gan-Ning bianqu jiaoyu shi* [History of education in the Shaanxi-Gansu-Ningxia Board Region]. Xi'an: Shaanxi remin chubanshe, 1994.

Liu Xun. "Xuewu yaoduan zhe" [A memorial on the important issues related to education]. *ZJXS* 2b: 587-88.

Liu Zhenjia. "Wan Li: Qing Er shi zhi qizhi, xian geming zhi da bo" [Wan Li: Bearing the flag of the second provincial teachers' school, advocating a great wave of revolution]. *SQGZ* 7A: 1-12.

Liu Ziyang. *Qingdai difang guan zhi kao* [A study of the Qing local bureaucratic system]. Beijing: Zijincheng chubanshe, 1988.

Lü Fangshang. *Cong xuesheng yundong dao yundong xuesheng: minguo ba nian zhi shiba nian* [From student movement to mobilizing students, 1919-29]. Taibei: Institute of Modern History, Academic Sinica, 1994.

Lü, Miawfen. "Practice as Knowledge: Yang-ming Learning and *Chiang-hui* in Sixteenth-Century China." PhD diss., University of California at Los Angeles, 1997.

Lu Jingshan. "Gei xiangcun xiaoxue jiaoshi de xin" [A letter to village elementary school teachers]. *Xiangjiao congxun* 2, 17 (1928): 2-4.

Lu Xun. "Fen, guafu zhuyi" [Graves and widowhood]. In *Lu Xun quanji* 1: 266.

–. *Lu Xun quanji* [Complete works of Lu Xun]. Beijing: Renmin wenxue chubanshe, 1981.

Lu Yin. *Lu Yin zizhuan* [Autobiography of Lu Yin]. Shanghai: Di yi chubanshe, 1934.

"Lun nüxue yi zhuzhong deyu" [Women's education should stress moral education]. *ZJXS* 2b (1906): 584-87.

Luo Suwen. *Nüxing yu jindai Zhongguo shehui* [Woman and modern Chinese society]. Shanghai: Shanghai renmin chubanshe, 1996.

Luo Tingguang. *Shifan jiaoyu xin lun* [A new perspective on teachers' education]. Shanghai: Nanjing shudian [Nanjing bookstore], 1933.

Luo Zhenyu. "Jiangsu shifan xuetang ji" [Memoir of Jiangsu Teachers' School]. *SJSJ:* 645.

Ma Tai-loi. "The Local Education Officials of Ming China, 1368-1644." *Oriens Extremes* 22, 1 (1975): 11-27.

McElroy, Sarah Coles. "Forging A New Role for Women: Zhili First Women's Normal School and the Growth of Women's Education in China, 1901-2." In Peterson, Hayoe, and Lu, *Education, Culture, and Identity in Twentieth-Century China*, 384-74.

Mann, Susan. "The Education of Daughters in the Mid-Ch'ing Period." In Elman and Woodside, *Education and Society in Late Imperial China*, 19-49.

–. "'Fuxue' [Women's Learning] by Zhang Xuecheng (1738-1801): China's First History of Women's Culture." *Late Imperial China* 13, 1 (1992): 40-62.

–. "Learned Women in the Eighteenth Century." In Gilmartin, Hershatter, Rofel, and White, *Engendering China*, 27-46.

–. *Precious Records: Women in China's Long Eighteenth Century*. Stanford: Stanford University Press, 1997.

Mao Zedong. "Hunan nongmin yundong kaocha baogao" [Report on an investigation of the Hunan peasant movement]. In *Mao Zedong xuanji* 1: 12-44.

–. *Mao Zedong xuanji* [Selected works of Mao Zedong]. Beijing: Renmin chubanshe, 1968.

Margadant, Jo Burr. *Madame le Professeur: Women Educators in the Third Republic*. Princeton: Princeton University Press, 1990.

Meng Guofang. "Meng Guofang ji Deng Chunlan ru Beida de jingguo" [Meng Guofang's recollection of Deng Chunlan's experience in entering Beijing University]. *ZJXS* 3b: 82-87.

Meskill, John. *Academies in Ming China: A Historical Essay*. Tucson: University of Arizona Press, 1982.

Min Keqin. "Zhongyang daxue di yi shiyan minzhong xuexiao baogao shu" [Report on Central University's Experimental School for Commoners Number One]. *Xiangjiao congxun* 2, 10 (1928): 1-2.

Miu Zheng. "Women de shiyan qu" [Our experimental region]. *Xiang xiao jikan* 1, 4 (1935): 55-60.

Miyazaki Ichisada. *China's Examination Hell: The Civil Service Examinations of Imperial China*. Trans. Conrad Shirokauer. New Haven: Yale University Press, 1981.

"Nan bei jiaoshi suo xin yundong zhi fen qi" [The rise of a movement of teachers in the south and the north demanding payment of back salaries]. *JYZZ* 22, 10 (1930): 125-26.

"Ni qing jiaoyu bu tuixing guoyu jiaoyu banfa wu tiao" [Five measures suggested to the Ministry of Education for promoting the national language]. *JYGB* yr. 6 (1919), 10.

"Nü shifan hua si wei guan" [The women's normal school changed from private to government-run]. In Li and Chang, *Jindai Zhongguo nüquan yundong shiliao* 2, 1231.

"Nü xuetang zhangcheng" [Women's school regulations, 1897]. *WSJ*: 188-92.

"Nüxue jishi: Bokuan xingxue" [News on female schooling: (Provincial authorities) allocated fund for girls' school]. In Li and Zhang, *Jindai Zhongguo nüquan yundong* 2, 1130.

Okubo Hideko. *Min Shin jidai shoin no kenkyu* [A study of academies during the Ming and Qing]. Tokyo: Kokusho kankokai, 1976.

Ono Kazuko. *Chinese Women in a Century of Revolution: 1850-1950*. Stanford: Stanford University Press, 1989.

Orb, Richard. "Chili Academies and Other Schools in the Late Ch'ing: An Institutional Survey." In Cohen and Schrecker, *Reform in Nineteenth-Century China*, 231-40.

Peake, Cyrus. *Nationalism and Education in Modern China*. New York: Howard Fertig, 1932.

Pei Zhi. "Ben xiao er shi er niandu ruxue shiyan de yanjiu" [A study of entrance examinations to this school in 1933]. *Xiancun gaizao xunkan* [Rural reform tri-monthly] 2, 13/14 (1933): 3-10.

Pepper, Suzanne. "The Political Odyssey of an Intellectual Construct: Peasant Nationalism and the Study of China's Revolutionary History – A Review Essay." *Journal of Asian Studies* 63, 1 (2004): 105-25.

–. *Radicalism and Education Reform in Twentieth-Century China*. New York: Cambridge University Press, 1996.

Peterson, Glen. "Peasant Education and the Reconstruction of Village Society." In Peterson, Hayhoe, and Lu, *Education, Culture, and Identity in Twentieth-Century China*, 207-37, 207-37.

–, Ruth Hayhoe, and Lu Yongling, eds. *Education, Culture, and Identity in Twentieth-Century China*. Ann Arbor: University of Michigan Press, 2001.

"Ping Su xuewuchu yu Ning xuewuchu zhi pishi" [Criticism of the instructions from the Jiangsu and Nanjing Education Bureaus]. *ZJXS* 2b: 654-57.

Pong, David, and Edmund S.K. Fung, eds. *Ideal and Reality: Social and Political Change in Modern China, 1860-1949*. New York: University Press of America, 1985.

Qian Manqian, and Jin Linxiang. *Zhongguo jindai xuezhi bijiao yanjiu* [Research on comparative schooling systems in modern China]. Guangzhou: Guangdong Jiaoyu chubanshe, 1996.

Qian, Nanxiu. "Revitalizing the Xianyuan (Worthy Ladies) Tradition: Women in the 1898 Reforms," *Modern China* 29, 4 (2003): 399-454.

Qian Yizhang. "Xiaoxue jiaoyuan shiji shenghuo diaocha" [A study of the actual lives of elementary schoolteachers]. *Zhonghua jiaoyu jie* 13, 12 (1924): 1-13.

Qian. "Nü xuesheng tian pian–zuotanhui jilu" [The record from female students' speeches in a forum]. *Funü shenghuo* 1, 4 (1934): 68-79.

Qiao Qiao. "Nü jiaoyuan" [The female teacher]. *Nüzi yuekan* 2, 12: 3289-95.

Qinghua Daxue, ed. *Zhandou zai yi er jiu yundong de qianlie* [Fighting on the front lines of the December Ninth Movement]. Beijing: Qinghua daxue chubanshe, 1985.

"Quanguo jiaoyu hui lianhe hui di liu ci huiyi jiyao" [Records of the sixth meeting of the National Federation of Educational Associations (1920, Shanghai)]. *JXJJT:* 227-34.

"Quanguo jiaoyu hui lianhe hui di yi ci kaihui ji lue" [A brief record of the first meeting of the National Federation of Educational Associations]. *JXJJT:* 200-5.

"Quanguo jiaoyu hui lianhe hui yijue an: Difang jiaoyu jingfei guihua an" [National Federation of Educational Associations proposals: Proposal on planning local education budgets]. *JYGB*, yr. 4 (1917), 7, "Zhuanjian": 1-2.

"Quanguo jiaoyu hui lianhe hui yijue an: Qing she nüzi gaodeng shifan xuexiao an" [The National Federation of Educational Associations' proposals: Proposal to establish a women's higher teachers' college). *JYGB*, yr. 4 (1917), 7, "Zhuanjian": 3-4.

"Quanguo shifan xuexiao xiaozhang huiyi yijue an: Guanyu zhengdun quanguo shifan xuexiao jiaoyu zhi yijian shu" [Proposals from the meeting of presidents of teachers' schools nationwide: Recommendations for rectifying teachers' schools nationwide ([August 1915)]. *SJSJ:* 819-21.

Rankin, Mary Backus. *Elite Activism and Political Transformation in China, Zhejiang Province, 1865-1911*. Stanford: Stanford University Press, 1986.

Rawlinsen, Frank. J. "Change and Progress in the Christian Movement in China during the Last Two Decades [1900-1920]." In Stauffer, *The Christian Occupation of China*, 32-39.

Rawski, Evelyn Sakakida. *Education and Popular Literacy in Ch'ing China*. Ann Arbor: University of Michigan Press, 1979.

Rowe, William T. "Education and Empire in Southwest China: Ch'en Hung-mou in Yunnan, 1733-38." In Elman and Woodside, *Education and Society in Late Imperial China*, 417-57.

Rudolph, Lloyd, and Susanne Rudolph. *The Modernity of Tradition: Political Development in India*. Chicago: University of Chicago Press, 1967.

Sang Bing. *Qing mo xin zhishijie de shetuan yu huodong* [The organizations and activities of new intellegensia in late Qing China]. Beijing: Sanlian shudian, 1995.

–. *Wan Qing xuetang xuesheng yu shehui bianqian* [New-style schools and their students in the social transformation during late Qing China]. Shanghai: Xuelin Press, 1995.

Schneewind, Sarah. "Community Schools and Improper Shrines: Local Institutions and the Chinese Society in the Ming Period (1368-1644)." PhD diss., Columbia University, 1999.

–. "Competing Institutions: Community Schools and 'Improper Shrines' in Sixteenth-Century China." *Late Imperial China* 20, 1 (1999): 85-106.

Schoppa, Keith R. *Chinese Elites and Political Change: Zhejiang Province in the Early Twentieth Century*. Cambridge: Harvard University Press, 1982.

Schwartz, Benjamin. "The Limits of 'Tradition versus Modernity' as Categories of Explanation: The Case of the Chinese Intellectuals." *Daedalus: Journal of the American Academy of Arts and Sciences* 101 (Spring 1972): 71-88.

–. *In Search of Wealth and Power: Yan Fu and the West*. Cambridge, MA: The Belknap Press of Harvard University Press, 1964.

Selden, Mark. *The Yenan Way in Revolutionary China*. Cambridge: Harvard University Press, 1971.

Seregny, Scott J. *Russian Teachers and Peasant Revolution: The Politics of Education in 1905*. Bloomington: Indiana University Press, 1989.

"Shaanxi jiaoyuting chengsong di yi, er shifan xuequ suoshuo xian fen biao qing jian he wen" [Shaanxi provincial bureau of education submitting the first and second teachers' school districts and the counties under their charge]. *JYGB*, yr. 5 (1918), 4, "Gongdu": 93-94.

Shaanxi sheng jiaoyu ting [Shaanxi provincial bureau of education]. "Ben ting guanyu di si qu xuexiao juban xiaoxue jiaoyuan jiaqi jiangxi hui banfa deng cailiao (minguo) 25 nian, 6 yue" [On the regulations and other materials regarding the summer training program of primary schoolteachers in the fourth district, June 1936]. Shaanxi Provincial archives, file 8-1-57.

Shang Yanliu. *Qingdai keju kaoshi shulu* [A description of the Qing civil service examinations]. Beijing: Sanlian Bookstore, 1958.

Shanghai qingyun shi yanjiu hui and Gongqingtuan Shanghai shiwei qingyun shi yanjiu shi, eds. *Shanghai xuesheng yundong shi* [A history of student movements in Shanghai]. Shanghai: Xuelin chubanshe, 1995.

"Shanghai nüzi Zhong Xi yi xuexiao zhangcheng" [Regulations for Shanghai Sino-West medical school for women], ZJXS 2b: 646-48.

"Shanghai Zhongxi nüshu zhangcheng" [The regulations for the McTyeire School for Girls in Shanghai]. *ZJXS* 4: 299-302.

Shanxi jiaoyu ting. "Shanxi jiaoyu ting cheng fu chen zun ling tuiguang nüzi jiaoyu ji xian zai chouban qingxing wen" [The Shanxi provincial bureau of education replys (to the Ministry of Education) on compliance with the order to promote women's education and recent situation]. *JYGB*, yr. 5 (1918), 12 "Gongdu": 77-78.

"Shanxi jiaoyuting cheng bao bennian jianding xiaoxue jiaoyuan qingxing qing he wen" [Shanxi provincial bureau of education reporting this result of the examination of primary school teachers in the year]. *JYGB*, yr. 5 (1918), 12, "Gongdu": 78.

"Shanxi jiaoyuting cheng fusong Shanxi shixiao xuequ biao wen" [Shanxi provincial bureau of education submitting the table of the province's teachers' school districts]. *JYGB*, yr. 5 (1918) 3, 109-19.

Shao Chongxiang. "Heimoyuan zhongxin chayuan" [Heimoyuan central tea house]. *Xiangjiao congxun* 2, 9 (1928): 3-4.

Sheng Langxi. "Shi nian lai Jiangsu zhongdeng xuexiao biyesheng chulu tongji" [Statistics on the number of graduates of secondary schools in Jiangsu over the past ten years]. *JYZZ* 17, 4 (1925): 1-13.

–. *Zhongguo shuyuan zhidu* [China's academy system]. Zhonghua shuju, 1934.

"Sheng Mali ya nü shuyuan xiaoshi" [The history of St. Mary's Hall for Chinese Girls]. *ZJXS* 4: 306-9.

Shi Sheng. "Zenyang shishi nongcun funü jiaoyu?" [How shall we implement rural women's education?]. *Funü shenghuo* 3, 5 (1936): 3-5.

Shifan Qunying, Guangyao Zhonghua [Heroic graduates of teachers' schools shine in Chinese history]. 21 vols. Shaanxi people's education publishing house, 1992-94.

Shu Xincheng. *Jindai Zhongguo Jiaoyu Shiliao* [Historical documents on Chinese modern education]. Shanghai: Commercial Press, 1927.

–. *Zhongguo jindai jiaoyu shi ziliao* [The source materials related to the modern education history of China]. 3 vols. Beijing: People's education publishing house, 1963.

"Shuntian shibao ji Yujiao nüxuetang xuesheng qingkuang" [The *Shuntian Times* reports on the student background of Inculcating Doctrine Women's School]. *ZJXS* 2b: 703-6.

"Shuyuan yixue tiao shiwen" [A glossary of terms related to academies and charitable schools]. *YZSJ:* 168-69.

"Si ci choubei huiyi jiyao" [Records of four preparatory meetings, 1897]. *WSJ*: 192-201.

"Sichuan tongsheng shifan xuetang de dansheng" [The birth of Sichuan Provincial Teachers' School]. *SJSJ:* 677-80.

"Sichuan zongdu Xi liang zou gaishe tongsheng shifan xuetang" [Memorial from Sichuan Governor Xi-liang on establishing the provincial teachers' school]. *SJSJ:* 677.

Sih, Paul K.T., ed. *The Strenuous Decade: China's Nation-Building Efforts, 1927-1937.* Baltimore: St. John's University Press, 1970.

Skinner, G. William, ed. *The City in Late Imperial China.* Stanford: Stanford University Press, 1977.

Smith, Richard J., Grace Fong, and Nanxiu Qian, eds. *Different Worlds of Discourse: New Views of Gender and Genre in Late Qing and Early Republican China.* Leiden: Brill Academic Publishers, forthcoming, 2007.

Stauffer, Milton T., ed. *The Christian Occupation of China: A General Survey of the Christian Forces in China.* Shanghai: China Continuation Committee, 1924.

Su Ying. "Susu nüxiao kaixue yanshuo" [Speech given at the opening ceremony of Susu Women's School (1904)]. *ZJXS* 2b: 582.

Su Yunfeng. *Zhang Zhidong yu Hubei jiaoyu gaige* [Zhang Zhidong and educational reform in Hubei]. Taipei: Zhongyang yanjiu yuan jindai shi suo [Institute of Modern History Academia Sinica], 1976.

Su Zhixin. "Teaching, Learning, and Reflective Acting: A Dewey Experiment in Chinese Teacher Education." *Teachers College Record* 98, 1 (1996): 126-52.

Sun Jixu. "Beijing nüzi gaodeng shifan" [Beijing Women's Higher Teachers' College]. *SJSJ:* 1028-35.

Sun Liping. "Cong minzhu zhengzhi dao quanwei zhengzhi" [From democratic politics to authoritarian politics]. In Xu and Chen, *Zhongguo xiandaihua shi*, 270-92.

Sun Mingxun, and Dai Zian, eds. *Xiaozhuang piban* [Critique of Xiaozhuang]. Shanghai: Ertong shuju, 1934.

Sun Shiyue. *Zhongguo jindai nüzi liuxue shi* [A modern history of Chinese female students studying abroad]. Beijing: Zhongguo heping chubanshe [Chinese peace press], 1995.

Sun Sibai, ed. *Beijing daxue yi er jiu yundong huiyi lu* [The students of Beijing University collectively recall the December Ninth Movement]. Beijing: Beijing daxue chubanshe, 1988.

Sun Yen-chu. "Chinese National Higher Education for Women in the Context of Social Reform, 1919-1929: A Case Study." PhD diss., New York University, 1985.

Tan Guangsheng. "Xiaoxue jiaoyu zhi weiji" [The crisis of primary education]. *Xin Jiaoyu* [New Education] 3, 1 (1921): 110-15.

Tang Chenglie. "Xuexiao pian" [The chapter on schools]. *YZSJ*: 156-57.

Tang Chindon Yiu. "Women's Education in China," *Bulletins on Chinese Education* 9, 2 (1923): 1-36.

Tang Jue. "Xiangxiang zhong de xiangcun zhongxue" [How I imagine rural middle schools]. *Xin jiaoyu* 9, 4 (1924): 733-39.

Tang Yuan and Han Zhiyou (compil.). *Zhongguo xiandai wenxue qikan mulu huibian* [Compendium of the contents of modern Chinese literature magazines]. Tianjin: Tianjin people press, 1988.

Tang Zhijun, and Chen Zuen (compil.). *Wuxu shiqi jiaoyu* [Chinese education during the 1898 Reform period]. Shanghai: Shanghai Education Press, 1993. One of *ZJJZH* series.

Tao Xingzhi. "Cun hun ge" [Song of village spirit]. *Tao Xingzhi wenji*: 265.

–. "Da Zhu Duanyan zhi wen" [Responding to Zhu Duanyan's questions]. In *Tao Xingzhi wenji* (1981): 226-31.

–. "Gei Feng Huanzhang xiansheng de xin" [A letter to Mr. Feng Huanzhang (Yuxiang)]. *Xiangjiao congxun* 2, 22 (1928): 1-4.

–. "Jiao xue zuo he yi" [Teaching, learning, and doing in one]. In *Tao Xingzhi wenji*: 184-86.

–. "Jiao xue zuo he yi xia zhi jiao ke shu" [Textbooks in teaching-learning-doing-in-one]. In *Tao Xingzhi wenji:* 294-305.

–. "Ju du yundong dagang" [Outline of the campaign to end opium smoking]. *Xiangjiao congxun* 2, 22 (1928): 1-4.

–. "Liancun jinyan weiyuanhui zhangcheng" [Regulations of the united villages committee to end opium smoking]. *Xiangjiao congxun* 2, 22 (1928): 1-4.

–. "Liancun ziweituan di yi hao bugao" [The first proclamation of the united villages selfdefence squad]. *Xiangjiao congxun* 2, 22 (1928): 1-4.

–. "Ruhe jiao nongmin chu tou" [How can we teach peasants to free themselves?]. In *Tao Xingzhi wenji* (1981): 177.
–. "Shenghuo gongju zhuyi zhi jiaoyu" [On instrumentalist education for life]. In *Tao Xingzhi wenji*: 172-73.
–. "Shenghuo ji jiaoyu" [Life is education]. In *Tao Xingzhi wenji:* 243-50.
–. "Shifan jiaoyu zhi chedi gaige" [The thorough reform of teachers' education]. In *Tao Xingzhi wenji:* 167-68.
–. "Shifan jiaoyu zhi xin qushi" [The new direction of teacher's education]. *Shishi xinbao* [The new current affairs daily], 22 October 1921.
–. "Shiyan xiangcun shifan di yi yuan jianzhang caoan" [Drafted regulations for Department Number One of the (Xiaozhuang) Experimental Village Teachers' School]. In *Tao Xingzhi wenji*: 145-47.
–. "Shiyan xiangcun shifan xuexiao da ke wen" [Answering questions from visitors regarding (Xiaozhuang) Experimental Village Teachers' School]. In *Tao Xingzhi wenji*: 149-54.
–. *Tao Xingzhi wenji* [Collected works of Tao Xingzhi]. Nanjing: Jiangsu renmin chubanshe, 1981.
–. "'Wei zhishi' jieji" [A class for "bogus knowledge"]. In *Tao Xingzhi wenji:* 191-201.
–. "Women de xintiao" [Our new creed]. In *Zhongguo jiaoyu gaizao* [The reform of Chinese education]. Beijing: Dongfang chubanshe, 1996: 73-74.
–. "Xiaozhuang liancun ziwei xintiao" [The self-defence creed of the united villages of Xiaozhuang]. *Xiangjiao congxun* 2, 22 (1928): 1-4.
–. "Xiaozhuang liancun ziweituan zuzhi dagang" [An organizational outline of the self-defence squad of the united villages of Xiaozhuang]. *Xiangjiao congxun* 2, 22 (1928): 1-4.
–. "Xing shi zhi zhi shi" [Practice is the beginning of knowledge]. In *Tao Xingzhi wenji*: 182-83.
–. "Zai lao li shang lao xin" [Improving one's mind through physical labor]. In *Tao Xingzhi wenjin*: 187-88.
–. "Zhongguo xiangcun jiaoyu yundong zhi yi ban" [A glimpse into China's rural education movement]. In *Tao Xingzhi wenji* (1981): 203-13.
–. "Zhonghua jiaoyu gaijin she gaizao quanguo xiangcun jiaoyu xuanyan" [A manifesto from the Chinese National Association for the Advancement of Education on reforming rural education]. In *Tao Xingzhi wenji:* 142.
Thaxton, Ralph. *China Turned Rightside Up: Revolutionary Legitimacy in the Peasant World*. New Haven: Yale University Press, 1983.
Thøgersen, Stig. *A County of Culture: Twentieth-Century China Seen from the Village Schools of Zouping, Shandong*. Ann Arbor: University of Michigan Press, 2002
– "Learning in Lijiazhuang: Education, Skills, and Careers in Twentieth-Century Rural China." In Peterson, Hayoe and Lu, *Education, Culture, and Identity in Twentieth-Century China*, 238-64.
Tian Guangsheng. "Xiaoxue jiaoyu zhi weiji" [The crisis of primary education]. *Xin jiaoyu* 3, 1 (1921): 110-15.
Tian Shiqian. "Kaocha Jiangsu zhongdeng jiaoyu baogao" [An examination of secondary education in Jiangsu]. *JYGB*, yr. 6 (1919), 3, "Baogao": 19-20.
Tie Ying. "Baoding ershi qiuxue jishi" [Recollections of Baoding Provincial Teachers' School Number Two]. *SQGZ* 8: 89-101.
Tong Jupu, and Shang Zhensheng. "He'nan shengli xiangshi shiyanqu tuiguang gaikuang ji jihua caohan" [Draft plan and general situation of the experimental region associated with Henan Provincial Village Teachers' School]. *Xiangcun gaizao* [Rural reform] 2, 11 (1933): 17-24.
Tong Runzhi. "Tichang xiangcun zhongdeng jiaoyu de ba da liyou" [The eight main reasons for advocating rural secondary education]. *Zhonghua jiaoyu jie* 24, 2 (1936): 1-10.
VanderVen, Elizabeth. "Educational Reform and Village Society in Twentieth-Century Northeast China: Haicheng, 1905-1931." Ph.D. diss., University of California at Los Angeles, 2003.
Vaughan, Mary Kay. *Cultural Politics in Revolution: Teachers, Peasants, and Schools in Mexico, 1930-1940*. Tucson: University of Arizona Press, 1997.

Wakeman, Frederic, and Carolyn Grant, eds. *Conflict and Control In Late Imperial China*. Berkeley: University of California Press, 1975.

Wang Baolian. *Shandong shengli di yi nüzi shifan xuexiao yi lan* [Shandong Provincial Women's Normal School Number One: a brochure]. Shandong Provincial Archives, file J101-14-30.

Wang Chaoxi. "Gao Junyue: Wei le dadi de mingtian" [Gao Junyue: For the sake of this land's future]. *SQGZ* 7B: 44-58.

–. "Li Zhuru: Juanjuan bixue xie chunqiu" [Li Zhuru: Making history by sacrificing his life]. *SQGZ* 7A: 170-82.

Wang Chuncai. "Cao Zhenqiu: Shuang zhong ye geng hong, huanghua wan jie xiang" [Cao Zhenqiu: Frost makes maple leaves redder and yellow flowers become more aromatic to its end: An educator's biography]. *SQGZ* 4: 100-9;

Wang Jiliang. "Sichuan de funü" [Women in Sichuan]. *Nüzi yuekan* 1, 4 (1933): 46-52.

Wang Maozu. "Shifan jiaoyu san da wenti" [Three great problems facing teachers' education]. *Jiaoyu huikan* [The chronicle of education] 2, 1 (1924): 1-9.

Wang Ruowang. *Wang Ruowang zizhuan* [Autobiography of Wang Ruowang]. Hong Kong: Mingbao chubanshe, 1991.

Wang Xi, and Frederic Wakeman, Jr., eds. *Zhongguo xiandai hua wenti: Yi ge duo fangwei de lishi tansuo* [China's quest for modernization: A historical perspective]. Shanghai: Fudan daxue chubanshe, 1994.

Wang, Zheng. *Women in the Chinese Enlightenment: Oral and Textual Histories*. Berkeley: University of California Press, 1999.

Wasserstrom, Jeffrey. *Student Protests in Twentieth-Century China: The View from Shanghai*. Stanford: Stanford University, 1991.

Weber, Eugen. *Peasants into Frenchmen: The Modernization of Rural France, 1870-1914*. Stanford: Stanford University Press, 1976.

Wei Ruichi, and Ma Zhenfu. "Nongcun funü jiaoyu de lilun yu shiji" [The theory and practice of rural women's education]. *Nüzi yuekan* 2, 7 (1934): 2509-16.

Wei Xixun. "Zhongguo nüzi jiaoyu zhi genben gaizao" [Making a fundamental change to women's education in China]. *Nüzi yuekan* 2, 1 (1934): 1739-48.

Wo Yi. "Linshi jiaoyu huiyi riji" [A journal from the Provisional Conference on Education (July 1912)]. In *YZYB:* 640.

Woodside, Alexander. "The Divorce between the Political Center and Educational Creativity in Late Imperial China." In Elman and Woodside, *Education and Society in Late Imperial China*, 458-92.

–. "Real and Imagined Continuities in the Chinese Struggle for Literacy." In Hayhoe, *Education and Modernization*, 23-45.

–. "Some Mid-Qing Theorists of Popular Schools: Their Innovations, Inhibitions, and Attitudes toward the Poor." *Modern China* 9, 1 (1983): 3-35.

Wou, Odoric. *Mobilizing the Masses: Building Revolution in Henan*. Stanford: Stanford University Press, 1994.

Wright, Mary Clabaugh. *The Last Stand of Chinese Conservatism: The T'ung-Chih Restoration, 1862-1874*. Stanford: Stanford University Press, 1975.

Wu Chucai, and Wu Diaohou. *Gu wen guan zhi* [A primer of classical Chinese texts]. Beijing: Zhonghua shuju [Zhonghua publishing house], 1959.

Wu Dingchu. *Zhongguo shifan jiaoyu jianshi* [A brief history of Chinese teachers' education]. Chengdu: Sichuan jiaoyu chubanshe [Sichuan education press], 1990.

Wu Guangsong. "Xianghu shifan xuexiao: Zhejiang de Xiaozhuang" [Xianghu Village Teachers' School: Zhejiang's Xiaozhuang]. *SQGZ* 18: 255-62.

Wu Ni, and Hu Yan. *Zhongguo gudai sixue yu jindai sili xuexiao yanjiu* [A study of private schools in ancient and modern China]. Ji'nan: Shandong jiaoyu chubanshe [Shandong education press], 1997.

Wu Ruoan. "Huiyi Shanghai Wuben nüshu" [Recollections of Nurturing Roots Women's Academy in Shanghai]. *ZJXS* 2b: 602-9.

Wu Xiangxiang. *Yan Yangchu zhuan: Wei quanqiu xiangcun gaizao fendou liushi nian* [A biography of James Yen: Sixty years of struggle for global rural reform]. Taibei: Shibao chubanshe, 1981.

Wu Xiangxiang, and Liu Shaotang (compil.). *Di er ci quanguo jiaoyu huiyi shi mo ji, 1930* [Records of the second National Conference of Education, 1930]. Taibei: Zhuangji wenxu chubanshe, 1971 (reprint).

Wu Xin. "Wuben nüxue shilue" [A brief history of Wuben Women's School]. *ZJXS* 2b: 589-90.

Wu Zhihe. *Mingdai de ruxue jiaoguan* [Education officials of the Ming Dynasty]. Taipei: Taibei xuesheng shuju [Taipei student publishing house], 1991.

"Wuben nüshu zengshe chudeng, gaodeng nüzi xiaoxue guize shezhi dayi" [The regulations of the newly added lower and higher elementary school at Wuben Women's School (1905)]. *ZJXS* 2b: 594-96.

"Wuben nüxuexiao di er ci gailiang guize" [The second revised regulations of Wuben Women's School (1905)]. *ZJXS* 2b: 590-94.

Xi'nan lianda chuxi fukan [Editorial group for the supplementary edition of the Southwest United University Journal], ed. *Lianda ba nian* [Eight years in the Southwest United University]. Kunming: Xi'nan lianda xuesheng chubanshe, 1946.

Xia Chengfeng. "Gaizhi hou zhongdeng jiaoyu zhengce shangque" [A discussion of the secondary education system after the reform]. *JYZZ* 17, 7 (1925): 1-5.

Xia Junxia. "Lun wan qing shuyuan gaige" [On the reform of academies in the late Qing]. *Jindaishi Yanjiu* [Modern China research] 4 (1993): 64-82.

Xia Mingfang. *Minguo shiqi de ziran zaihai yu xiangcun shehui* [Natural disasters and rural society in Republican China]. Beijing: Zhonghua shuju, 2000.

Xia Xiaohong. "Daodu: wan Qing nübao de xingbie guanzhao–*Nüzi shijie* yianjiu [Readers' guide: gender vision of women's newspapers in the late Qing–a study of *Women's world*]. In Xia Xiaohong (compil.), *Nüzi shijie wenxuan* [Selected reading from *Women's world*]: 1-52.

Xia Xiaohong (compil.). *Nüzi shijie wenxuan* [Selected reading from *Women's world*]. Guiyang: Guizhou jiaoyu chubanshe, 2003.

–. *Wan Qing nüxing yu jindai Zhongguo* [Late Qing women and modern China]. Beijing: Beijing daxue chubanshe [Beijing University press], 2004.

Xiangjiao congxun [Collective newsletter on rural education].

"Xiangjiao yanjiu hui di yi jie nianhui jilu" [The records of the first annual meeting of the Association for Rural Education]. *Xiangcun jiaoyu* 26/27 (1935): 49.

"Xiao wen yi shu" [School news briefs]. *Xiangjiao congxun* 2, 18 (1928): 4.

"Xiaoxue fa" [Primary school law]. In *Zhongyang minguo zhengfu gonggao* [Central republican government bulletin]. *KJKHJ* (Republican period) 3: 182.

"Xiaoxue jiaoyuan youdai tiaoli" [Terms on the special treatment of primary schoolteachers]. *ZJSJZ*: 819-22.

"Xiaoxue jiaoyuan zhi suo xin yundong" [A movement among primary schoolteachers' demanding payment of back salaries]. *JYZZ* 23, 3 (1931): 129.

Xiaozhuang shifan xuexiao. "Shiyan xiangcun shifan xuexiao gaikuang" [The general condition of experimental village teachers' schools]. *Zhonghua jiaoyu jie* 17, 3 (1928): 1-10.

Xie Bao. "Lun Xiaozhuang shifan bei feng shi" [On the closing of the Xiaozhuang teachers' school]. In Sun and Zian, *Xiaozhuang pipan*, 137.

Xin Wu. "Yunnan funü gaiguan" [The general situation of women in Yunnan]. *Nüzi yuekan* 1, 10 (1933): 57-60.

Xin Yuan, and Xie Fang, eds. *Tao Xingzhi yu Xiaozhuang shifan* [Tao Xingzhi and Xiaozhuang Teachers' School]. Nanjing: Jiangsu jiaoyu chubanshe, 1986.

"Xingjian gaoshi, xiangwen" [Government edicts and documents on establishing (charitable schools)]. *YZSJ:* 314-28.

Xinjiang Sheng. "Xinjiang quan sheng jiaoyu jinxing jihua shu" [Report: Education plan for Xinjiang province]. *JYGB*, yr. 4 (1917), 8, "Baogao": 1-10.

Xiong Ming'an. *Zhonghua minguo jiaoyu shi* [A history of education in the Republic of China]. Chongqing: Chongqing chubanshe, 1990.

Xiu Sheng. "Nü tongxue shou xun lue shu" [A brief report on the training of female students]. *Funü shenghuo* 3, 2 (1936): 22-24.

Xu Bing. "Yi ge xiaoxue jiaoshi de husheng" [The voice of a primary school teacher]. *Funü shenghuo* 3, 4 (1936): 31-33.

Xu Jilin, and Chen Dakai, eds. *Zhongguo xiandaihua shi* [A history of modernization in China]. Shanghai: Sanlian shudian, 1995.

Xu Naixiang (chief compiler). *Zhongguo xiandai wenxue cidian* [Encyclopedia of Chinese modern literature]. Nanning: Guangxi people press, 1989.

Xue bu [Board of Education]. "Chudeng xiao xuetang zhangcheng" [Regulations for the primary level of elementary schools]. *XZYB*: 291-306.

–. "Chuji shifan xuetang zhangcheng" [Regulations for primary teachers' schools]. *XZYB*: 398-414.

–. "Da xuetang zhangcheng" [The regulations for universities]. *XZYB*: 339-92.

–. "Gaoden xuetang zhangcheng" [Regulations for colleges]. *XZYB*: 317-39.

–. "Meng yang jia jiao he yi" [Unity of early education and family education]. *XZYB:* 396.

–. "Tongxing gesheng tuiguang shifan sheng ming'e dian" [A telegram urging all of the provinces to promote enrolment in teachers' schools]. *XBGB* 1 (1906): 6b.

–. "Xue bu zou yi nüzi shifan xuetang zhangcheng zhe (fu zhangcheng)" [Memorial from the Education Bureau on women's normal school regulations (regulation attached)]. *SJSJ:* 573.

–. "Youji shifan xuetang zhangcheng" [Regulations for advanced teachers' colleges]. *XZYB:* 414-15.

–. "Zhong xuetang zhangcheng" [Regulations for middle schools]. *XZYB*: 317-39.

–. "Zou ding ge xuetang jiangli zhangcheng" [Imperially approved memorial on the regulations for degrees awarding to various graduates of new schools]. *XZYB*: 514-23.

–. "Zou zun ni nü xuesheng fuse changcheng" [Board of Education made the regulations on the colour and style of clothing for female students (10 January 1910)]. *ZJXS* 2b: 675-76.

–. "Zouding mengyang yuan zhangcheng ji jiating jiaoyu fa zhangcheng" [Imperially approved regulations for kindergartens and family education methods]. *XZYB:* 393-96.

–. "Zouding nüzhi shifan xuetang ji nüzi xiaoxuetang zhangcheng" [Imperial Approved Regulations on Women's Normal Schools and Girls' Elementary Schools]. *JZJS* 2: 169-73.

–. "Zouding renyong jiaoyuan zhangcheng" [Imperial approved regulations on the appointment of teachers]. *XZYB*: 428-30.

Xue bu zongwu si [General information office of board of education]. *Di yi ci jiaoyu tongji tubiao 1907* [An almanac of the first educational statistics, 1907]. Taipei: Wenhai chubanshe [Wenhai press], 1987 (reprint).

–. "Ge sheng shifan xuetang xuesheng tongji biao" [A statistical table of teachers' schools and students in every province]. In *Di yi ci jiaoyu tongji tubiao 1907:* 23-24.

–. "Ge sheng shiye xuetang xuesheng tongji biao" [Statistical table on students at vocational schools in the provinces]. In *Di yi ci jiaoyu tongji tubiao*: 21-22.

–. "Ge sheng xuetang li nian zeng jian bijiao biao" [A comparative table showing the increase and decrease of modern schools in every province]. In *Di yi ci jiaoyu tongji tubiao 1907*: 27-28.

–. "Ge sheng zhuanmen xuetang xuesheng tongji biao" [A statistical table of specialty colleges and students in every province]. In *Di yi ci jiaoyu tongji tubiao 1907:* 19-20.

–. "Guangxu san shi si nanfen di er ci jiaoyu tongji tubiao" [The second compilation of educational statistics, 1908]. *SJSJ:* 620-21.

–. "Guangxu sanshi si nian gesheng shifan xuetang xuesheng tongjibiao" [1908 statistics of teachers' schools and students in each province]. *ZJXS* 2b: 466-67.

–. "Xuantong yuan nian fen di san ci jiaoyu tongji tubiao" [The third compilation of educational statistics, 1909]. *SJSJ:* 624-25.

–. "Xuantong yuan nian jiaoyu tongji biao" [Tabular educational statistics for 1909]. *SJSJ:* 623-25.

Xue Zheng, "Xue Zheng ji Shanghai Zhongxi nüshu de kecheng" [Xue Zheng's recollection on the curricula of the McTyeire School for Girls in Shanghai]. *ZJXS* 4: 303-5.

"Xuexiao dang yu zhi manyan" [The spreading terror: Communists in schools arrested]. *JYZZ* 22, 12 (1930): 126-27.

"Xuezhi xitong caoan" [A draft proposal for the school system]. *XZYB:* 860-64.

Ya Lu. "Ai nüjie" [Women's sorrow]. *ZJXS* 2b (1904): 577-81.

Yan Yangchu. "Zhonghua pingmin jiaoyu cujin hui Dingxian gongzuo dagai" [Report on the Chinese National Association for the Promotion of Mass Education program in Dingxian]. In Zhang and Xu, *Xiangcun jianshe shiyan*, 1:53-61.

–, and Chen Zhushan. "Dingxian shiyan qu gongzuo gailue" [A general description of the program in the Dingxian experimental district]. In *Xiangcun jianshe shiyan* 3: 225-60.

Yang Bojun (trans. and annotater). *Mengzi yi zhu* [Mengzi translated and annotated]. Trans. Yang Bojun. Beijing: Zhonghua shuju, 1981.

Yang Jiayu. "Sichuan funü shenghuo gaiguan" [The general situation of women's lives in Sichuan]. *Nüzi yuekan* 2, 1 (1934): 1819-26.

Yang Jie. "Sishu wenti" [The issue of Sishu-style schools], *Jiaoyu xinchao* [New educational tide]. Ed. and published by Anhui daxue xueshe, 3, 4 (1934): 5-10.

Yang Kaimin, and Yang Xuepeng. "Xiri men qian lengluo, jinri zheng ru jiaotan: Jiangsu zhongduo kaosheng shouxuan shifan" [Teaching was formerly an unpopular major, and now everyone fights to get in: Many who took the college entrance examination in Jiangsu selected teachers' colleges as their first choice]. *Guangming ribao* [Guangming daily], 29 August 1996, 2.

Yang Qiliang. "Xiang wo de muxiao Baoding ershi huibao" [A report to my alma mater, Baoding Teachers' School Number Two]. *SQGZ* 8: 124-37.

Yang Rongchun. *Zhongguo fengjian shehui jiaoyu shi* [Educational history of feudal China]. Guangzhou: Guangdong renmin chubanshe [Guangdong people's press], 1985.

Yang Xiaochun. "Huanglu shifan yu Huanglu hanzai kangzhan" [Huanglu teachers' school and Huanglu's drought-relief]. *Zhonghua jiaoyu jie* 23, 10 (1936): 69-73.

–. *Xiangcun jiaoyu lunwen ji* [Collection on rural education]. Caohu: Huanglu xiangcun shifan, 1935.

–. "Xiangcun xiaoxue jiaoshi wenti" [The problems faced by rural elementary school teachers]. *Jiaoyu huikan* 2, 1921: 1-8.

–. "Xing jiang yi sui de Nanjing shiyan xiangcun shifan" [Approaching the end of the first year of the Nanjing Experimental Village Teachers' School]. *Zhonghua jiaoyu jie* 17, 5 (1928): 1-20.

"Yanjin fandong kanwu, 1932" [Prohibited Reactionary Publications, 1932]. In Hebei Provincial Archives, files 645-1-1.

"Yanjin fandong xuanchuan, 1930" [Prohibited Reactionary Propaganda, 1930]. In Hebei Provincial Archives, files 645-1-7.

Yao, Yusheng. "National Salvation through Education: Tao Xingzhi's Educational Radicalism." PhD diss., University of Minnesota, 1999.

Ye Jianxin. *Kangzhan qian Zhongguo zhongdeng jiaoyu zhi yanjiu, 1928-1937* [A study of Chinese secondary education before the Sino-Japanese War, 1928-37]. Taipei: Wenshezhe chubanshe, 1982.

Ye Weili. "'Nü Liuxuesheng': The Story of American-Educated Chinese Women, 1880-1920s." *Modern China* 20, 3 (1994): 315-46.

Ye Wenxin. "Baoshou yu jijin: Shi lun wusi yundong zai Hangzhou" [Conservative and radical: The May Fourth Movement in Hangzhou]. In Wang and Wakeman, Jr., *Zhongguo xiandai hua wenti*, 200-15.

Ye Zonglin. "You ben sheng xiaoxue jiaoshi shang lai toushi *He'nan jiaoyu*" [A review of the primary schoolteachers based on *Henan Educational Review*]. *Xiangcun gaizao* [Rural reform] 6, 6 (1937): 1-8.

Yeh, Wen-hsin. *The Alienated Academy: Culture and Politics in Republican China, 1919-1937*. Cambridge: Harvard University Press, 1990.

–. *Provincial Passages: Culture, Space, and the Origins of Chinese Communism*. Berkeley: University of California Press, 1996.

"Yi ding nüxue zhangcheng" [A discussion of how to regulate women's schooling]. In Li and Zhang, *Jindai Zhongguo nüquan yundong* 2, 1117.

Yip Ka-che. "Warlordism and Educational Finances, 1916-1927." In Fogel and Rowe, *Perspectives on a Changing China*, 183-95.

"Yixue zhangcheng" [Regulations of charitable schools]. *YZSJ:* 335-55.

"Yiyi Nü Xuetang zhangcheng" [Regulations for Girls' School of Language Translation], in Yuning and Zhang Yüfa, *Jindai Zhongguo nüquan yundong shiliao, 1842-1911*, 1101-6.

Young, Ernest. *The Presidency of Yuan Shih-k'ai: Liberalism and Dictatorship in Early Republican China*. Ann Arbor: University of Michigan Press, 1977.

Yu Jiaju. *Shifan jiaoyu* [Teachers' education]. Shanghai: Chung Kwa Book Co., 1926.

–. "Xiangcun jiaoyu de weiji" [The crisis in rural education]. *Zhonghua jiaoyu jie* 10, 1 (1920): 83-86.

–. "Xiangcun jiaoyu yundong de hanyi he fangxiang" [The meaning and direction of the rural education movement]. *Zhonghua jiaoyu jie* 10, 10 (1921): 11-25.

Yu Xueren. *Zhongguo xiandai xuesheng yundong shi changbian* [A detailed history of modern student movements in China]. Changchun: Dongbei daxue chubanshe, 1988.

Yu Ying-shih. "Some Preliminary Observations on the Rise of Ch'ing Confucian Intellectualism." *Tsing Hua Journal of Chinese Studies* 11 (1975): 105-43.

Yu Zhi, ed. *De yi lu*: "Yue dong qimeng yishu guitiao 1869" [Record of charitable deeds: Regulations for primary charitable schools in East Guangdong, 1869). *YZSJ*: 349-53.

Yu Ziyi. "Ji Aiguo nüxue yu Guanfuhui" [A recollection of Patriotic Women's School and the Restoration Society]. *ZJXS* 2b: 627-31.

Yuan Shikai. "Da zongtong ling ge sheng xingzheng gongshu nei she jiaoyu si, 1913" [President orders establishment of bureau of education in provincial government]. *JXJJT*: 122.

–. "Teding jiaoyu gangyao" [Special education directive, 1915]. *XZYB*: 747-58.

–. "Zhili zongdu Yuan Shikai zou ban Zhili shifan xuetang ji xiao xuetang zhe (fu zhangcheng)" [Memorial from governor general of Zhili Yuan Shikai on establishing Zhili Teachers' School and Elementary School (the regulations are attached)]. *SJSJ:* 628-37.

–. "Zou wei sheli beiyang shifan xuetang yi guang jiaoyu zhe" [A memorial on establishing Beiyang Teachers' College in order to promote education]. *SJSJ*: 659-61.

Yun Liu. "Xianxing shifan xuezhi de liubi jiqi gaige fa" [The drawbacks to the current system of teachers' schools and how to reform it]. *SJSJ:* 856-59.

Yunnan sheng zhengxie wenshi ziliao yanjiu weiyuanhui [Historical and cultural documents research committee of the Yunnan Provincial Political Consultative Conference]. Xi'nan lianghe daxue Beijing Kunming xiaoyouhui [The alumni associations in Beijing and Yunnan of the Southwest United University], and Yunnan shifan daxue [Yunnan teachers' university], compilation. *Yunnan wenshi ziliao xuanji* [Selection on Yunnan historical and cultural documents, 34). *Xi'nan lianhe daxue jianxiao wushi zhounian jinan zhuanji* [A special collection in commemoration of the fiftieth anniversary of the establishment of the Southwest United University]. Kunming: Yunnan Remin chubanshe, 1988.

Zhan Lu. "Duiyu zhuchi nüxue zhe zhi zhi yan" [Frank words to those who are running women's education]. *Funü zazhi* 1, 6 (1915): 1-4.

Zhang Ailing. "Liuli wa" [Glazed tiles]. In *Zhang Ailing wenji* 1: 111-23.

–. *Zhang Ailing wenji* [A collection of Zhang Ailing's works]. Hefei: Anhui wenyi chubanshe, 1992.

Zhang Baixi, Zhang Zhidong, and Rong-qing. "Guanxue dachen yi fu yanxuan shifan biantong xin jinshi rutang yiye pian" [Memorial from the ministers of education in response to the discussion of how to apply rigorous standards to choosing students for teachers' schools and of the need for flexibility in choosing newly advanced *jinshi* degree-holders to study in teachers' schools]. *DFZZ* 1 (1904): 11-12.

Zhang Bin. *Cong Zhejiang kan Zhongguo jiaoyu jindai hua* [Education modernization in Zhejiang]. Guangzhou: Guangdong Education Press, 1996.

Zhang Jianren. "Ji jiu jiachen nian nüzi zhi fangfa" [Urgent way to save women in the year of Jiachen 1904]. Xia, *Nüzi shijie wenxuan*, 148-49.

–. "Yu chang pingdeng xian xing nüxue lun" [Promoting equality must promote women's education first], Xiao Xiaohong, *Nüzi shijie wenxuan*, 137-38.

Zhang Jihe, ed. *Dan xin bi xue: jiu Zhongguo lici xue chao shilu* [Crimson hearts and cherry blood: Historical records of student movements in old China]. Shijiazhuang: Hebei daxue chubanshe, 1996.

Zhang Shufeng. *Shandong jiaoyu tongshi: Jinxiandai juan* [A comprehensive history of education in Shandong: Modern section]. Jinan: Shandong renmin chubanshe, 2001.

Zhang Tingyu, ed. *Ming Shi* [History of the Ming Dynasty]. Beijing: Zhonghua shuju [Zhonghua press], 1974.

Zhang Wenchang. "Qingnian wenti yanjiu: Hang shi 577 gaozhong xuesheng diaocha tongji jieguo" [A study of youth problems: A survey of 577 students from Hangzhou's upper middle schools]. *JYZZ* 26, 1 (1936): 87-98.

Zhang Yimin. "Xiandai hua bianqian zhong de tudi gaige" [Land reform in the course of modernization]. In Xu and Chen, *Zhongguo xiandai hua shi*, 1: 452-77.

Zhang Yuanshan, and Xu Shilian, eds. *Xiangcun jianshe shiyan* [Rural reconstruction experiment]. Vol. 1-3. Shanghai: Zhonghua shuju, 1934.

Zhang Zhidong. "Zha xuewuchu gai xiu Liang Hu shifan xuetang" [Memo to the provincial bureau of education on repairing the Liang Hu teachers' school]. *SJSJ:* 680.

Zhang Zhidong, Zhang Baixi, and Rong-qing. "Guanxue dachen deng zou qing shiban dijian keju zhuzhong xuetang zhe" [A memorial from the ministers of education on the experiment of attenuating the civil service examinations and reinforcing new schools]. *DFZZ* 1 (1904): 151-54.

–. "Xuewu gangyao" [A program for educational affairs]. *JZJS* 2: 8-30.

–. "Zou Jiangnan chuangjian sanjiang shifan xuetang zhe" [A memorial on establishing Sanjiang Teachers' College in Jiangnan]. *SJSJ*: 712-14.

Zhang Zhongyuan. "Zhongguo shifan jiaoyu de zong jiantao" [An overall self-criticism on Chinese teachers' schools]. *JYZZ* 25, 7 (1935): 45-84.

Zhang Zhu Hanfen. "Tuiguang nüzi chudeng xiaoxue siyi" [A personal opinion on promoting lower primary schools for girls]. *Funü zazh* 1, 6 (1915): 4-5.

Zhang Zonglin. "Man le yi sui ban yihou de Xiaozhuang" [Xiaozhuang, one and a half years later]. *Xiangjiao congxun* 2, 20 (1928): 1-3.

–. "Xueyuan zhi de xiangcun shifan" [Village teachers' schools in school field]. *Zhonghua jiaoyu jie* 23, 11 (1936): 25-32.

Zhao Erxun. *Qingshi gao* [A draft of the Qing history]. Beijing: Zhonghua shuju [Zhonghua press], 1977.

–. "Xuanyu zhi" [A record of the examination system]. In Zhao, *Qingshi gao* 12. Beijing: Zhonghua shuju, 1977: 3099-119.

"Zhe fu Zhang Zengyang zou ban quan Zhe shifan xuetang zhe" [A memorial from Zhejiang Governor Zhang Zengyang on establishing Zhejiang Teachers' School]. *SJSJ:* 694-95.

"Zhe sheng shixing xin xue zhi zhi zhunbei" [Zhejiang province is preparing for the implementation of new school system]. *Xin jiaoyu* [New education] 6, 1: 120-21.

"Zhe yi qi" [This issue]. *Xiangjiao congxun* 2, 22 (1928): 1.

"Zhejiang jiaoyuting chengsong shengli ge shifan xuequ nei suoshu ge xian qingdan qing he wen" [Zhejiang provincial bureau of education submitting the list for province's teachers' school districts and the counties they cover]. *JYGB*, yr. 5 (1918), 5, "Gongdu": 97-98.

Zhejiang Sheng. "Zhejiang shengli Xianghu xiangcun shifan de xiangcun tuiguang jiaoyu" [Zhejiang's Xianghu Provincial Village Teachers' Schools' promotion of rural education]. In *Xiangcun jianshe shiyan* 3: 491-512.

Zheng Chao. "Jiaoyu bu yunniang quxiao shifan sheng, jiaoshi zige jiang dingqi renzheng" [The Ministry of Education is brewing a plan to abolish teachers' schools while periodically examining teachers for certificates]. See "Shijie luntan wang: wenjiao xinwen" [World forum web: news on culture and education]. http://www.wforum.com/newspool/articles/culedu/55668.html.

Zheng Dahua. *Minguo xiangcun jianshe yundong* [Rural construction movement in the Republican period]. Shehui kexue wenxian chubanshe, Beijing, 2000.

Zheng Xiaocang. "Zhejiang liangji shifan he di yi shifan xiao shi zhi yao" [Highlights from the history of Zhejiang Combined Teachers' College and the Number One Teachers' School]. *SJSJ:* 696-712.

"Zhenjiang nüshu gongke jianbiao" [A brief curriculum of the Zhenjiang Girls' School]. *ZJXS* 4: 342-43.

Zhi Xian. "Nü jiaoshi" [The female teacher]. *Jiaoshi zhi you* [Teachers' friend] 1, 10 (1935): 1612-14.

"Zhili deng sheng jiaoyu hui lianhe cheng qing shezhi difang jiaoyu duli guanting" [Requested by Zhili and other provincial educational associations to establish local independent education administration bureau]. *JXJJT:* 127-28.

"Zhili jiaoyuting chengsong shengli ge shifan xuequ shangdai gengding wen" [Zhili provincial bureau of education responding to (Ministry of Education) on the program of teachers' school district in revision]. *JYGB*, yr. 5 (1918), 5, "Gongdu": 99-100.

"Zhili Tianjin xian xiang song shiban nüxuetang zhangcheng" [Attentative regulations on girls' schools submitted by Tianjin county, Zhili province]. In Li and Zhang, *Jindai Zhongguo nüquan yundong* 2, 1023-24.

Zhili xuewu chu [Education bureau of Zhili]. "Benchu cheng shifan xuetang kaoxuan youji fen like wenke jiaoyou qing li'an bing, 1905" [The bureau's report requesting confirmation on the selection of students for the advanced program of the teachers' school and on the division of students into science and humanistics for the purpose of teaching separately]. *SJSJ:* 643-44.

"Zhixia gaodeng shifan yi lan biao" [Table of higher teachers' colleges under the direction of the central government]. *SJSJ*: 881.

Zhong Lu. "Wo zhi nüxue tan" [My opinion on women's education]. *JYZZ* 6, 2 (1914): 1-2.

Zhongguo jiaoyu nianjian bianjibu [Editorial department for the Chinese education year book]. *Zhongguo jiaoyu nianjian, 1949-81* [Chinese education yearbook, 1949-81]. Beijing: Zhongguo dabaikequanshu chubanshe, 1984.

Zhonghua jiaoyu gaijin she, "Zhonghua jiaoyu gaizao she Xiaozhuang xuexiao baogao shu" [A report on the Xiaozhuang school by the Chinese National Association for the Advancement of Education]. *Xiangjiao congxun* [Collective newsletter on rural education] 2, 11 (1928): 1-2.

Zhonghua Jidu jiaohui nianjian [The yearbook of Chinese Christians (1917)]. *ZJXS* 4: 296-97.

Zhonghua Jidujiao jiaoyu diaochahui, *Zhonghua Jidujiao jiaoyu shiye* [The educational cause of the Chinese Christian]. Shanghai: Commercial Press, 1922.

Zhongyang da xue qu, "Zhongyang da xuequ jianding xiaoxue jiaoyuan zhanxing guicheng" [Central District of the University Council: Provisional regulations on examining primary schoolteachers]. *DXYGB* 9 (1928): 122-27.

Zhongyang jiaoyu kexue yanjiu suo [Central research institute of educational science] (compilation), *Zhonghua renmin gongheguo jiaoyu dashiji, 1949-82* [Chronology of education in the People's Republic of China, 1949-82]. Beijing: Jiaoyu kexue chubanshe, 1983.

Zhongyang minguo zhengfu gonggao [Central government bulletin], "Xiaoxue fa" [Primary school law]. *KJKHJ* (Republican period) 3: 182.

Zhongyang yanjiuyuan jindai shi yanjiu suo, *Jindai Zhongguo funü shi yanjiu* [Studies in modern Chinese women's history], 8.

"Zhongyao jiaoyu xingzheng renyuan yi lan" [List of major educational personnel]. *DYCZJNJ* 5: 205-6.

Zhou Hanguang. *Zhang Zhidong yu Guangya shuyuan* [Zhang Zhidong and the Guangya Academy]. Taibei: Zhongguo wenhua daxue chubanshe [University of Chinese culture press], 1983.

Zhou Jianfan. "Zhounan nüzi shifan xuexiao jingying zhuangkuang" [The management of Zhounan Women's Normal School]. *SJSJ:* 976-77.

Zhou Kai. "Xiangyang fu shu yixue zhangcheng" [Regulations for the charitable schools subordinated to Xiangyang Prefecture]. *YZSJ*: 337.

Zhou Xuqi. *1910-1920 niandai douhui funü shenghuo fengmao* [The lifestyle of new women in the metropolis in the 1910s and 1920s]. Taipei: Guoli Taiwan Daxue [National Taiwan University], 1996.

Zhu Jiading, and Chen Guanglian. "Hongse tudi shang de baochun xinya: Zhongyang suqu Liening shifan" [Buds predicting spring in the red earth: Central soviet Lenin teachers' schools]. *SQGZ* 5: 219-31.

Zhu Youhuan, Qi Mingxiu, Qian Manqian, and Huo Yiping (compil.). *Jiaoyu xingzheng jigou ji jiaoyu tuanti* [Education administrations and organizations]. Shanghai Education Press, 1993. One of *ZJJZH* series.

–. *Zhongguo jindai xuezhi shiliao* [Historical materials on the school system of modern China]. 4 vols. Shanghai: East China Normal University Press, 1989.
Zhu Yuanshan. "Jiaoyu duli" [Educational independence]. *JYZZ* 8, 1 (1916): 1-4.
Zhuang Zexuan. "Gansu jiaoyu xianzhuang yi pie" [A glimpse of education in Gansu Province today]. *Zhonghua jiaoyu jie* 24, 7 (1937): 157-63.
Zong Shunhua. "Changshu funü de weiji" [Women's crisis in Changshu]. *Nüzi yuekan* 2, 1 (1934): 1829-31.
Zurndorfer, Harriet T. "Beyond Good Wifehood and Good Scholarship: Wang Zhaoyuan (1763-1851) and the Vanished 'Talented Women.'" In Smith, Fong, and Qian, eds., *Different Worlds of Discourse*.

Index

References to tables are in **bold**.

Printed in Canada by Friesens
Set in Stone by Artegraphica Design Co. Ltd.
Copy editor: Joanne Richardson
Proofreader: Dianne Tiefensee
Indexer: Dianne Tiefensee
Cartographer: Eric Leinberger